i g o r t

5

is the perfect number

(1994 - 2002)

i g o r t

5

**dedicated to
georges simenon
george herriman**

DRAWN AND
D&Q
QUARTERLY

Translated by Ioana Georgescu.

Publisher: Chris Oliveros.
Book design: Igort, Coconino Press.
Publicity: Elizabeth Walker.

Drawn & Quarterly
Post Office Box 48056
Montreal, Quebec
Canada H2V 4S8
www.drawnandquarterly.com

Printed by Coconino Press in Bologna, Italy in May 2003.
www.igort.com

National Library of Canada Cataloguing in Publication
Igort, 1958-
5 is the perfect number / Igort; translator, Ioana Georgescu.
Translation of: 5 è il numero perfetto.
ISBN 1-896597-68-8
I. Georgescu, Ioana, 1955- II. Title. III. Title: Five is the perfect number.
PN6767.I34C5513 2003   741.5'945   C2002-905021-9

Distributed in the USA and abroad by:
Chronicle Books
85 Second Street
San Francisco, CA 94105
800.722.6657

Distributed in Canada by:
Raincoast Books
9050 Shaughnessy Street
Vancouver, BC V6P 6E5
800.663.5714

chapter 1
tears from Napoli

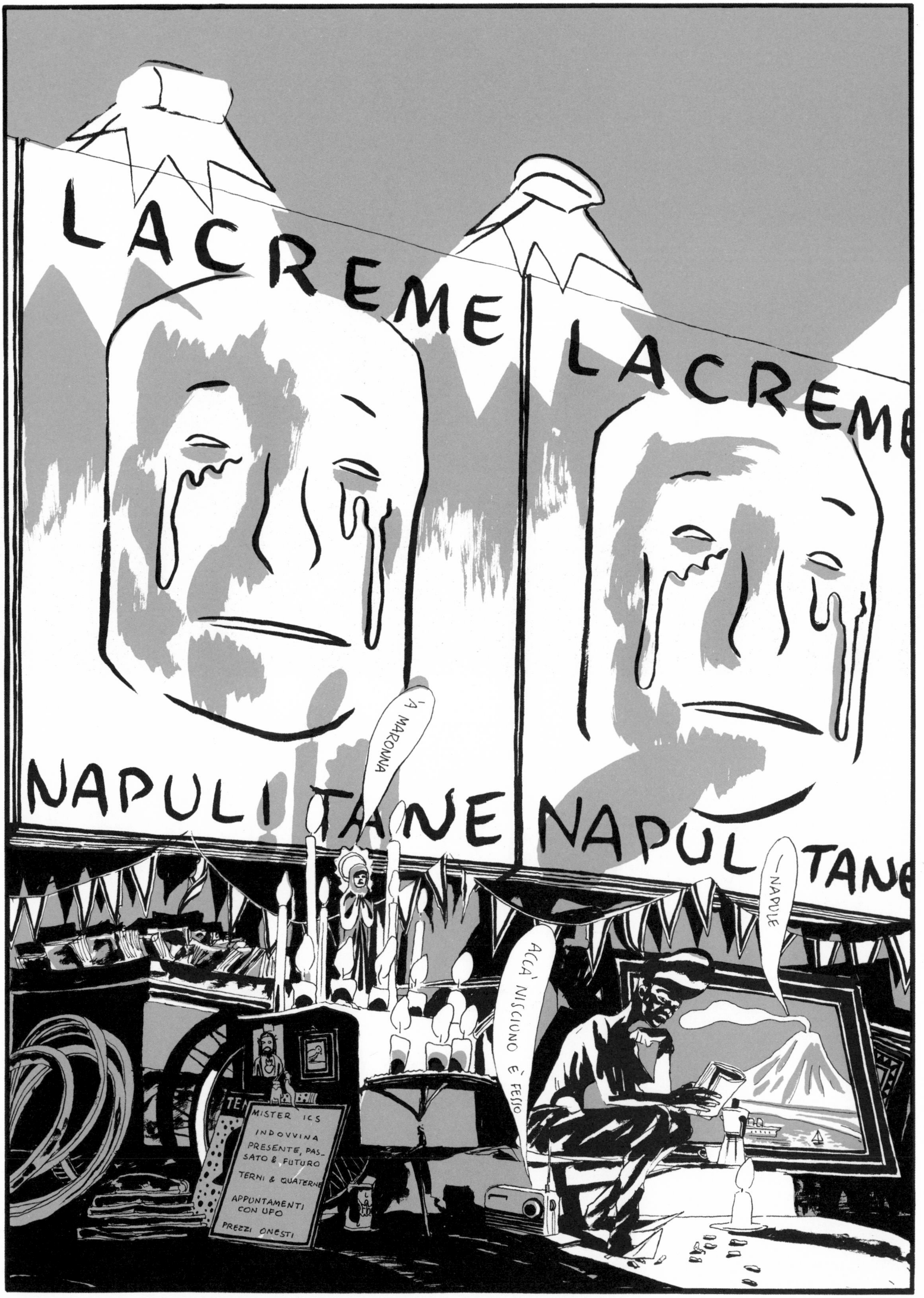
LACREME NAPULITANE
LACREME NAPULITANE
'A MARONNA
ACCÀ NISCIUNO È FESSO
—NAPULE
MISTER ICS
INDOVVINA PRESENTE, PASSATO & FUTURO
TERNI & QUATERNE
APPUNTAMENTI CON UFO
PREZZI ONESTI

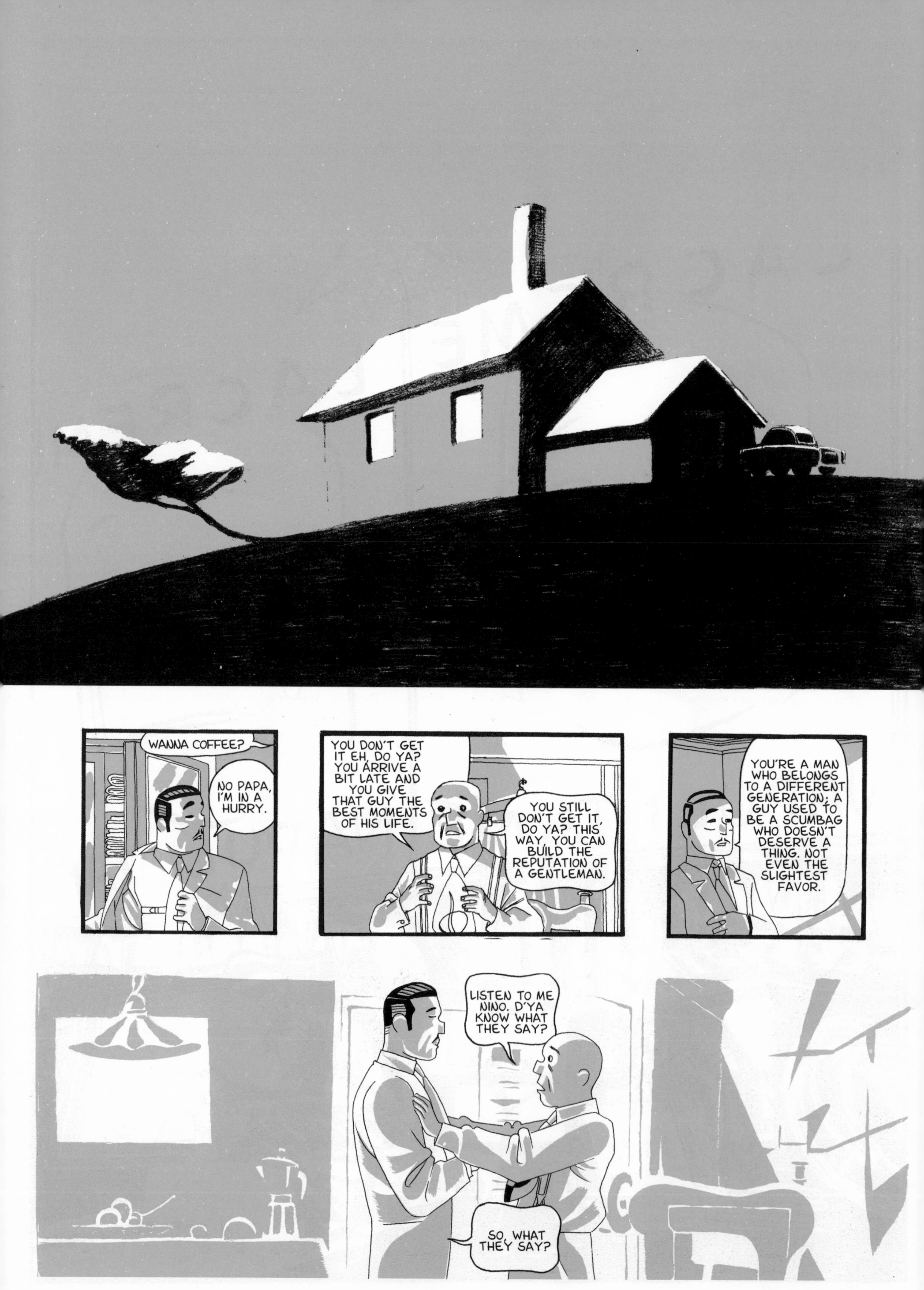
WANNA COFFEE?
NO PAPA, I'M IN A HURRY.
YOU DON'T GET IT EH, DO YA? YOU ARRIVE A BIT LATE AND YOU GIVE THAT GUY THE BEST MOMENTS OF HIS LIFE.
YOU STILL DON'T GET IT, DO YA? THIS WAY, YOU CAN BUILD THE REPUTATION OF A GENTLEMAN.
YOU'RE A MAN WHO BELONGS TO A DIFFERENT GENERATION; A GUY USED TO BE A SCUMBAG WHO DOESN'T DESERVE A THING. NOT EVEN THE SLIGHTEST FAVOR.
LISTEN TO ME NINO. D'YA KNOW WHAT THEY SAY?
SO, WHAT THEY SAY?

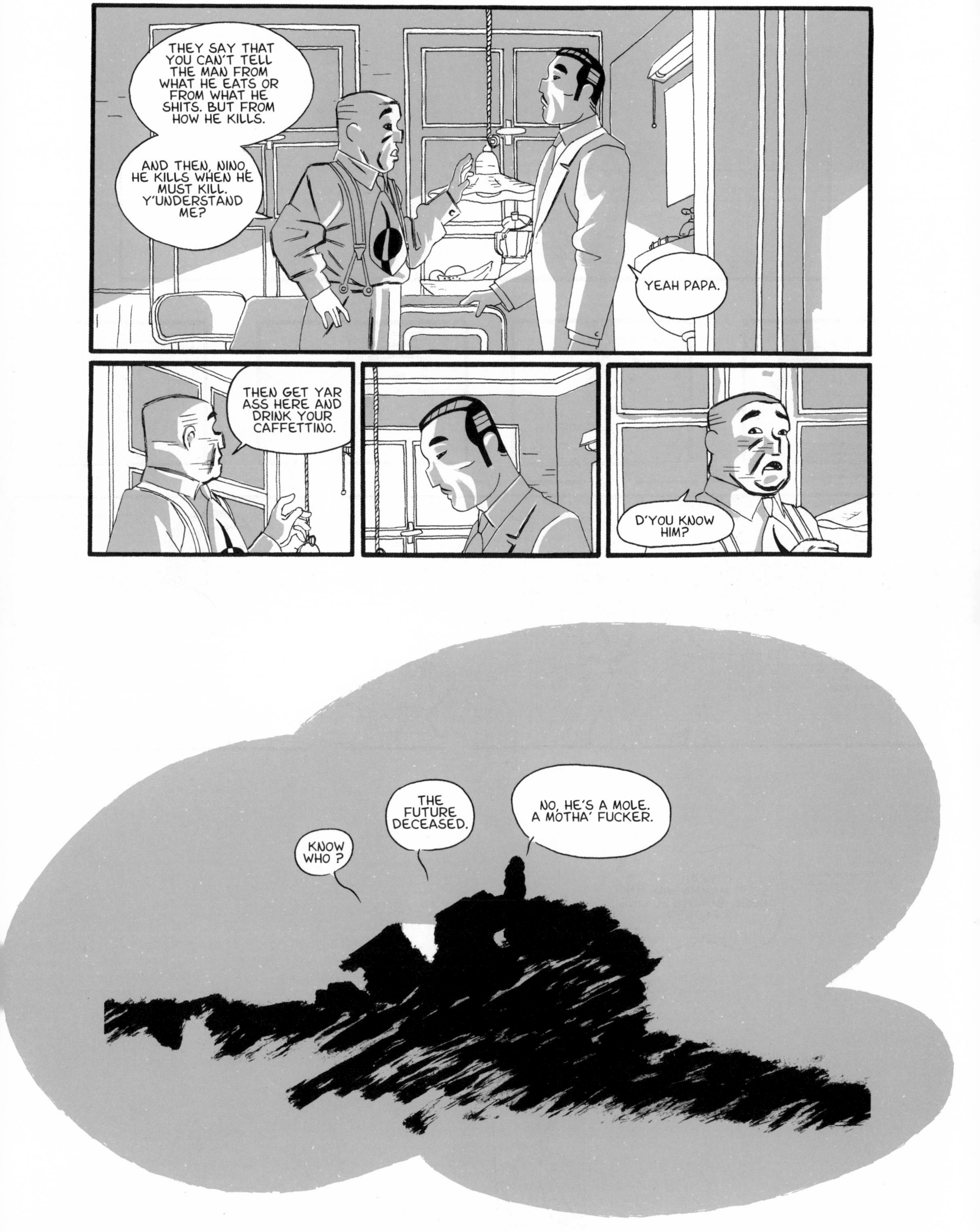
THEY SAY THAT YOU CAN'T TELL THE MAN FROM WHAT HE EATS OR FROM WHAT HE SHITS. BUT FROM HOW HE KILLS.
AND THEN, NINO, HE KILLS WHEN HE MUST KILL. Y'UNDERSTAND ME?
YEAH PAPA.
THEN GET YAR ASS HERE AND DRINK YOUR CAFFETTINO.
D'YOU KNOW HIM?
KNOW WHO ?
THE FUTURE DECEASED.
NO, HE'S A MOLE. A MOTHA' FUCKER.

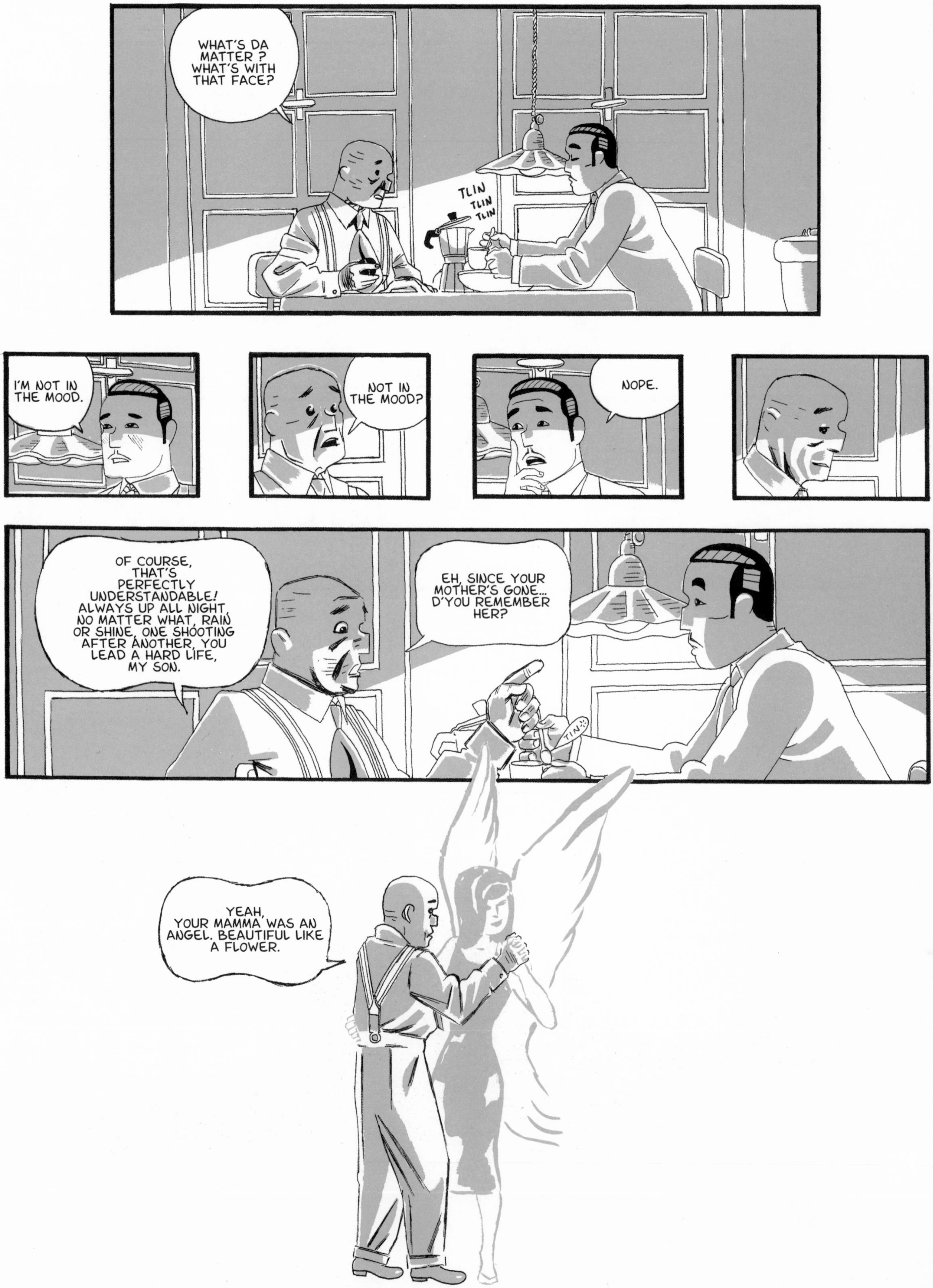
WHAT'S DA MATTER ? WHAT'S WITH THAT FACE?
TLIN TLIN TLIN
I'M NOT IN THE MOOD.
NOT IN THE MOOD?
NOPE.
OF COURSE, THAT'S PERFECTLY UNDERSTANDABLE! ALWAYS UP ALL NIGHT, NO MATTER WHAT, RAIN OR SHINE, ONE SHOOTING AFTER ANOTHER, YOU LEAD A HARD LIFE, MY SON.
EH, SINCE YOUR MOTHER'S GONE... D'YOU REMEMBER HER?
TIN
YEAH, YOUR MAMMA WAS AN ANGEL. BEAUTIFUL LIKE A FLOWER.

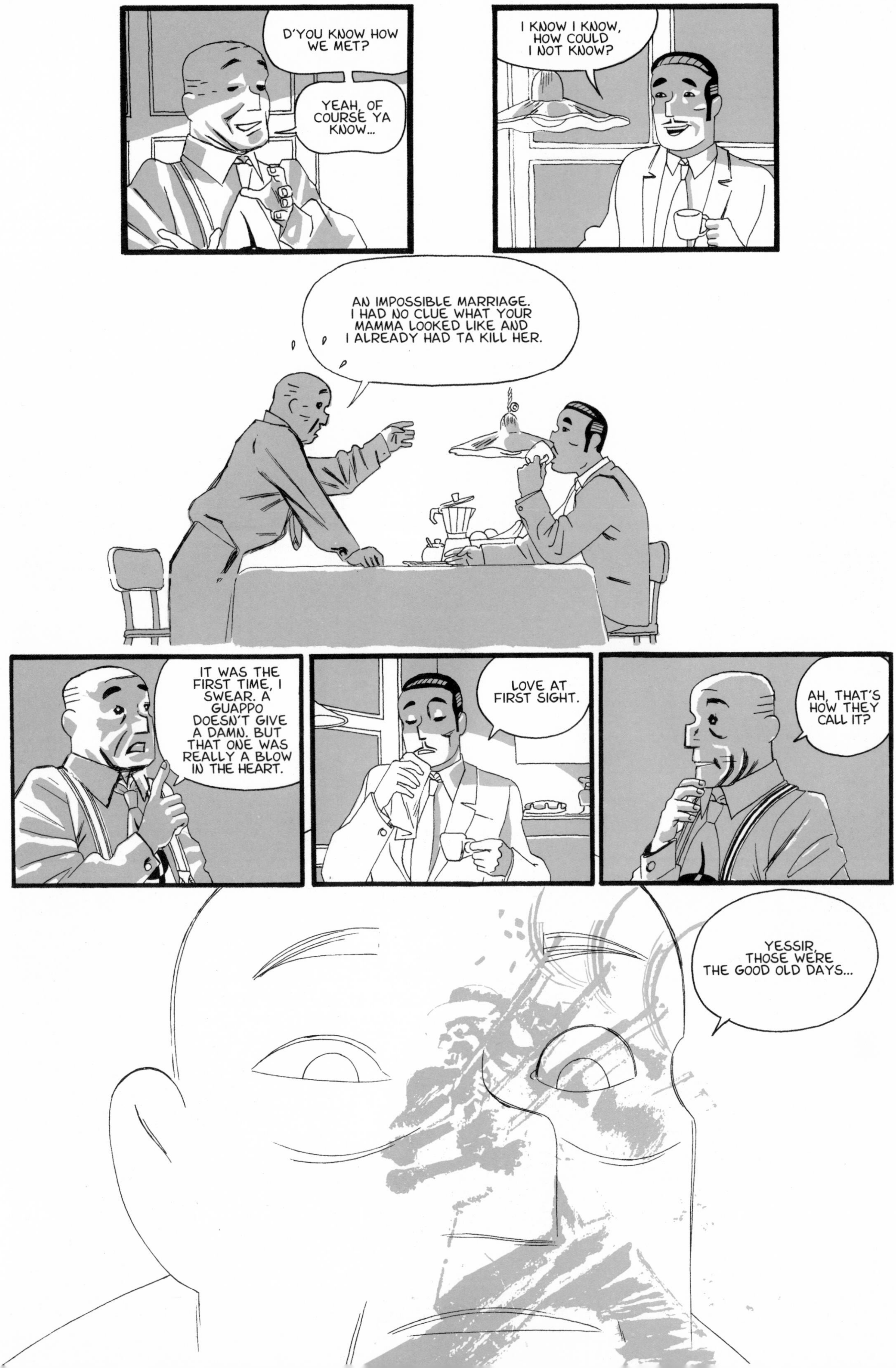
D'YOU KNOW HOW WE MET?
YEAH, OF COURSE YA KNOW...
I KNOW I KNOW, HOW COULD I NOT KNOW?
AN IMPOSSIBLE MARRIAGE. I HAD NO CLUE WHAT YOUR MAMMA LOOKED LIKE AND I ALREADY HAD TA KILL HER.
IT WAS THE FIRST TIME, I SWEAR. A GUAPPO DOESN'T GIVE A DAMN. BUT THAT ONE WAS REALLY A BLOW IN THE HEART.
LOVE AT FIRST SIGHT.
AH, THAT'S HOW THEY CALL IT?
YESSIR, THOSE WERE THE GOOD OLD DAYS...

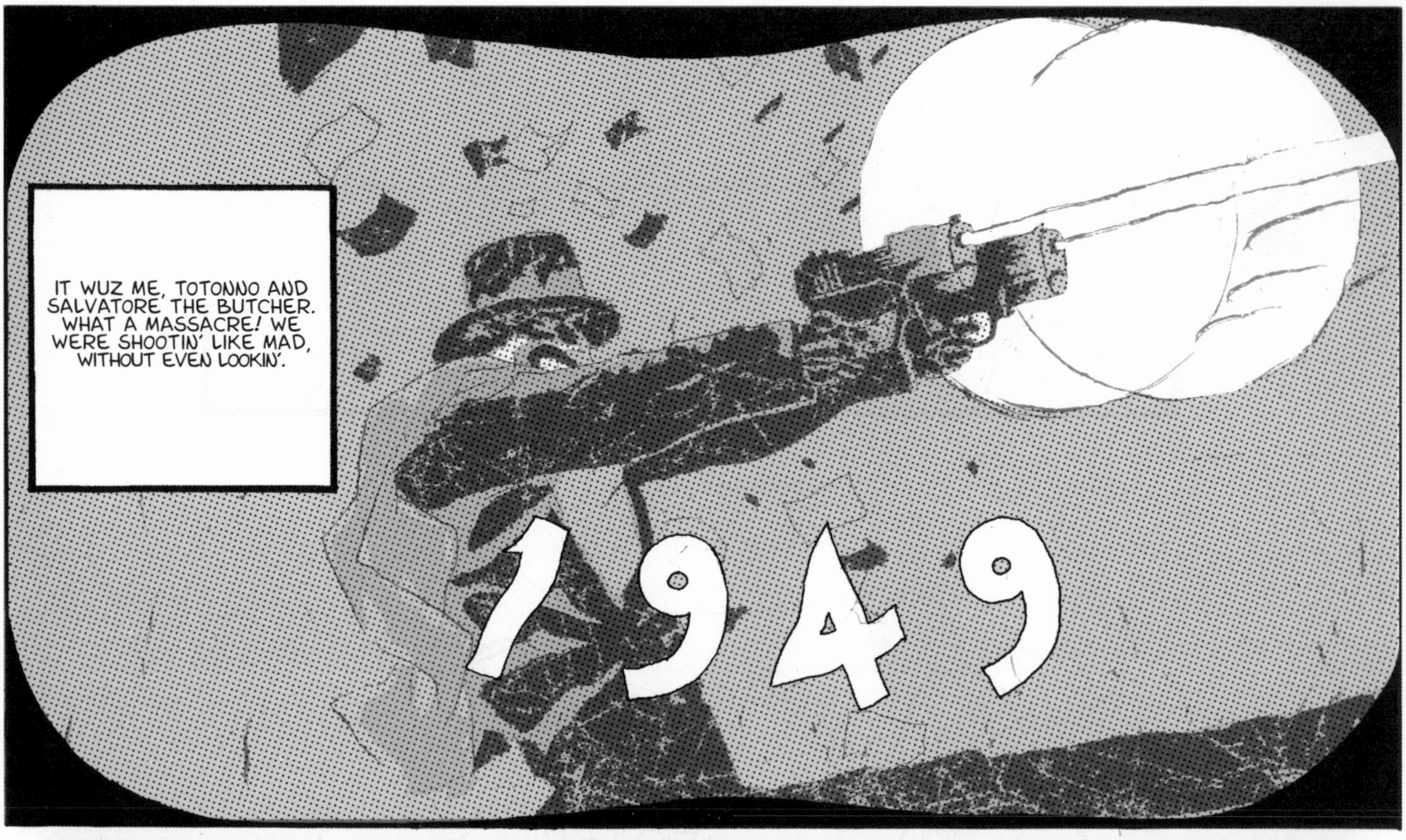
IT WUZ ME, TOTONNO AND SALVATORE THE BUTCHER. WHAT A MASSACRE! WE WERE SHOOTIN' LIKE MAD, WITHOUT EVEN LOOKIN'.
1949

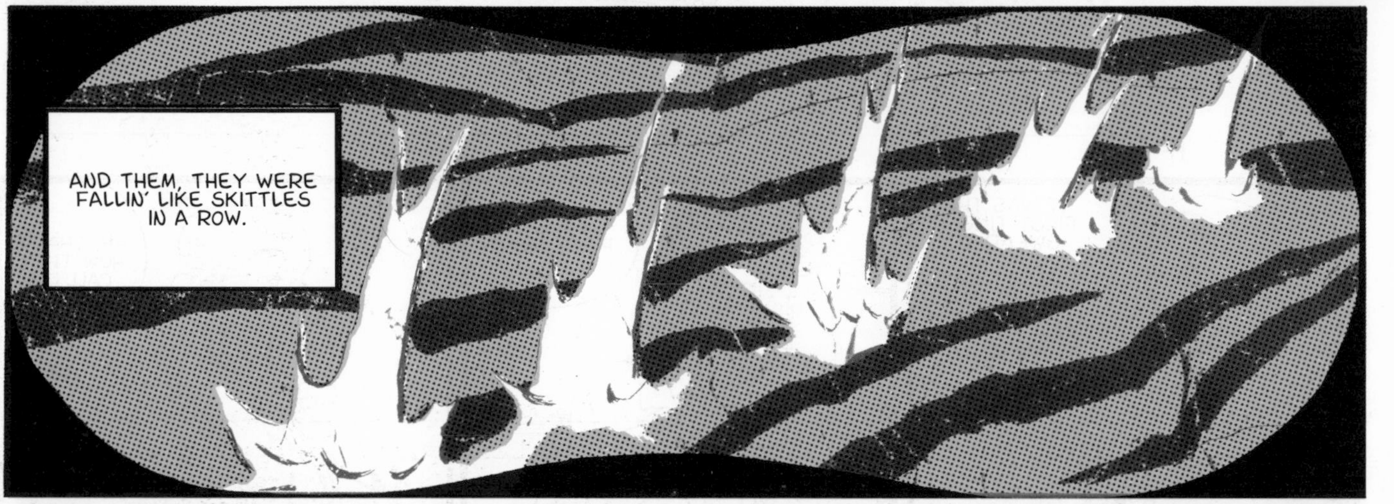
AND THEM, THEY WERE FALLIN' LIKE SKITTLES IN A ROW.

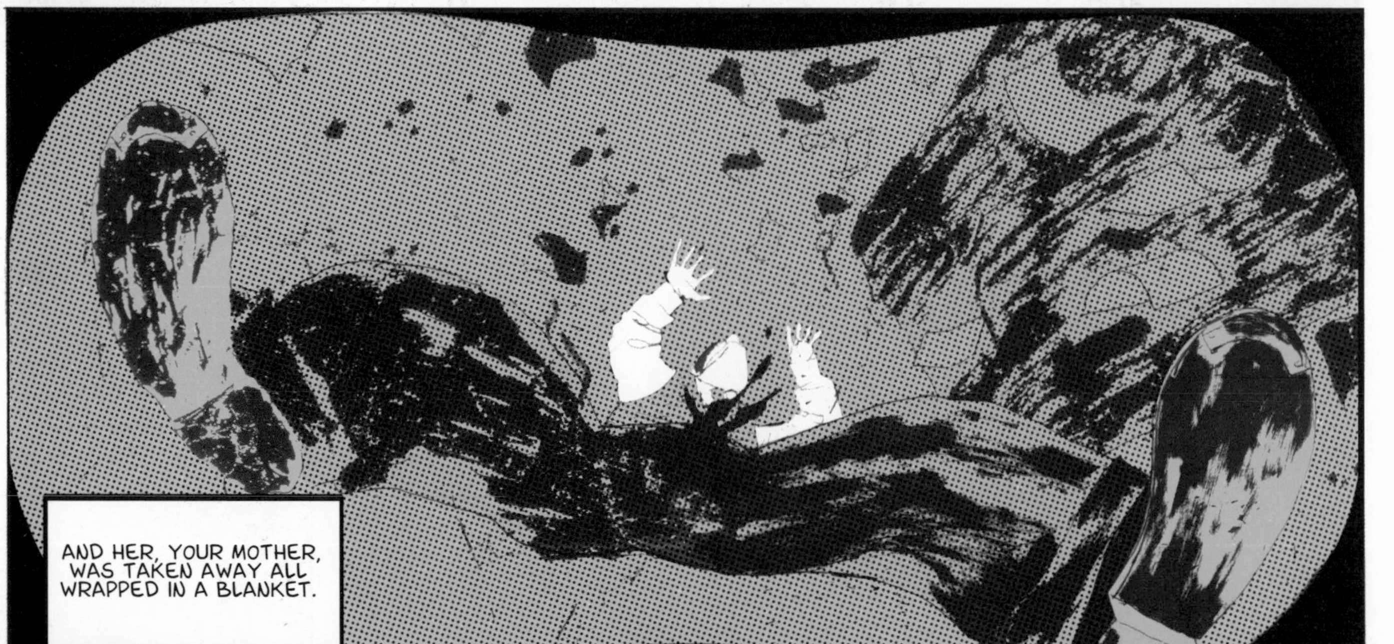
AND HER, YOUR MOTHER, WAS TAKEN AWAY ALL WRAPPED IN A BLANKET.

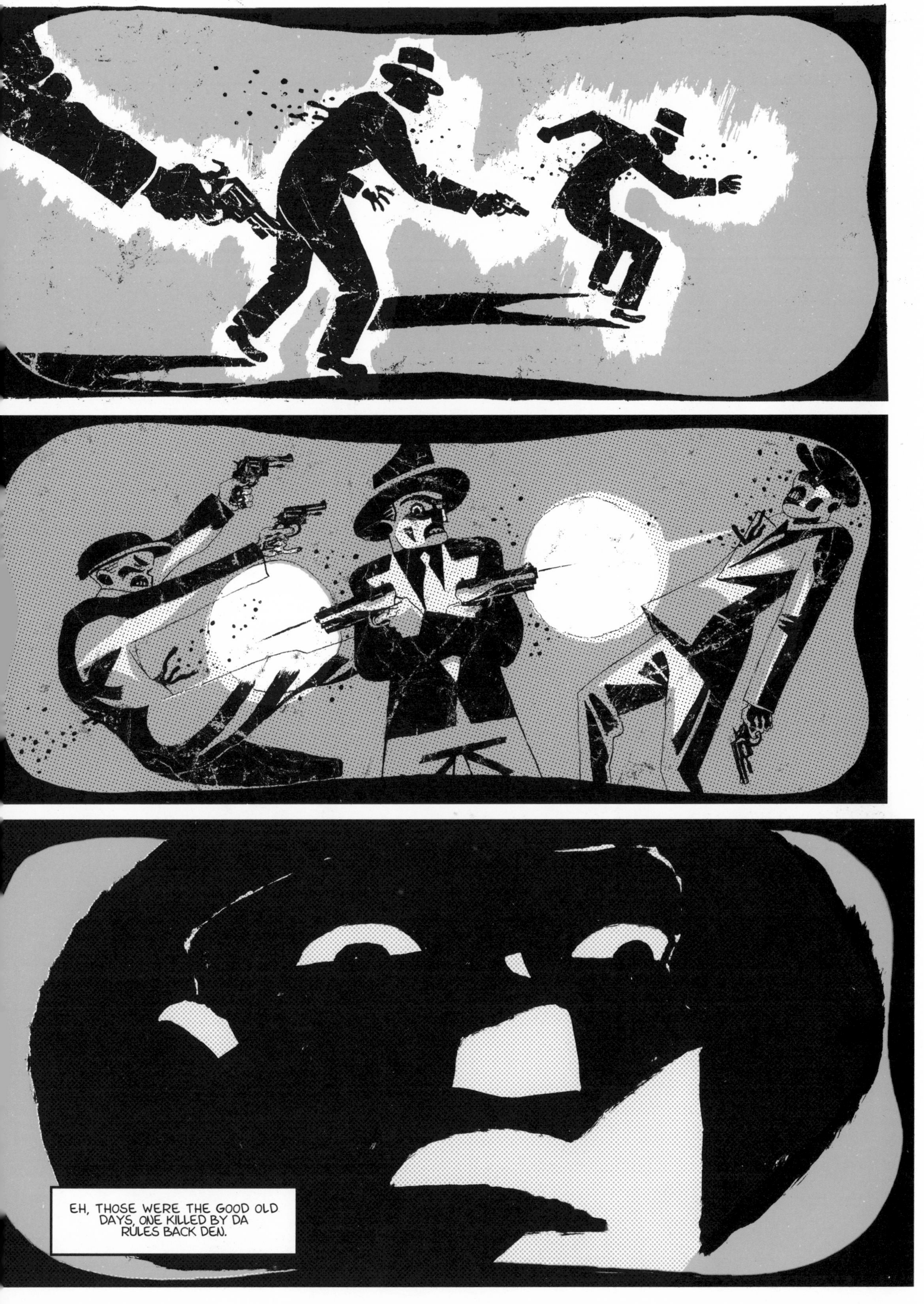
EH, THOSE WERE THE GOOD OLD DAYS, ONE KILLED BY DA RULES BACK DEN.

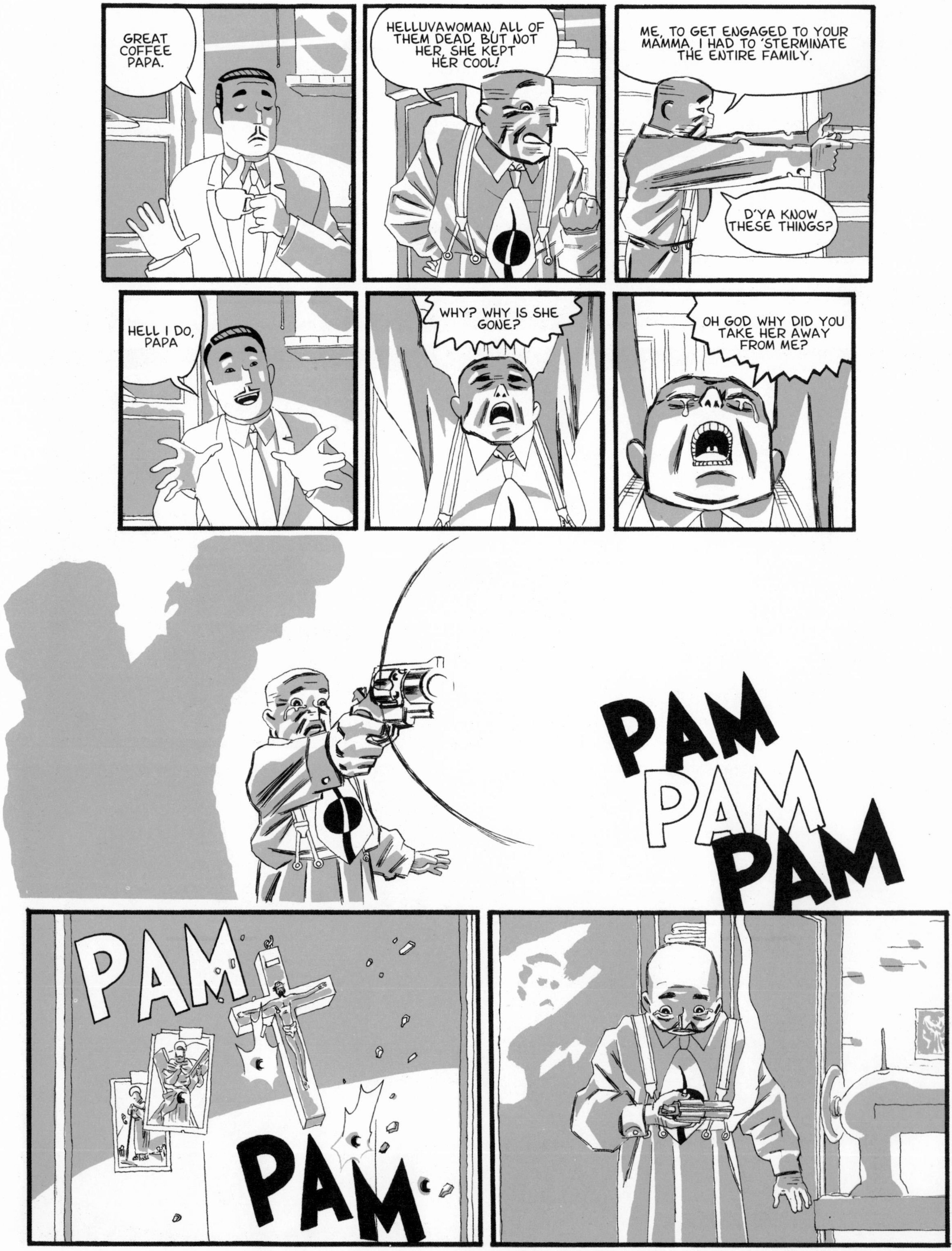

GREAT COFFEE PAPA.
HELLUVAWOMAN, ALL OF THEM DEAD, BUT NOT HER, SHE KEPT HER COOL!
ME, TO GET ENGAGED TO YOUR MAMMA, I HAD TO 'STERMINATE THE ENTIRE FAMILY.
D'YA KNOW THESE THINGS?
HELL I DO, PAPA
WHY? WHY IS SHE GONE?
OH GOD WHY DID YOU TAKE HER AWAY FROM ME?
PAM
PAM
PAM
PAM
PAM

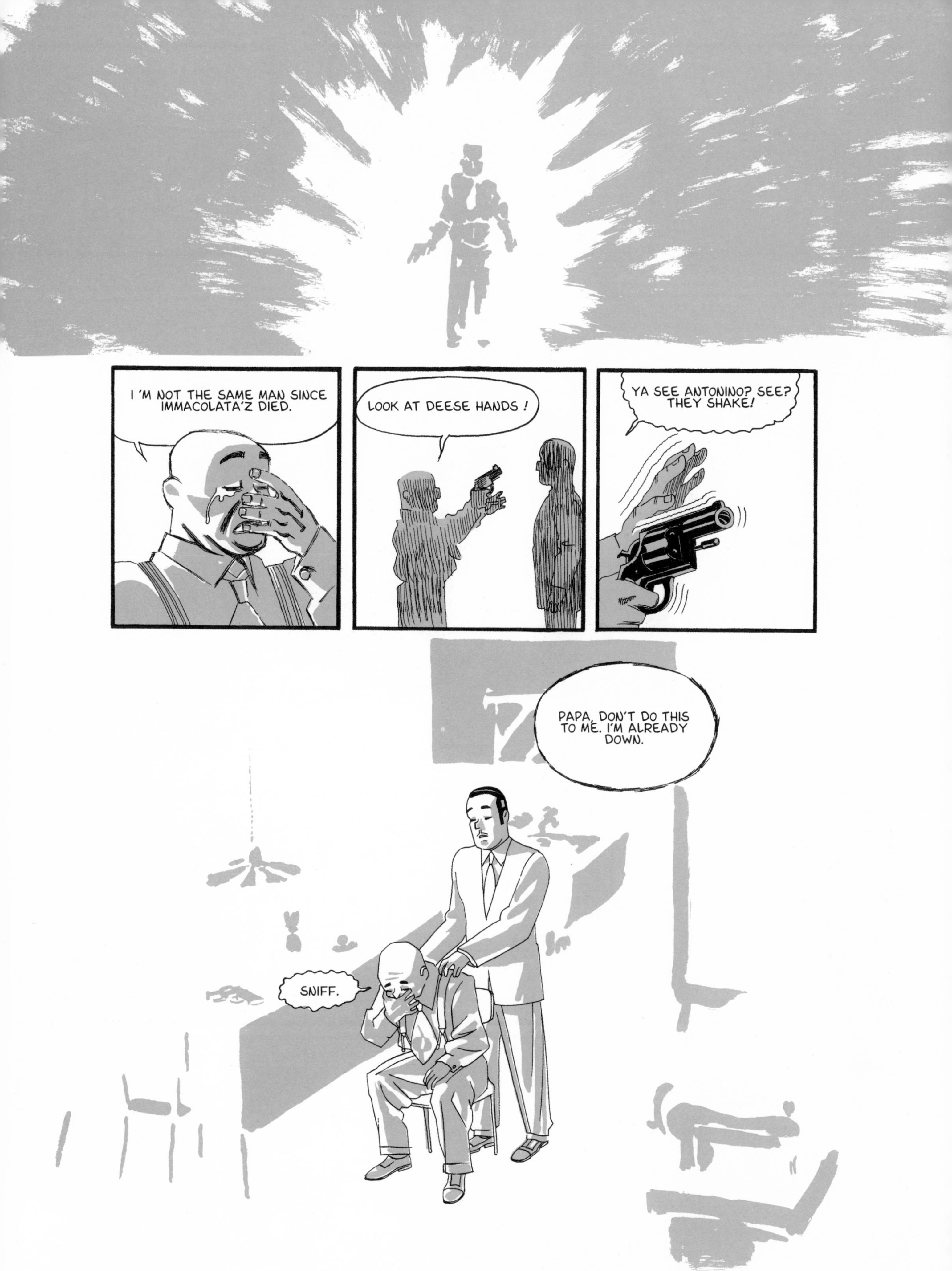
I 'M NOT THE SAME MAN SINCE IMMACOLATA'Z DIED.
LOOK AT DEESE HANDS !
YA SEE ANTONINO? SEE? THEY SHAKE!
PAPA, DON'T DO THIS TO ME. I'M ALREADY DOWN.
SNIFF.

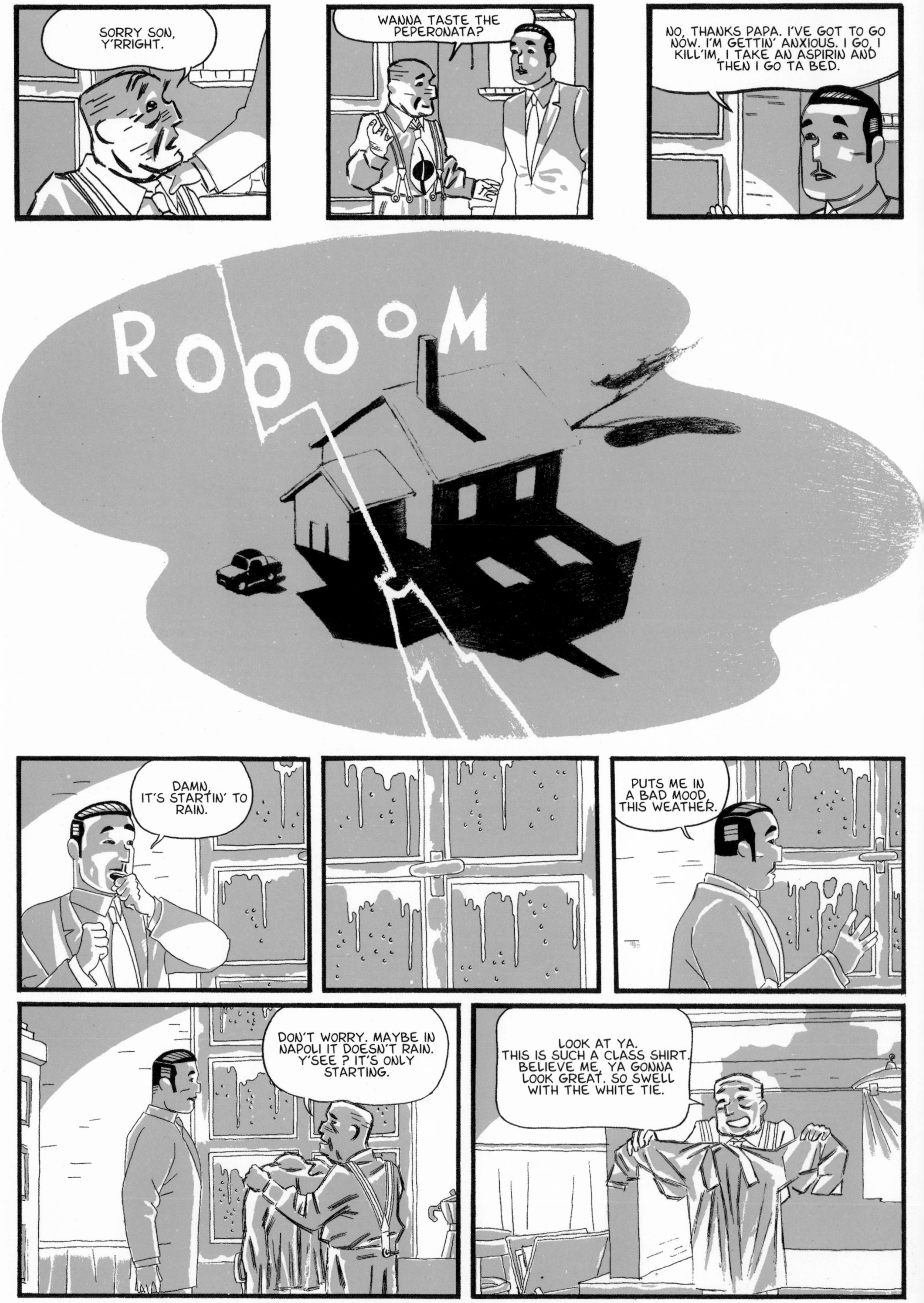
SORRY SON, Y'RRIGHT.
WANNA TASTE THE PEPERONATA?
NO, THANKS PAPA. I'VE GOT TO GO NOW. I'M GETTIN' ANXIOUS. I GO, I KILL'IM, I TAKE AN ASPIRIN AND THEN I GO TA BED.
ROOOOM
DAMN, IT'S STARTIN' TO RAIN.
PUTS ME IN A BAD MOOD THIS WEATHER.
DON'T WORRY. MAYBE IN NAPOLI IT DOESN'T RAIN. Y'SEE ? IT'S ONLY STARTING.
LOOK AT YA. THIS IS SUCH A CLASS SHIRT. BELIEVE ME, YA GONNA LOOK GREAT. SO SWELL WITH THE WHITE TIE.

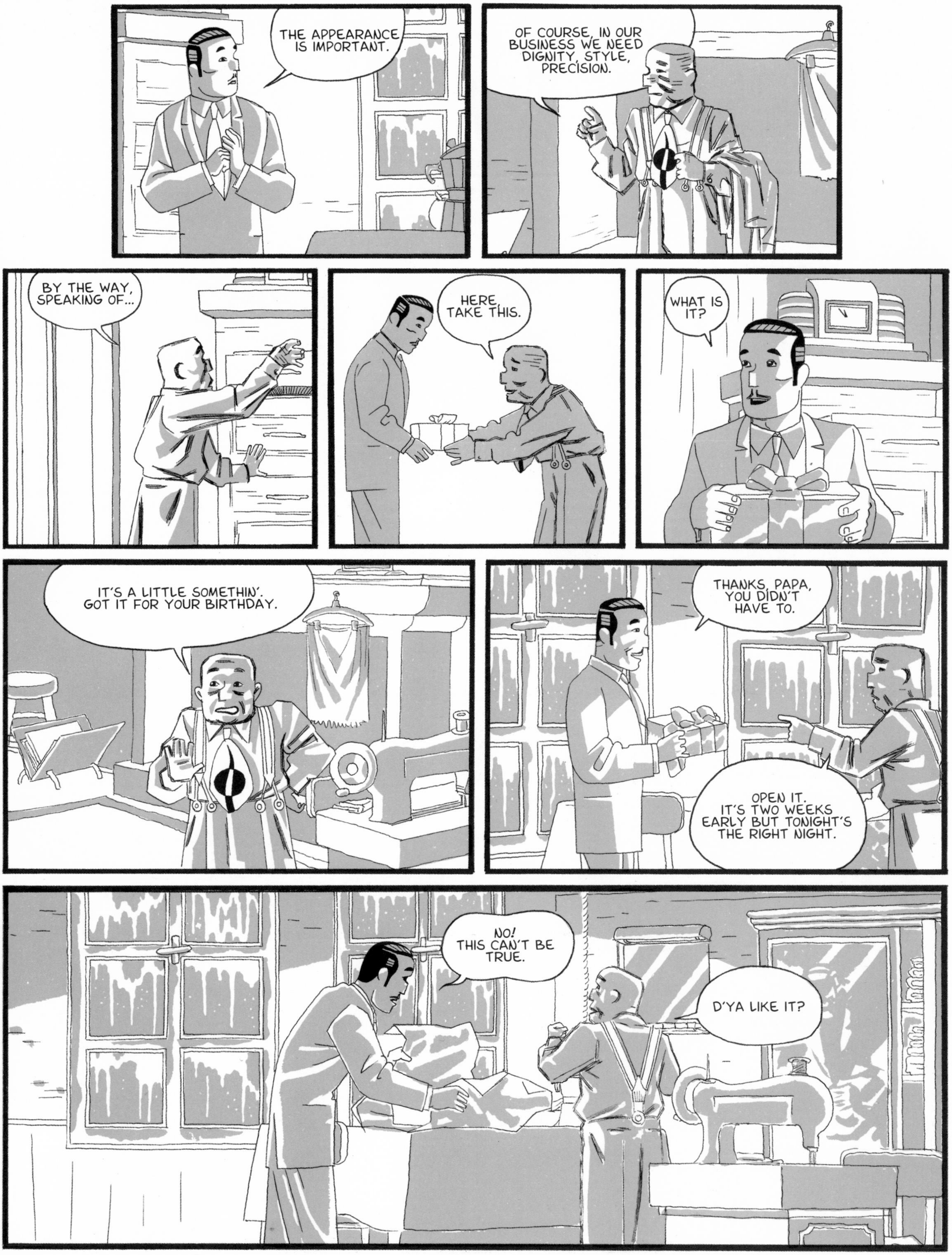
THE APPEARANCE IS IMPORTANT.
OF COURSE, IN OUR BUSINESS WE NEED DIGNITY, STYLE, PRECISION.
BY THE WAY, SPEAKING OF...
HERE, TAKE THIS.
WHAT IS IT?
IT'S A LITTLE SOMETHIN'. GOT IT FOR YOUR BIRTHDAY.
THANKS, PAPA, YOU DIDN'T HAVE TO.
OPEN IT. IT'S TWO WEEKS EARLY BUT TONIGHT'S THE RIGHT NIGHT.
NO! THIS CAN'T BE TRUE.
D'YA LIKE IT?

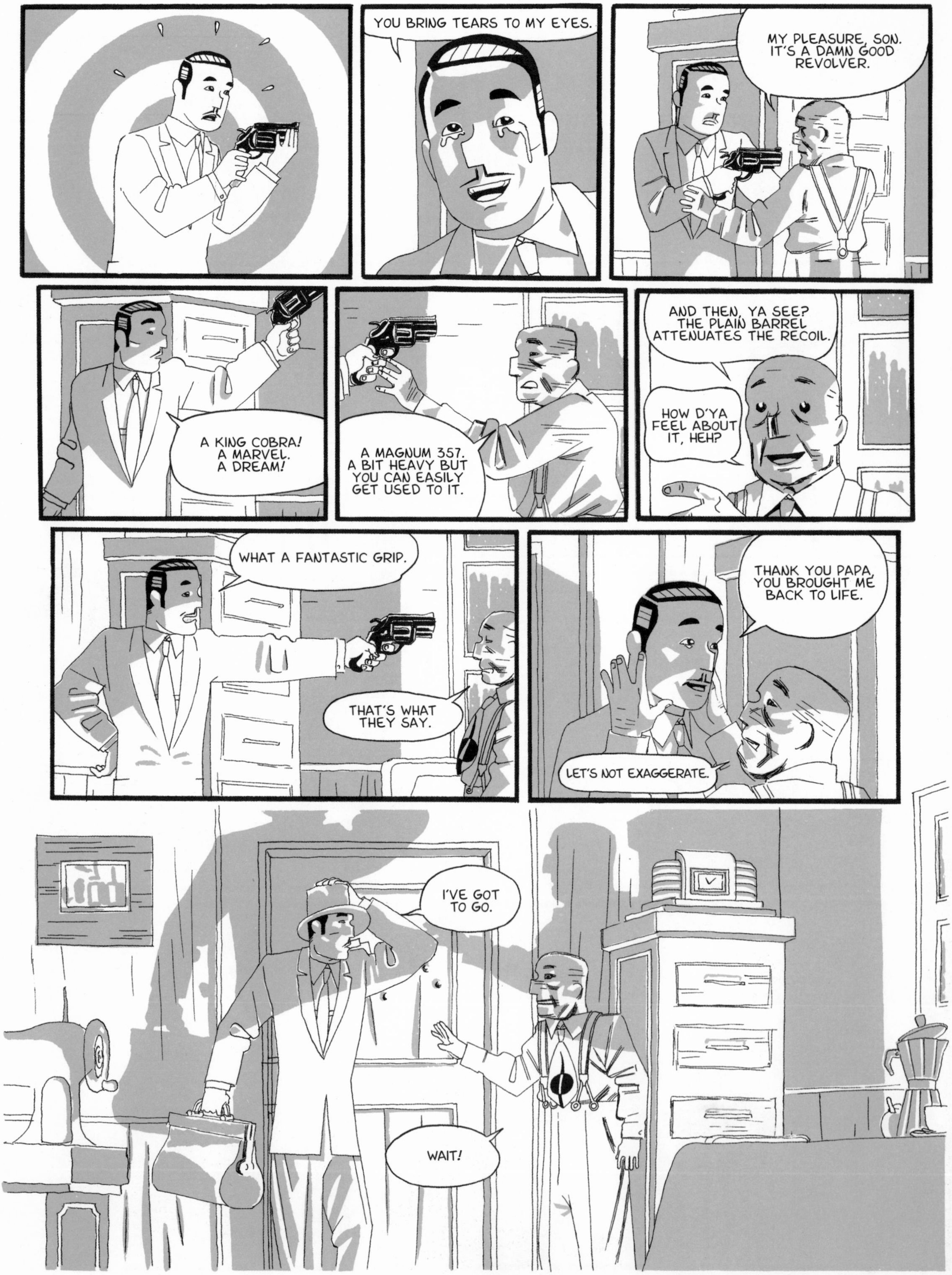
YOU BRING TEARS TO MY EYES.
MY PLEASURE, SON. IT'S A DAMN GOOD REVOLVER.
A KING COBRA! A MARVEL. A DREAM!
A MAGNUM 357. A BIT HEAVY BUT YOU CAN EASILY GET USED TO IT.
AND THEN, YA SEE? THE PLAIN BARREL ATTENUATES THE RECOIL.
HOW D'YA FEEL ABOUT IT, HEH?
WHAT A FANTASTIC GRIP.
THAT'S WHAT THEY SAY.
THANK YOU PAPA, YOU BROUGHT ME BACK TO LIFE.
LET'S NOT EXAGGERATE.
I'VE GOT TO GO.
WAIT!

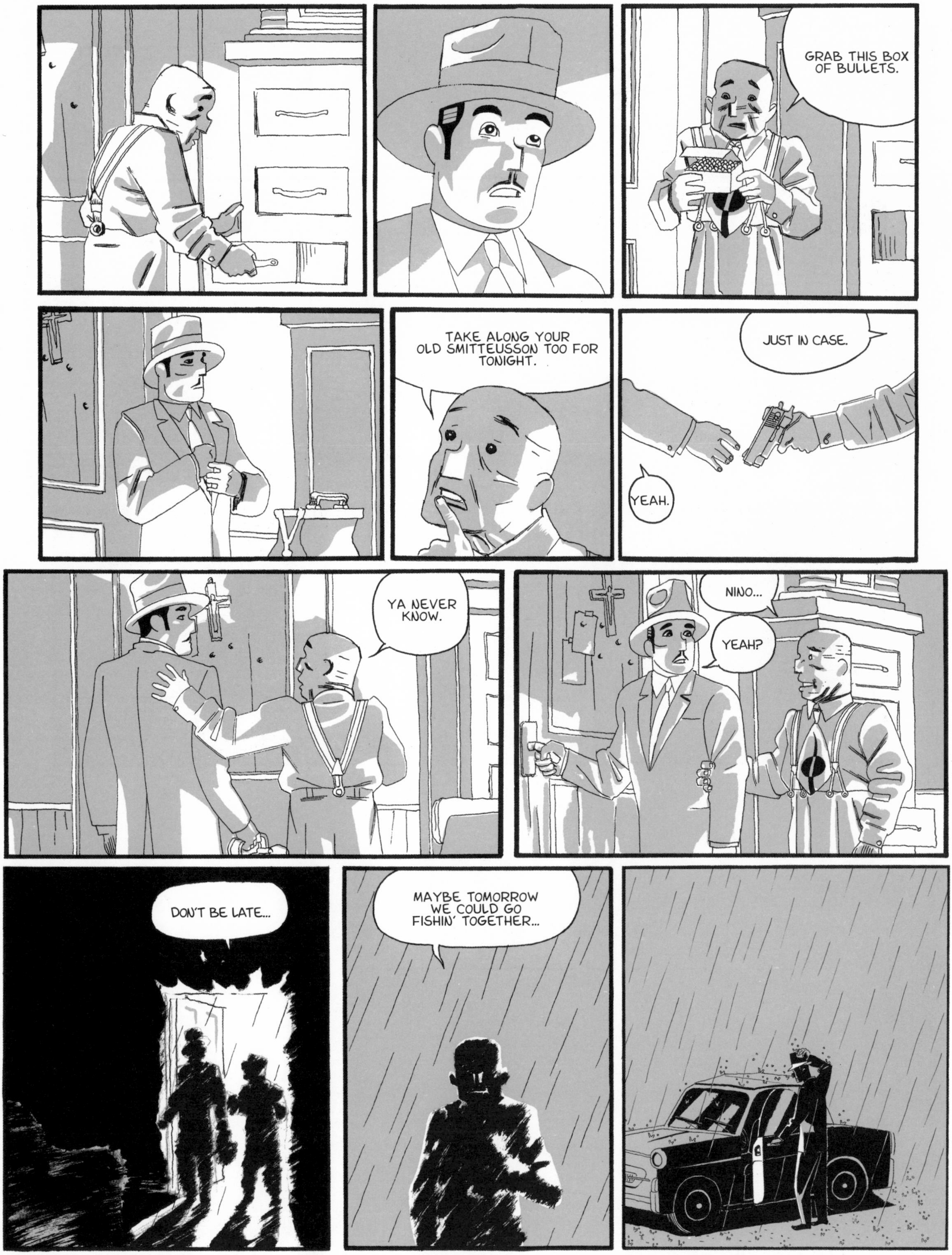
GRAB THIS BOX OF BULLETS.
TAKE ALONG YOUR OLD SMITTEUSSON TOO FOR TONIGHT.
JUST IN CASE.
YEAH.
YA NEVER KNOW.
NINO...
YEAH?
DON'T BE LATE...
MAYBE TOMORROW WE COULD GO FISHIN' TOGETHER...

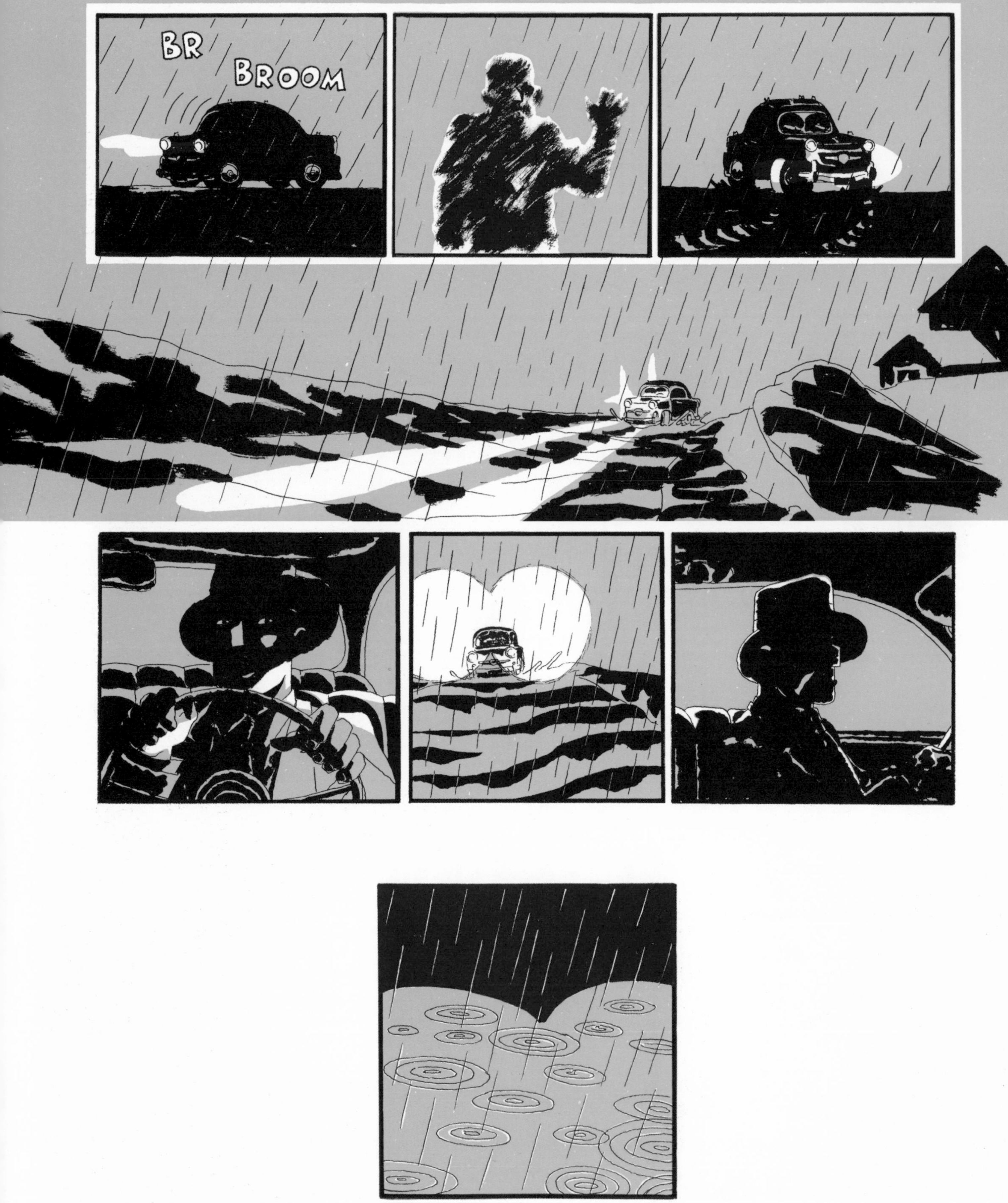
BR
BROOM

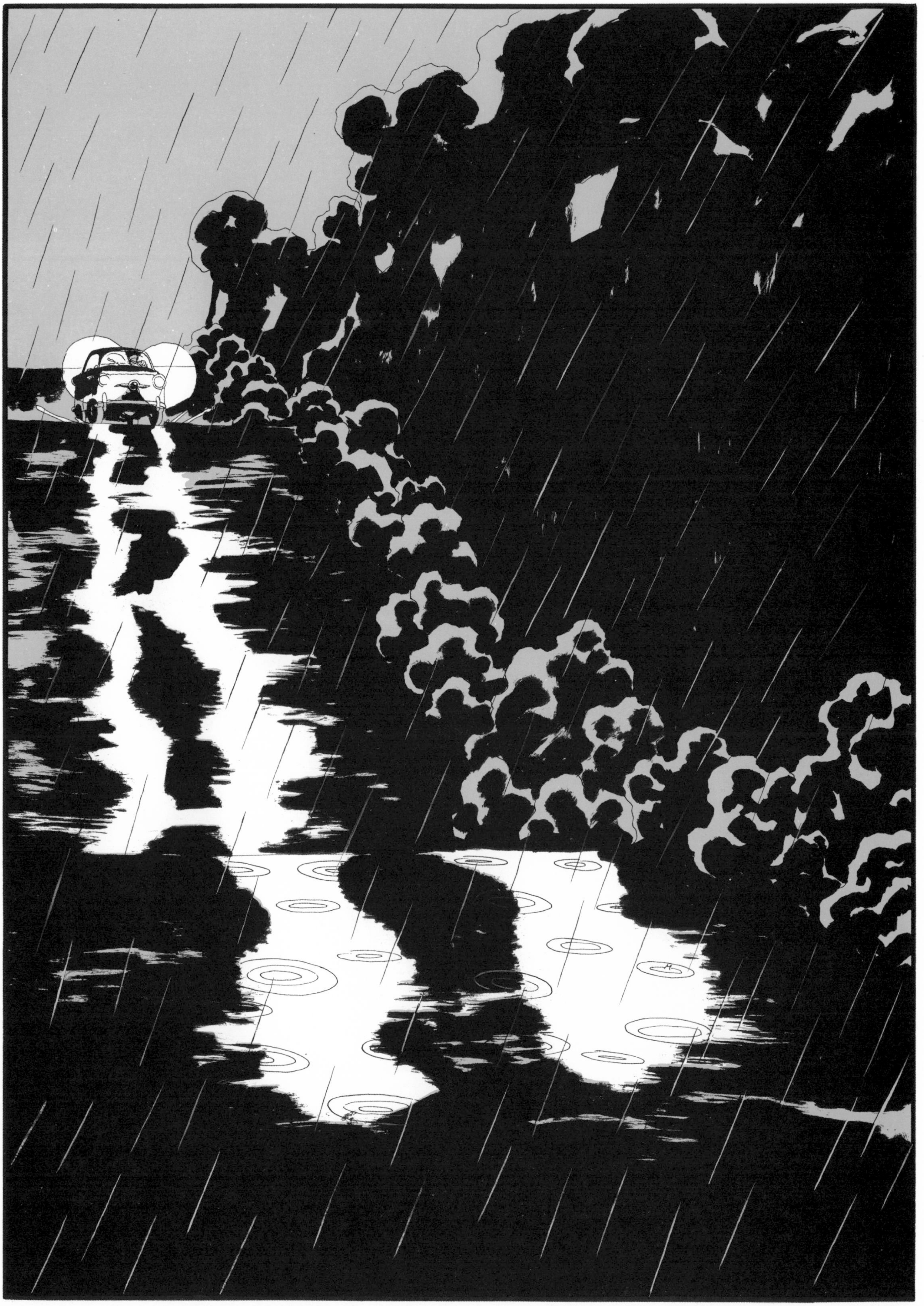

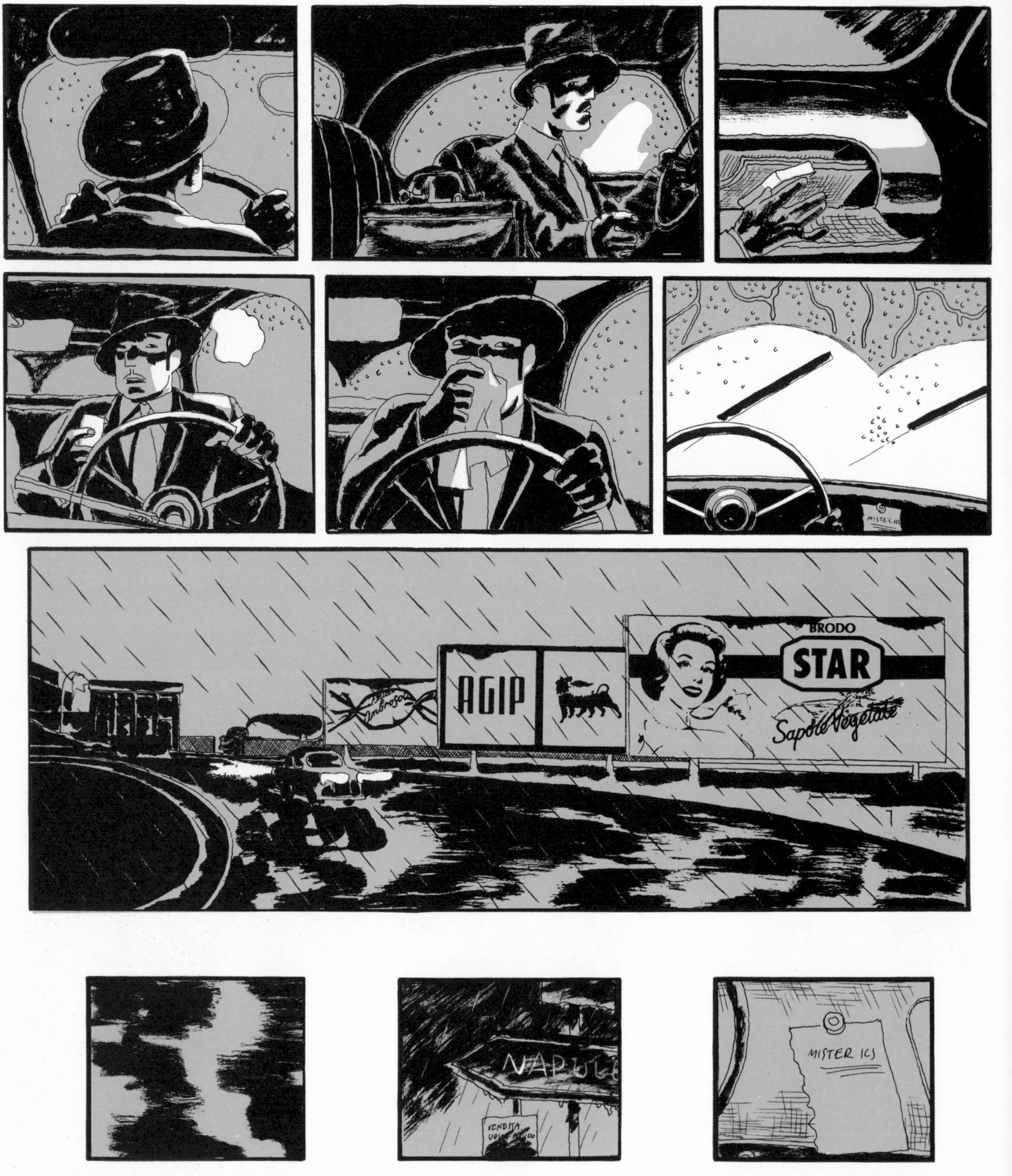
AGIP
BRODO
STAR
Sapore Vegetale
MISTER ICS

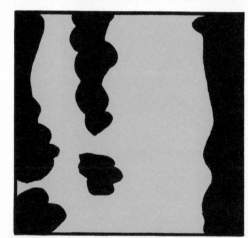

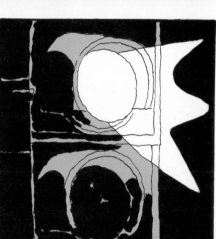

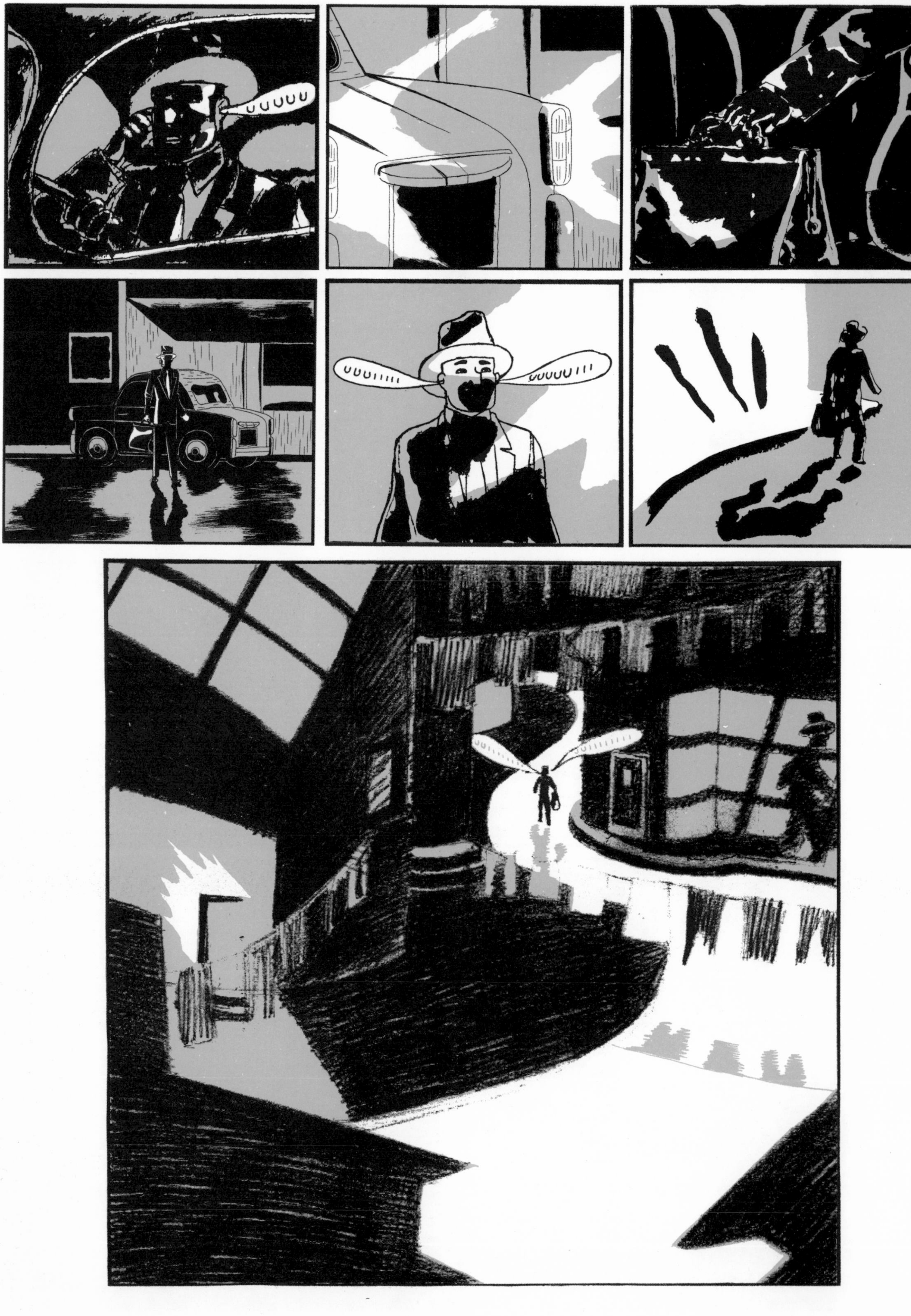

LACREME
NAPULITANE
NAPULITANE
ZKFFFFF

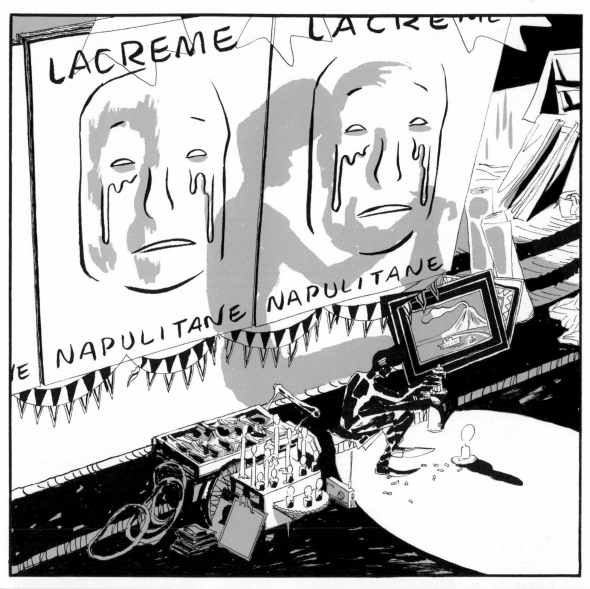

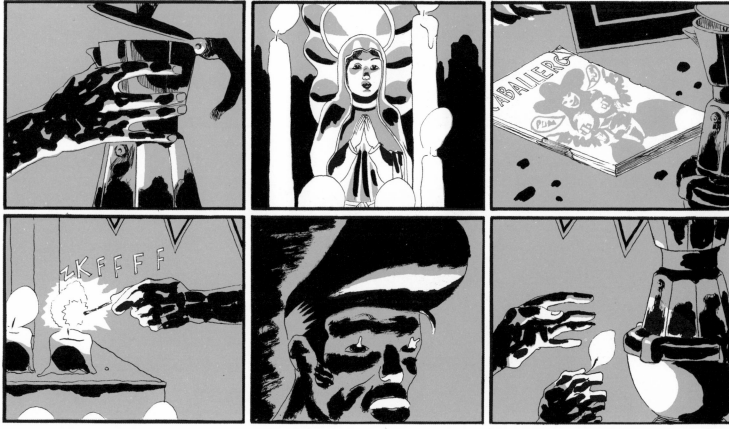

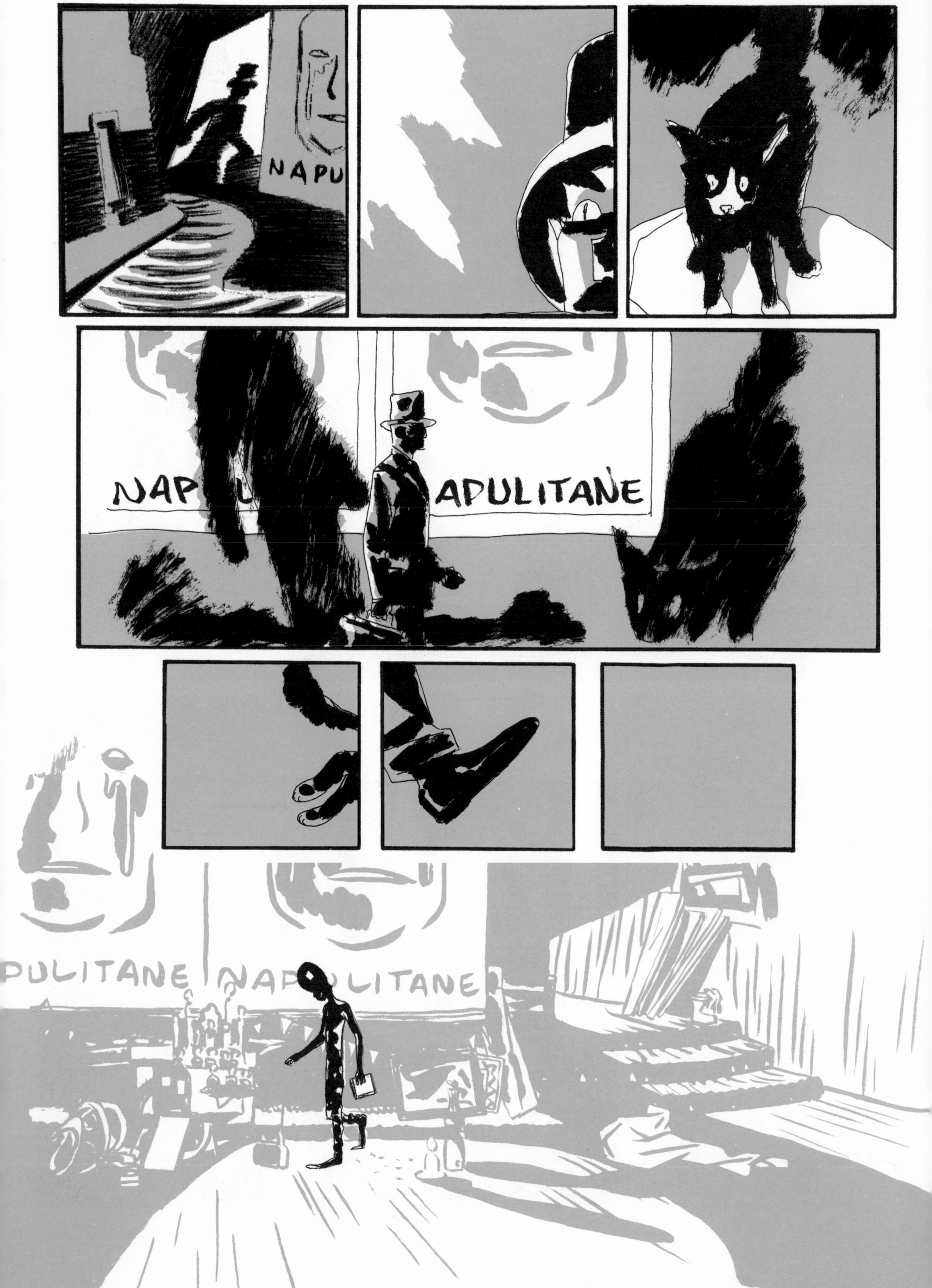
NAPU
NAP
APULITANE
PULITANE
NAP LITANE

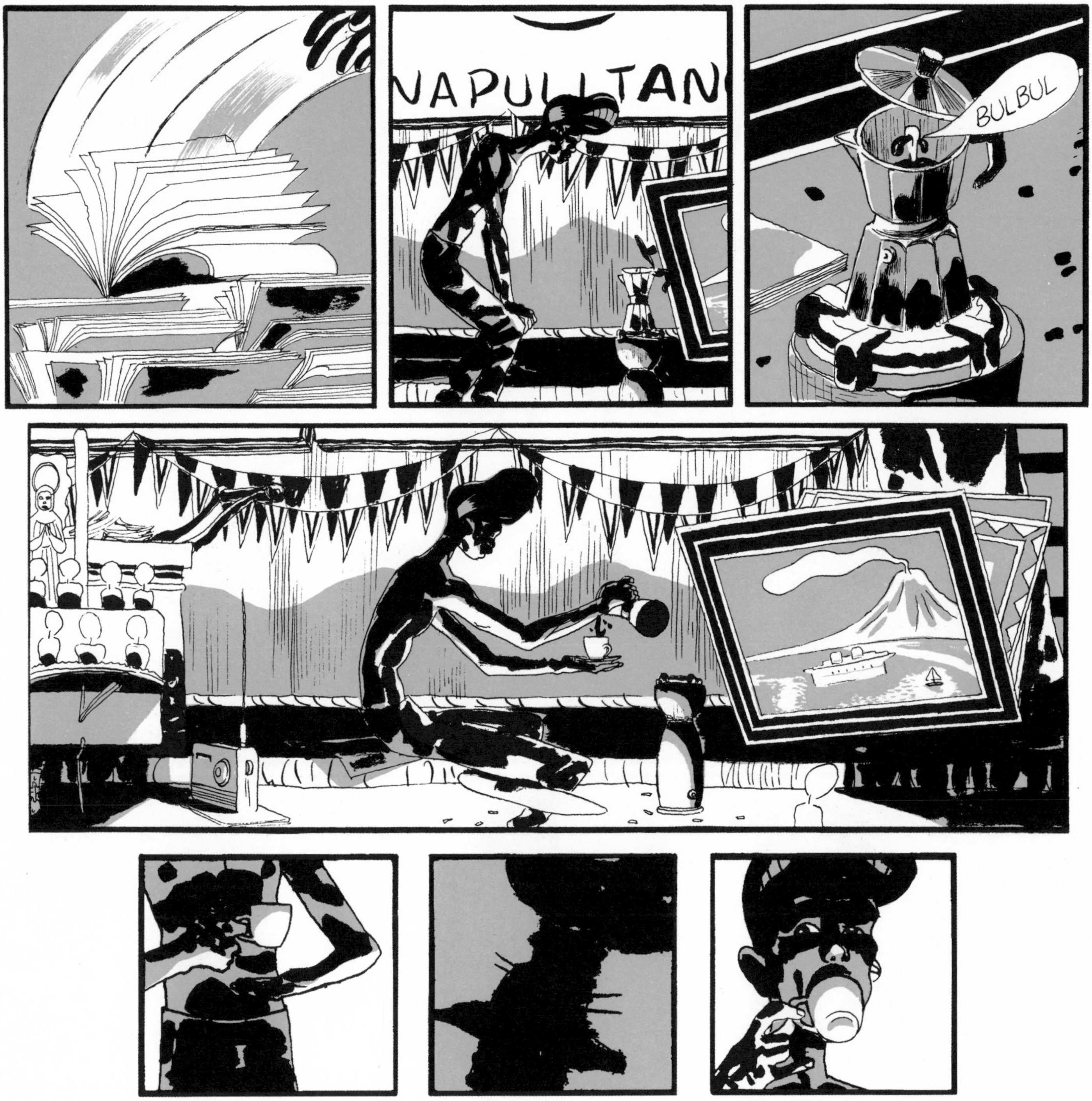
BULBUL

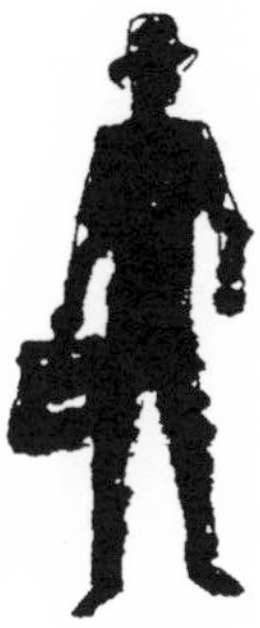

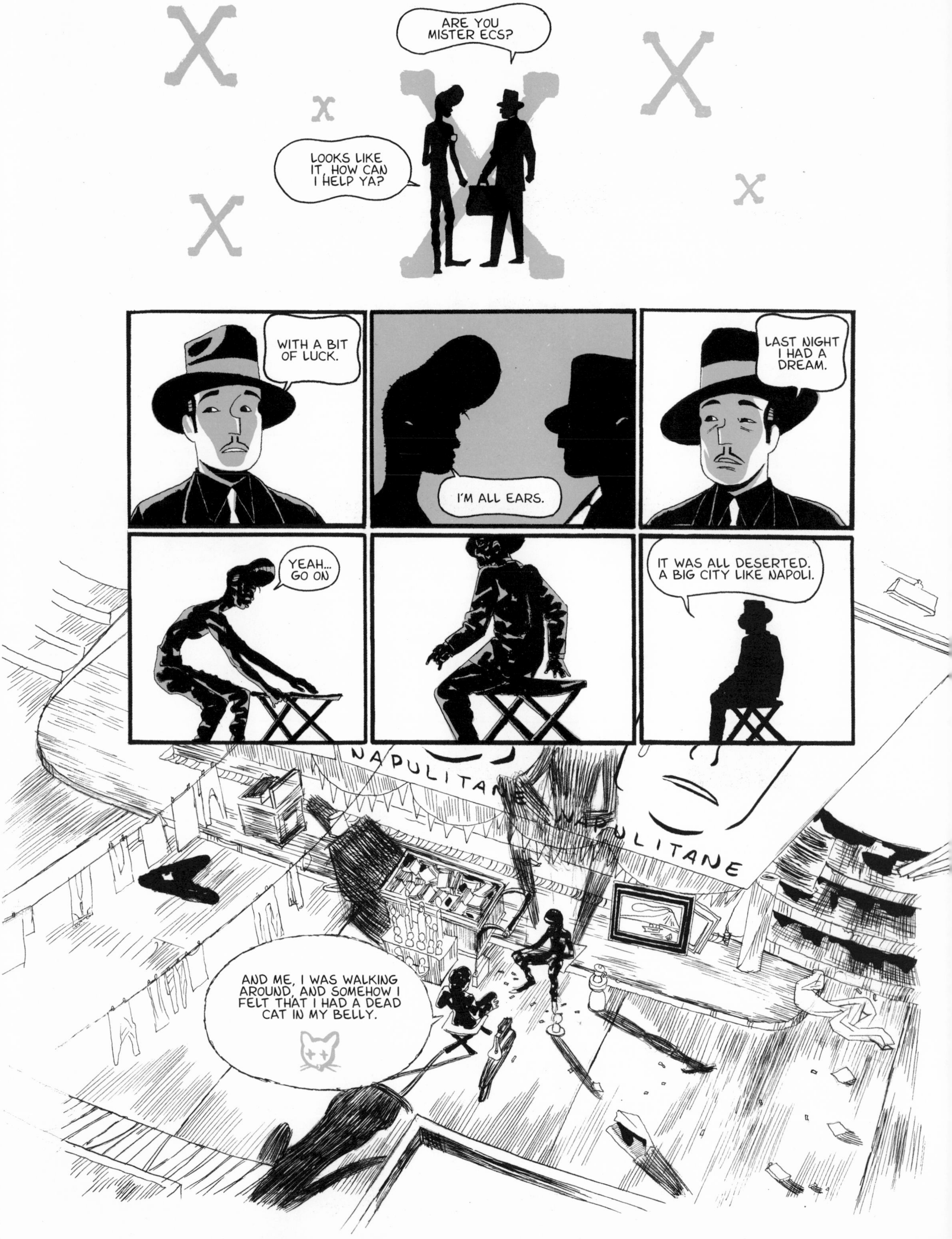
ARE YOU MISTER ECS?
LOOKS LIKE IT, HOW CAN I HELP YA?
WITH A BIT OF LUCK.
I'M ALL EARS.
LAST NIGHT I HAD A DREAM.
YEAH... GO ON
IT WAS ALL DESERTED. A BIG CITY LIKE NAPOLI.
NAPULITANE
NAPULITANE
AND ME, I WAS WALKING AROUND, AND SOMEHOW I FELT THAT I HAD A DEAD CAT IN MY BELLY.

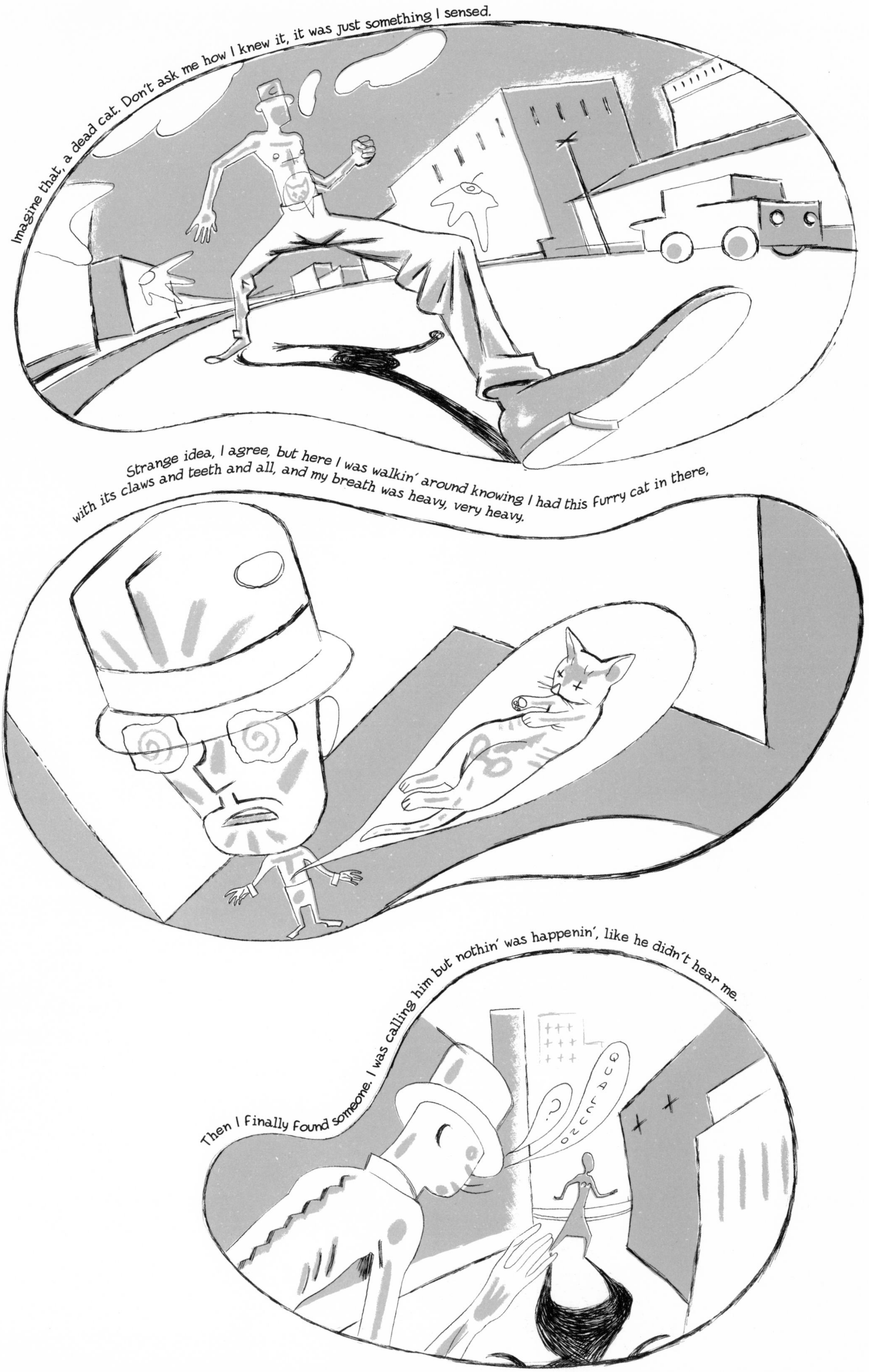
Imagine that, a dead cat. Don't ask me how I knew it, it was just something I sensed.
Strange idea, I agree, but here I was walkin' around knowing I had this furry cat in there, with its claws and teeth and all, and my breath was heavy, very heavy.
Then I finally found someone. I was calling him but nothin' was happenin', like he didn't hear me.

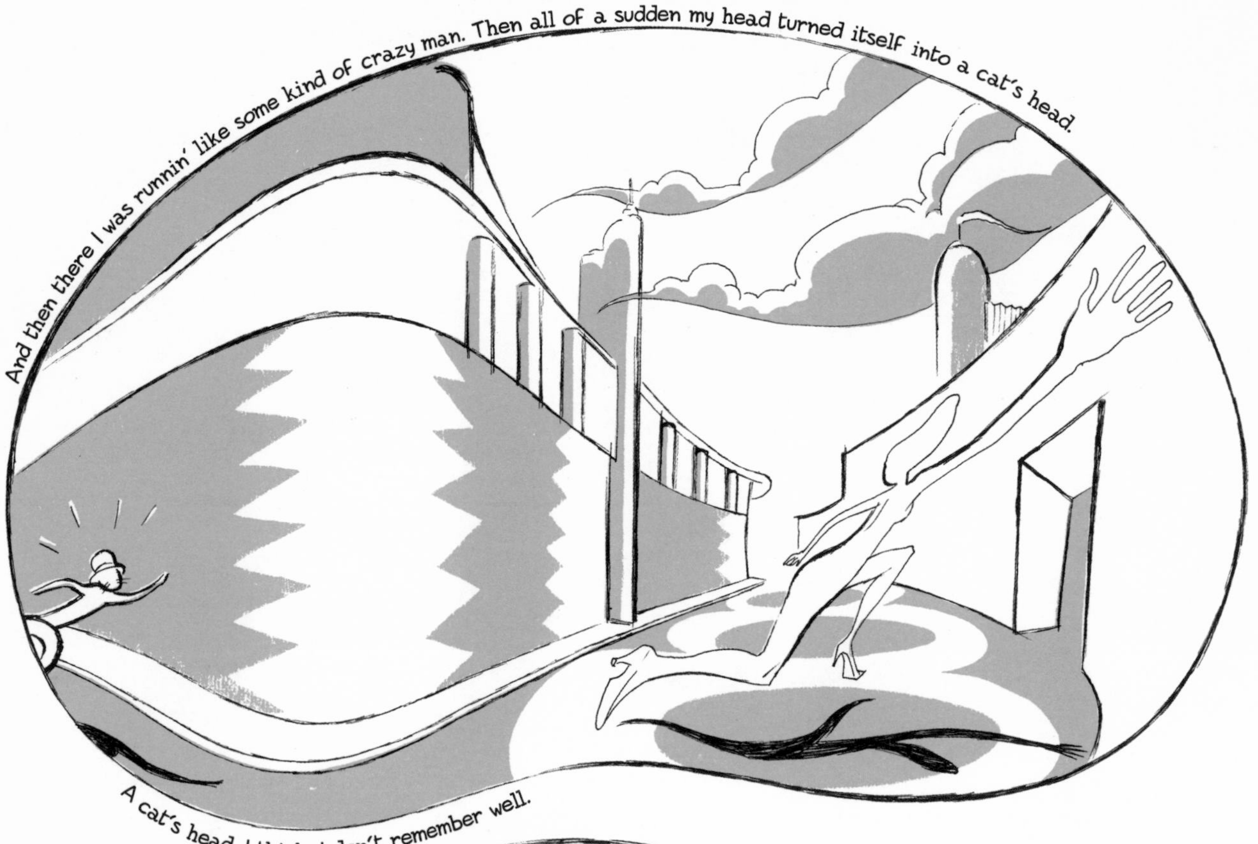
And then there I was runnin' like some kind of crazy man. Then all of a sudden my head turned itself into a cat's head.
A cat's head, I think, I don't remember well.

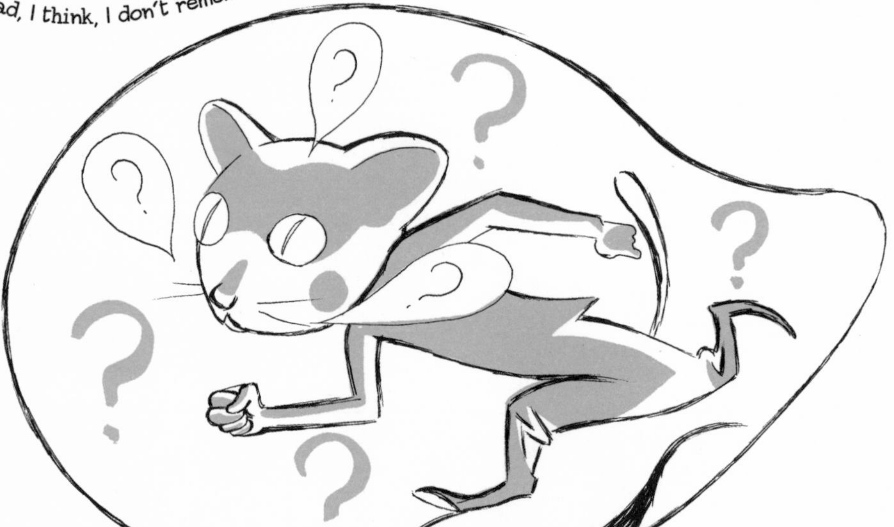
?
?
?
?
?
?
?

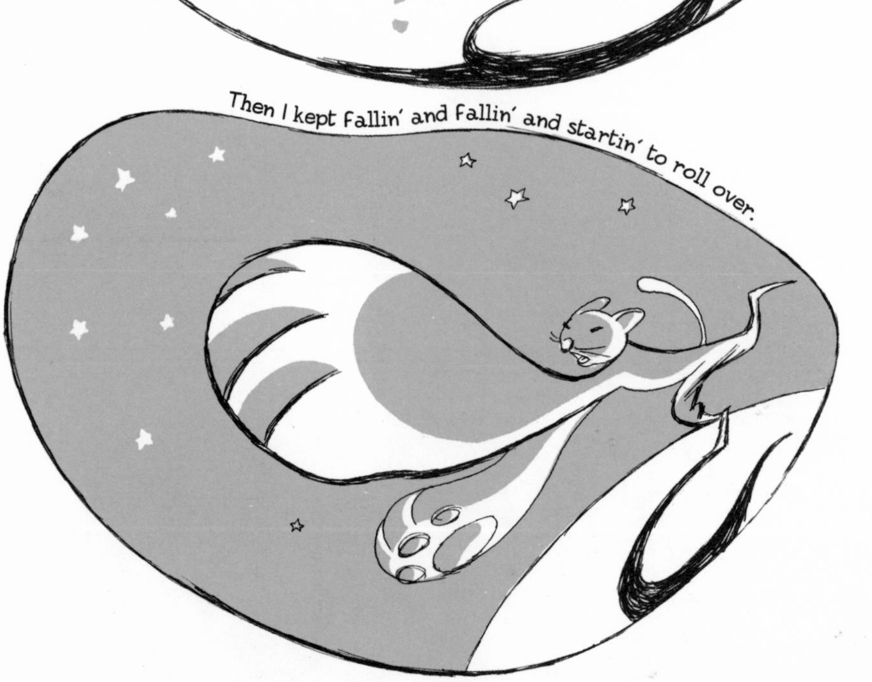
Then I kept fallin' and fallin' and startin' to roll over.

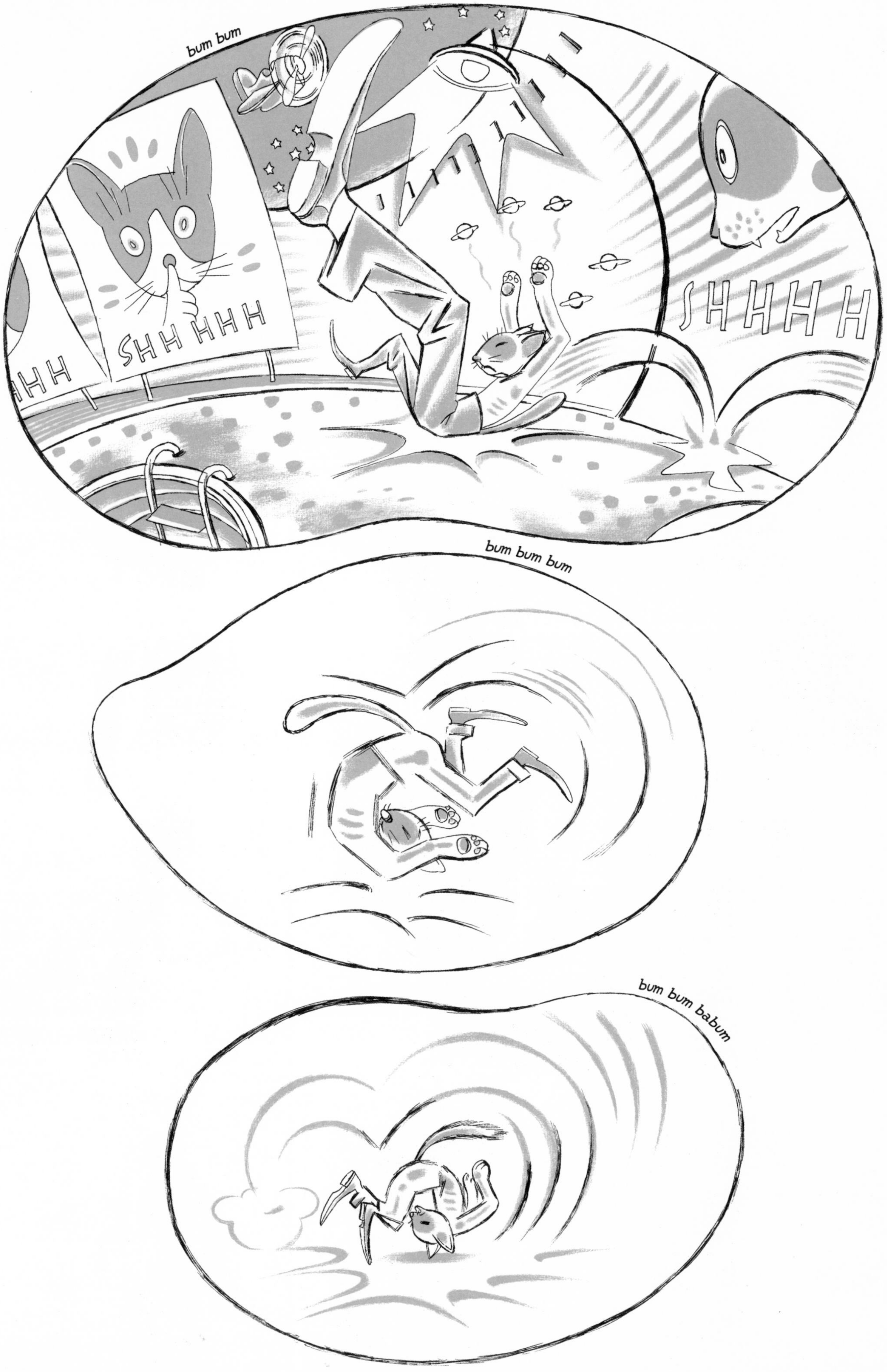
bum bum
SHHHHH
SHHHHH
bum bum bum
bum bum babum

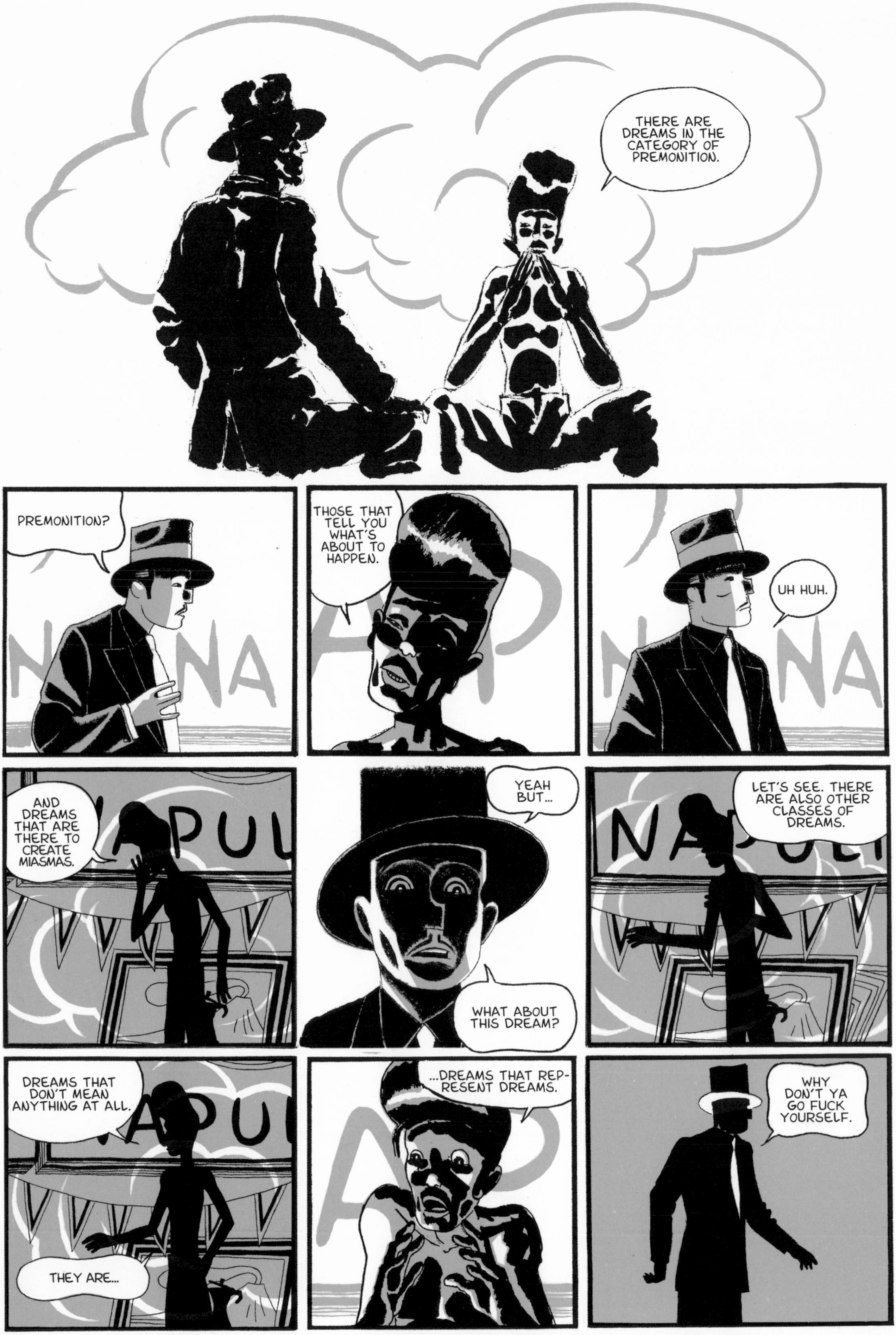
THERE ARE DREAMS IN THE CATEGORY OF PREMONITION.
PREMONITION?
THOSE THAT TELL YOU WHAT'S ABOUT TO HAPPEN.
NA
UH HUH.
NA
AND DREAMS THAT ARE THERE TO CREATE MIASMAS.
YEAH BUT...
WHAT ABOUT THIS DREAM?
LET'S SEE. THERE ARE ALSO OTHER CLASSES OF DREAMS.
DREAMS THAT DON'T MEAN ANYTHING AT ALL.
THEY ARE...
...DREAMS THAT REPRESENT DREAMS.
WHY DON'T YA GO FUCK YOURSELF.

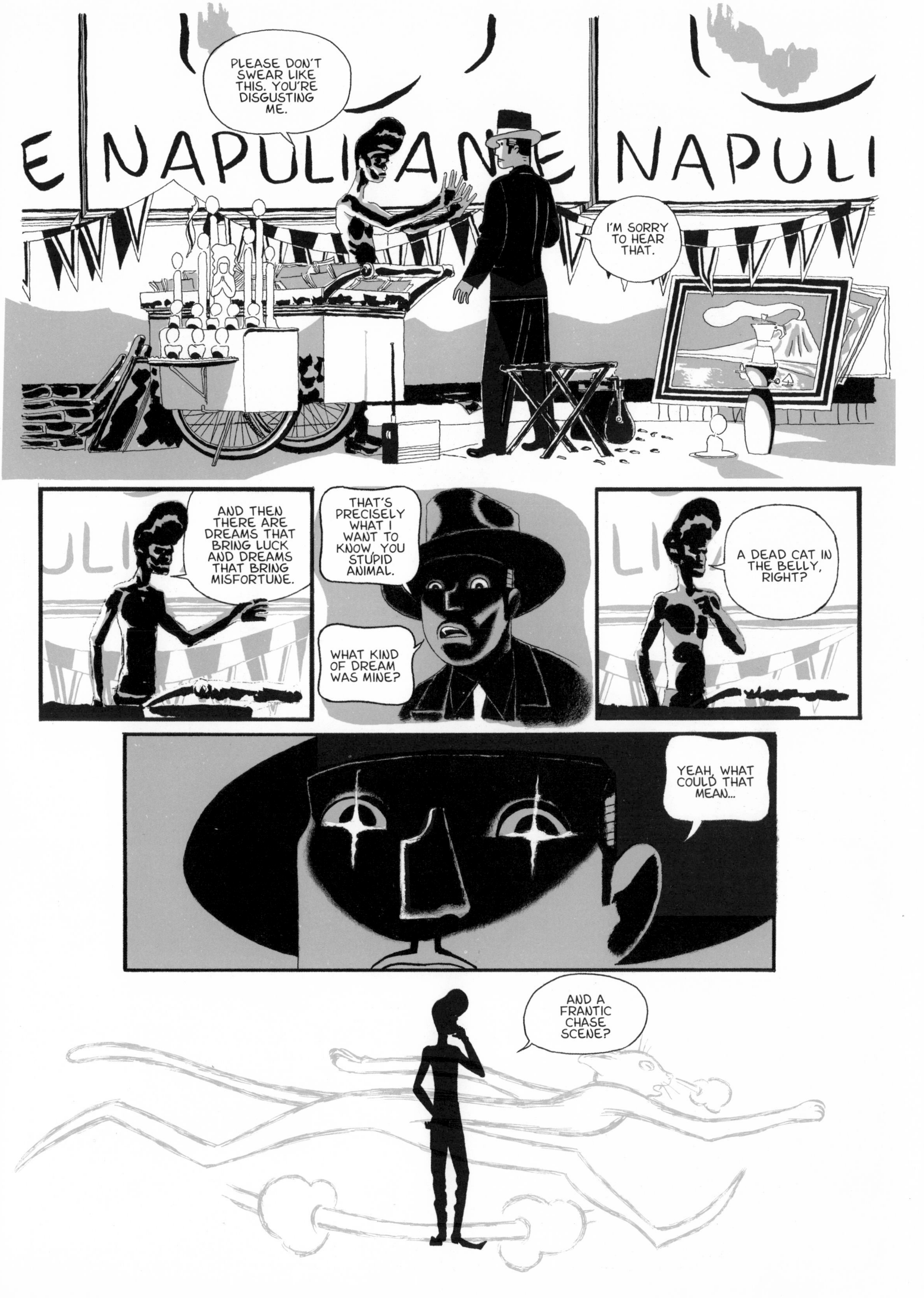
PLEASE DON'T SWEAR LIKE THIS. YOU'RE DISGUSTING ME.
E NAPULI ANE NAPULI
I'M SORRY TO HEAR THAT.
AND THEN THERE ARE DREAMS THAT BRING LUCK AND DREAMS THAT BRING MISFORTUNE.
THAT'S PRECISELY WHAT I WANT TO KNOW, YOU STUPID ANIMAL.
WHAT KIND OF DREAM WAS MINE?
A DEAD CAT IN THE BELLY, RIGHT?
YEAH, WHAT COULD THAT MEAN...
AND A FRANTIC CHASE SCENE?

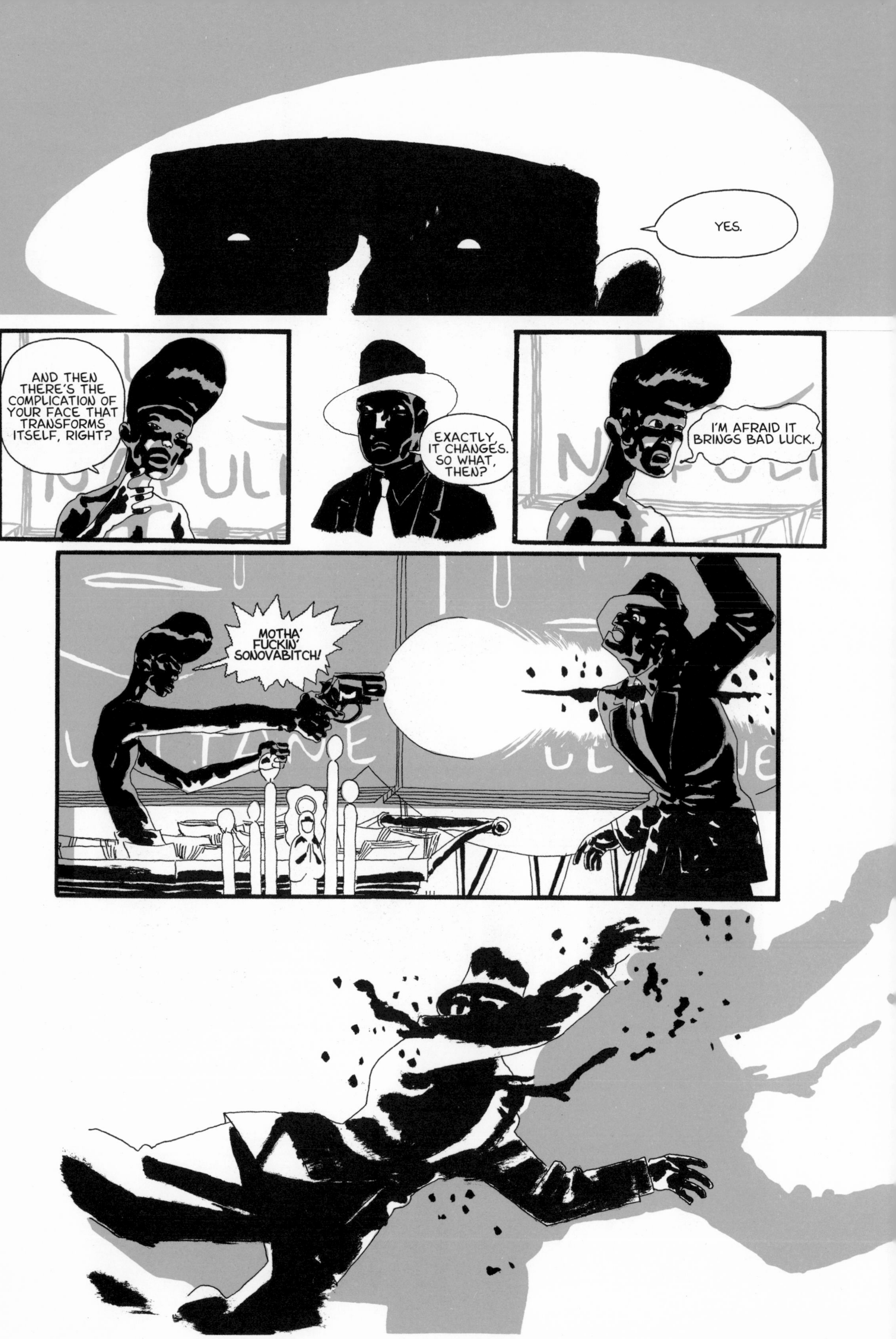
YES.
AND THEN THERE'S THE COMPLICATION OF YOUR FACE THAT TRANSFORMS ITSELF, RIGHT?
EXACTLY, IT CHANGES. SO WHAT, THEN?
I'M AFRAID IT BRINGS BAD LUCK.
MOTHA' FUCKIN' SONOVABITCH!

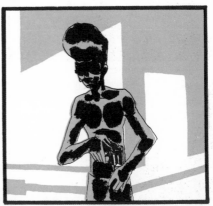

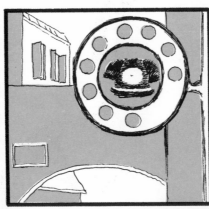

GET READY. LET'S TAKE CARE OF THE FATHER NOW.

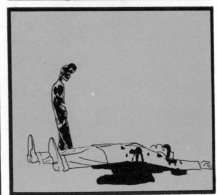

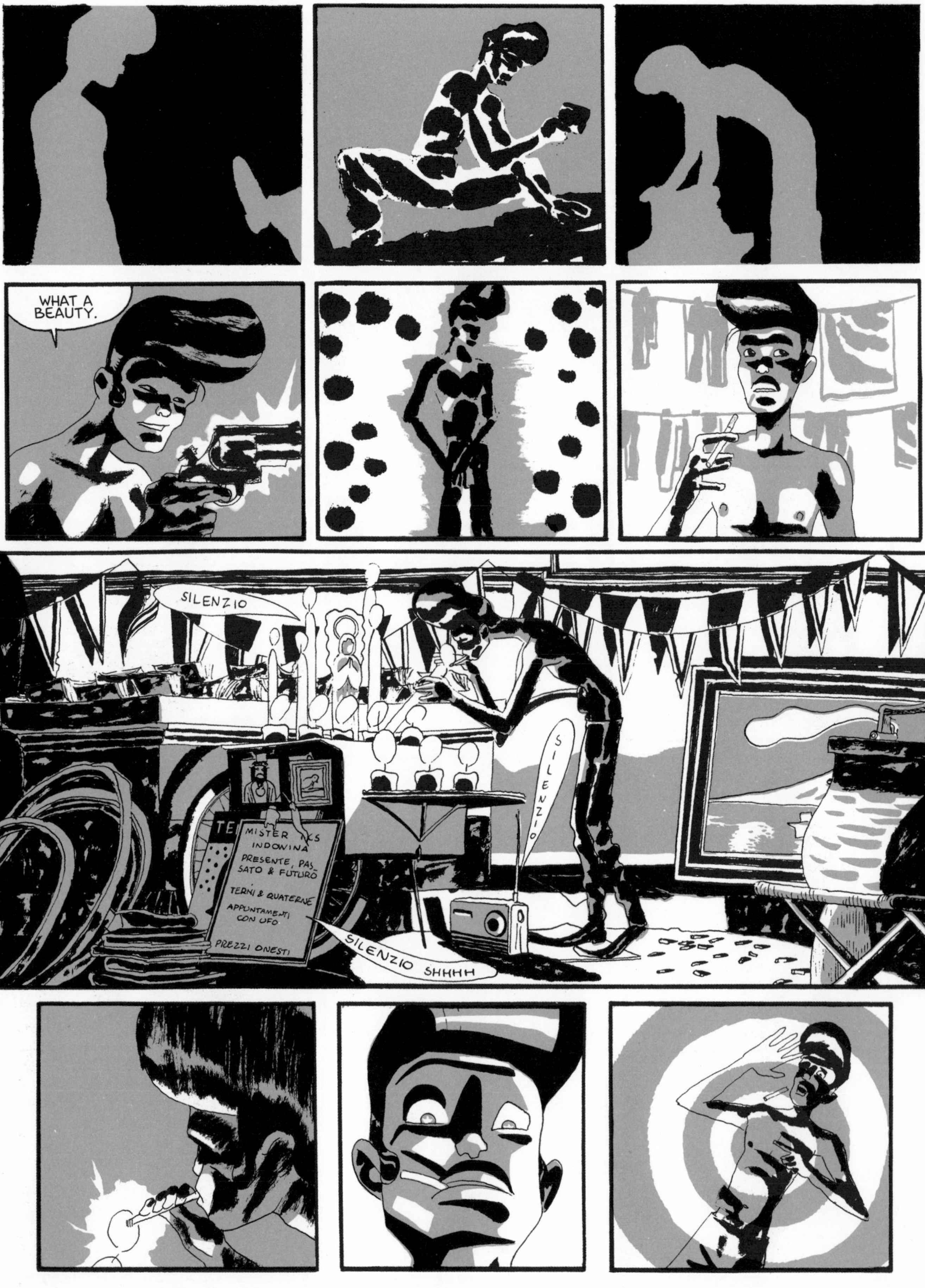
WHAT A BEAUTY.
SILENZIO
SILENZIO
MISTER
INDOWINA
PRESENTE, PASSATO & FUTURO
TERNI & QUATERNE
APPUNTAMENTI CON UFO
PREZZI ONESTI
SILENZIO SHHHH

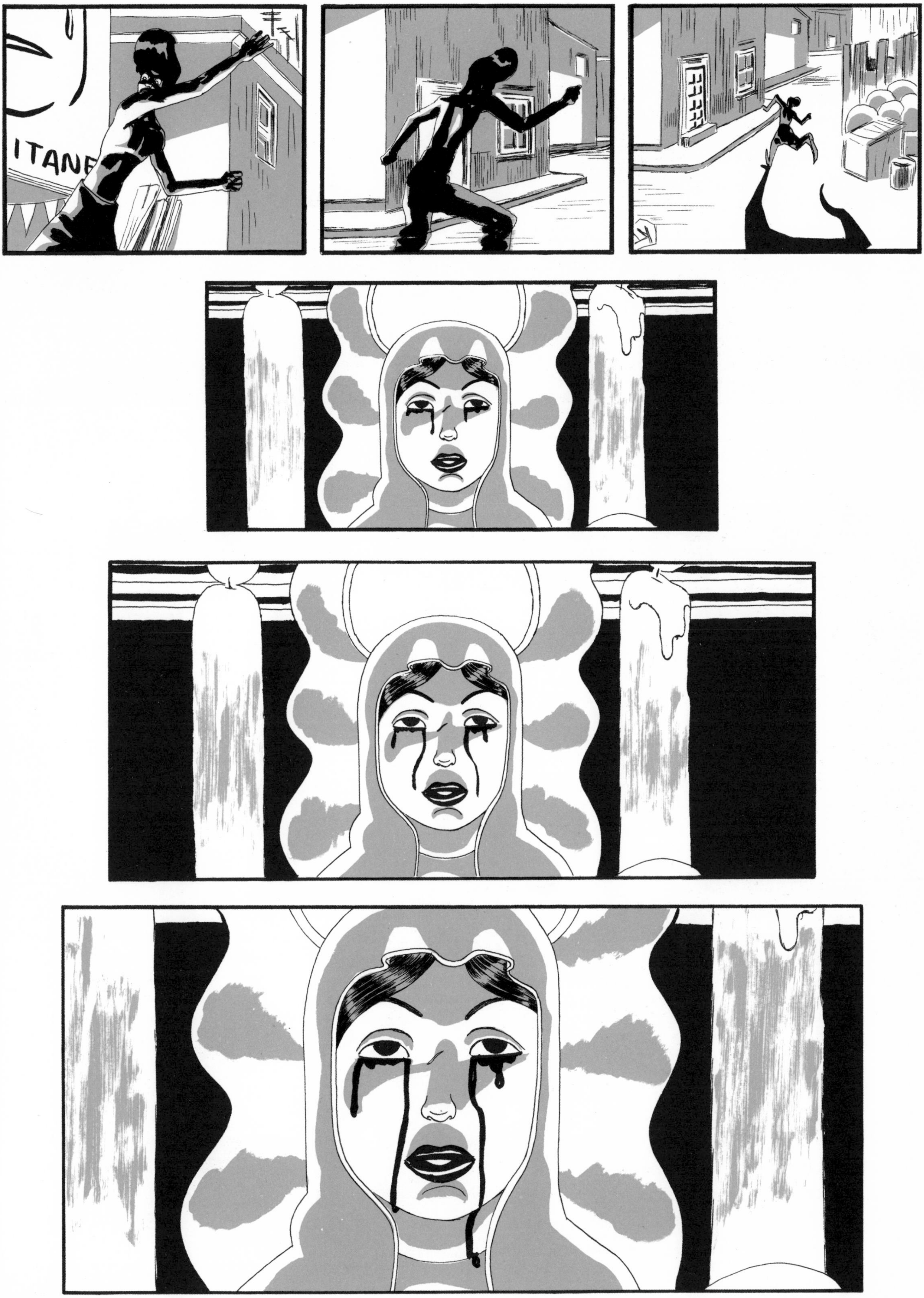
ITANE

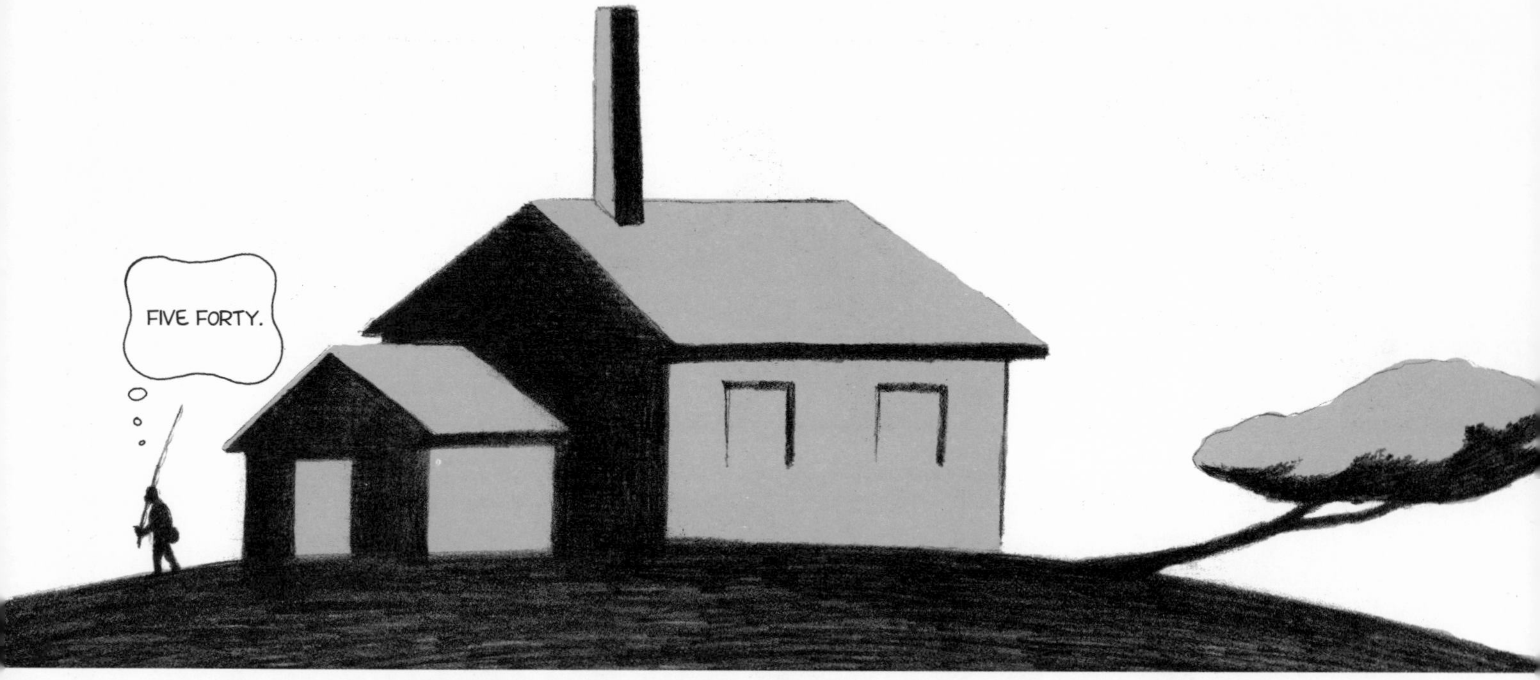
FIVE FORTY.

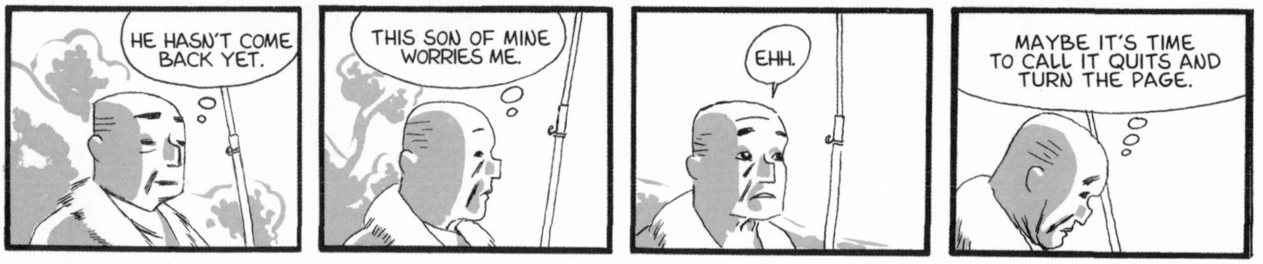
HE HASN'T COME BACK YET.
THIS SON OF MINE WORRIES ME.
EHH.
MAYBE IT'S TIME TO CALL IT QUITS AND TURN THE PAGE.

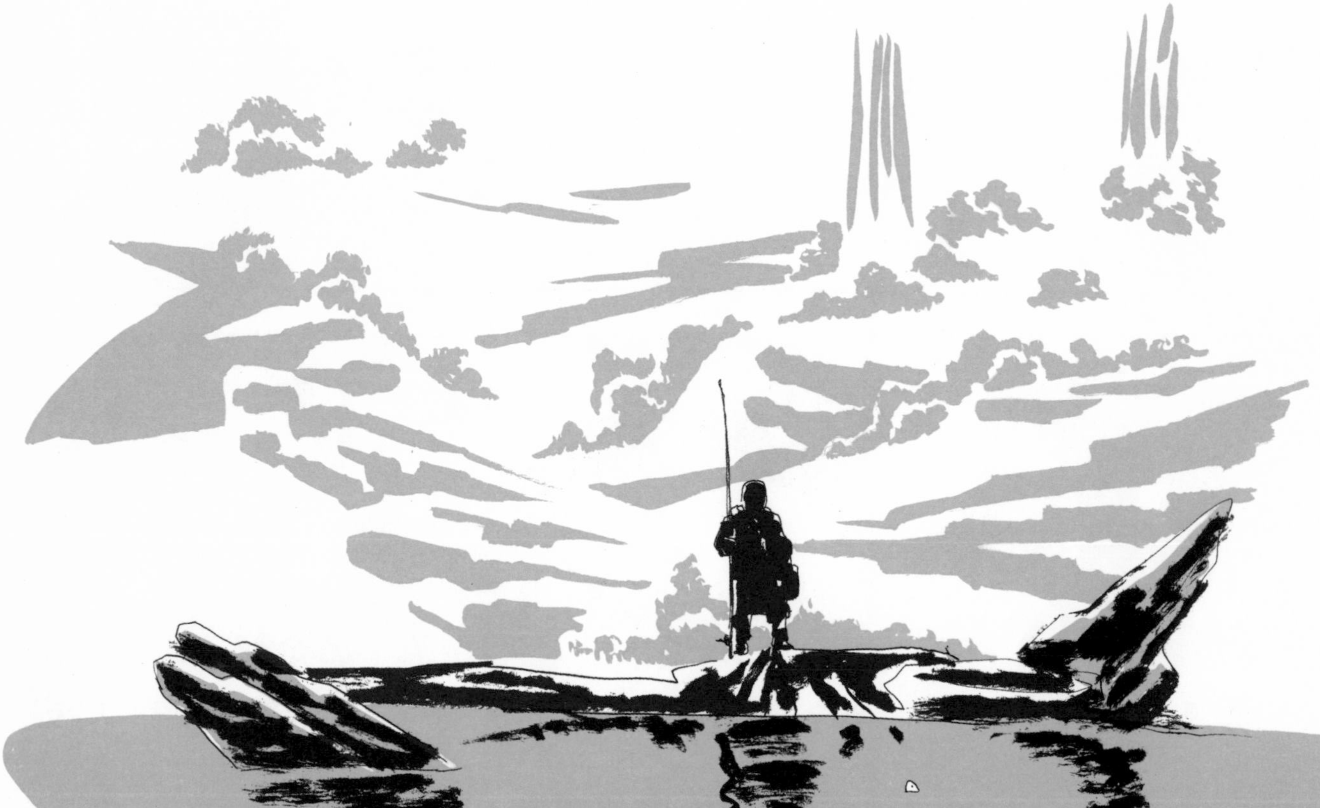

chapter two
Crosswords

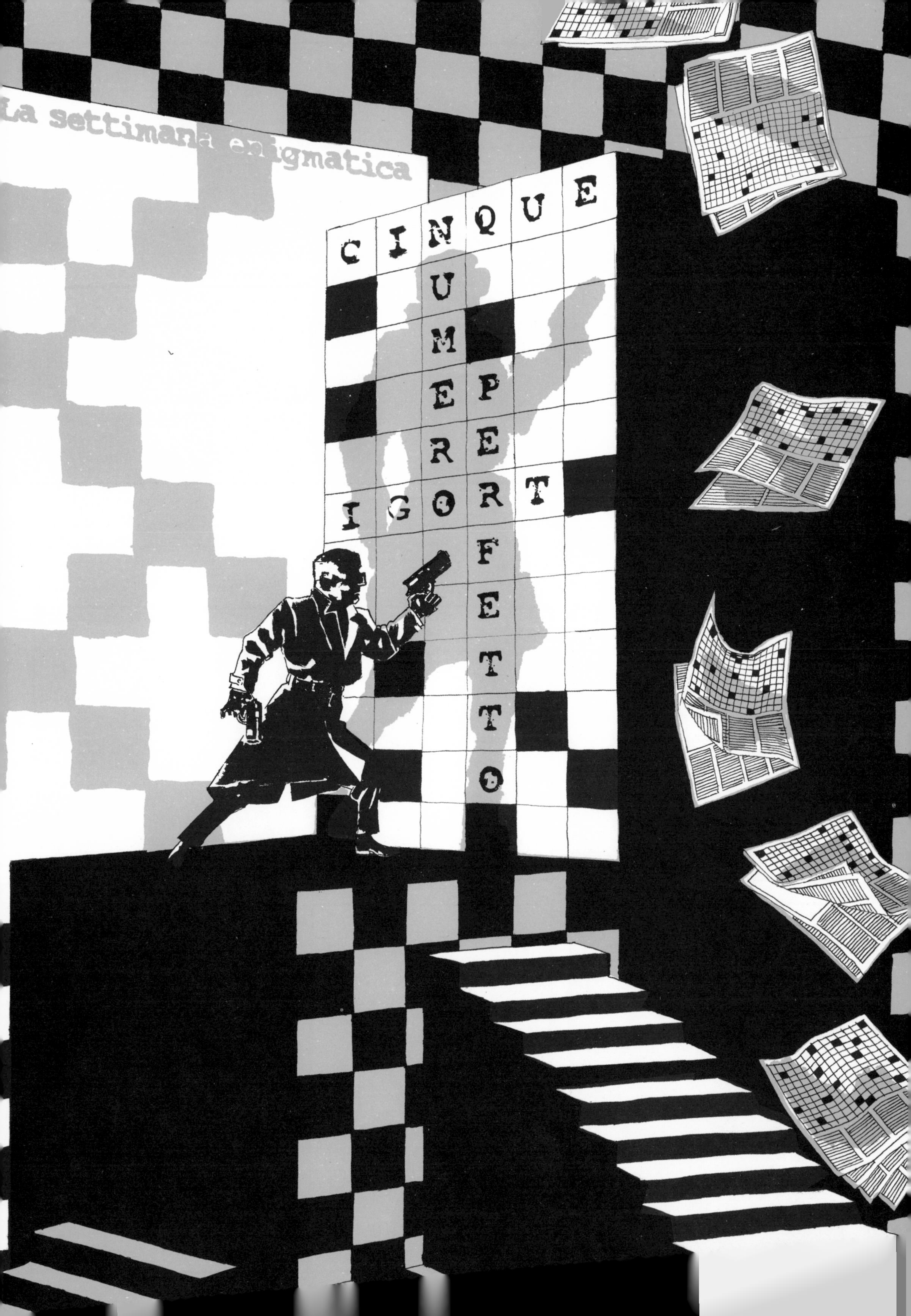
La settimana enigmatica
CINQUE
NUMERI
IGORT
PERFETTO

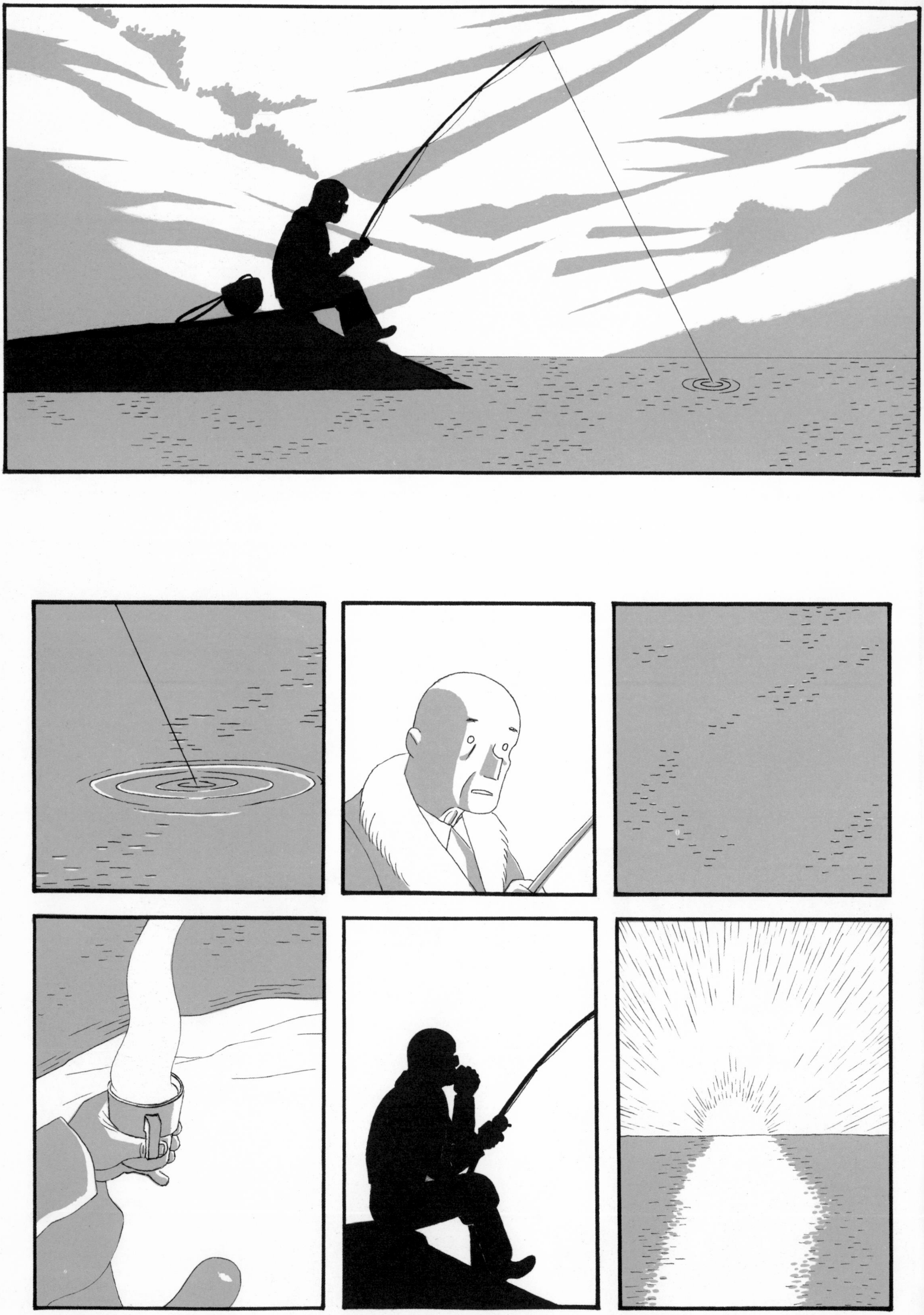

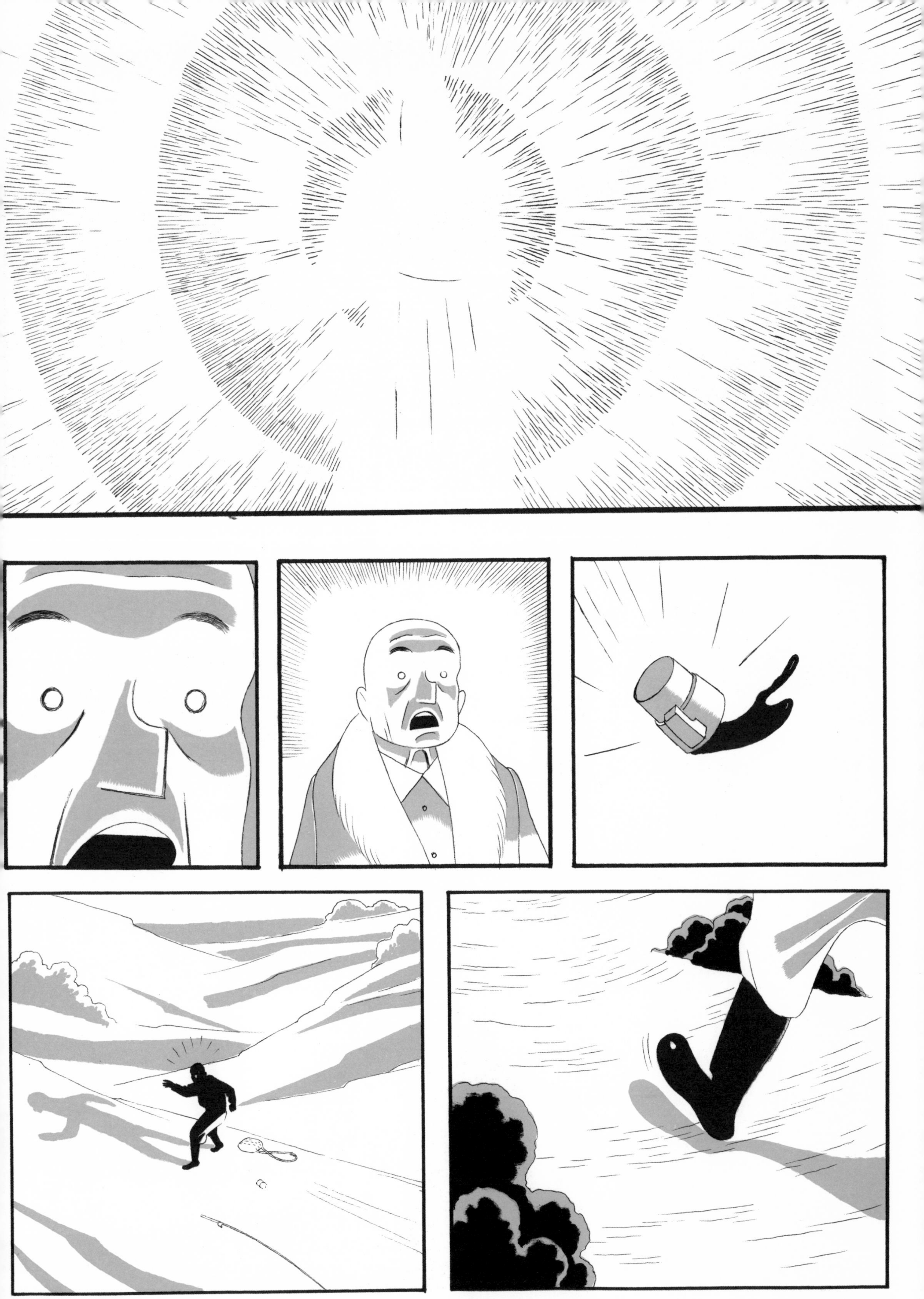

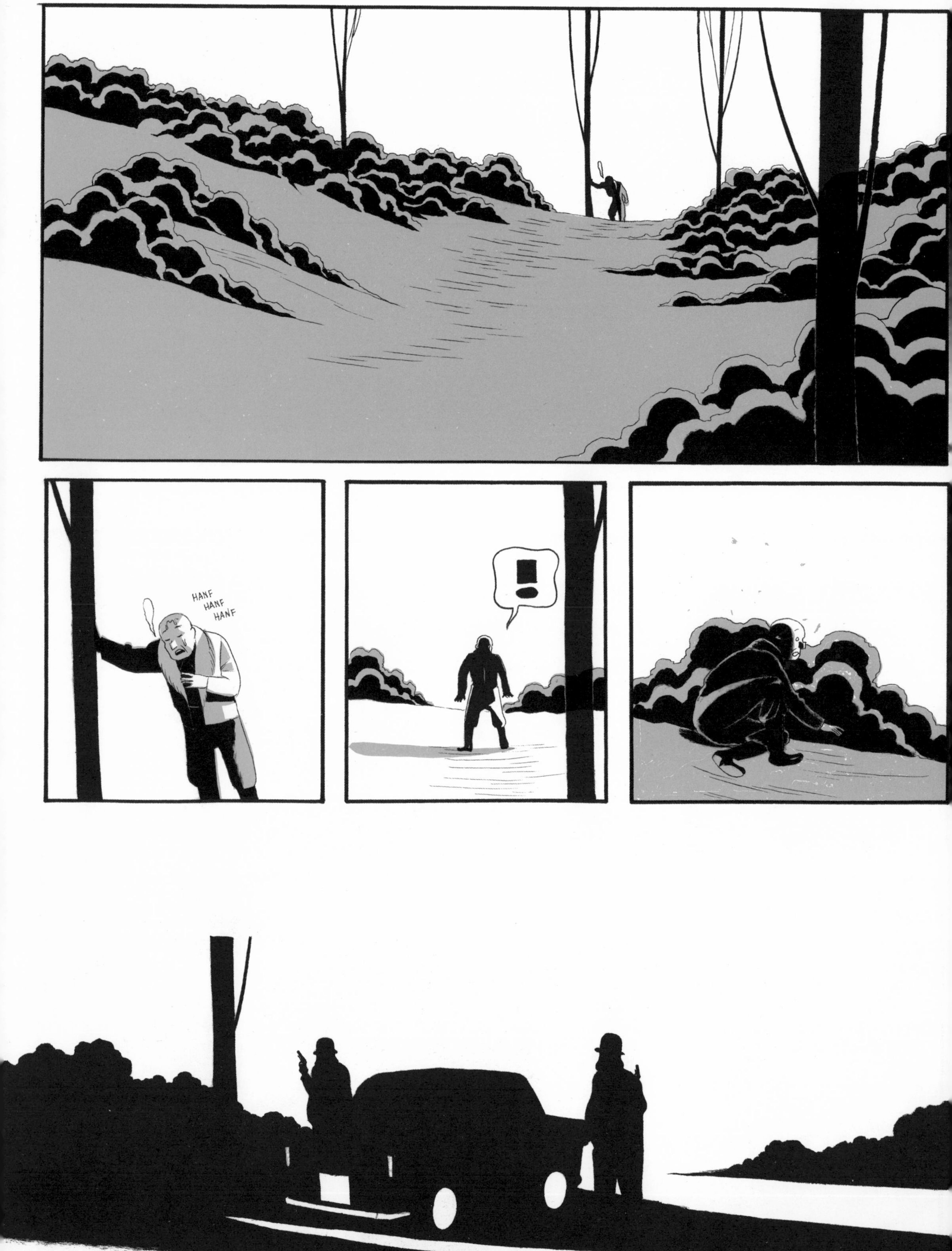
HANF
HANF
HANF

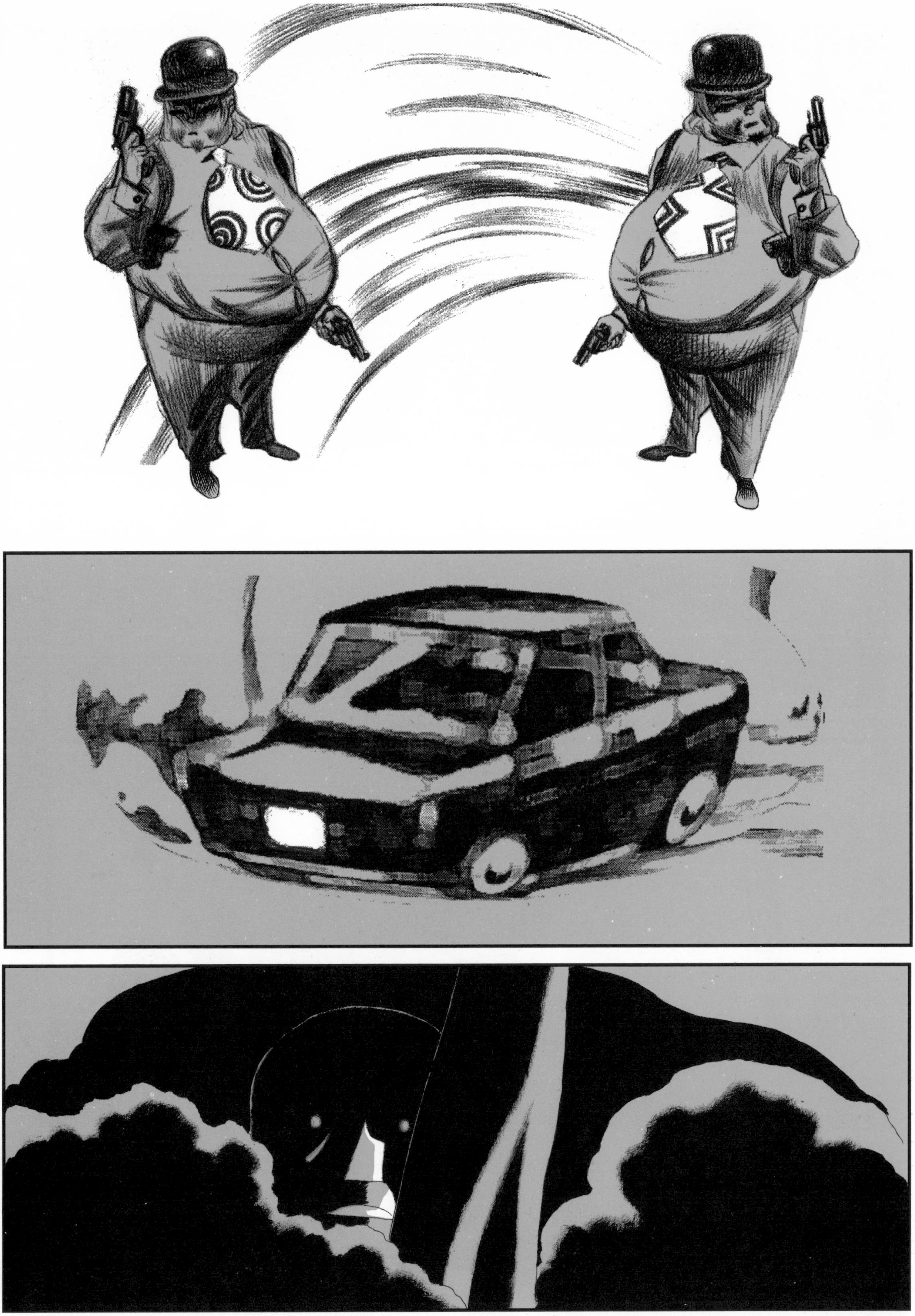

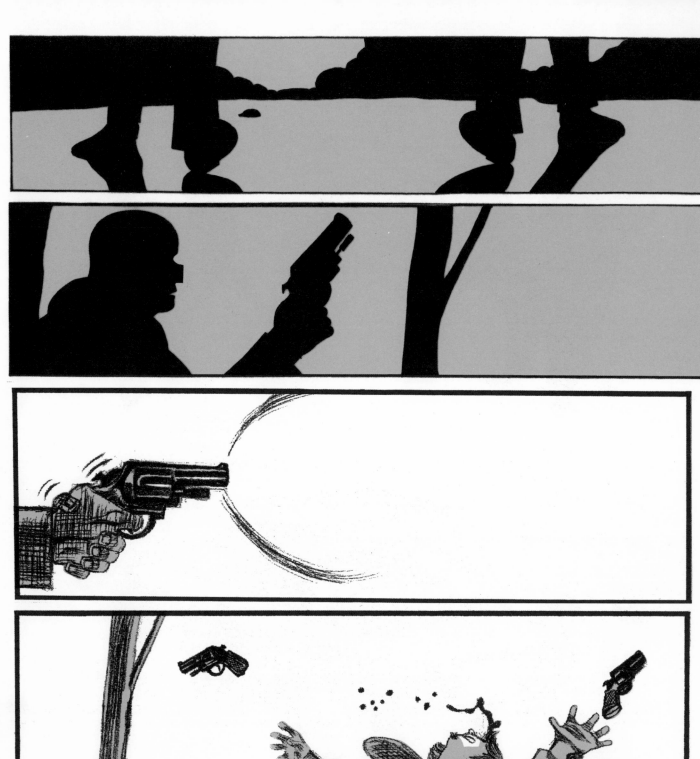

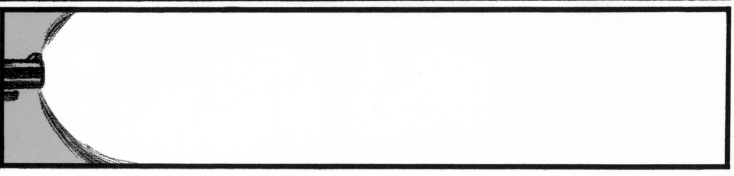

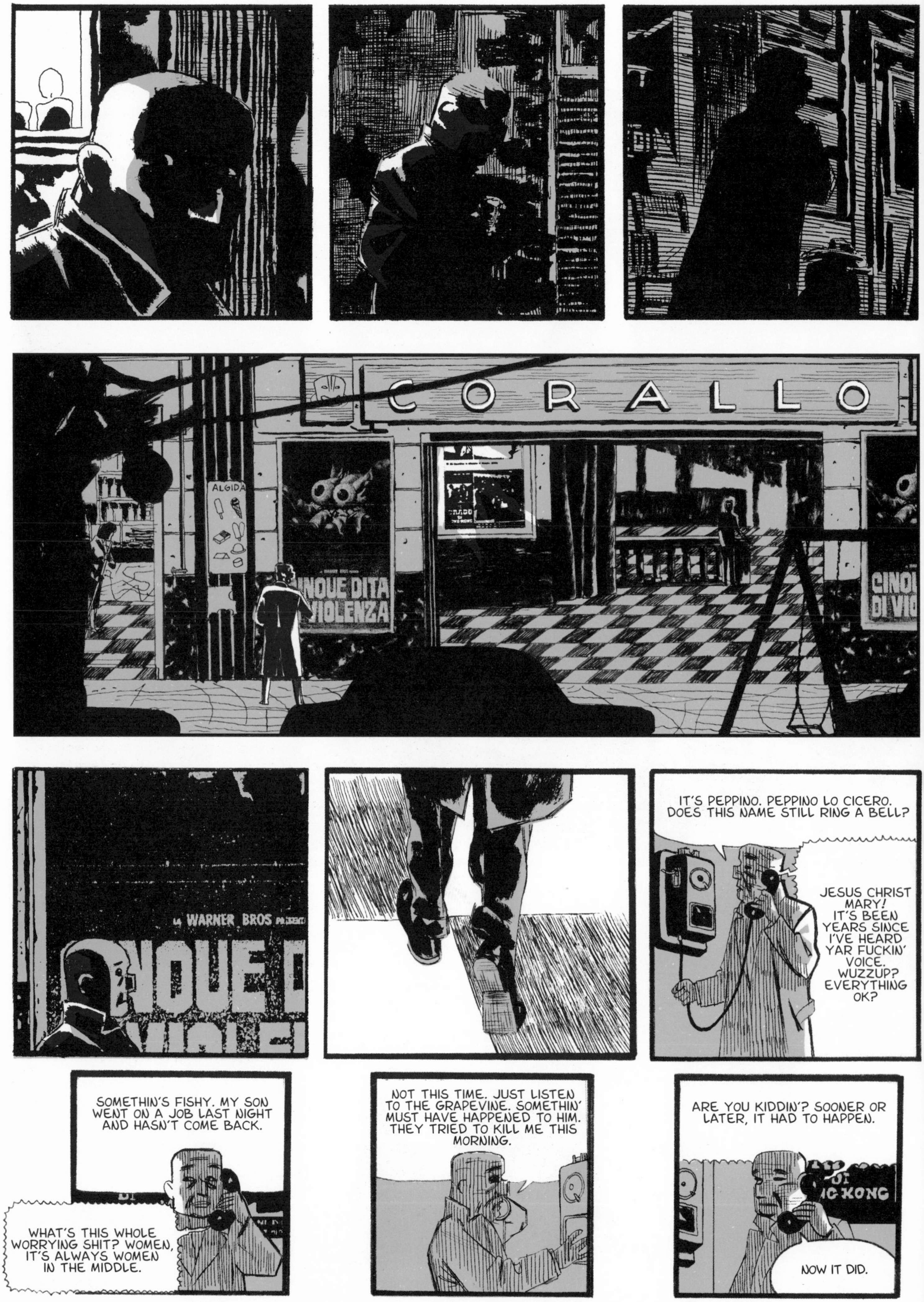
CORALLO
ALGIDA
INQUE DITA
VIOLENZA
WARNER BROS
IT'S PEPPINO. PEPPINO LO CICERO. DOES THIS NAME STILL RING A BELL?
JESUS CHRIST MARY! IT'S BEEN YEARS SINCE I'VE HEARD YAR FUCKIN' VOICE. WUZZUP? EVERYTHING OK?
SOMETHIN'S FISHY. MY SON WENT ON A JOB LAST NIGHT AND HASN'T COME BACK.
WHAT'S THIS WHOLE WORRYING SHIT? WOMEN, IT'S ALWAYS WOMEN IN THE MIDDLE.
NOT THIS TIME. JUST LISTEN TO THE GRAPEVINE. SOMETHIN' MUST HAVE HAPPENED TO HIM. THEY TRIED TO KILL ME THIS MORNING.
ARE YOU KIDDIN'? SOONER OR LATER, IT HAD TO HAPPEN.
NOW IT DID.

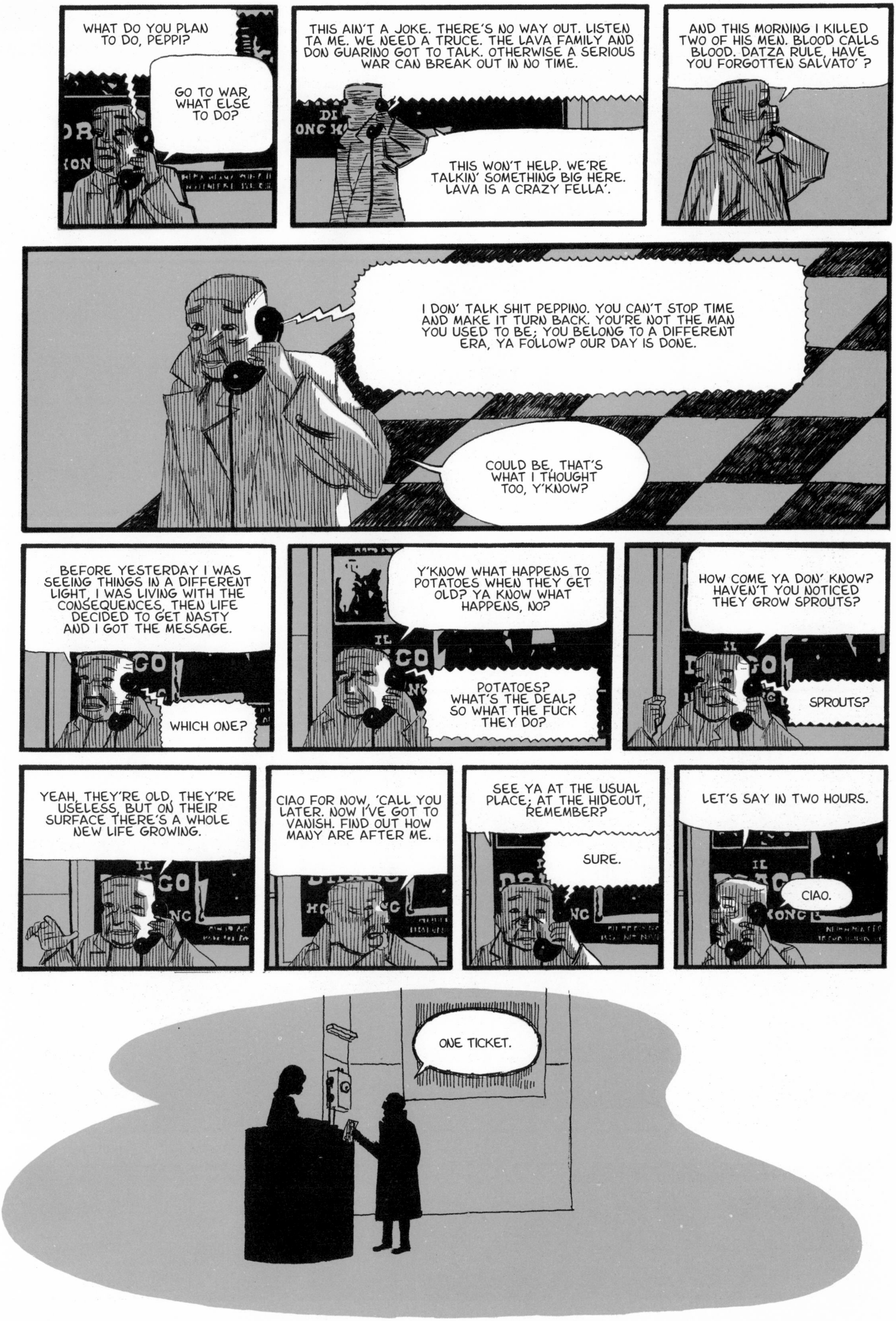
WHAT DO YOU PLAN TO DO, PEPPI?
GO TO WAR, WHAT ELSE TO DO?
THIS AIN'T A JOKE. THERE'S NO WAY OUT. LISTEN TA ME. WE NEED A TRUCE. THE LAVA FAMILY AND DON GUARINO GOT TO TALK. OTHERWISE A SERIOUS WAR CAN BREAK OUT IN NO TIME.
THIS WON'T HELP. WE'RE TALKIN' SOMETHING BIG HERE. LAVA IS A CRAZY FELLA'.
AND THIS MORNING I KILLED TWO OF HIS MEN. BLOOD CALLS BLOOD. DATZA RULE, HAVE YOU FORGOTTEN SALVATO' ?
I DON' TALK SHIT PEPPINO. YOU CAN'T STOP TIME AND MAKE IT TURN BACK. YOU'RE NOT THE MAN YOU USED TO BE; YOU BELONG TO A DIFFERENT ERA, YA FOLLOW? OUR DAY IS DONE.
COULD BE, THAT'S WHAT I THOUGHT TOO, Y'KNOW?
BEFORE YESTERDAY I WAS SEEING THINGS IN A DIFFERENT LIGHT, I WAS LIVING WITH THE CONSEQUENCES, THEN LIFE DECIDED TO GET NASTY AND I GOT THE MESSAGE.
WHICH ONE?
Y'KNOW WHAT HAPPENS TO POTATOES WHEN THEY GET OLD? YA KNOW WHAT HAPPENS, NO?
POTATOES? WHAT'S THE DEAL? SO WHAT THE FUCK THEY DO?
HOW COME YA DON' KNOW? HAVEN'T YOU NOTICED THEY GROW SPROUTS?
SPROUTS?
YEAH, THEY'RE OLD, THEY'RE USELESS, BUT ON THEIR SURFACE THERE'S A WHOLE NEW LIFE GROWING.
CIAO FOR NOW, 'CALL YOU LATER. NOW I'VE GOT TO VANISH. FIND OUT HOW MANY ARE AFTER ME.
SEE YA AT THE USUAL PLACE; AT THE HIDEOUT, REMEMBER?
SURE.
LET'S SAY IN TWO HOURS.
CIAO.
ONE TICKET.

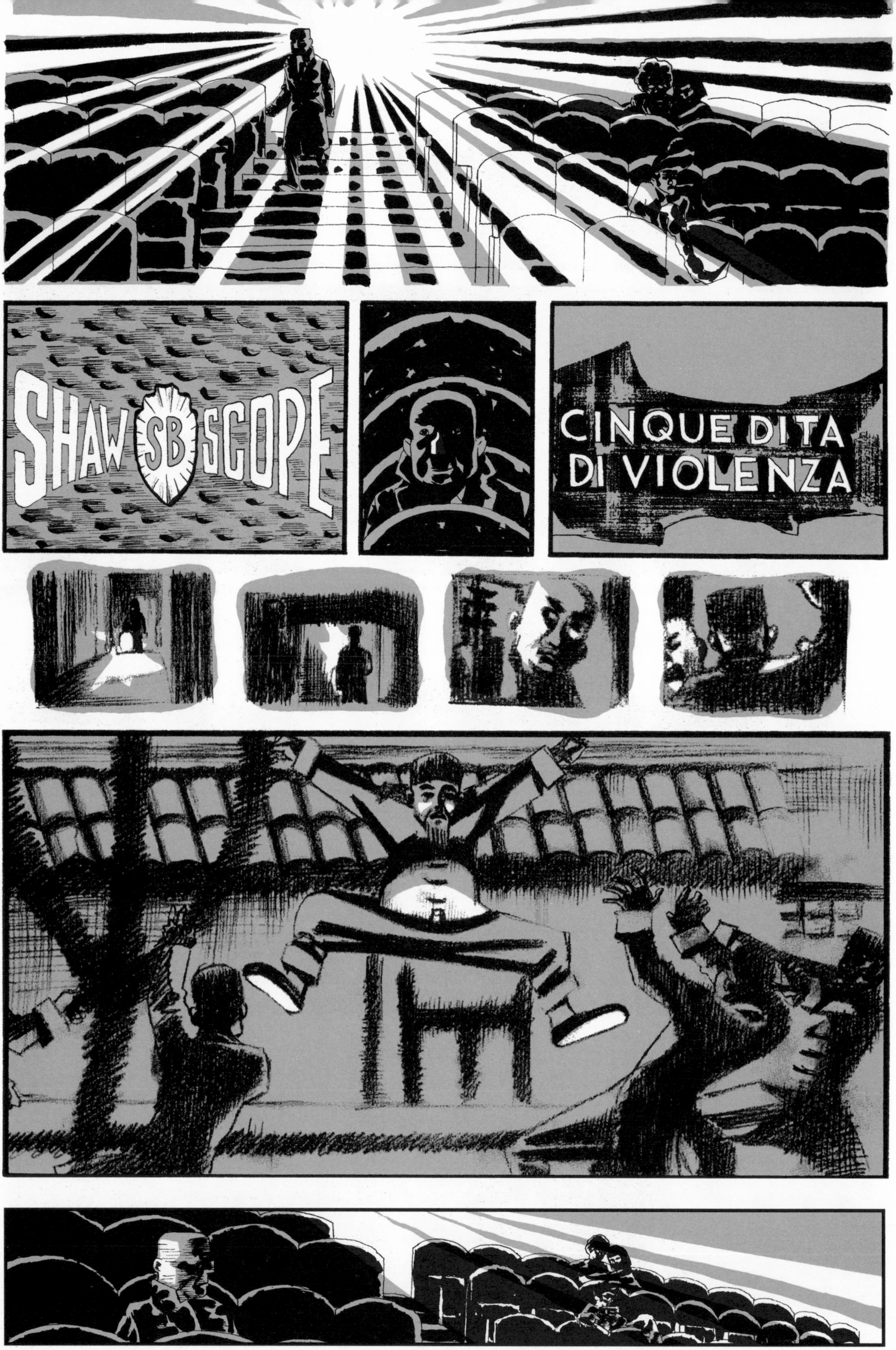
SHAW SB SCOPE
CINQUE DITA DI VIOLENZA

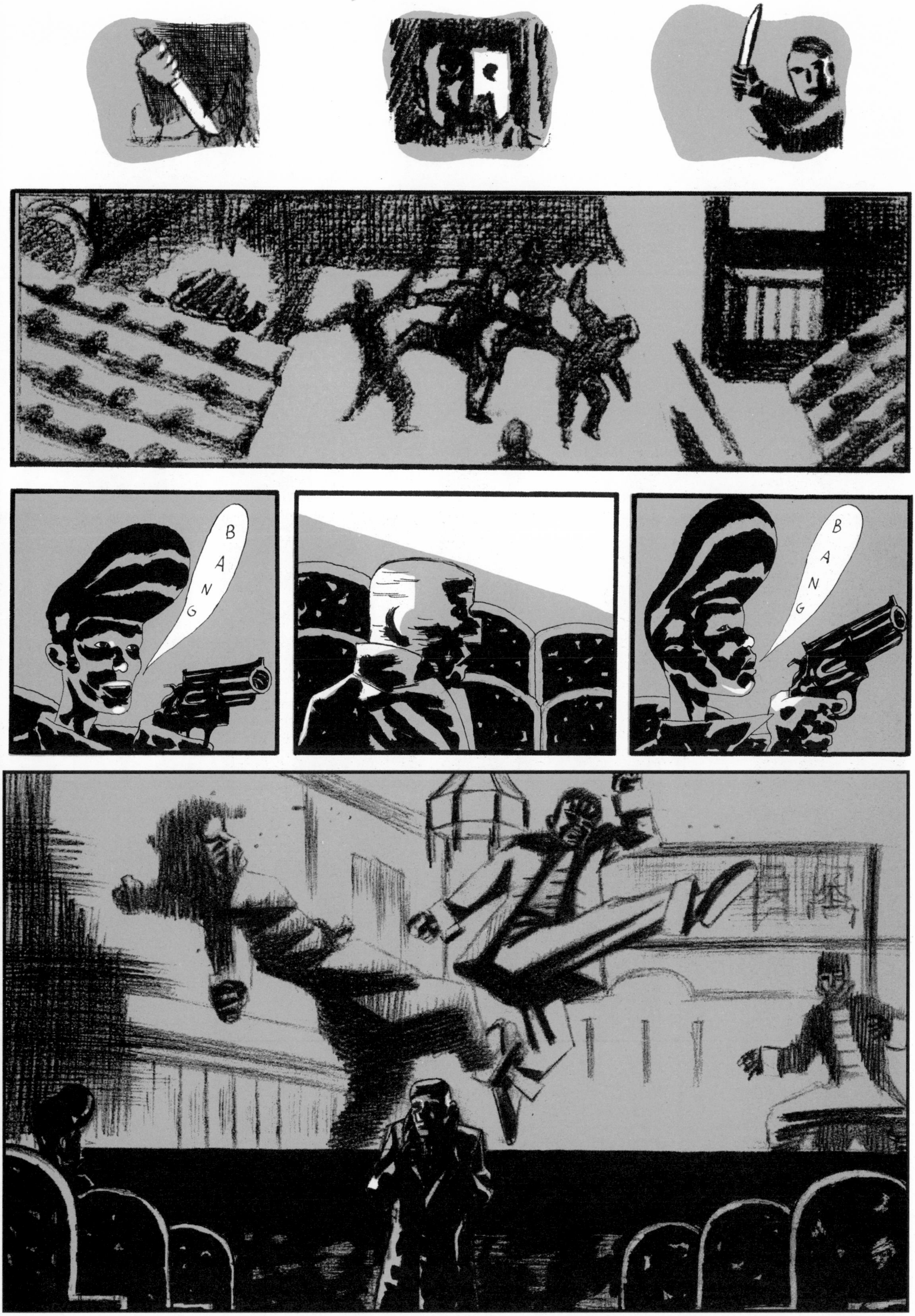
BANG
BANG

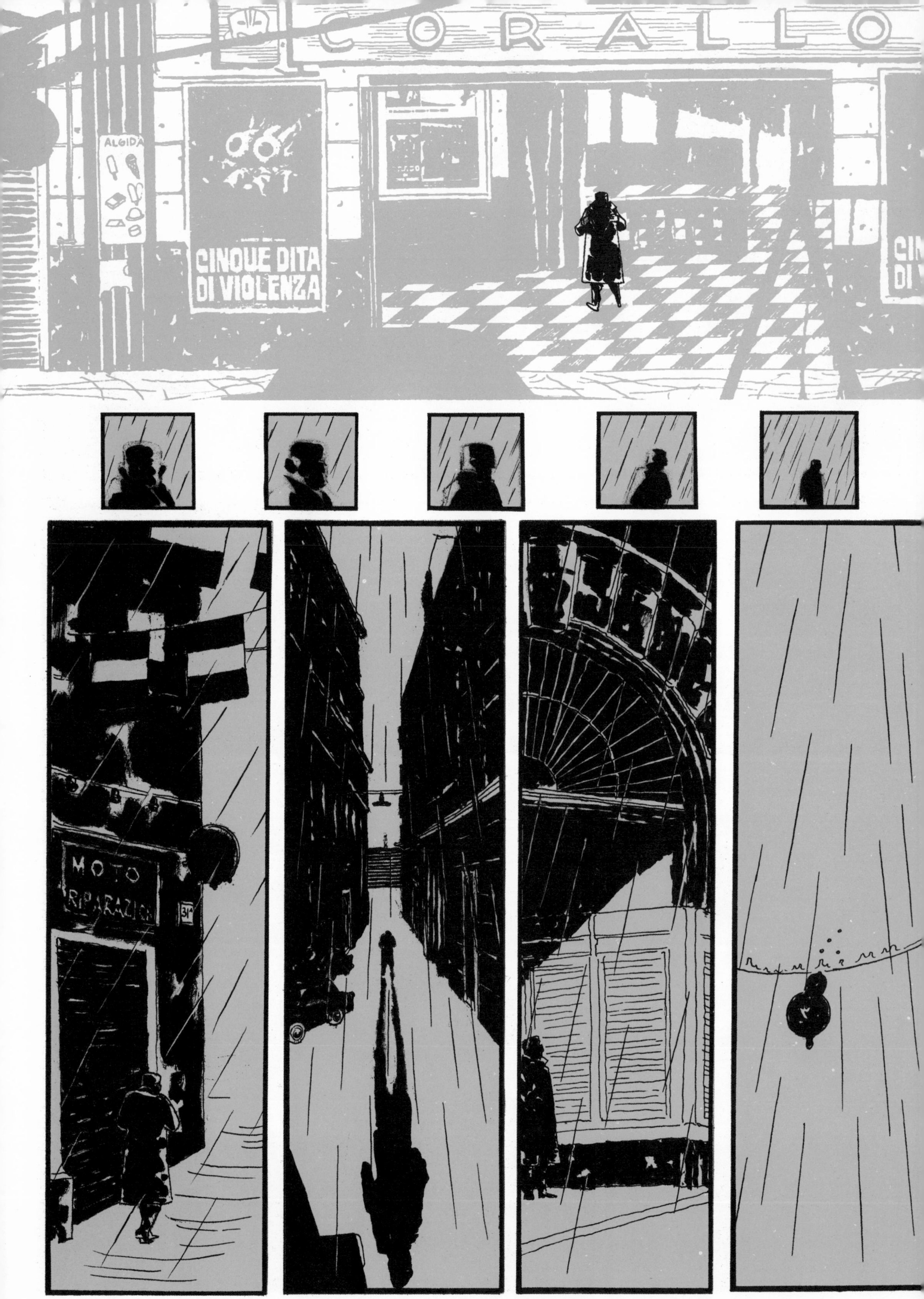
CORALLO
ALGIDA
CINQUE DITA
DI VIOLENZA
MOTO

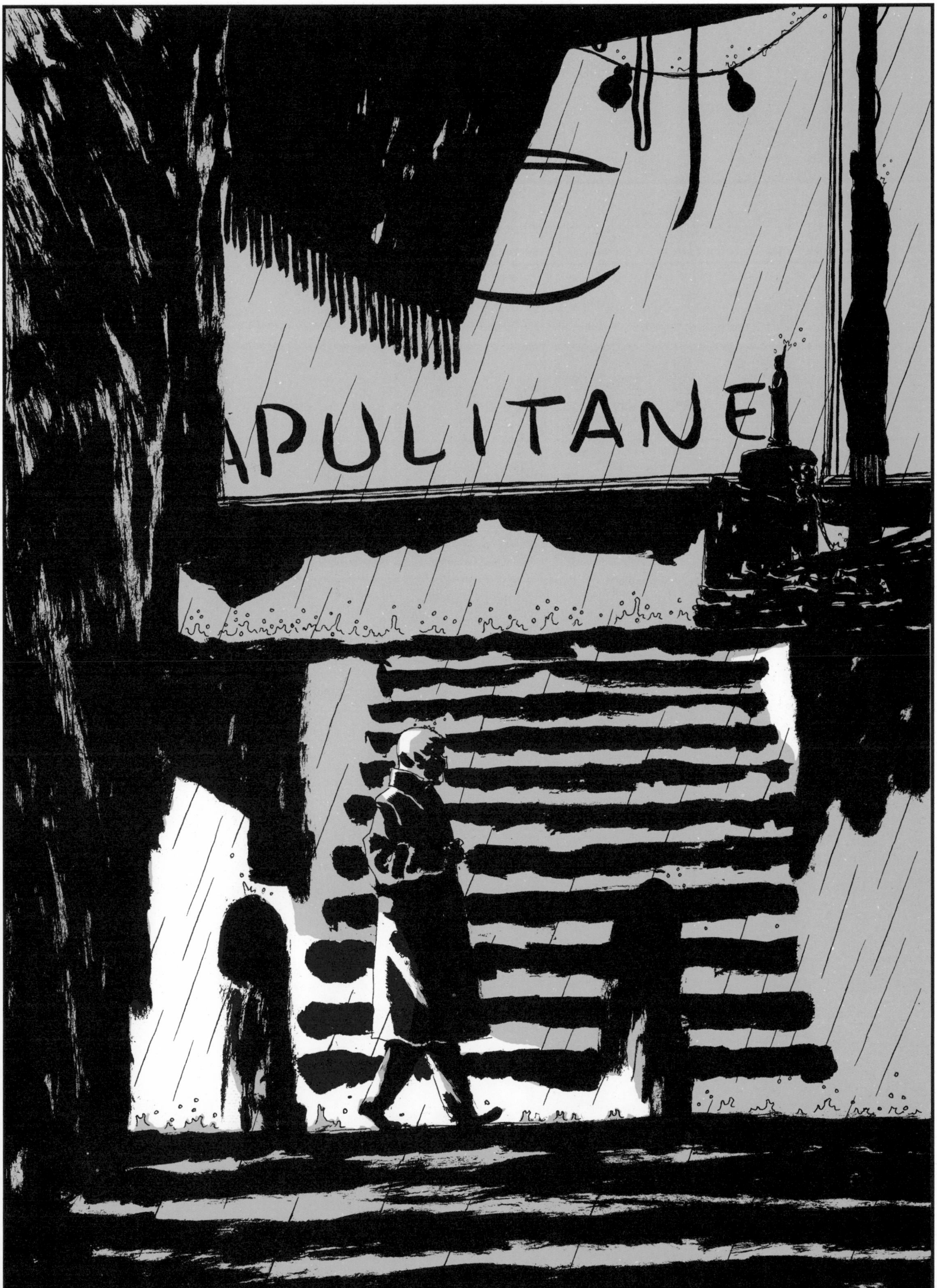

APULITANE

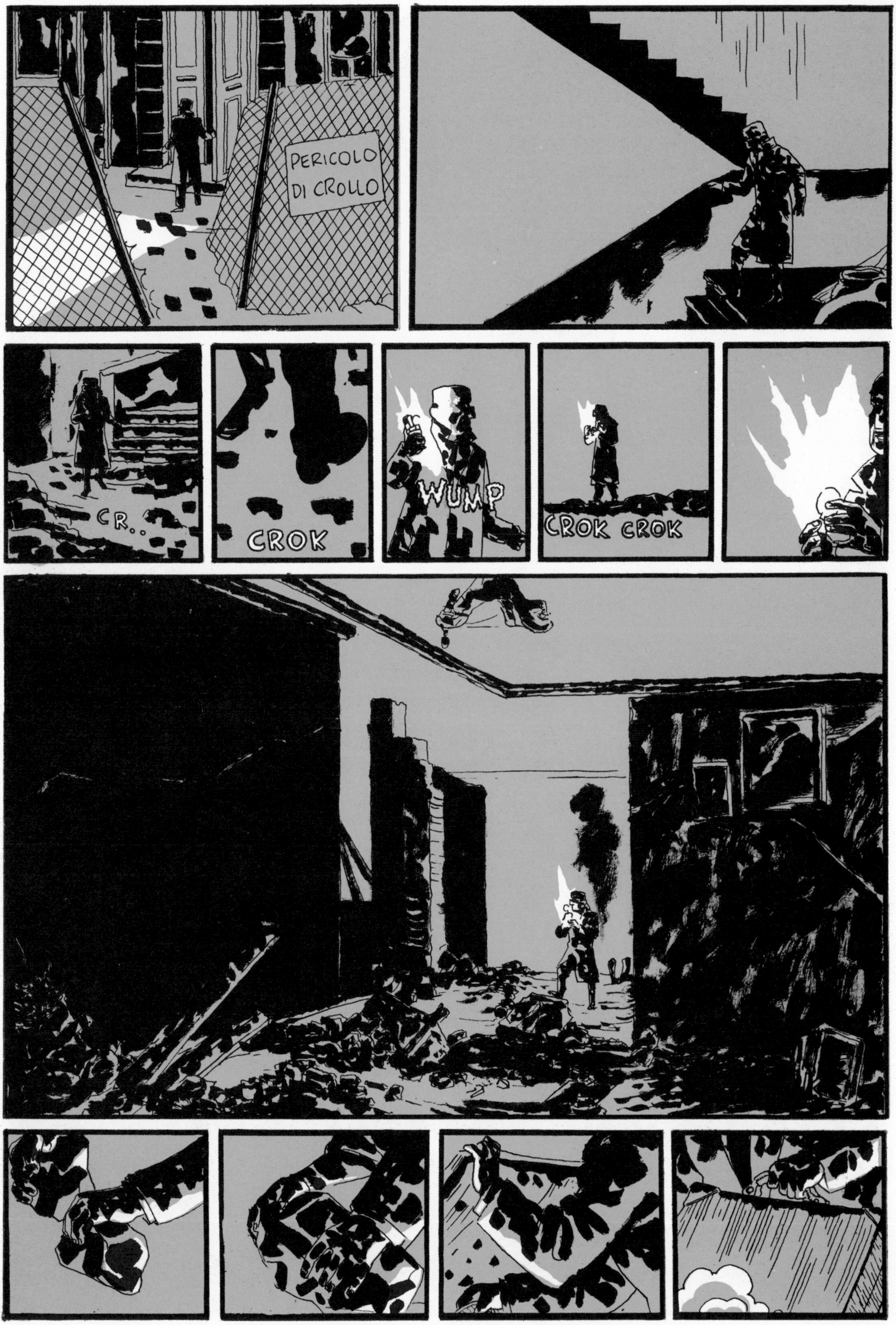
PERICOLO
DI CROLLO
CR..
CROK
WUMP
CROK CROK

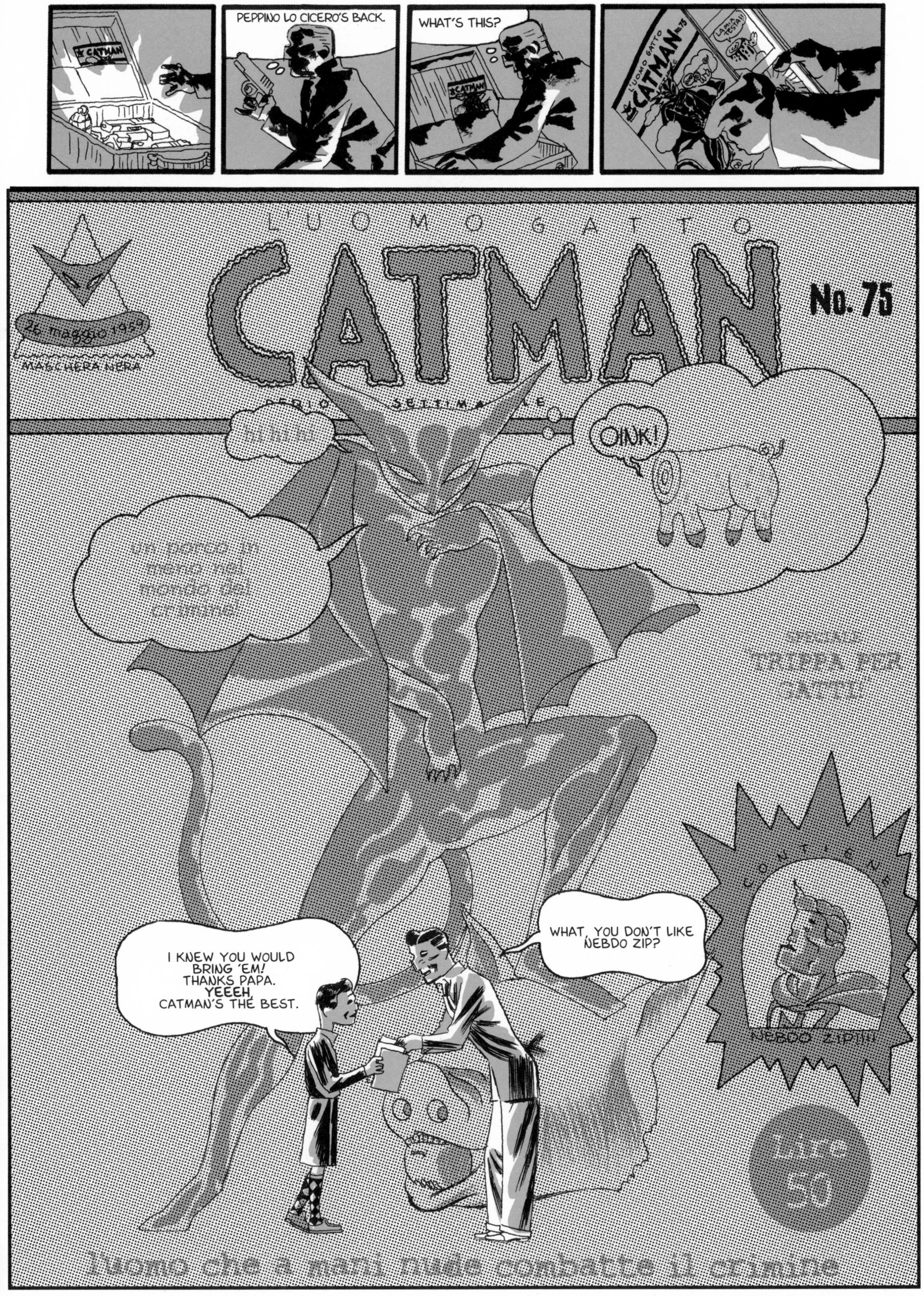
PEPPINO LO CICERO'S BACK.
WHAT'S THIS?
L'UOMO GATTO
CATMAN
No. 75
26 maggio 1939
MASCHERA NERA
OINK!
CONTIENE
NEBDO ZIP!!!
WHAT, YOU DON'T LIKE NEBDO ZIP?
I KNEW YOU WOULD BRING 'EM! THANKS PAPA. **YEEEH,** CATMAN'S THE BEST.

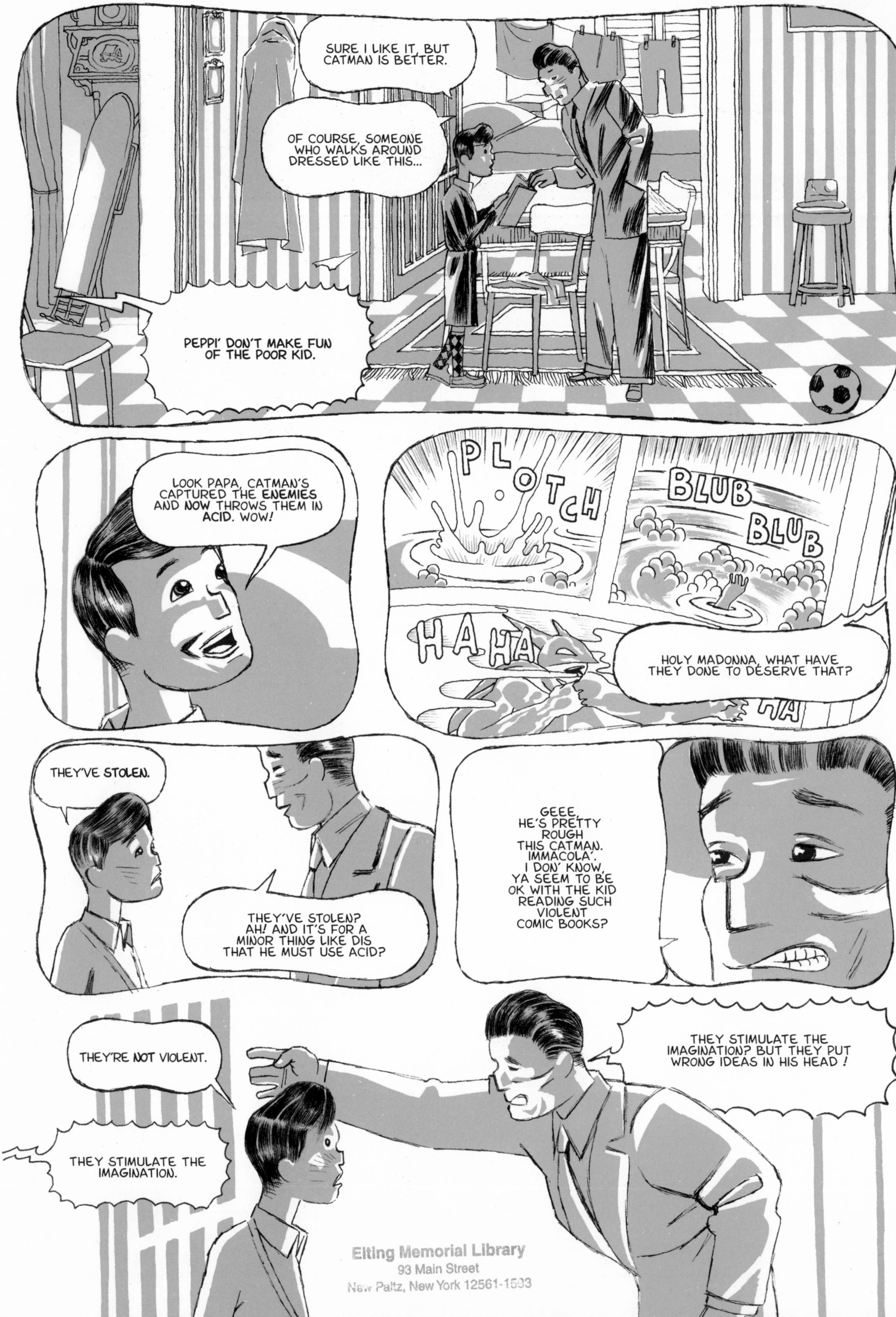

SURE I LIKE IT, BUT CATMAN IS BETTER.
OF COURSE, SOMEONE WHO WALKS AROUND DRESSED LIKE THIS...
PEPPI' DON'T MAKE FUN OF THE POOR KID.
LOOK PAPA, CATMAN'S CAPTURED THE ENEMIES AND NOW THROWS THEM IN ACID. WOW!
PLOTCH
BLUB BLUB
HA HA
HA
HOLY MADONNA, WHAT HAVE THEY DONE TO DESERVE THAT?
THEY'VE STOLEN.
THEY'VE STOLEN? AH! AND IT'S FOR A MINOR THING LIKE DIS THAT HE MUST USE ACID?
GEEE, HE'S PRETTY ROUGH THIS CATMAN. IMMACOLA'. I DON' KNOW, YA SEEM TO BE OK WITH THE KID READING SUCH VIOLENT COMIC BOOKS?
THEY'RE NOT VIOLENT.
THEY STIMULATE THE IMAGINATION.
THEY STIMULATE THE IMAGINATION? BUT THEY PUT WRONG IDEAS IN HIS HEAD !

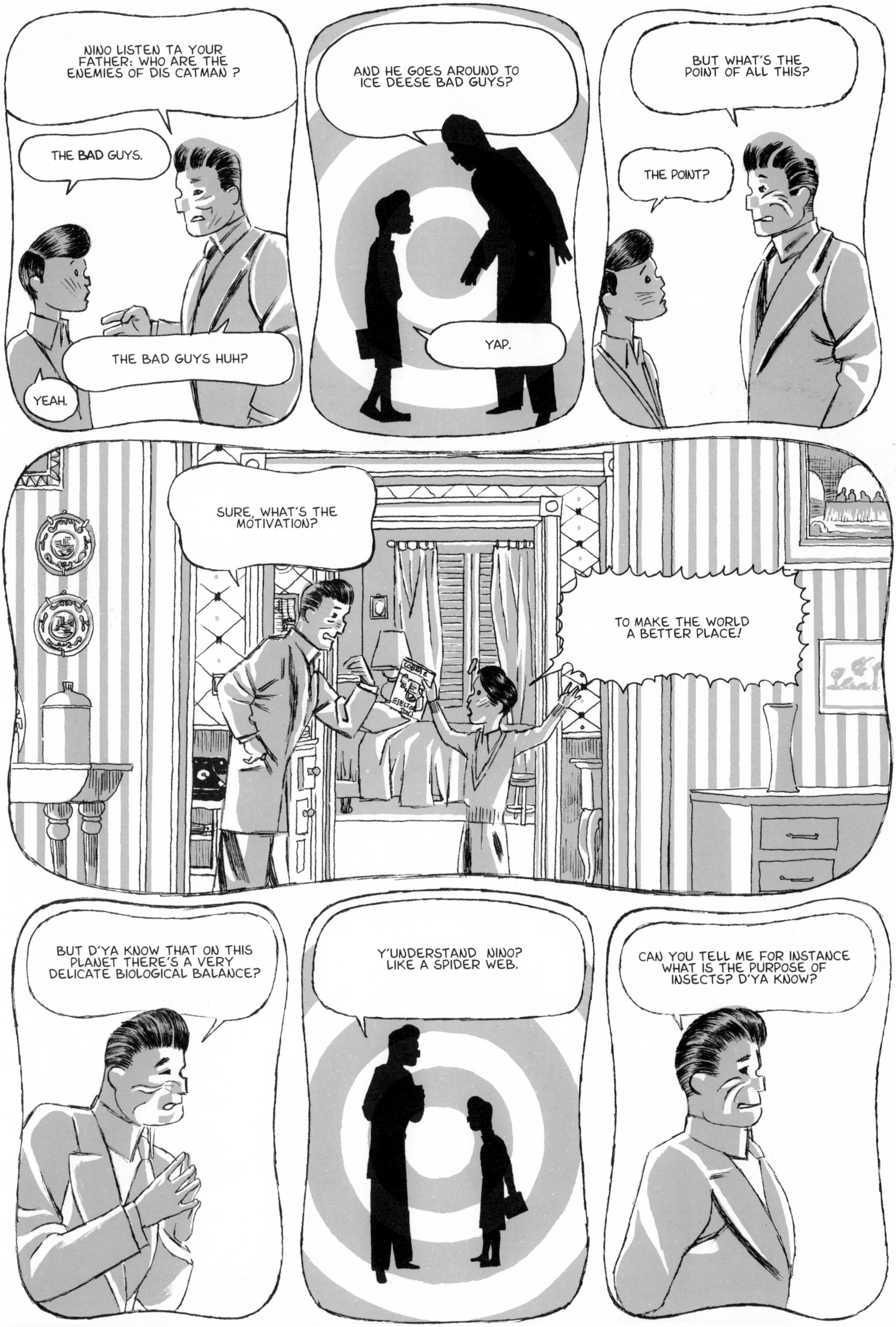
NINO LISTEN TA YOUR FATHER: WHO ARE THE ENEMIES OF DIS CATMAN ?
THE **BAD** GUYS.
THE BAD GUYS HUH?
YEAH.
AND HE GOES AROUND TO ICE DEESE BAD GUYS?
YAP.
BUT WHAT'S THE POINT OF ALL THIS?
THE POINT?
SURE, WHAT'S THE MOTIVATION?
TO MAKE THE WORLD A BETTER PLACE!
BUT D'YA KNOW THAT ON THIS PLANET THERE'S A VERY DELICATE BIOLOGICAL BALANCE?
Y'UNDERSTAND NINO? LIKE A SPIDER WEB.
CAN YOU TELL ME FOR INSTANCE WHAT IS THE PURPOSE OF INSECTS? D'YA KNOW?

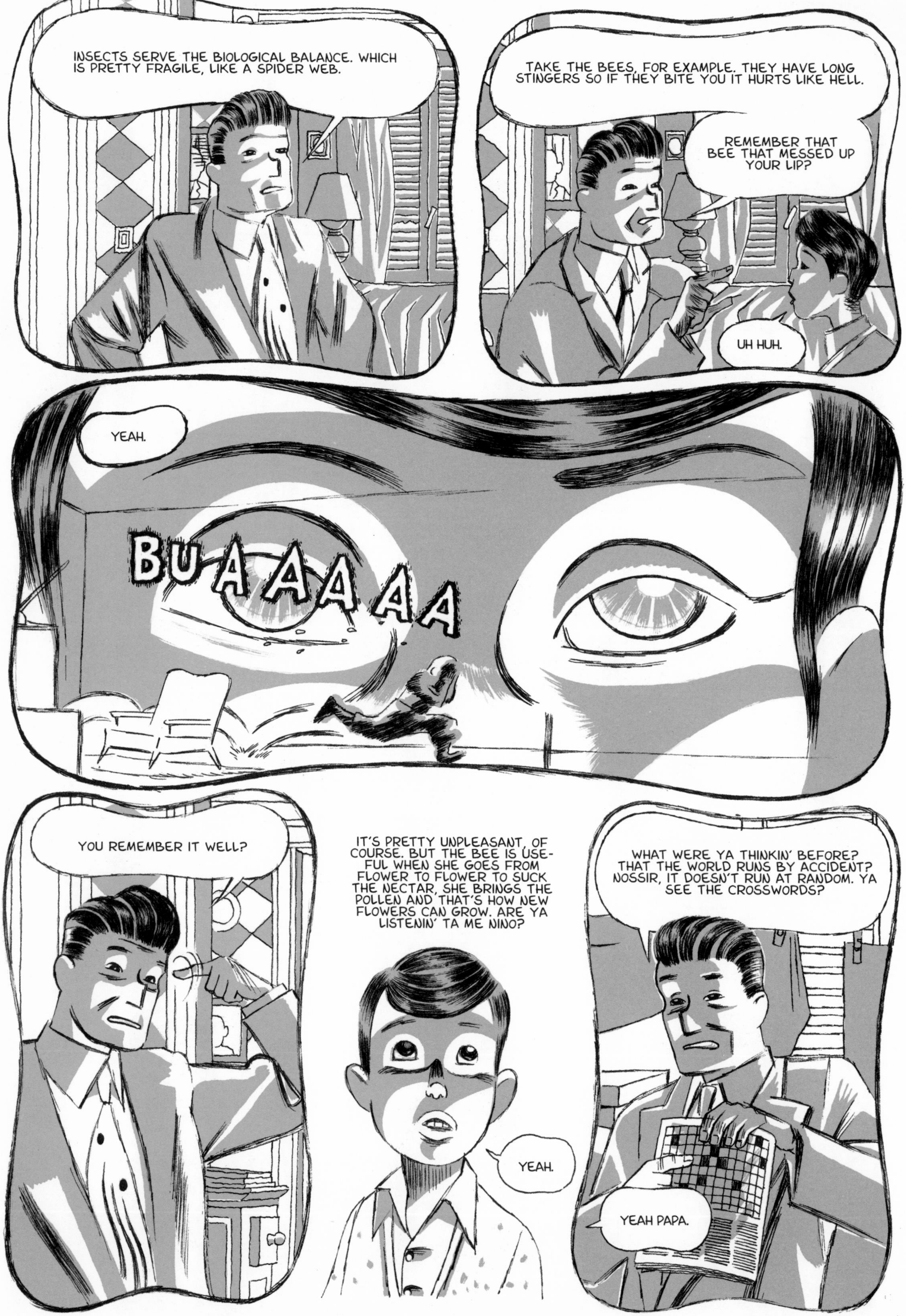
INSECTS SERVE THE BIOLOGICAL BALANCE. WHICH IS PRETTY FRAGILE, LIKE A SPIDER WEB.
TAKE THE BEES, FOR EXAMPLE. THEY HAVE LONG STINGERS SO IF THEY BITE YOU IT HURTS LIKE HELL.
REMEMBER THAT BEE THAT MESSED UP YOUR LIP?
UH HUH.
YEAH.
BUAAAAAA
YOU REMEMBER IT WELL?
IT'S PRETTY UNPLEASANT, OF COURSE. BUT THE BEE IS USEFUL WHEN SHE GOES FROM FLOWER TO FLOWER TO SUCK THE NECTAR, SHE BRINGS THE POLLEN AND THAT'S HOW NEW FLOWERS CAN GROW. ARE YA LISTENIN' TA ME NINO?
YEAH.
WHAT WERE YA THINKIN' BEFORE? THAT THE WORLD RUNS BY ACCIDENT? NOSSIR, IT DOESN'T RUN AT RANDOM. YA SEE THE CROSSWORDS?
YEAH PAPA.

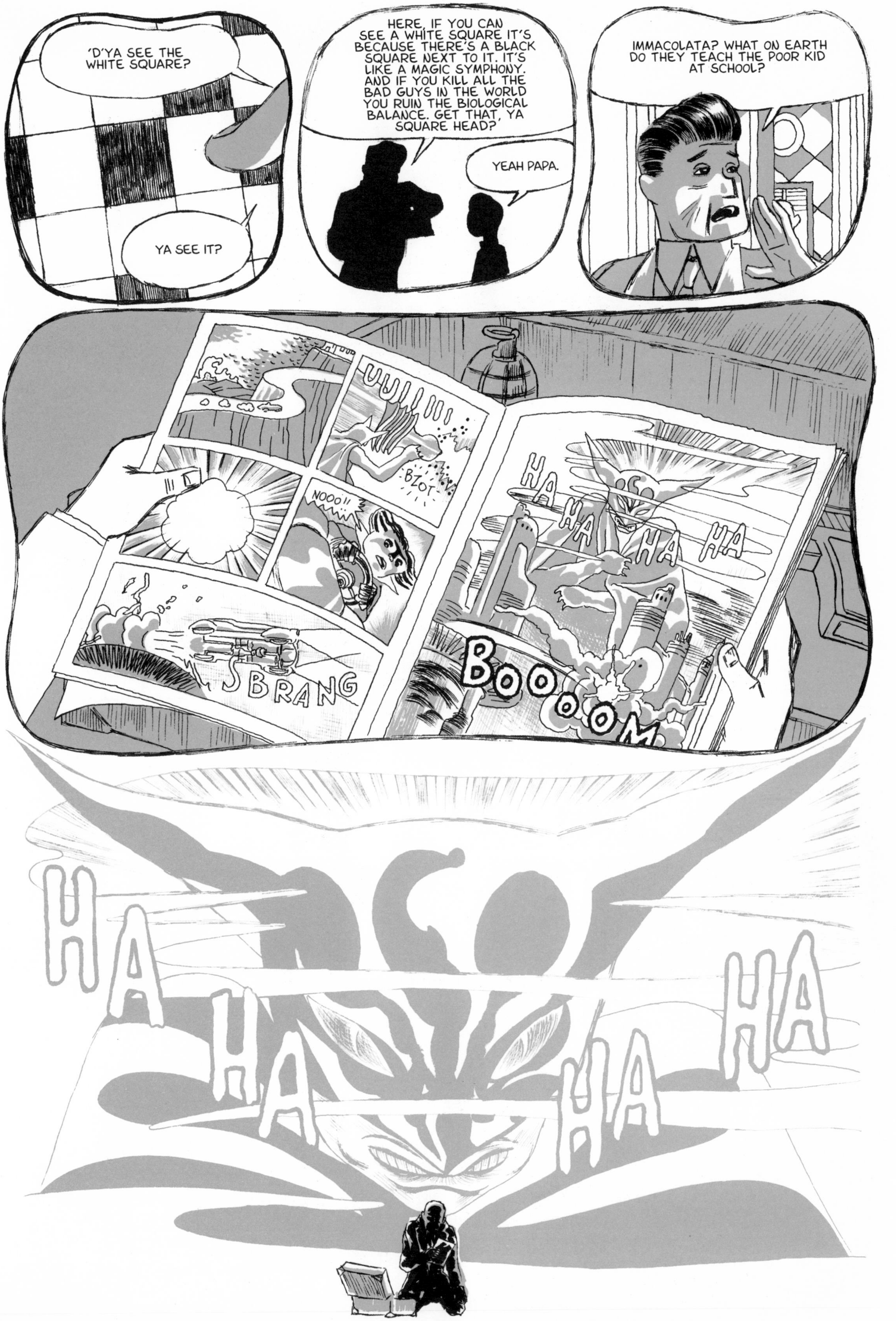
'D'YA SEE THE WHITE SQUARE?
YA SEE IT?
HERE, IF YOU CAN SEE A WHITE SQUARE IT'S BECAUSE THERE'S A BLACK SQUARE NEXT TO IT. IT'S LIKE A MAGIC SYMPHONY. AND IF YOU KILL ALL THE BAD GUYS IN THE WORLD YOU RUIN THE BIOLOGICAL BALANCE. GET THAT, YA SQUARE HEAD?'
YEAH PAPA.
IMMACOLATA? WHAT ON EARTH DO THEY TEACH THE POOR KID AT SCHOOL?
UUIIIIII
BZOT
NOOO!!
SBRANG
HA HA HA HA HA
BOOOOOM
HA HA HA HA HA

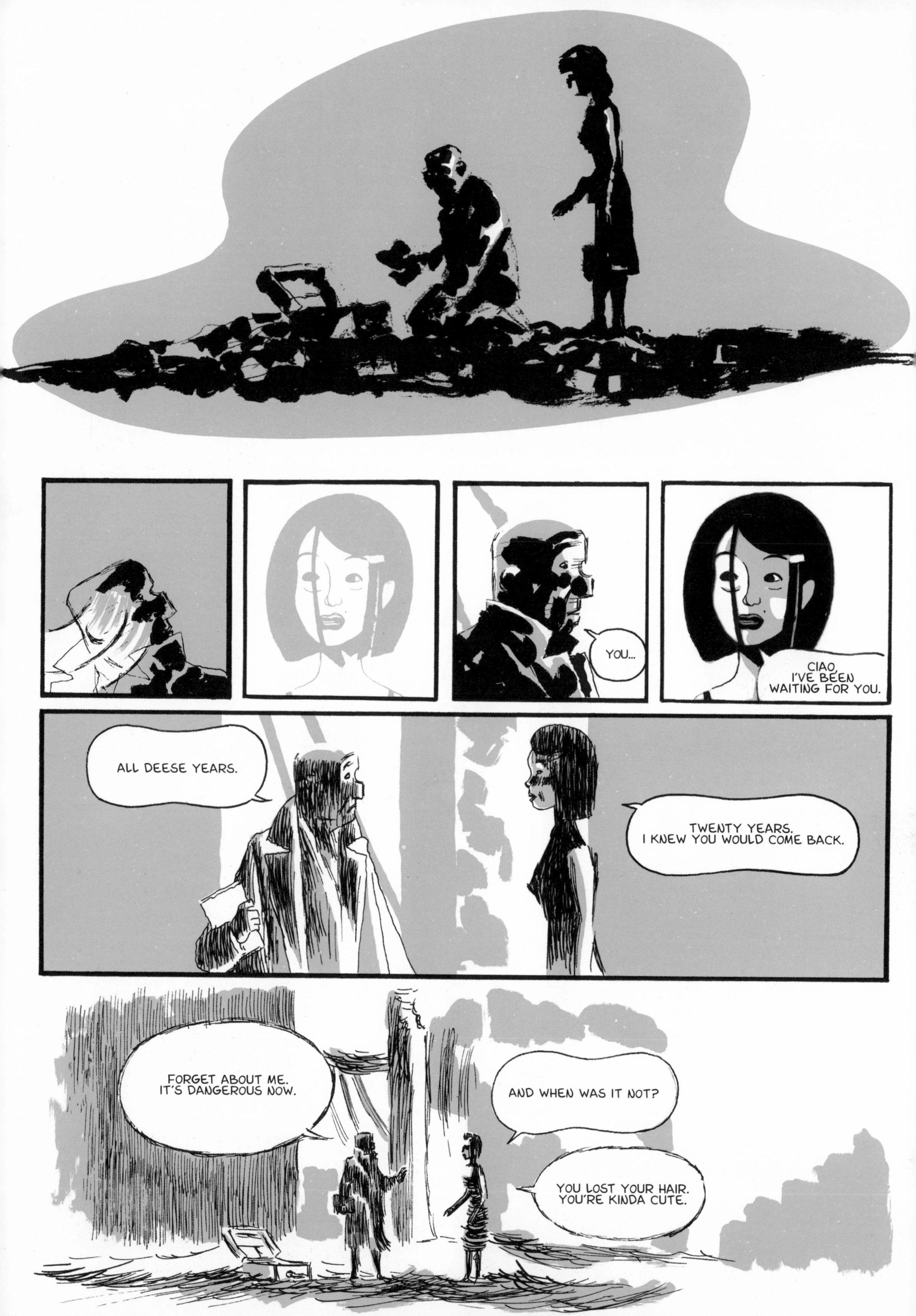

YOU...
CIAO, I'VE BEEN WAITING FOR YOU.
ALL DEESE YEARS.
TWENTY YEARS. I KNEW YOU WOULD COME BACK.
FORGET ABOUT ME. IT'S DANGEROUS NOW.
AND WHEN WAS IT NOT?
YOU LOST YOUR HAIR. YOU'RE KINDA CUTE.

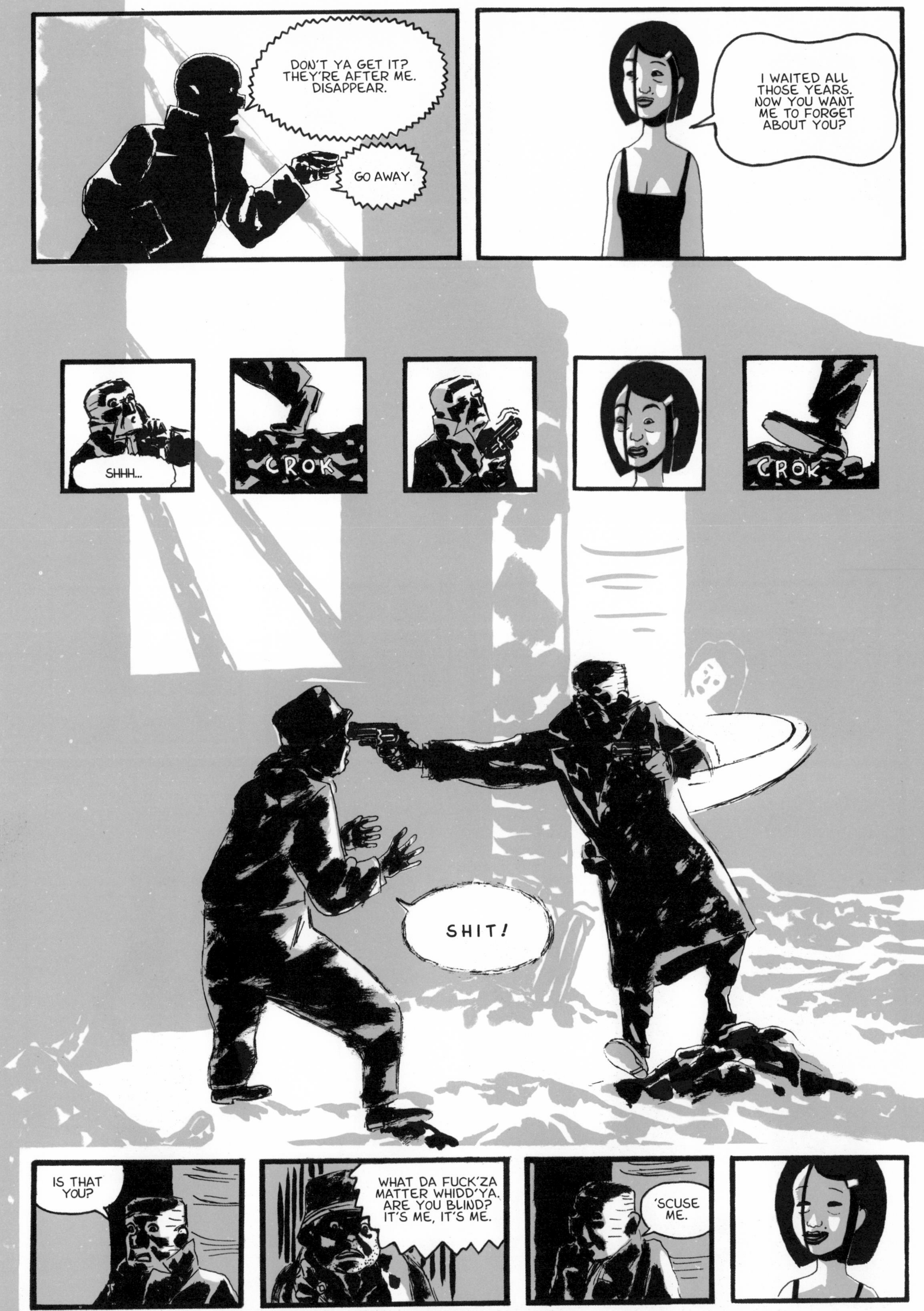
DON'T YA GET IT? THEY'RE AFTER ME. DISAPPEAR.
GO AWAY.
I WAITED ALL THOSE YEARS. NOW YOU WANT ME TO FORGET ABOUT YOU?
SHHH...
CROK
CROK
SHIT!
IS THAT YOU?
WHAT DA FUCK'ZA MATTER WHIDD'YA. ARE YOU BLIND? IT'S ME, IT'S ME.
'SCUSE ME.

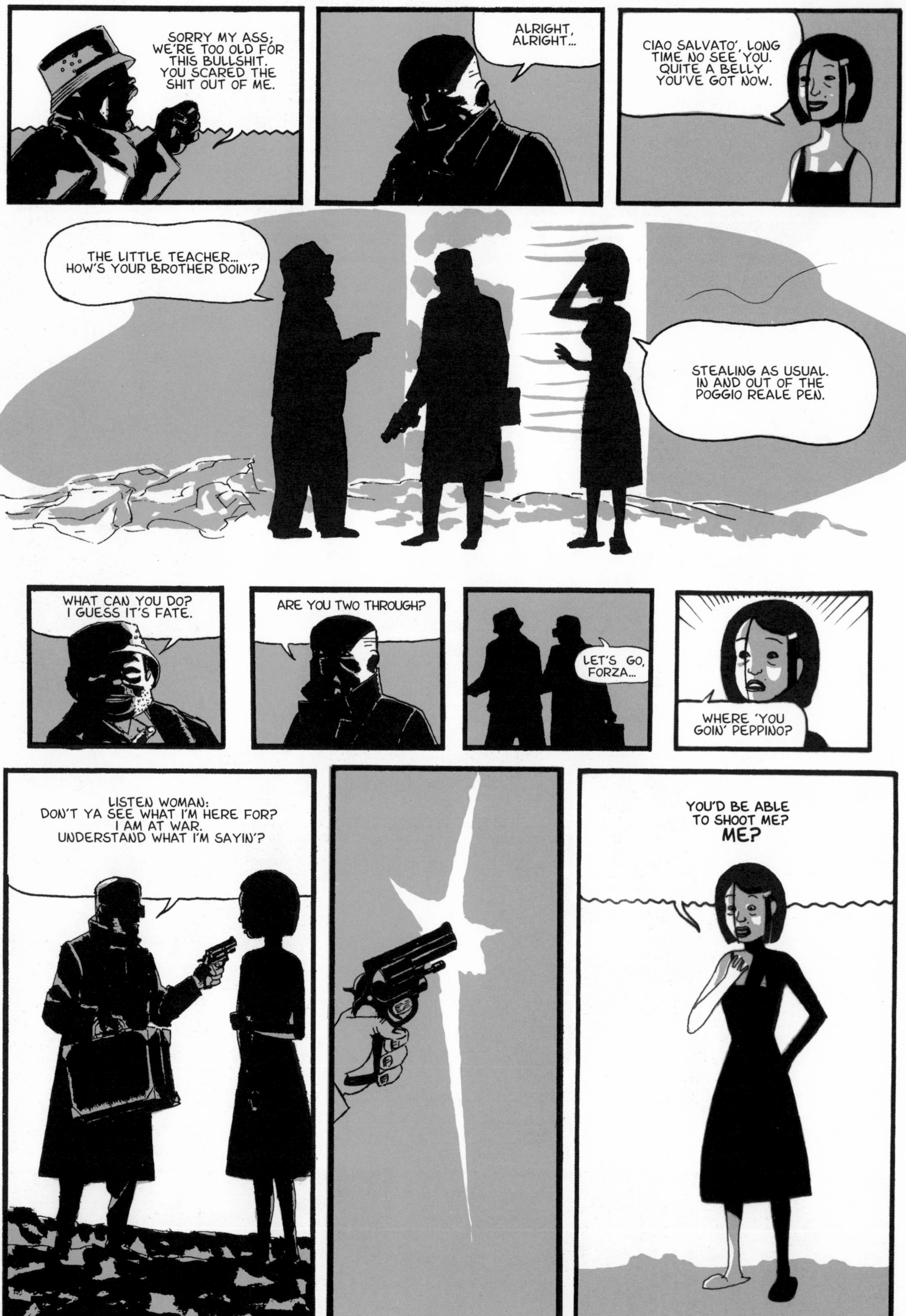
SORRY MY ASS; WE'RE TOO OLD FOR THIS BULLSHIT. YOU SCARED THE SHIT OUT OF ME.
ALRIGHT, ALRIGHT...
CIAO SALVATO', LONG TIME NO SEE YOU. QUITE A BELLY YOU'VE GOT NOW.
THE LITTLE TEACHER... HOW'S YOUR BROTHER DOIN'?
STEALING AS USUAL. IN AND OUT OF THE POGGIO REALE PEN.
WHAT CAN YOU DO? I GUESS IT'S FATE.
ARE YOU TWO THROUGH?
LET'S GO, FORZA...
WHERE 'YOU GOIN' PEPPINO?
LISTEN WOMAN: DON'T YA SEE WHAT I'M HERE FOR? I AM AT WAR. UNDERSTAND WHAT I'M SAYIN'?
YOU'D BE ABLE TO SHOOT ME? ME?

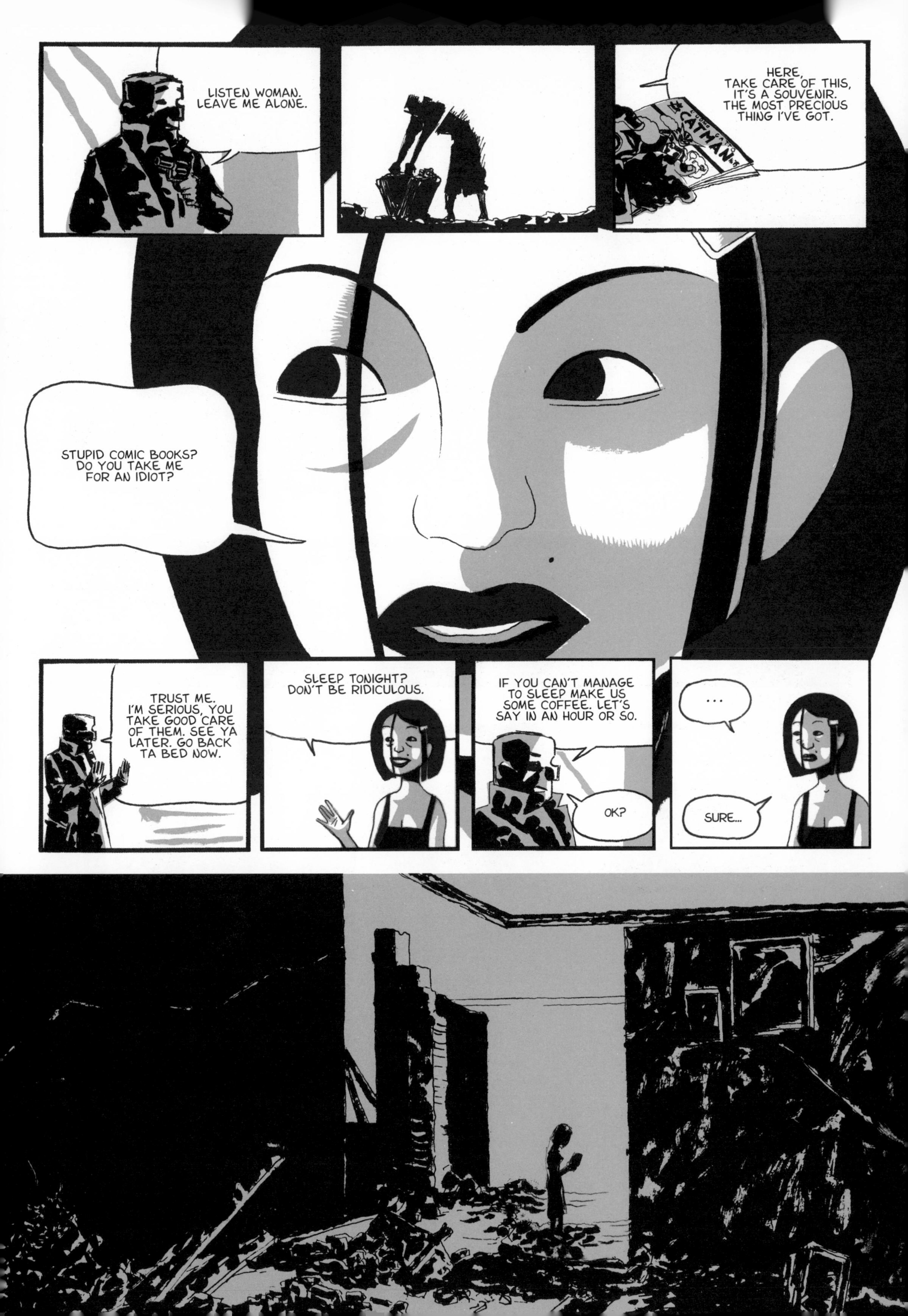
LISTEN WOMAN. LEAVE ME ALONE.
HERE, TAKE CARE OF THIS, IT'S A SOUVENIR. THE MOST PRECIOUS THING I'VE GOT.
CATMAN
STUPID COMIC BOOKS? DO YOU TAKE ME FOR AN IDIOT?
TRUST ME. I'M SERIOUS, YOU TAKE GOOD CARE OF THEM. SEE YA LATER. GO BACK TA BED NOW.
SLEEP TONIGHT? DON'T BE RIDICULOUS.
IF YOU CAN'T MANAGE TO SLEEP MAKE US SOME COFFEE. LET'S SAY IN AN HOUR OR SO.
OK?
...
SURE...

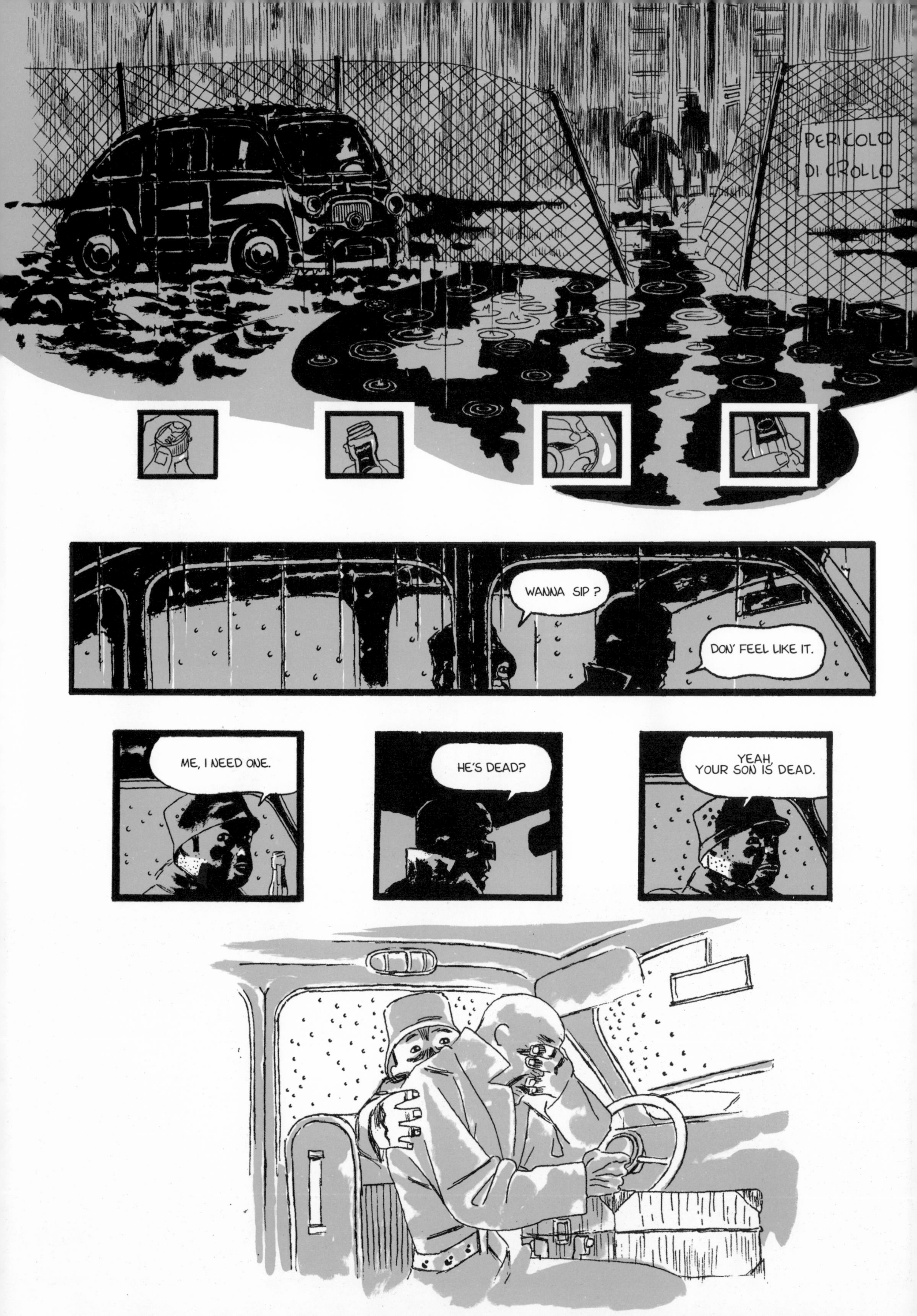

PERICOLO
DI CROLLO
WANNA SIP ?
DON' FEEL LIKE IT.
ME, I NEED ONE.
HE'S DEAD?
YEAH,
YOUR SON IS DEAD.

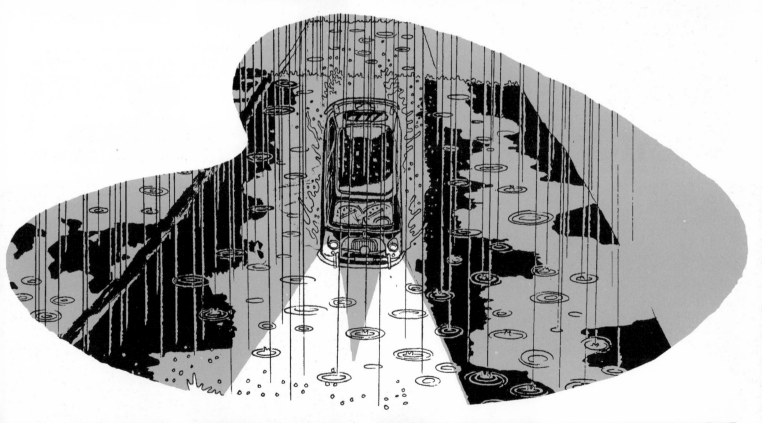

WHAT'S ON YOUR MIND PEPPI? WHAT ARE YA THINKING OF DOIN' NOW?

ARE YOU UP TO THIS?

UP TO WHAT? YOU GOT ME INTO SHIT, SO NOW DO ME A FAVOR AND START THINKIN' FAST.

WE'RE NOT THE FELLAS WE USED TO BE. TIME FLIES FOR ALL OF US. WE'VE GOT TO TALK TO DON GUARINO.

ARE YA WITH ME PEPPI'?

YOUR SON WAS WORKING FOR DON GUARINO AND DON GUARINO WILL TAKE CARE OF THE ENTIRE PROBLEM; DATZ DA RULES.

'KNOW WHAT?

YOU'RE SCARED SALVATO'. YOU USED TO BE SO BRAVE, NOW YOU'RE AFRAID OF YOUR OWN SHADOW.

I'VE GOT A STRANGE FEELIN' THE FUTURE WON'T BE ROSY.

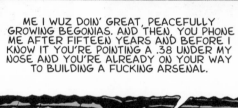

ME I WUZ DOIN' GREAT, PEACEFULLY GROWING BEGONIAS. AND THEN, YOU PHONE ME AFTER FIFTEEN YEARS AND BEFORE I KNOW IT YOU'RE POINTING A .38 UNDER MY NOSE AND YOU'RE ALREADY ON YOUR WAY TO BUILDING A FUCKING ARSENAL.

ARE YOU DONE? TONIGHT THERE WAS A GUY AT THE CINEMA, WITH A FUCKING ROCK'N' ROLL HAIRDO. AND HE HAD A GUN.

WELL, WHAT'S SO SPECIAL ABOUT IT? THEY ALL CARRY ONE...

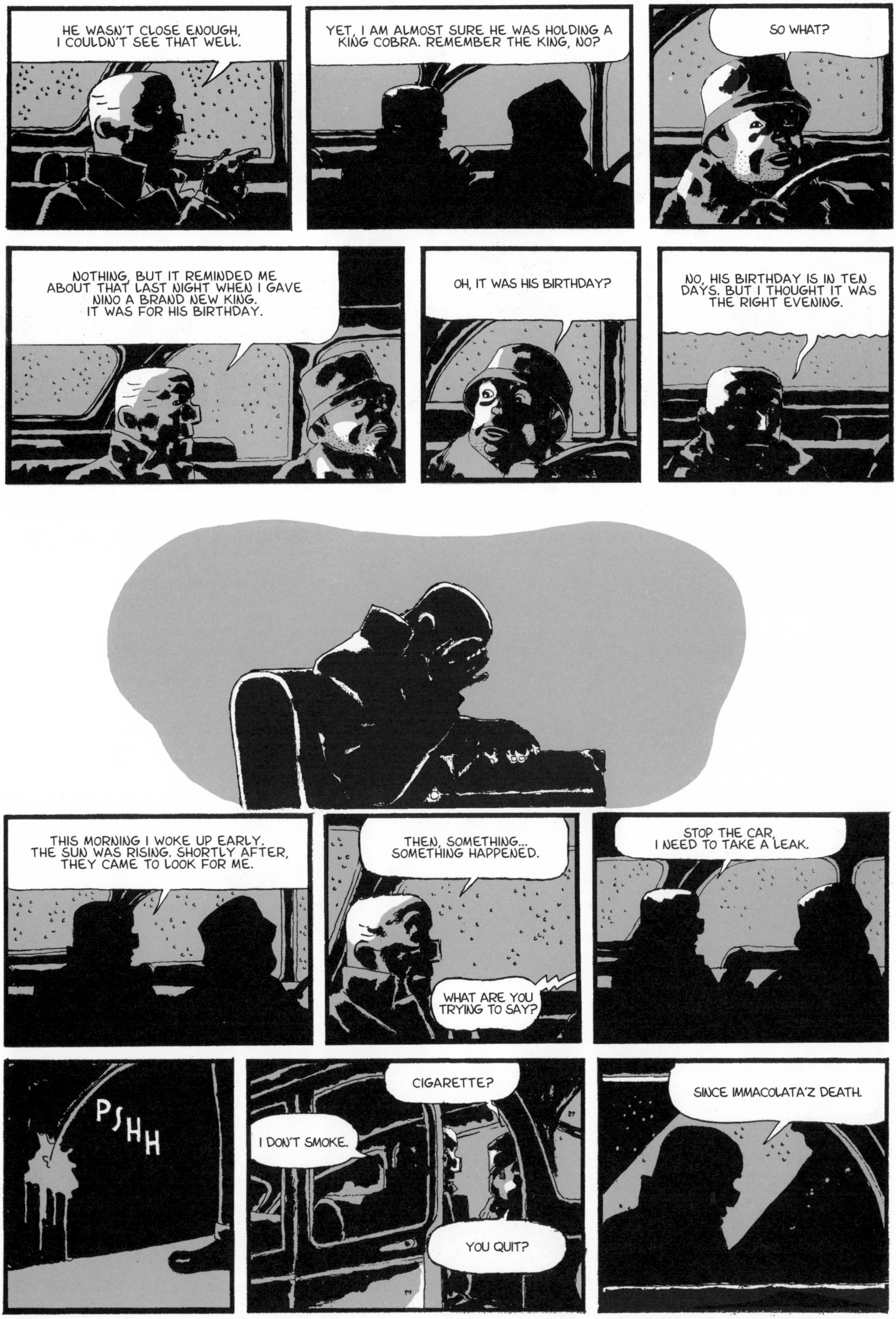
HE WASN'T CLOSE ENOUGH, I COULDN'T SEE THAT WELL.
YET, I AM ALMOST SURE HE WAS HOLDING A KING COBRA. REMEMBER THE KING, NO?
SO WHAT?
NOTHING, BUT IT REMINDED ME ABOUT THAT LAST NIGHT WHEN I GAVE NINO A BRAND NEW KING. IT WAS FOR HIS BIRTHDAY.
OH, IT WAS HIS BIRTHDAY?
NO, HIS BIRTHDAY IS IN TEN DAYS. BUT I THOUGHT IT WAS THE RIGHT EVENING.
THIS MORNING I WOKE UP EARLY. THE SUN WAS RISING. SHORTLY AFTER, THEY CAME TO LOOK FOR ME.
THEN, SOMETHING... SOMETHING HAPPENED.
WHAT ARE YOU TRYING TO SAY?
STOP THE CAR, I NEED TO TAKE A LEAK.
PSHH
CIGARETTE?
I DON'T SMOKE.
YOU QUIT?
SINCE IMMACOLATA'Z DEATH.

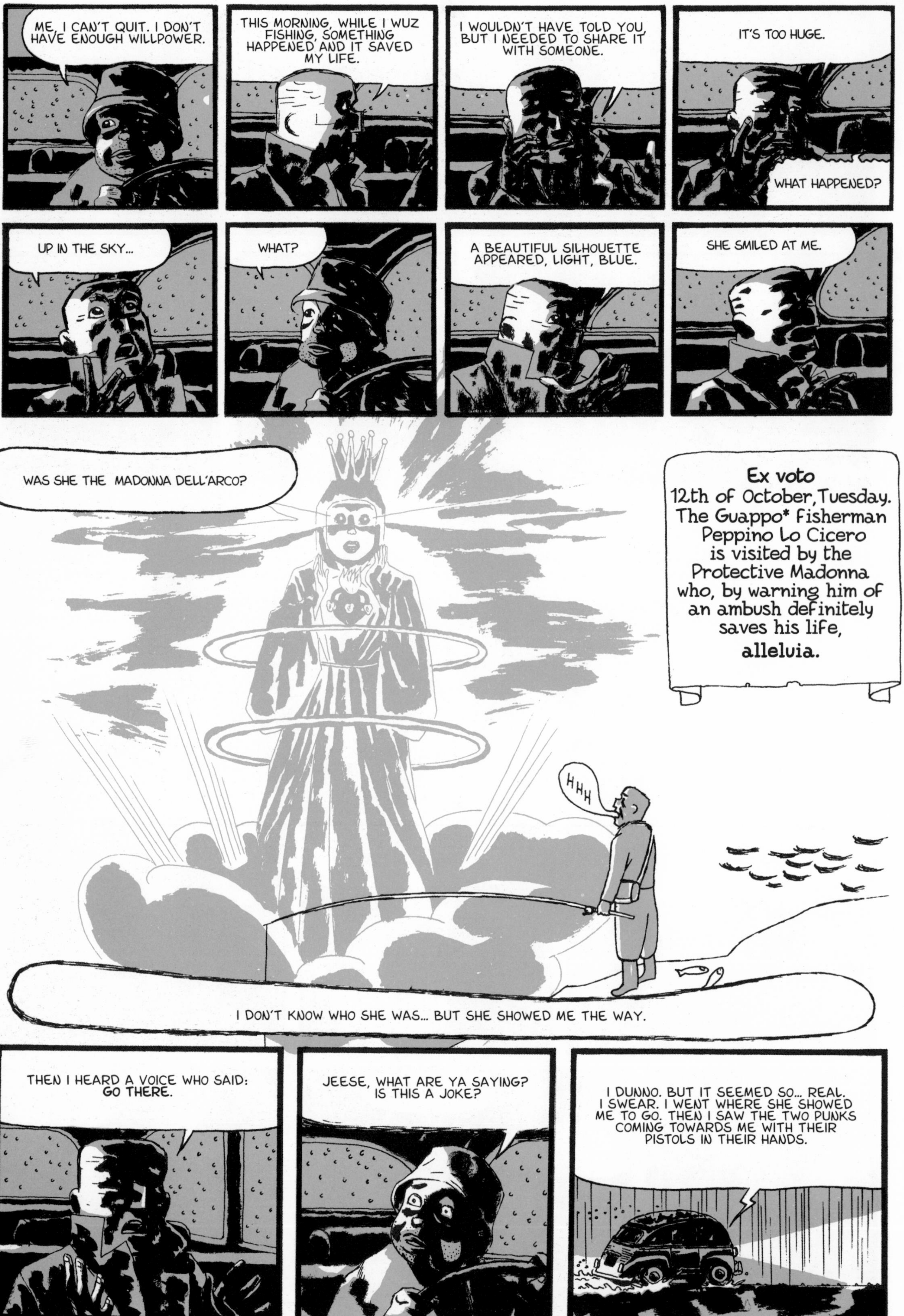

ME, I CAN'T QUIT. I DON'T HAVE ENOUGH WILLPOWER.
THIS MORNING, WHILE I WUZ FISHING, SOMETHING HAPPENED AND IT SAVED MY LIFE.
I WOULDN'T HAVE TOLD YOU, BUT I NEEDED TO SHARE IT WITH SOMEONE.
IT'S TOO HUGE.
WHAT HAPPENED?
UP IN THE SKY...
WHAT?
A BEAUTIFUL SILHOUETTE APPEARED, LIGHT, BLUE.
SHE SMILED AT ME.
WAS SHE THE MADONNA DELL'ARCO?
Ex voto
12th of October, Tuesday.
The Guappo* fisherman Peppino Lo Cicero is visited by the Protective Madonna who, by warning him of an ambush definitely saves his life,
alleluia.
HHH
I DON'T KNOW WHO SHE WAS... BUT SHE SHOWED ME THE WAY.
THEN I HEARD A VOICE WHO SAID: GO THERE.
JEESE, WHAT ARE YA SAYING? IS THIS A JOKE?
I DUNNO. BUT IT SEEMED SO... REAL. I SWEAR. I WENT WHERE SHE SHOWED ME TO GO. THEN I SAW THE TWO PUNKS COMING TOWARDS ME WITH THEIR PISTOLS IN THEIR HANDS.

* GUAPPO: a mafioso from the Napoli area

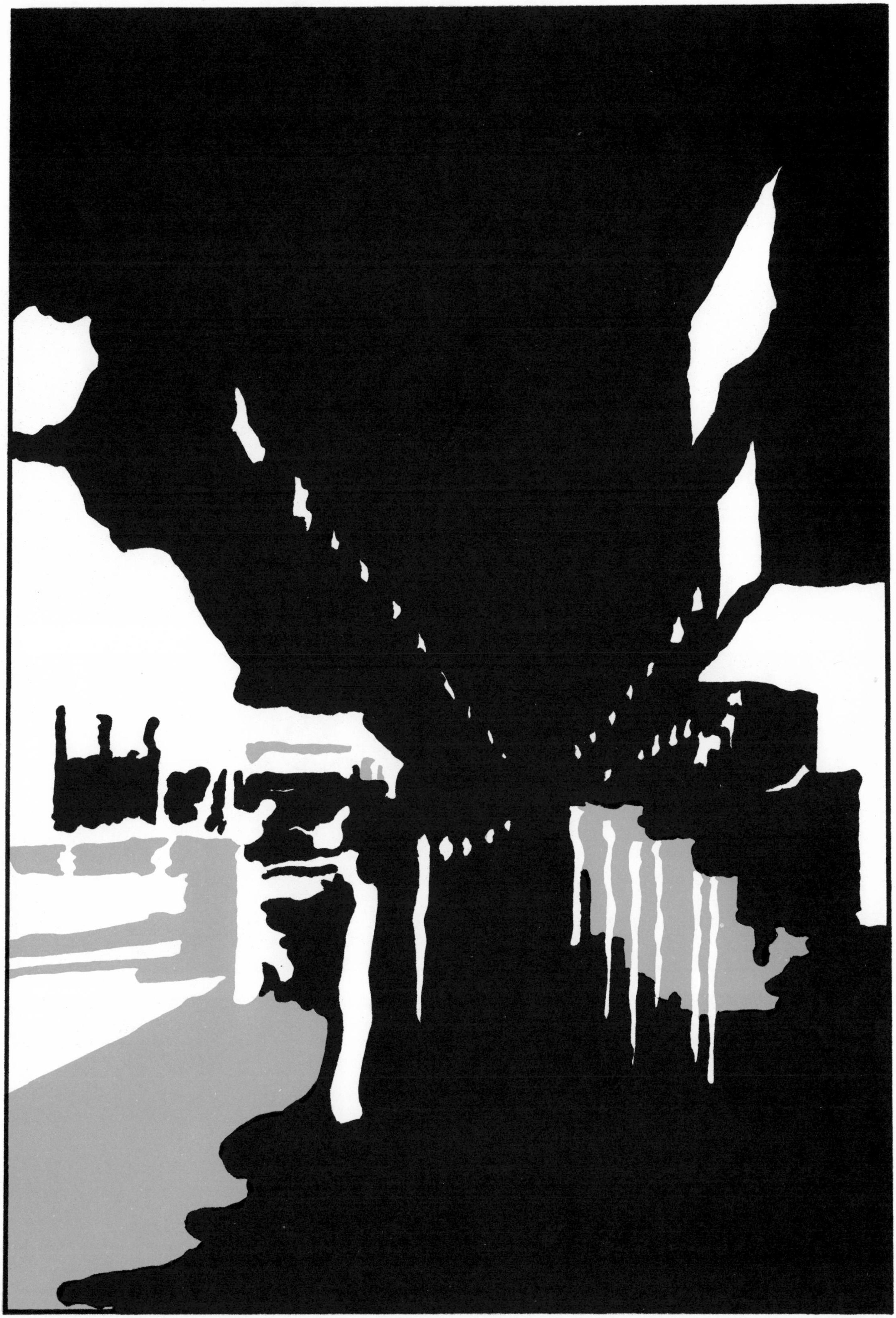

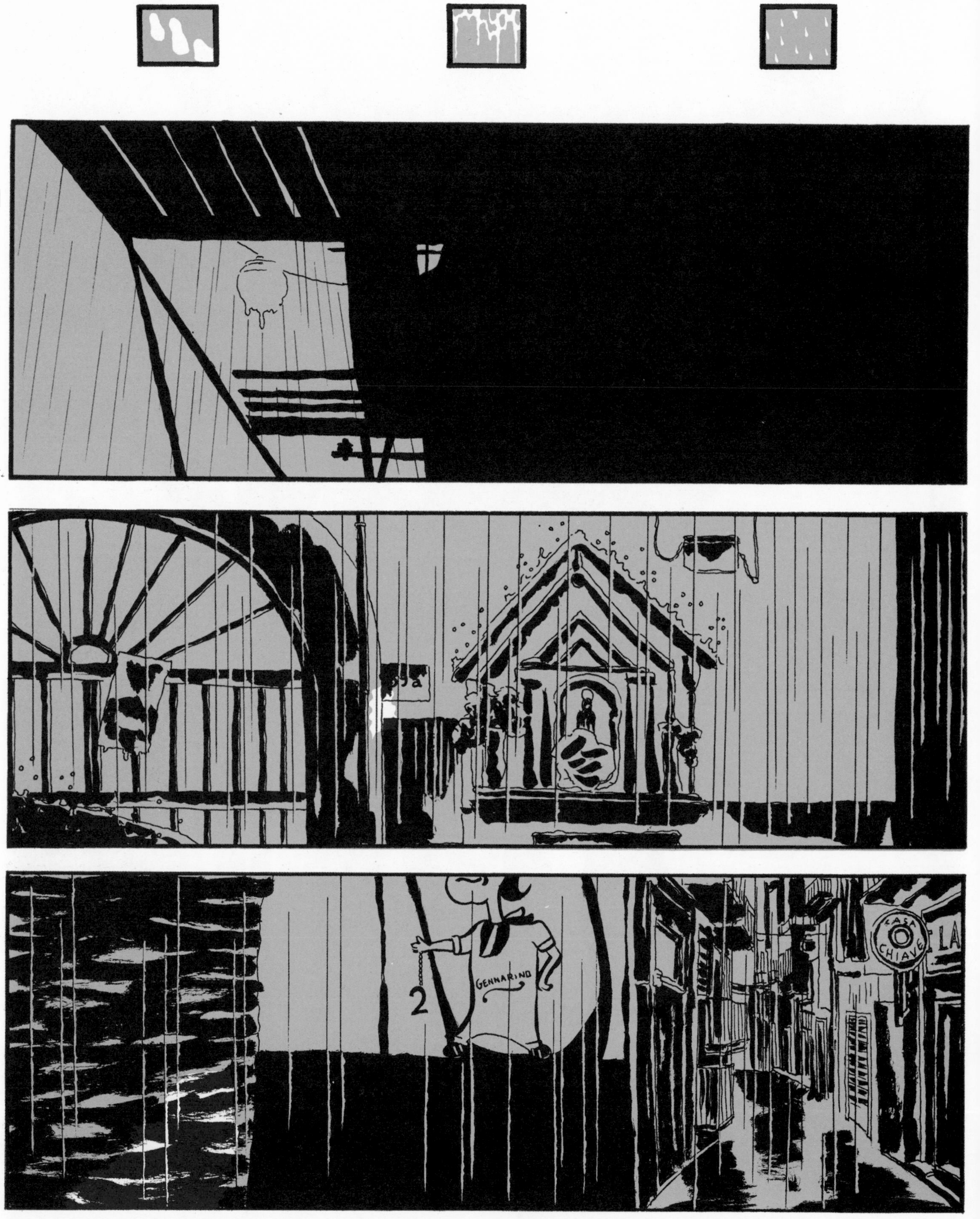
2
GENNARINO
CASA
CHIAVE
LA

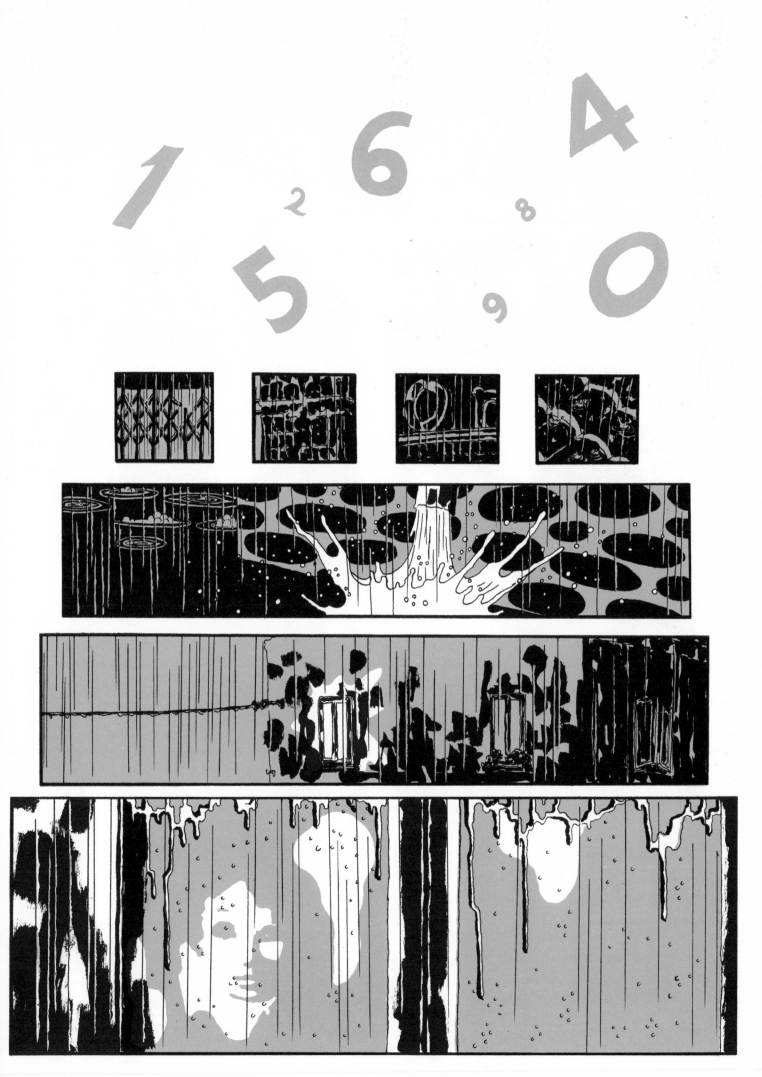

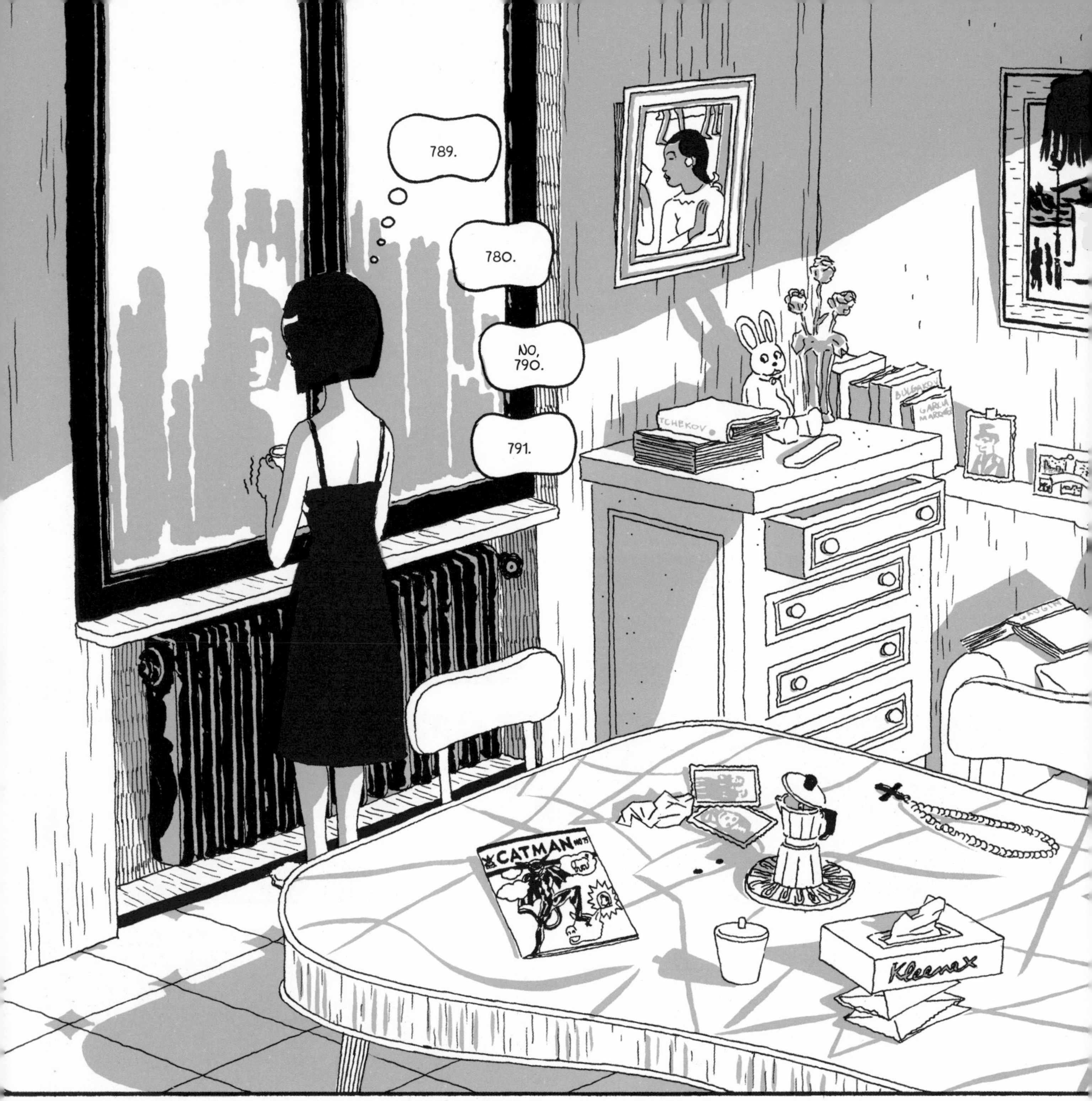
789.
780.
NO,
790.
791.
TCHEKOV
BULGAKOV
GARCIA
MARQUEZ
CATMAN
Kleenex

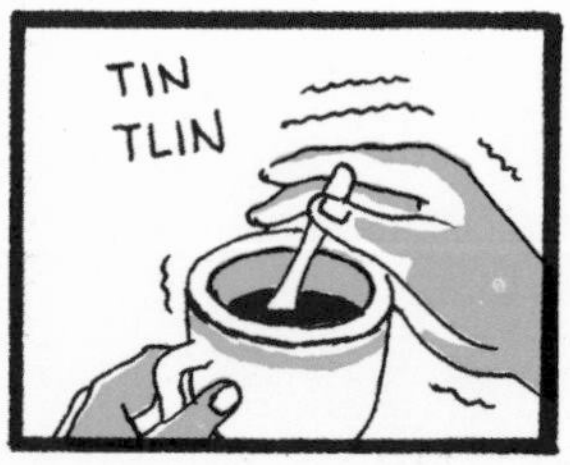
TIN
TLIN

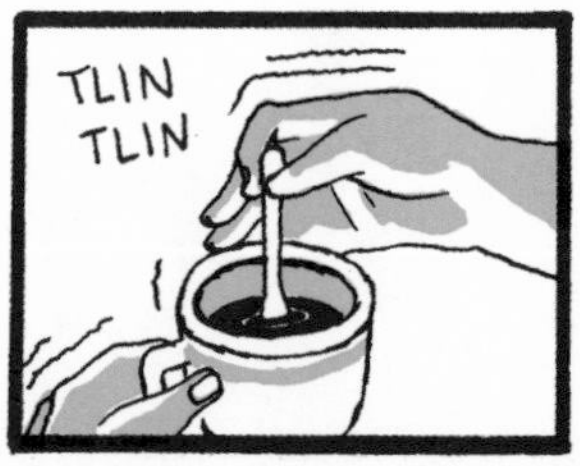
TLIN
TLIN

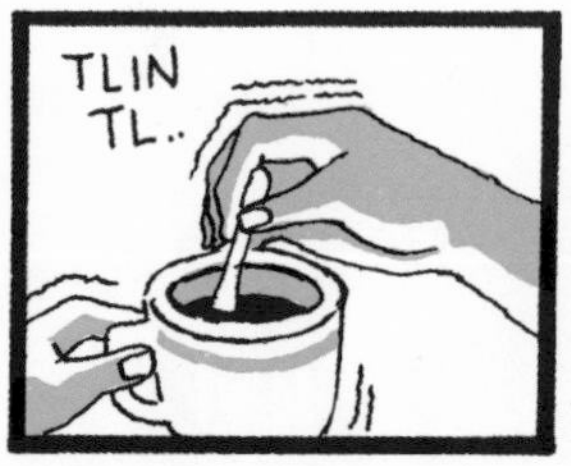
TLIN
TL..

chapter three
mafia waltz

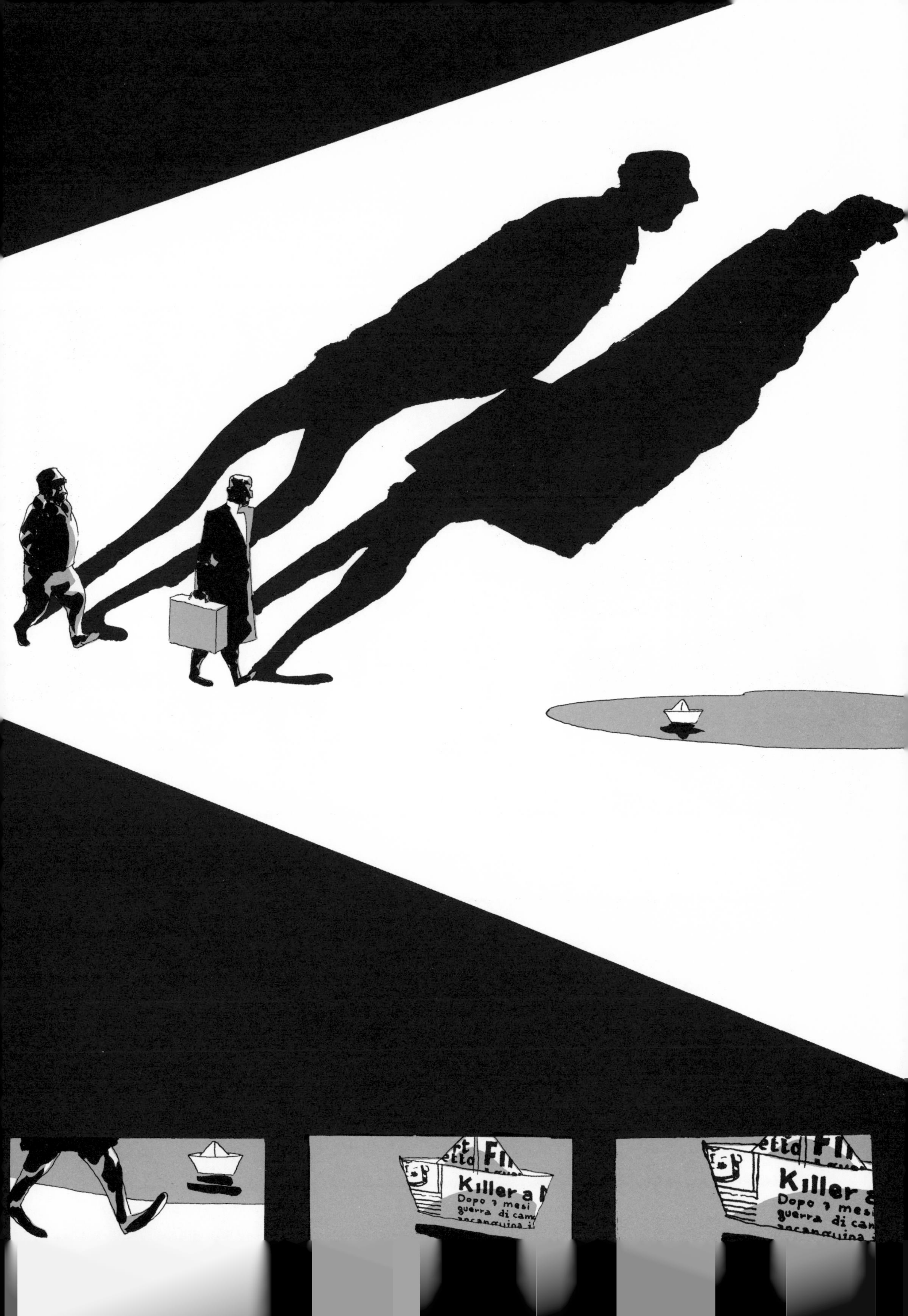
Killer a
Dopo 7 mesi
guerra di cam

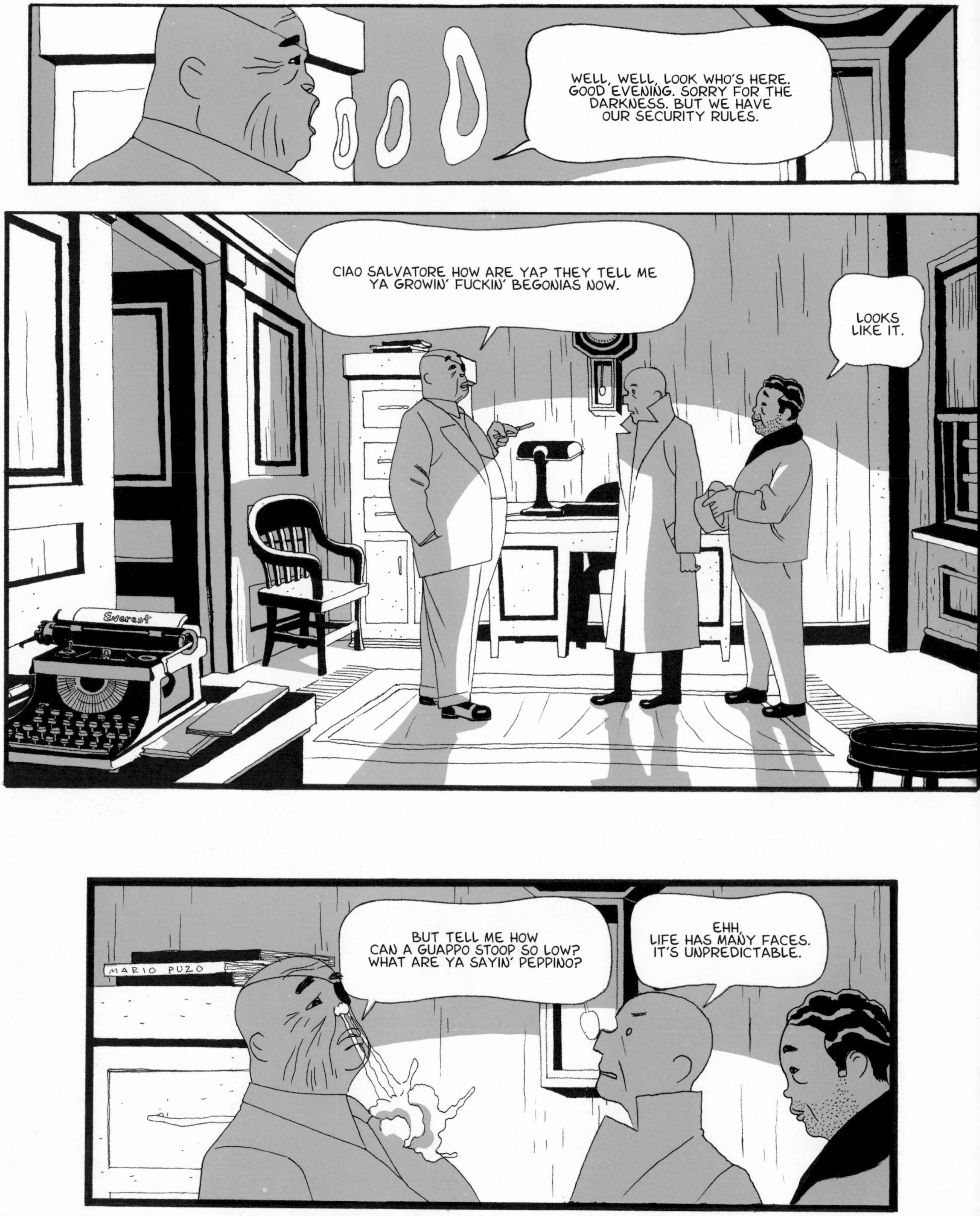
WELL, WELL, LOOK WHO'S HERE. GOOD EVENING. SORRY FOR THE DARKNESS. BUT WE HAVE OUR SECURITY RULES.
CIAO SALVATORE HOW ARE YA? THEY TELL ME YA GROWIN' FUCKIN' BEGONIAS NOW.
LOOKS LIKE IT.
Everest
MARIO PUZO
BUT TELL ME HOW CAN A GUAPPO STOOP SO LOW? WHAT ARE YA SAYIN' PEPPINO?
EHH, LIFE HAS MANY FACES. IT'S UNPREDICTABLE.

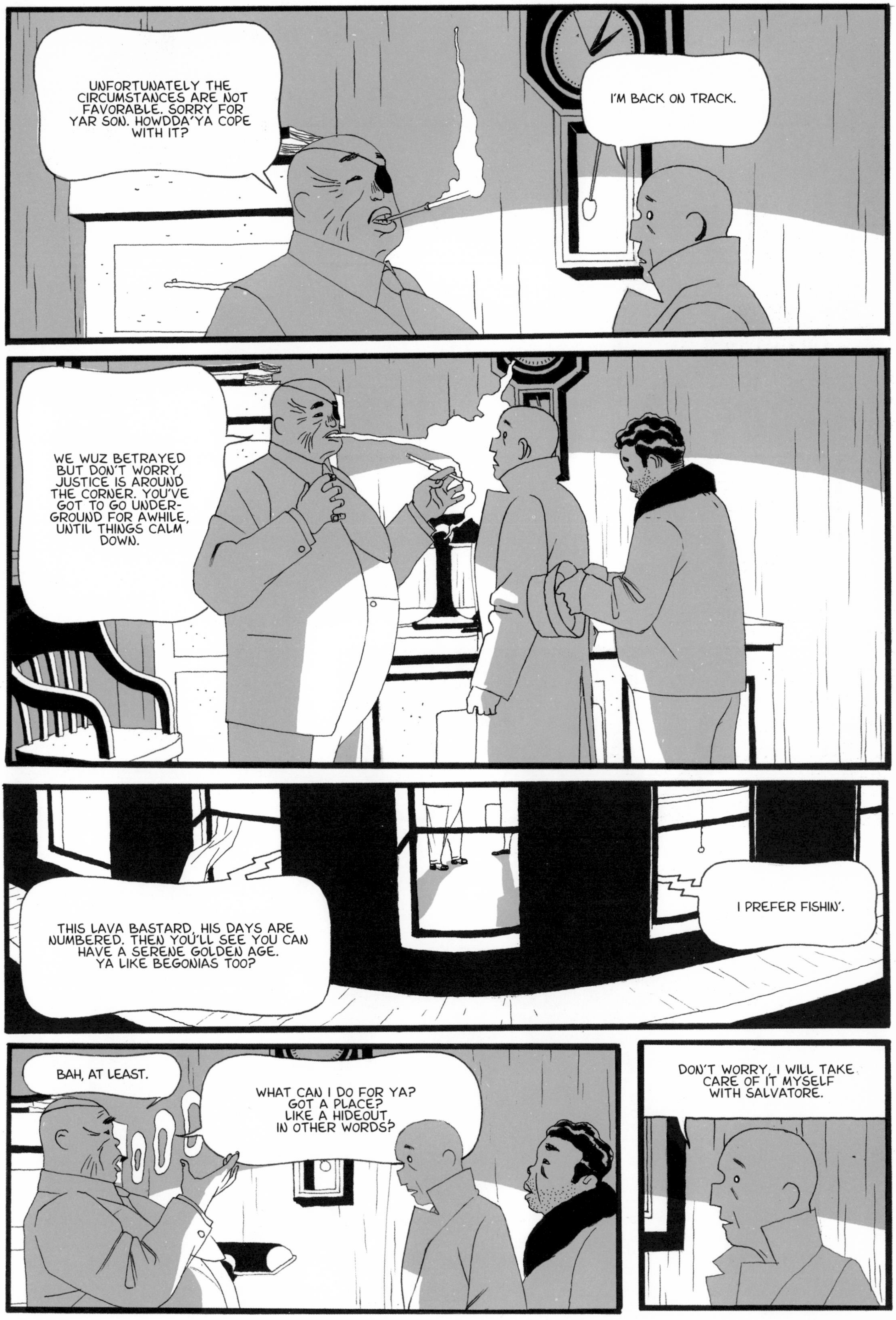
UNFORTUNATELY THE CIRCUMSTANCES ARE NOT FAVORABLE. SORRY FOR YAR SON. HOWDDA'YA COPE WITH IT?
I'M BACK ON TRACK.
WE WUZ BETRAYED BUT DON'T WORRY, JUSTICE IS AROUND THE CORNER. YOU'VE GOT TO GO UNDER-GROUND FOR AWHILE, UNTIL THINGS CALM DOWN.
THIS LAVA BASTARD, HIS DAYS ARE NUMBERED. THEN YOU'LL SEE YOU CAN HAVE A SERENE GOLDEN AGE. YA LIKE BEGONIAS TOO?
I PREFER FISHIN'.
BAH, AT LEAST.
WHAT CAN I DO FOR YA? GOT A PLACE? LIKE A HIDEOUT, IN OTHER WORDS?
DON'T WORRY, I WILL TAKE CARE OF IT MYSELF WITH SALVATORE.

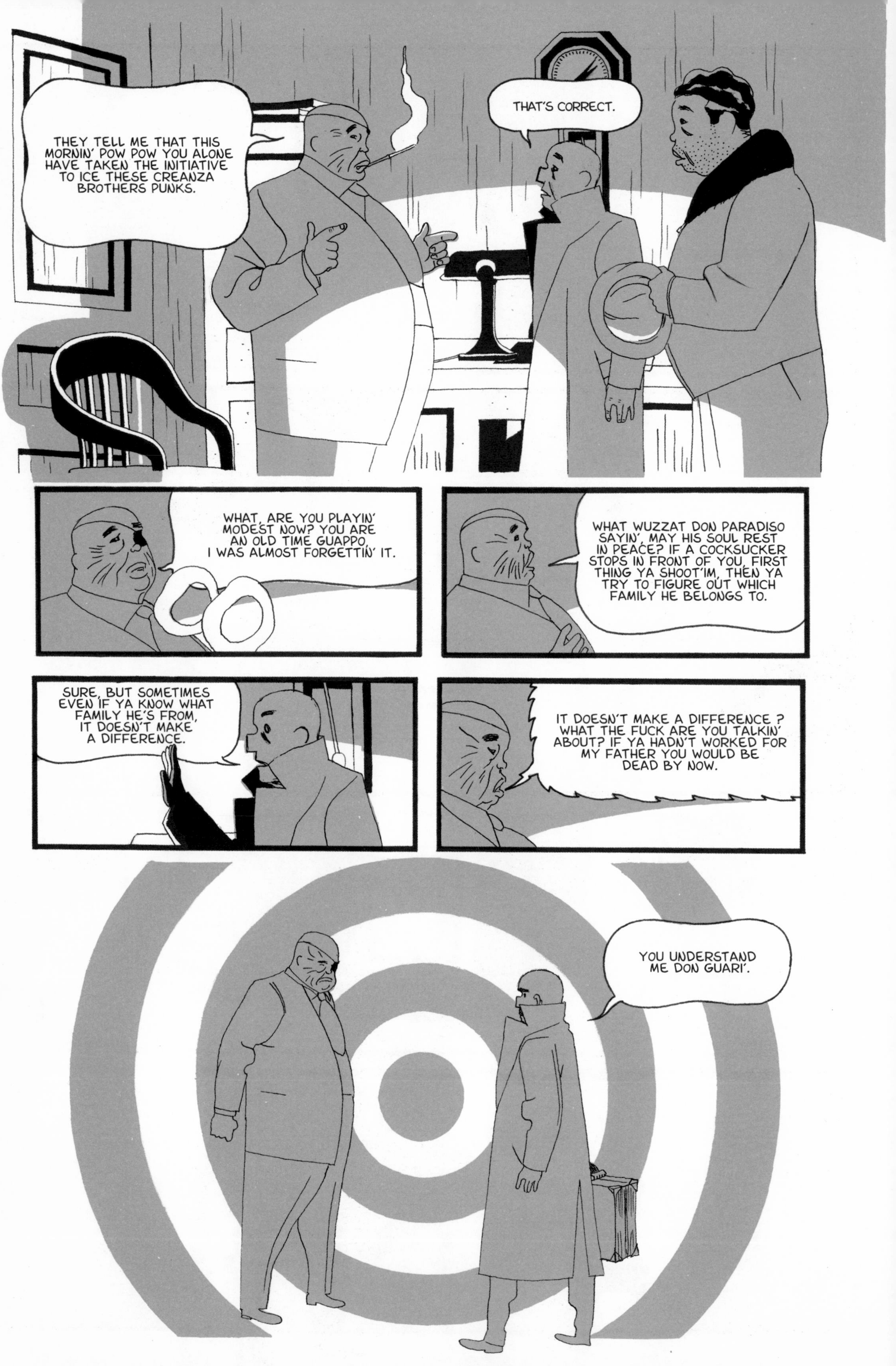
THEY TELL ME THAT THIS MORNIN' POW POW YOU ALONE HAVE TAKEN THE INITIATIVE TO ICE THESE CREANZA BROTHERS PUNKS.
THAT'S CORRECT.
WHAT, ARE YOU PLAYIN' MODEST NOW? YOU ARE AN OLD TIME GUAPPO, I WAS ALMOST FORGETTIN' IT.
WHAT WUZZAT DON PARADISO SAYIN', MAY HIS SOUL REST IN PEACE? IF A COCKSUCKER STOPS IN FRONT OF YOU, FIRST THING YA SHOOT'IM, THEN YA TRY TO FIGURE OUT WHICH FAMILY HE BELONGS TO.
SURE, BUT SOMETIMES EVEN IF YA KNOW WHAT FAMILY HE'S FROM, IT DOESN'T MAKE A DIFFERENCE.
IT DOESN'T MAKE A DIFFERENCE ? WHAT THE FUCK ARE YOU TALKIN' ABOUT? IF YA HADN'T WORKED FOR MY FATHER YOU WOULD BE DEAD BY NOW.
YOU UNDERSTAND ME DON GUARI'.

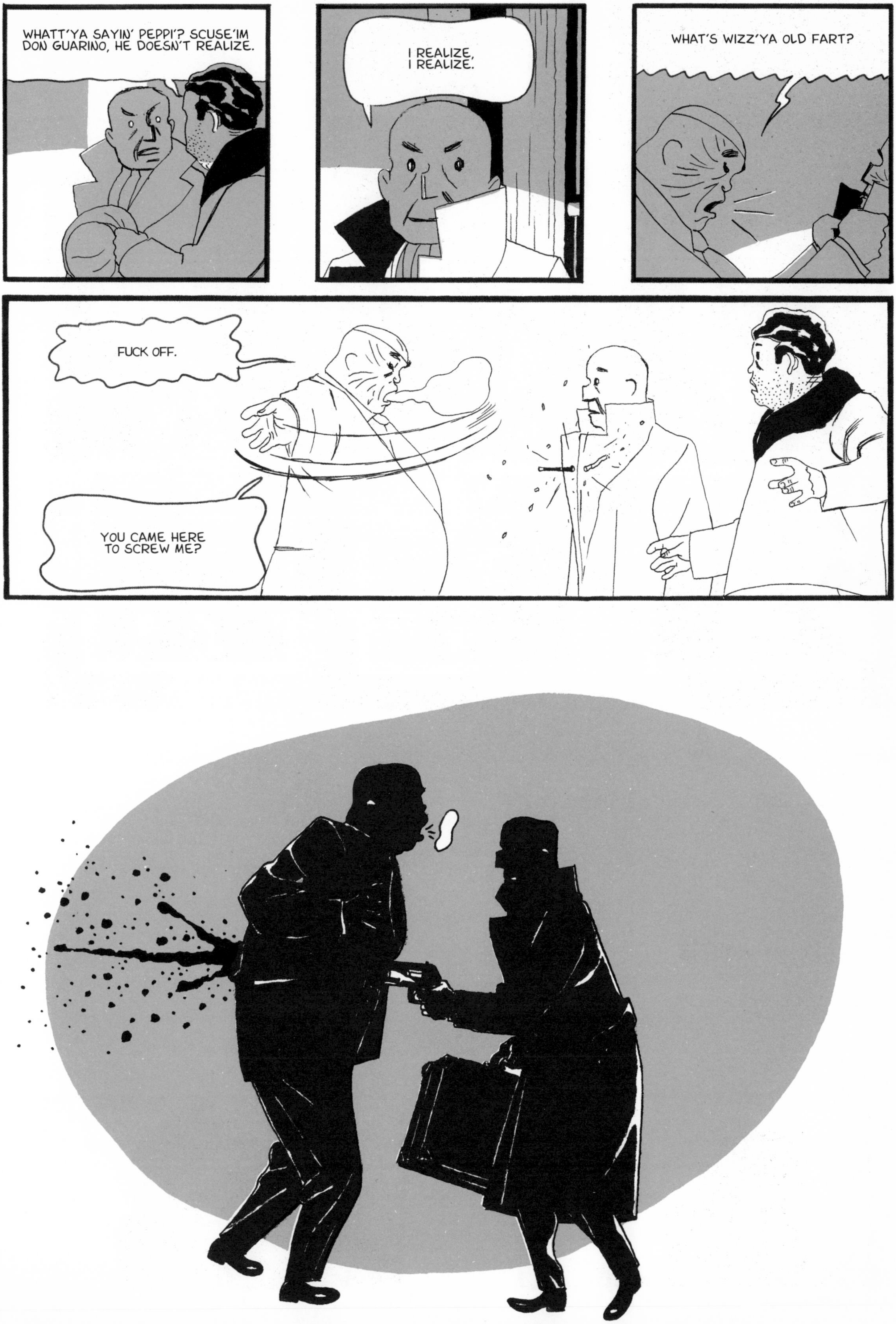
WHATT'YA SAYIN' PEPPI'? SCUSE'IM DON GUARINO, HE DOESN'T REALIZE.
I REALIZE, I REALIZE.
WHAT'S WIZZ'YA OLD FART?
FUCK OFF.
YOU CAME HERE TO SCREW ME?

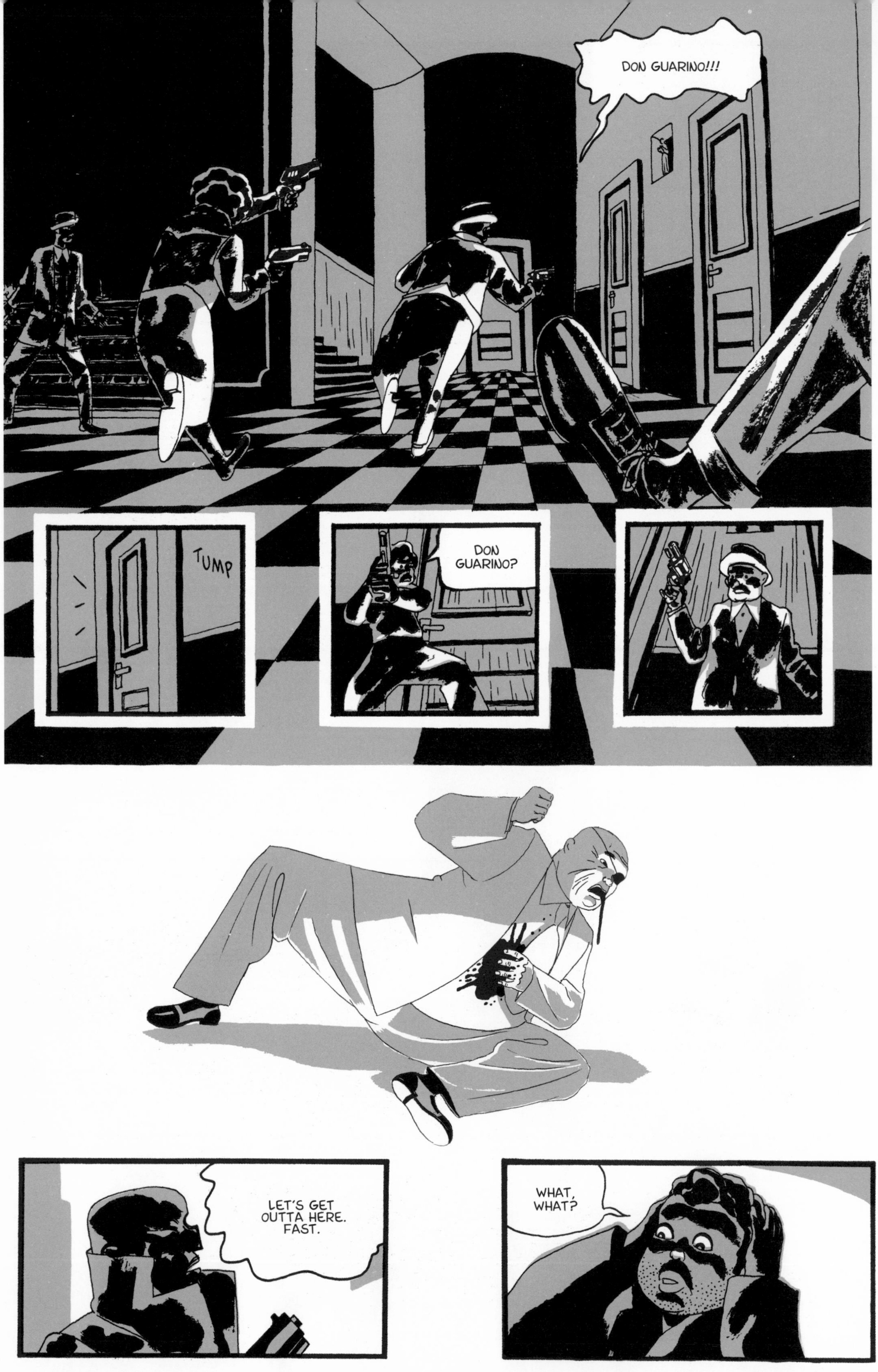
DON GUARINO!!!
TUMP
DON GUARINO?
LET'S GET OUTTA HERE. FAST.
WHAT, WHAT?

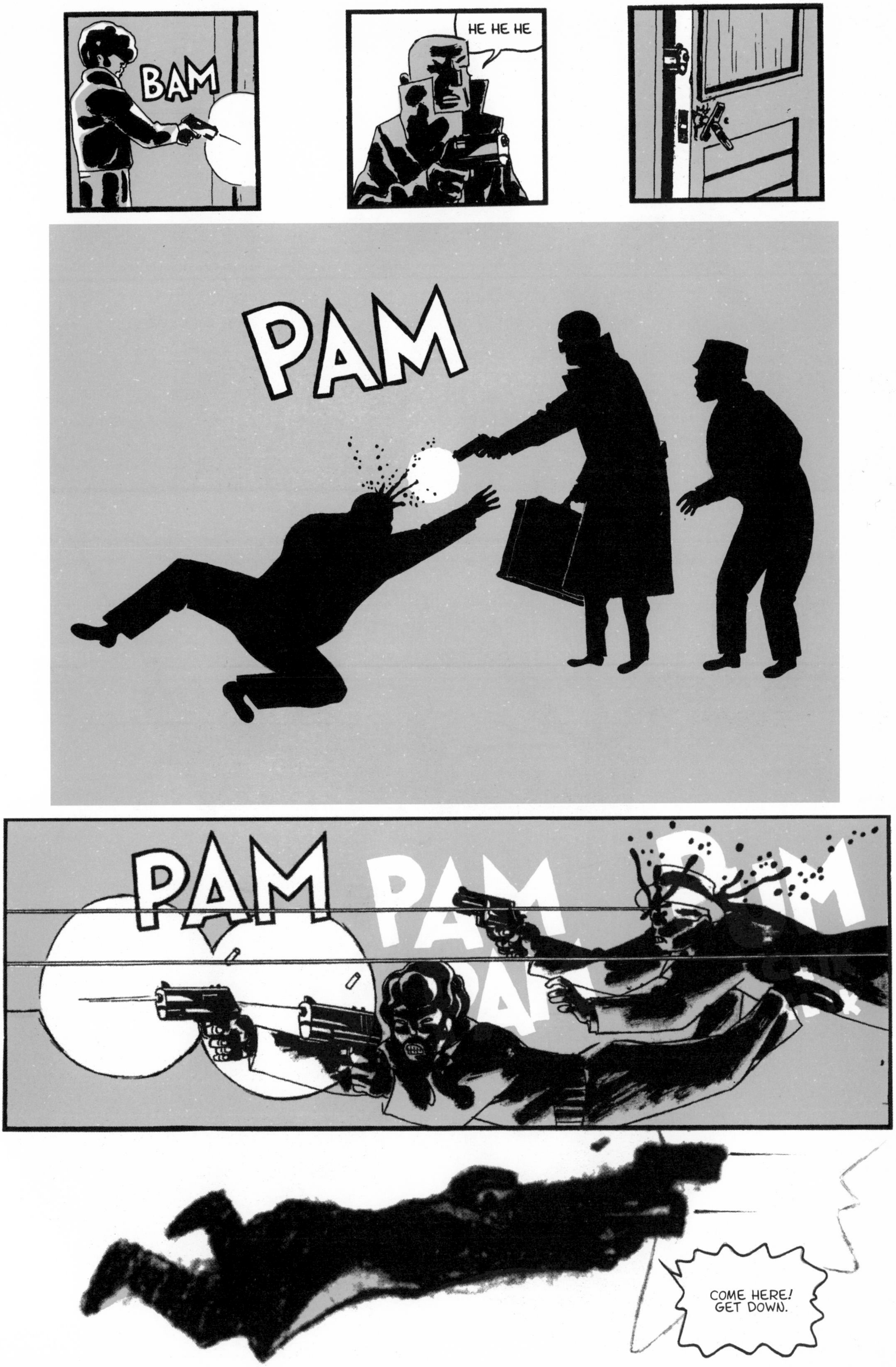
BAM
HE HE HE
PAM
PAM
PAM
COME HERE! GET DOWN.

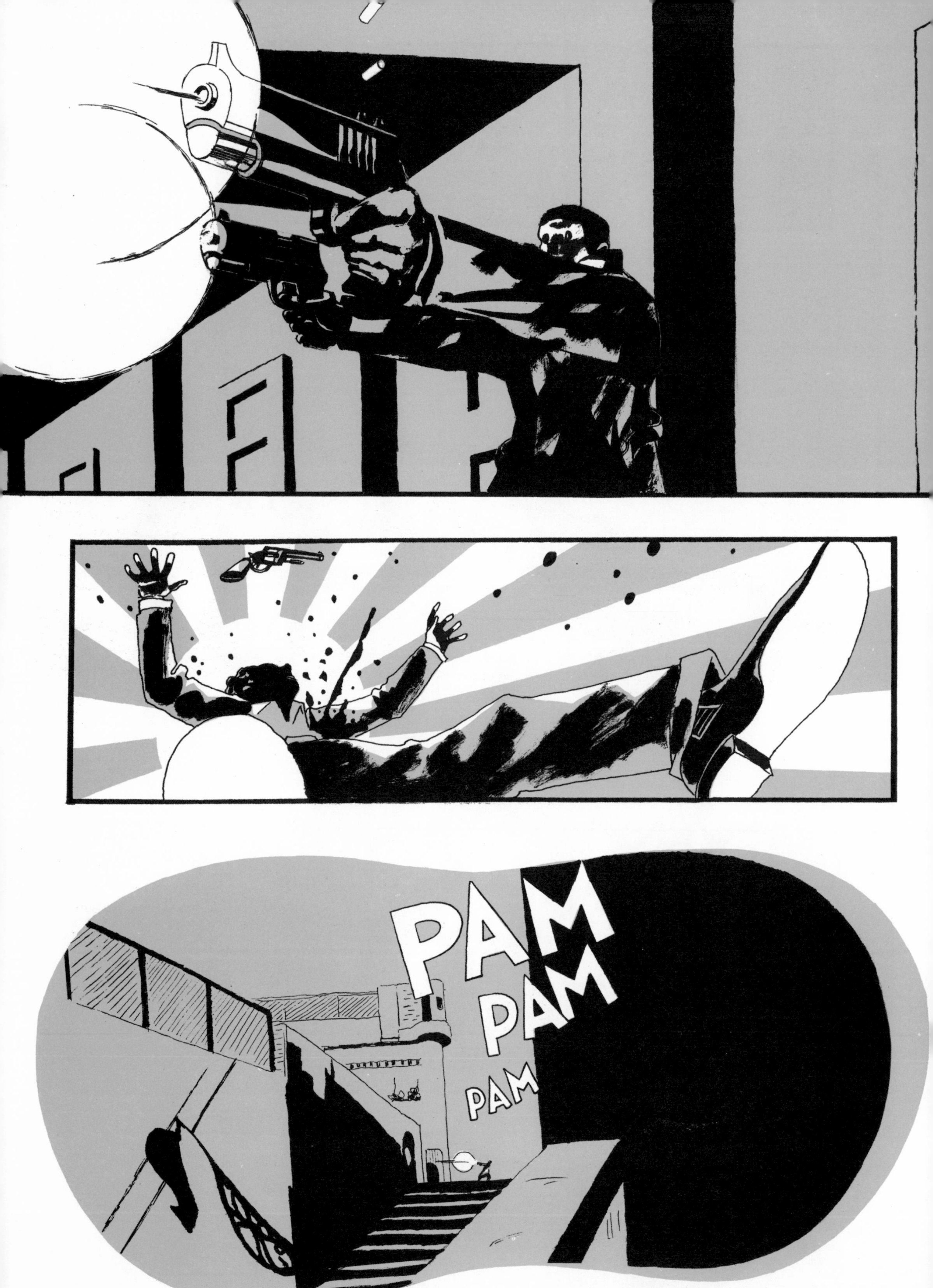
PAM
PAM
PAM

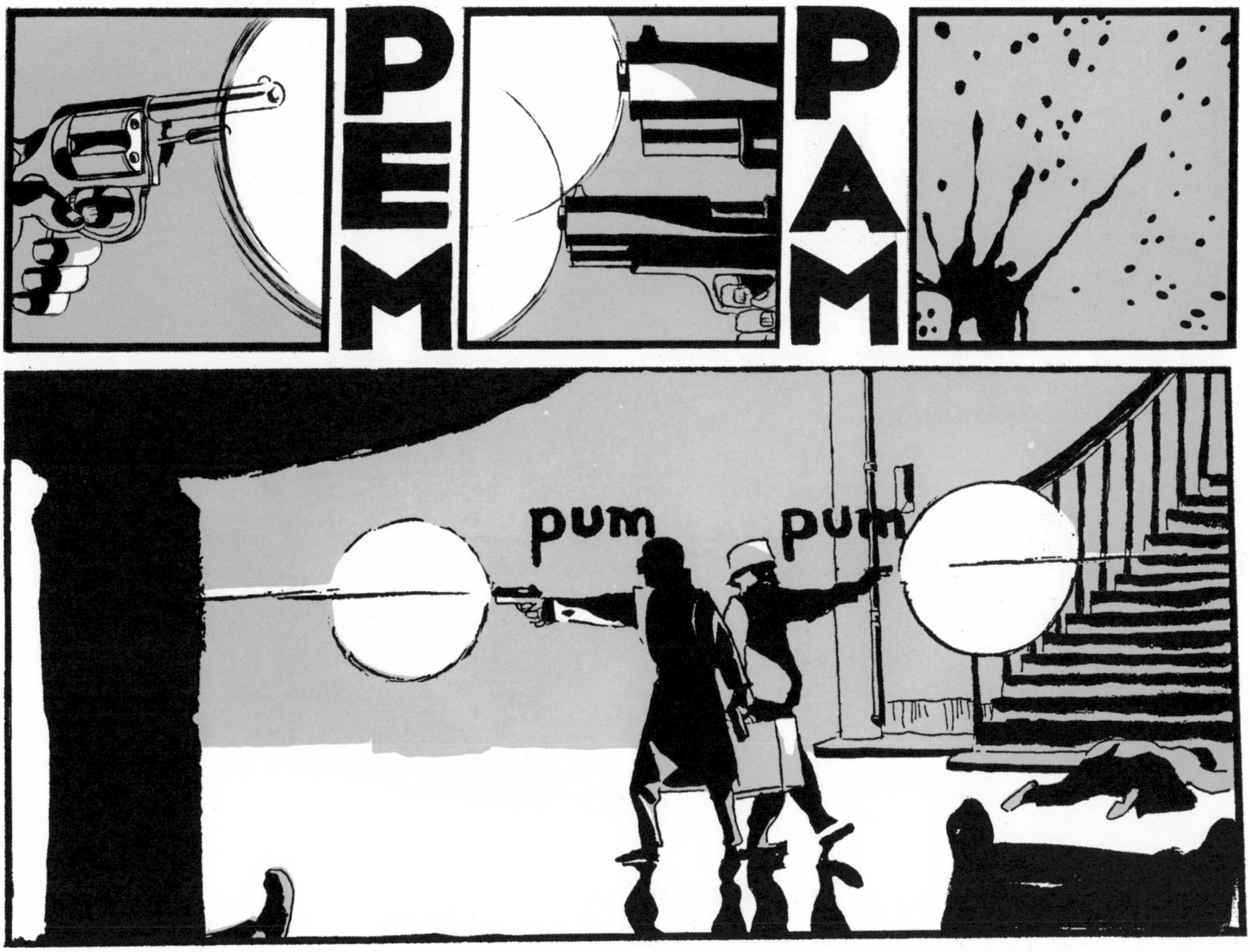
PEM
PAM
pum
pum

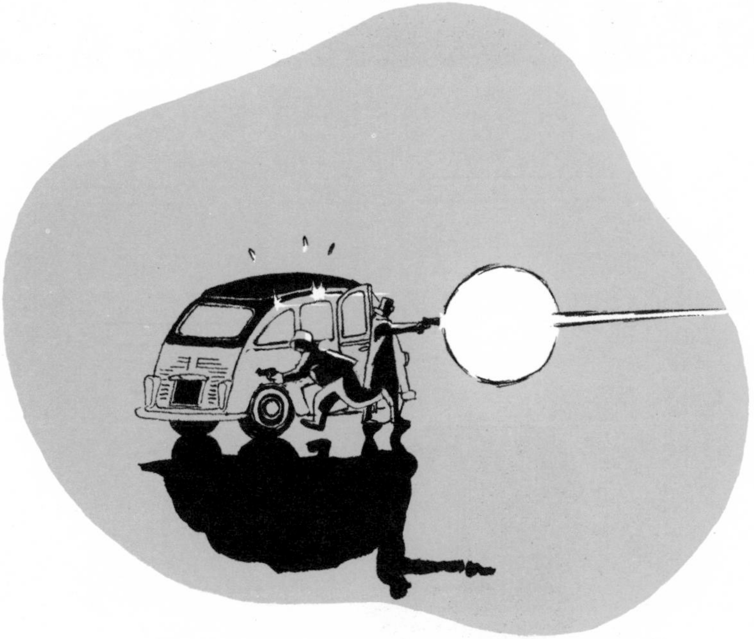

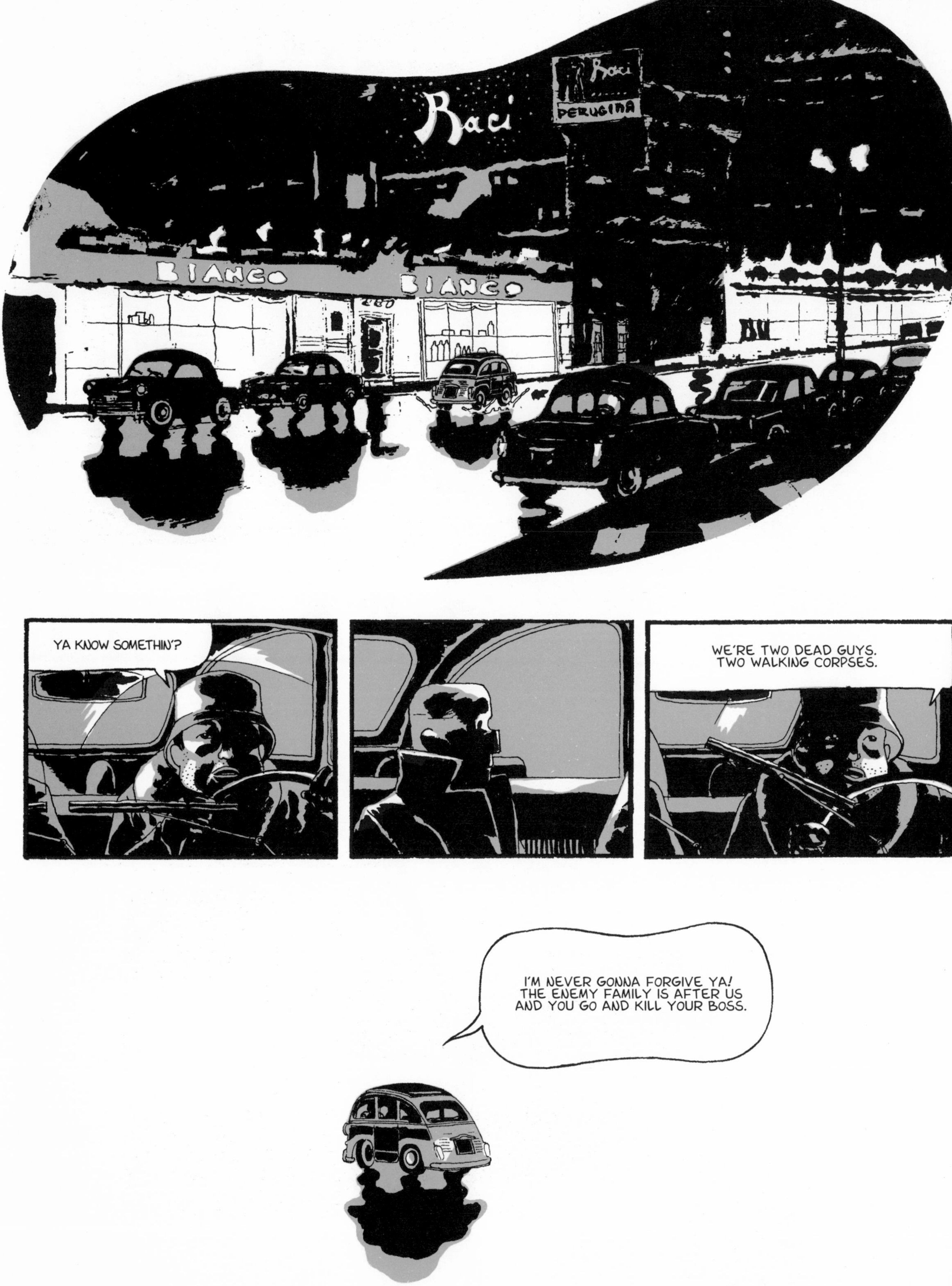
Baci
Baci
PERUGINA
BIANCO
BIANCO
YA KNOW SOMETHIN'?
WE'RE TWO DEAD GUYS.
TWO WALKING CORPSES.
I'M NEVER GONNA FORGIVE YA!
THE ENEMY FAMILY IS AFTER US
AND YOU GO AND KILL YOUR BOSS.

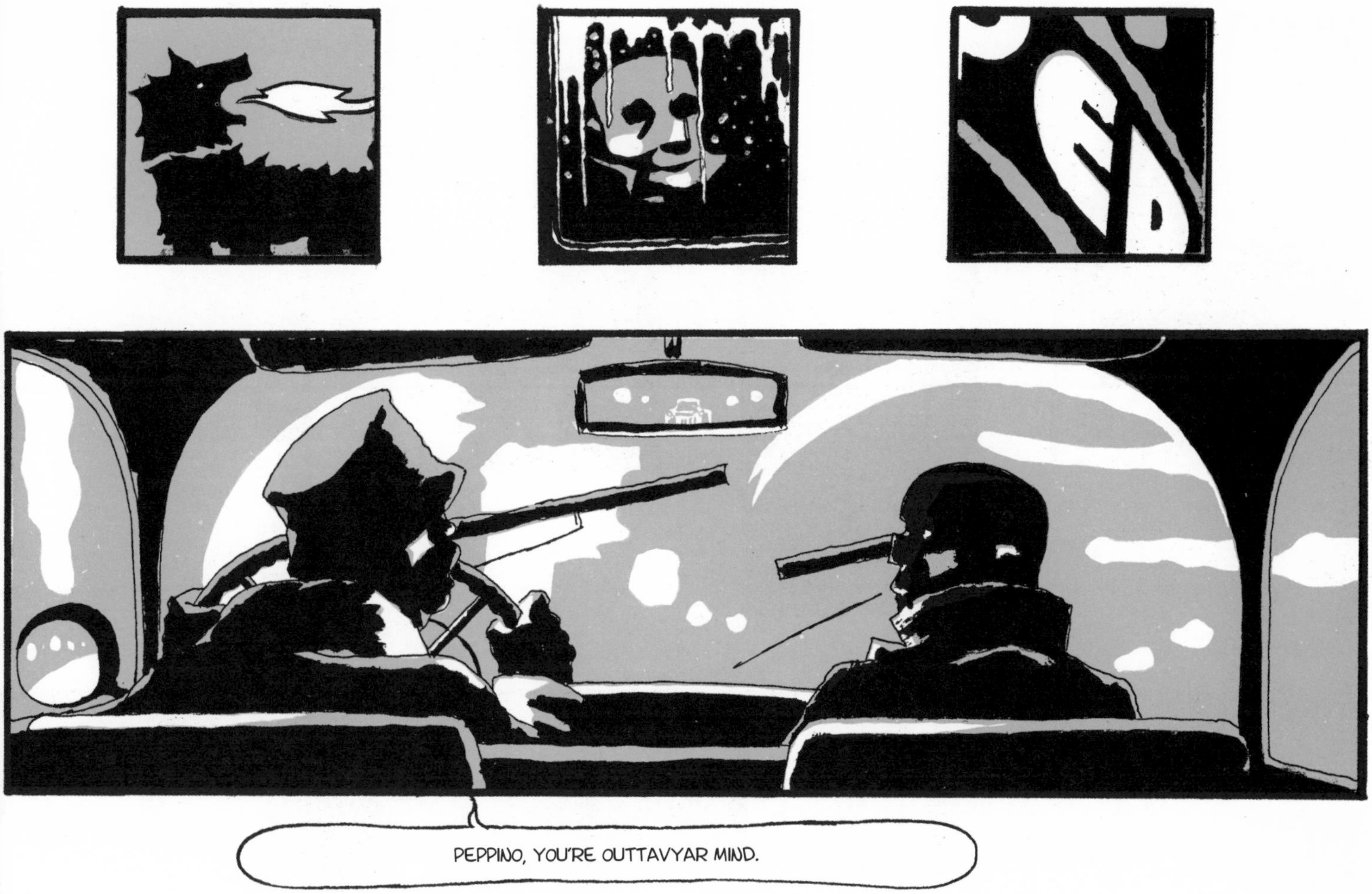
PEPPINO, YOU'RE OUTTAVYAR MIND.

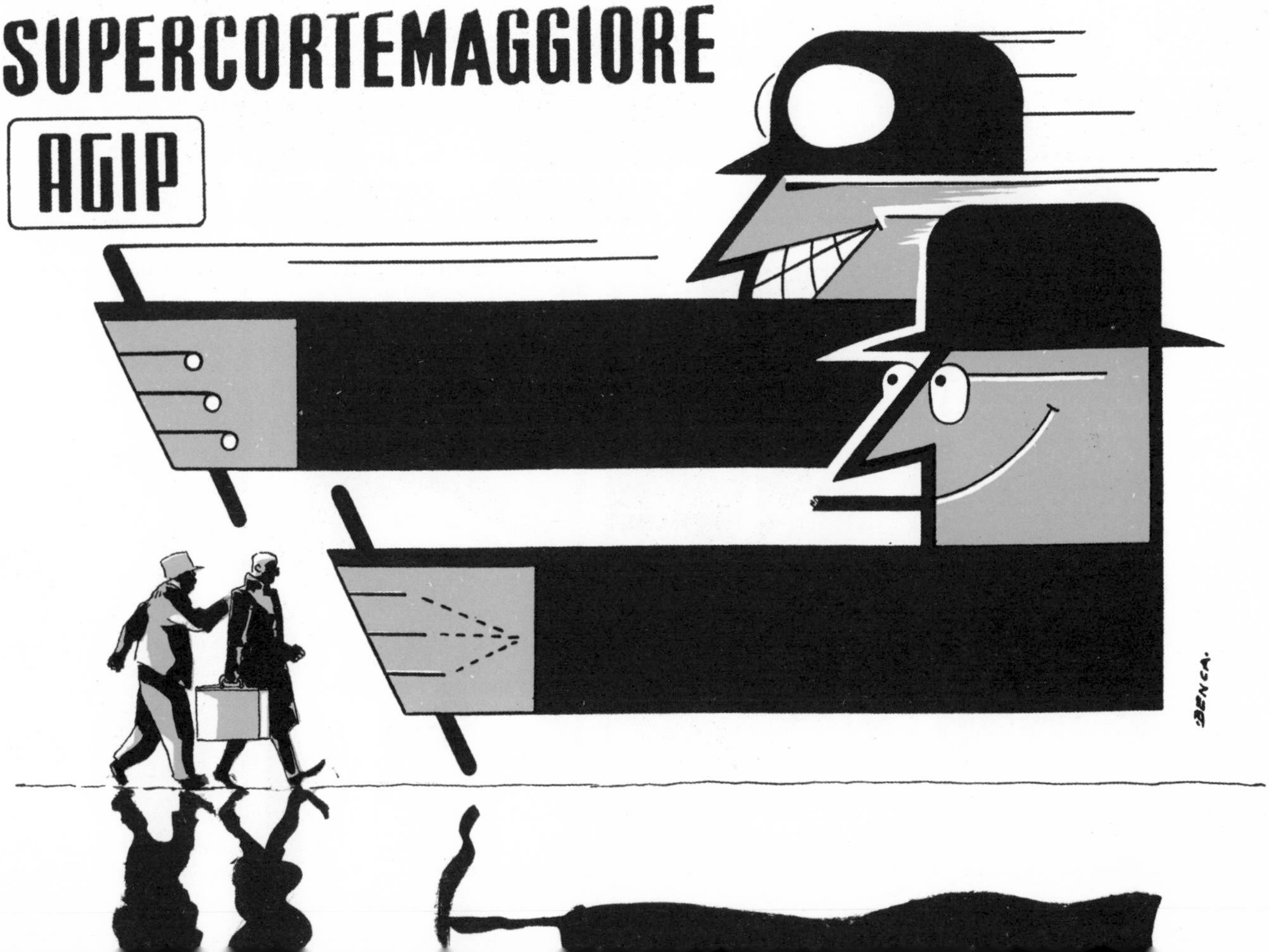
SUPERCORTEMAGGIORE
AGIP
BENCA.

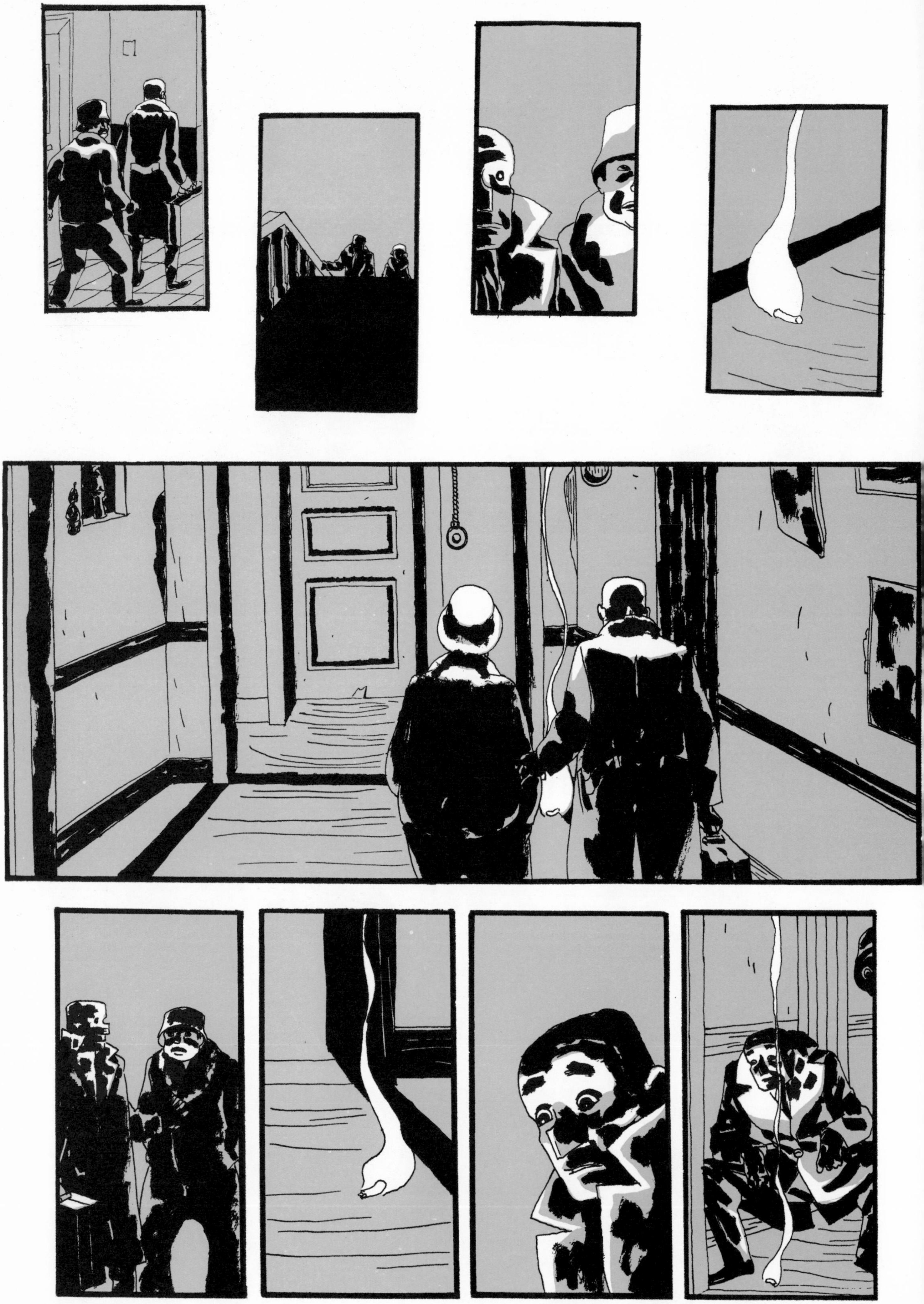

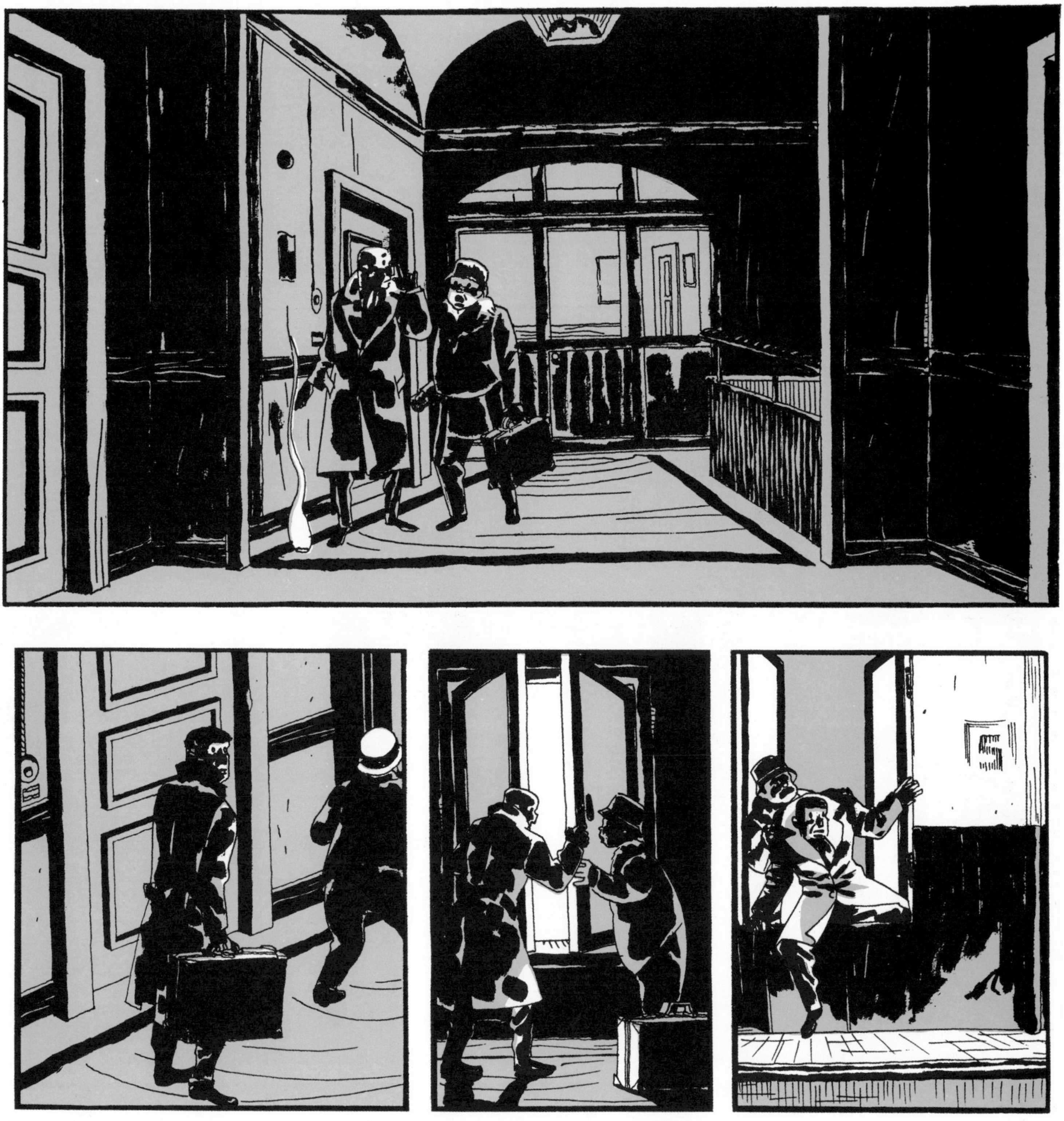

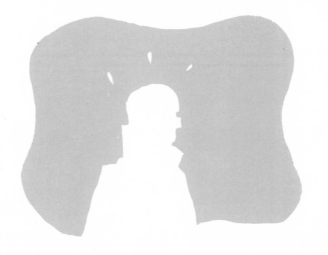

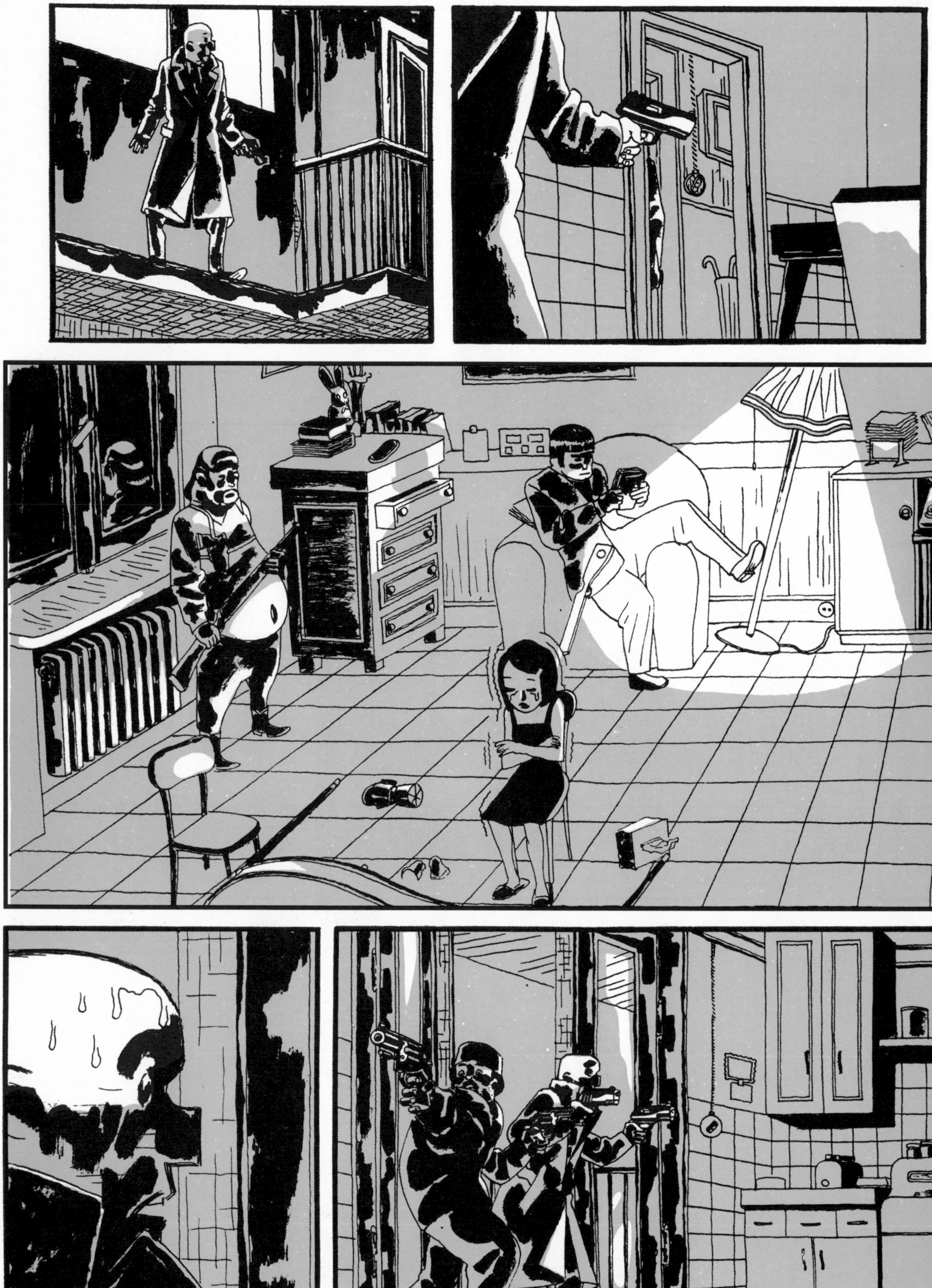

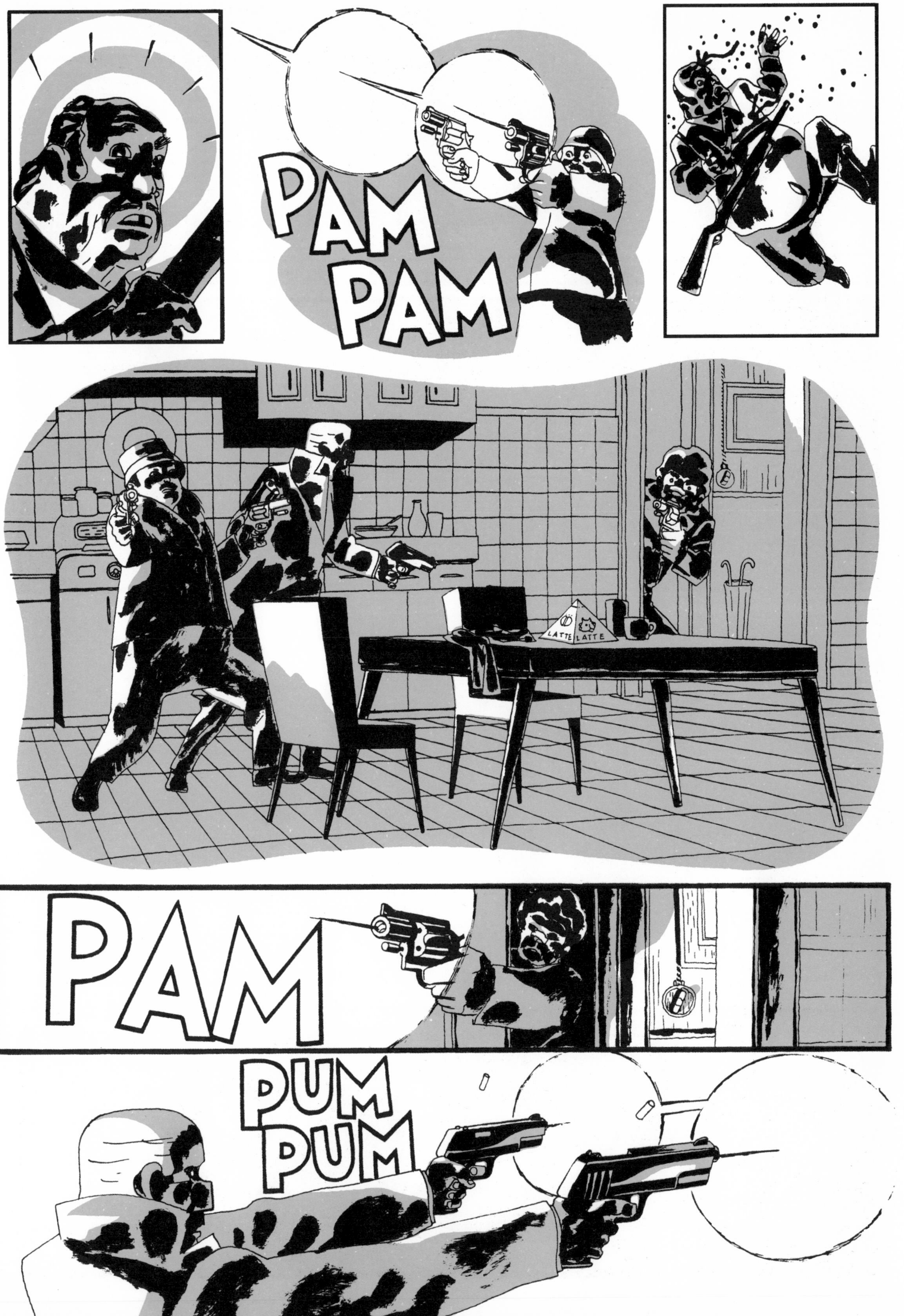
PAM
PAM
LATTE
LATTE
PAM
PUM
PUM

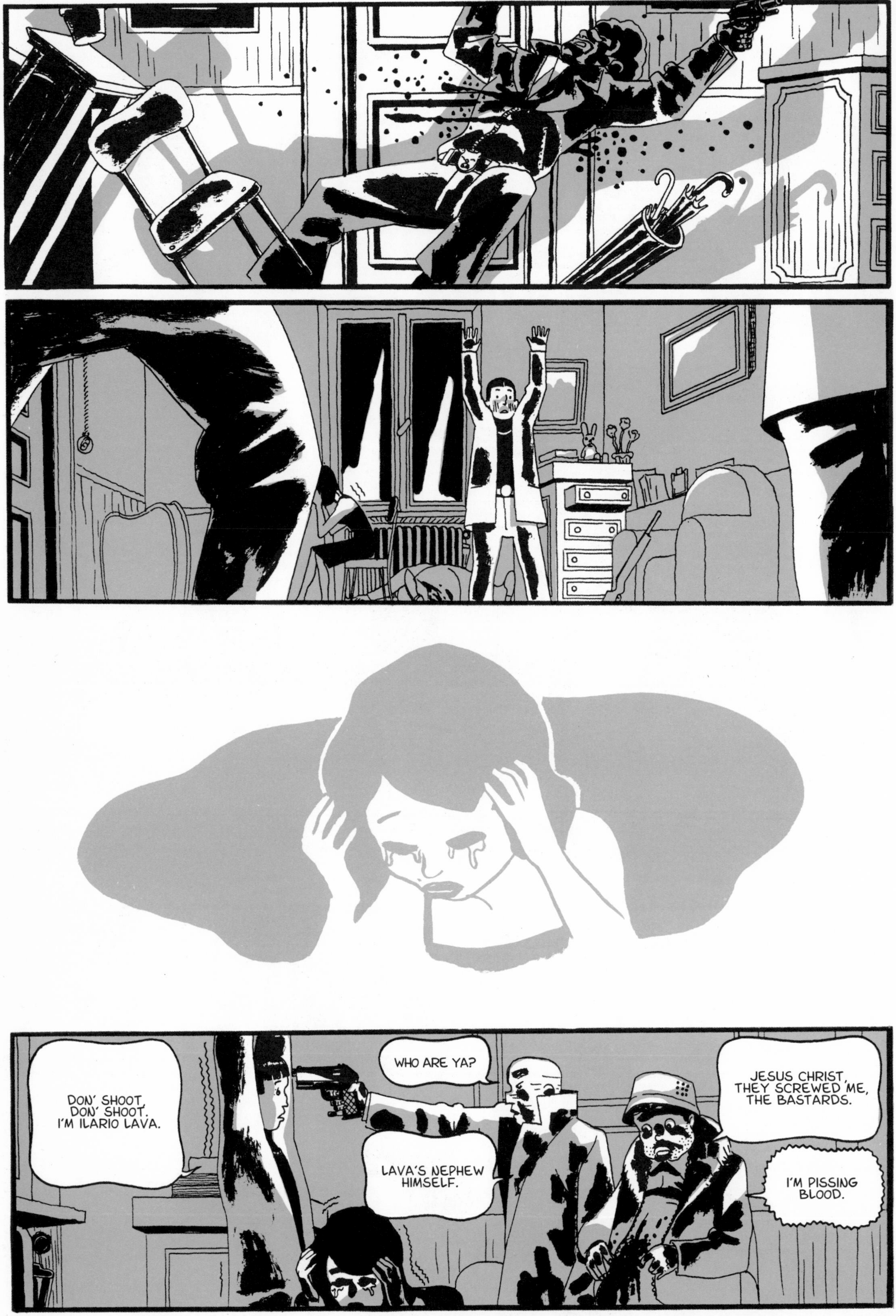
DON' SHOOT, DON' SHOOT. I'M ILARIO LAVA.
WHO ARE YA?
LAVA'S NEPHEW HIMSELF.
JESUS CHRIST, THEY SCREWED ME, THE BASTARDS.
I'M PISSING BLOOD.

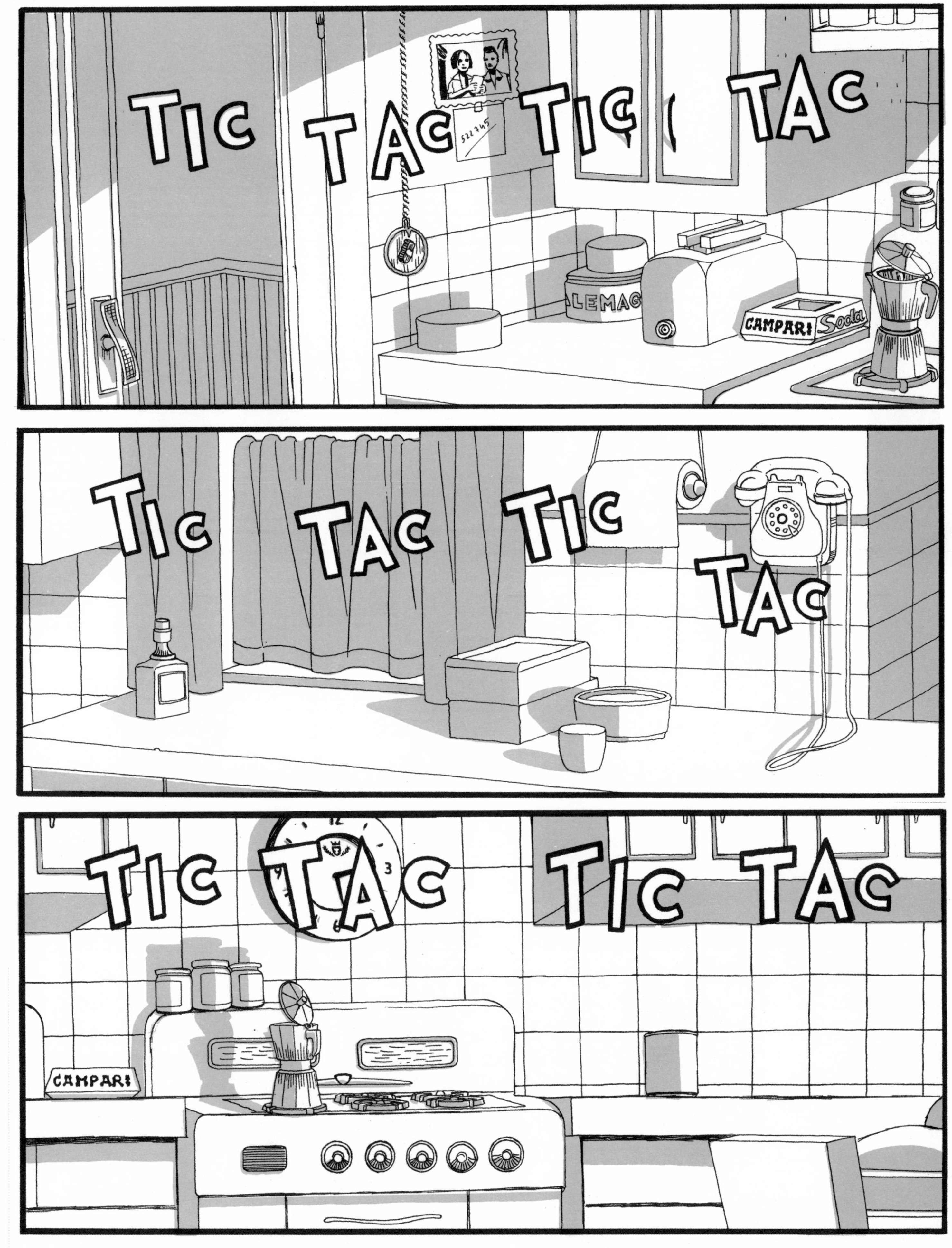

TIC TAC TIC TAC
LEMAG
CAMPARI Soda
TIC TAC TIC TAC
TIC TAC TIC TAC
CAMPARI

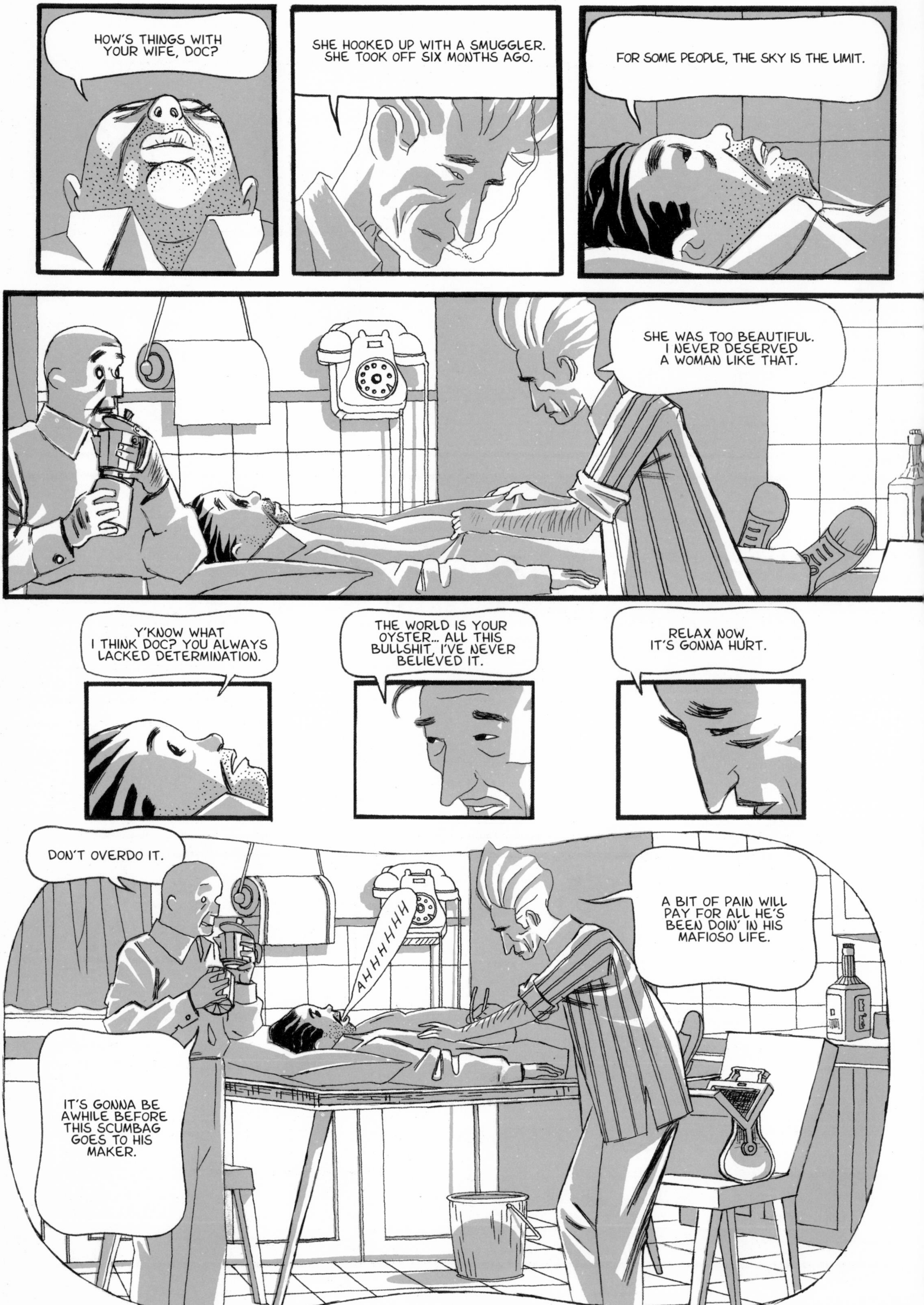
HOW'S THINGS WITH YOUR WIFE, DOC?
SHE HOOKED UP WITH A SMUGGLER. SHE TOOK OFF SIX MONTHS AGO.
FOR SOME PEOPLE, THE SKY IS THE LIMIT.
SHE WAS TOO BEAUTIFUL. I NEVER DESERVED A WOMAN LIKE THAT.
Y'KNOW WHAT I THINK DOC? YOU ALWAYS LACKED DETERMINATION.
THE WORLD IS YOUR OYSTER... ALL THIS BULLSHIT, I'VE NEVER BELIEVED IT.
RELAX NOW, IT'S GONNA HURT.
DON'T OVERDO IT.
AHHHHHHH
A BIT OF PAIN WILL PAY FOR ALL HE'S BEEN DOIN' IN HIS MAFIOSO LIFE.
IT'S GONNA BE AWHILE BEFORE THIS SCUMBAG GOES TO HIS MAKER.

YA TRULY BELIEVE IN THIS, DOC?

IN WHAT?

THE UNIVERSAL JUSTICE.

THE LACK OF RULES IS A LUXURY I CANNOT AFFORD.

SURE.

RIGHT.

STAY STILL.

IT'S BEEN QUITE A DAY DOC, YA KNOW?

I CAN STILL HEAR THE EXPLOSIONS RESOUNDING IN MY EARS.

BANG BANG BANG. WHAT A MESS.

HA! HA! HA!...

THIS IS NOT FUNNY.

THE DOCTOR IS RIGHT. THERE'S NOTHING TO LAUGH ABOUT.

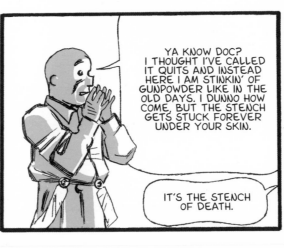

YA KNOW DOC? I THOUGHT I'VE CALLED IT QUITS AND INSTEAD HERE I AM STINKIN' OF GUNPOWDER LIKE IN THE OLD DAYS. I DUNNO HOW COME, BUT THE STENCH GETS STUCK FOREVER UNDER YOUR SKIN.

IT'S THE STENCH OF DEATH.

MAYBE, BUT IT DOESN'T SCARE ME ANYMORE.

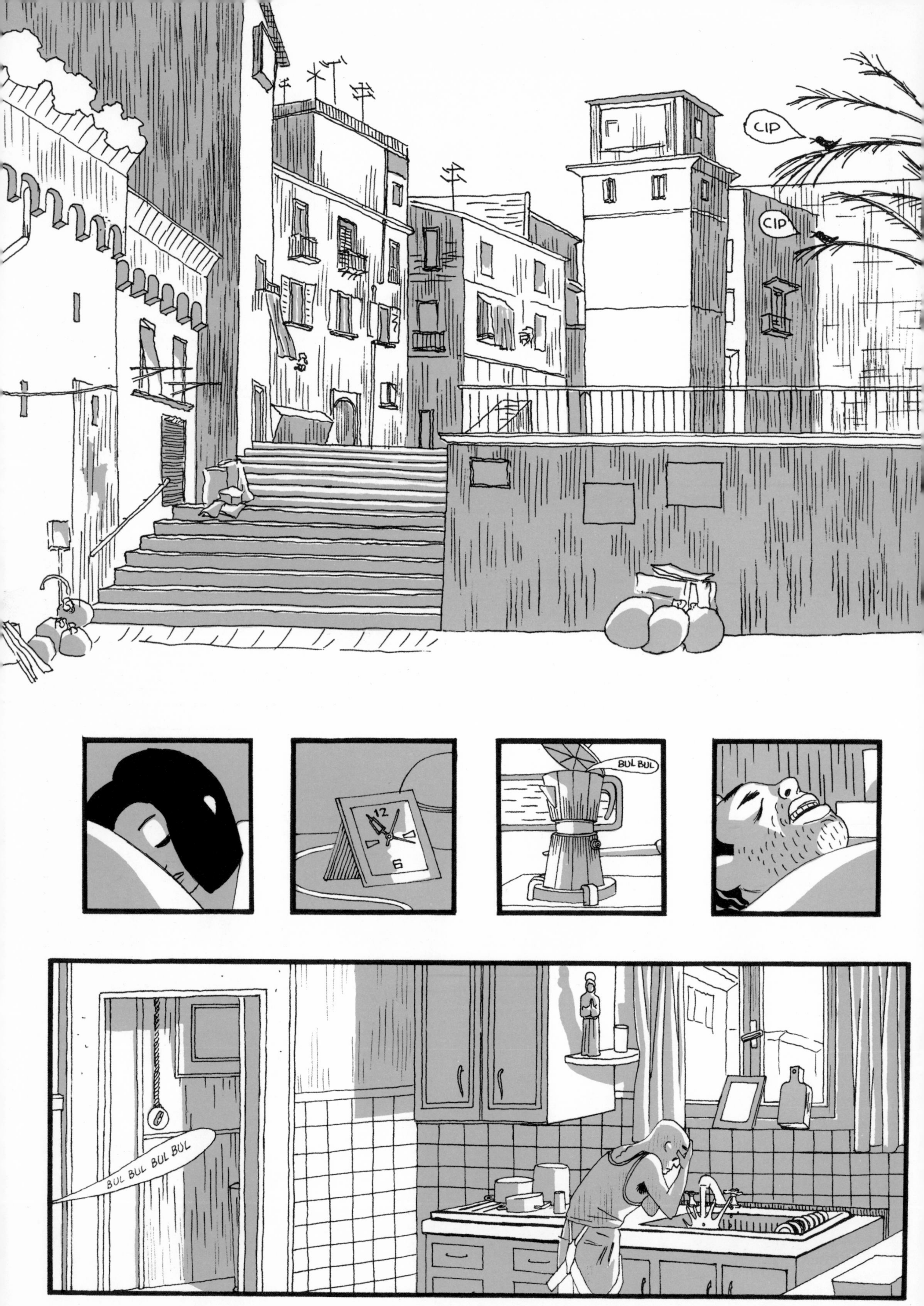
CIP
CIP
BUL BUL
BUL BUL BUL BUL

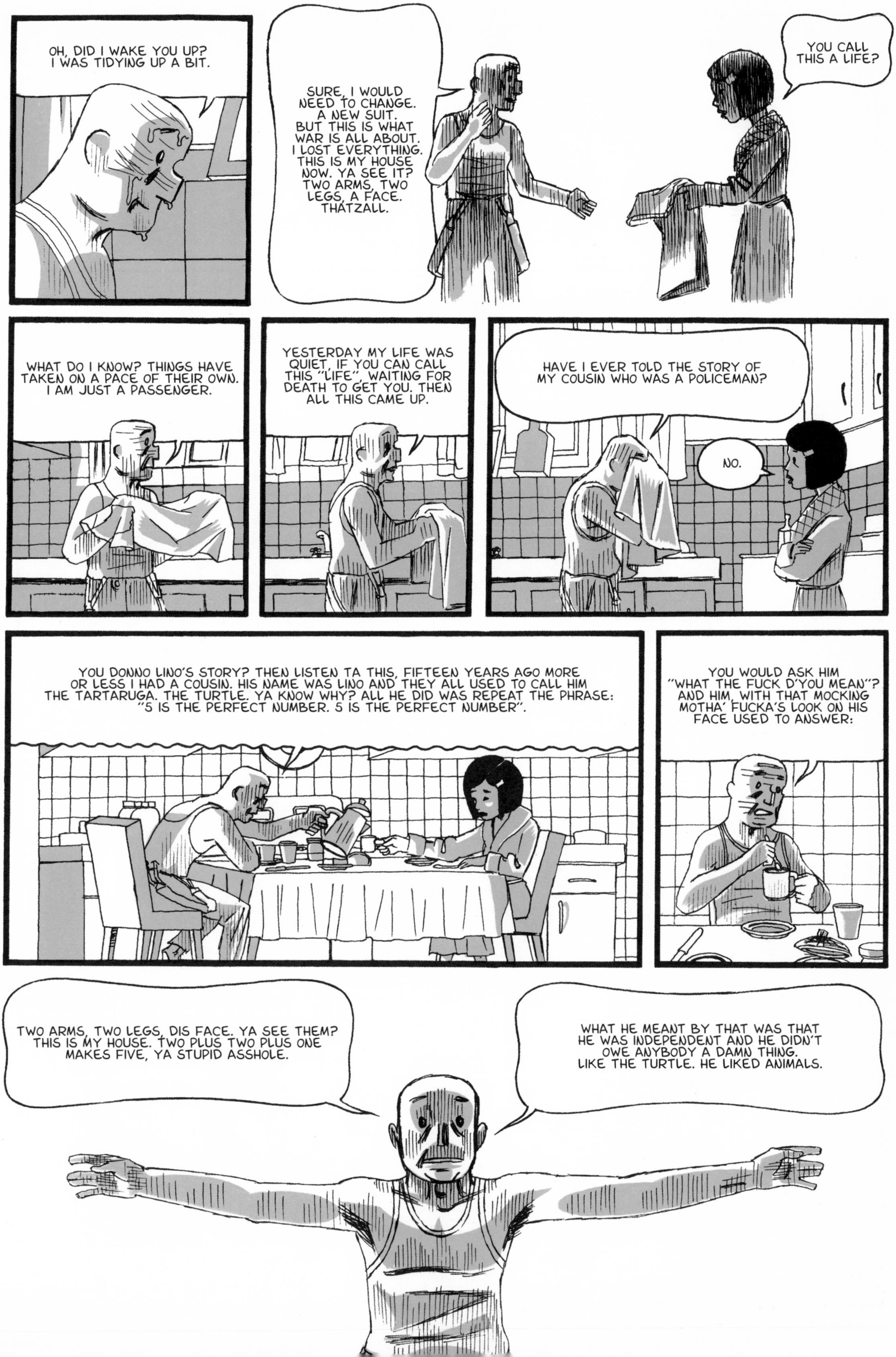
OH, DID I WAKE YOU UP? I WAS TIDYING UP A BIT.
SURE, I WOULD NEED TO CHANGE. A NEW SUIT. BUT THIS IS WHAT WAR IS ALL ABOUT. I LOST EVERYTHING. THIS IS MY HOUSE NOW. YA SEE IT? TWO ARMS, TWO LEGS, A FACE. THATZALL.
YOU CALL THIS A LIFE?
WHAT DO I KNOW? THINGS HAVE TAKEN ON A PACE OF THEIR OWN. I AM JUST A PASSENGER.
YESTERDAY MY LIFE WAS QUIET, IF YOU CAN CALL THIS "LIFE", WAITING FOR DEATH TO GET YOU. THEN ALL THIS CAME UP.
HAVE I EVER TOLD THE STORY OF MY COUSIN WHO WAS A POLICEMAN?
NO.
YOU DONNO LINO'S STORY? THEN LISTEN TA THIS, FIFTEEN YEARS AGO MORE OR LESS I HAD A COUSIN. HIS NAME WAS LINO AND THEY ALL USED TO CALL HIM THE TARTARUGA. THE TURTLE. YA KNOW WHY? ALL HE DID WAS REPEAT THE PHRASE: "5 IS THE PERFECT NUMBER. 5 IS THE PERFECT NUMBER".
YOU WOULD ASK HIM "WHAT THE FUCK D'YOU MEAN"? AND HIM, WITH THAT MOCKING MOTHA' FUCKA'S LOOK ON HIS FACE USED TO ANSWER:
TWO ARMS, TWO LEGS, DIS FACE. YA SEE THEM? THIS IS MY HOUSE. TWO PLUS TWO PLUS ONE MAKES FIVE, YA STUPID ASSHOLE.
WHAT HE MEANT BY THAT WAS THAT HE WAS INDEPENDENT AND HE DIDN'T OWE ANYBODY A DAMN THING. LIKE THE TURTLE. HE LIKED ANIMALS.

HE HAD A SPECIAL PASSION FOR PIGEONS, LINO.

HE WAS CROSSBREEDING PIGEONS AND WAS ALWAYS ON THE ROOF WHERE HE KEPT THEM.

HE WAS A POLICEMAN AND THAT ALONE WAS A DISHONOR FOR MY FAMILY.

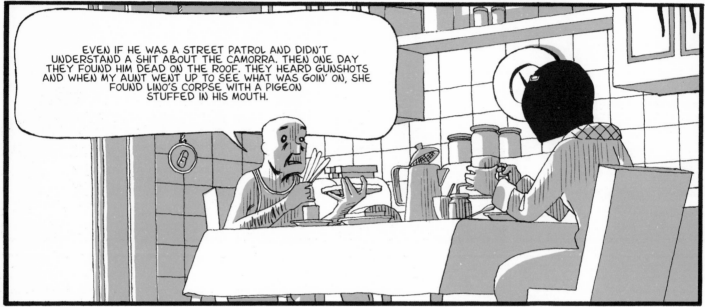

EVEN IF HE WAS A STREET PATROL AND DIDN'T UNDERSTAND A SHIT ABOUT THE CAMORRA. THEN ONE DAY THEY FOUND HIM DEAD ON THE ROOF. THEY HEARD GUNSHOTS AND WHEN MY AUNT WENT UP TO SEE WHAT WAS GOIN' ON, SHE FOUND LINO'S CORPSE WITH A PIGEON STUFFED IN HIS MOUTH.

THERE WAS A NOTE NEXT TO HIM SAYING "5 IS THE PERFECT NUMBER AND SCREW YOU!"

THEY SHOT HIM FIVE TIMES IN THE HEART. D'YA KNOW WHY? BECAUSE HIS PIGEONS...

...APPARENTLY SHAT ON DON GUARINO'S SILK SHEETS.

WELL, YEAH.

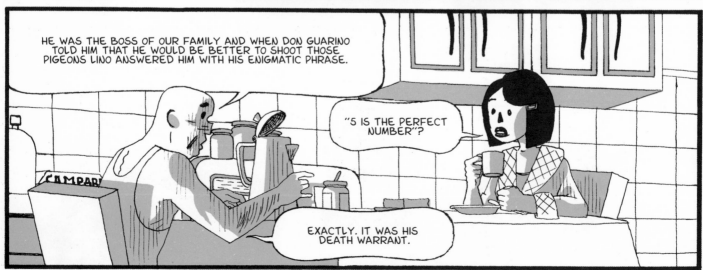

HE WAS THE BOSS OF OUR FAMILY AND WHEN DON GUARINO TOLD HIM THAT HE WOULD BE BETTER TO SHOOT THOSE PIGEONS LINO ANSWERED HIM WITH HIS ENIGMATIC PHRASE.

"5 IS THE PERFECT NUMBER"?

EXACTLY. IT WAS HIS DEATH WARRANT.

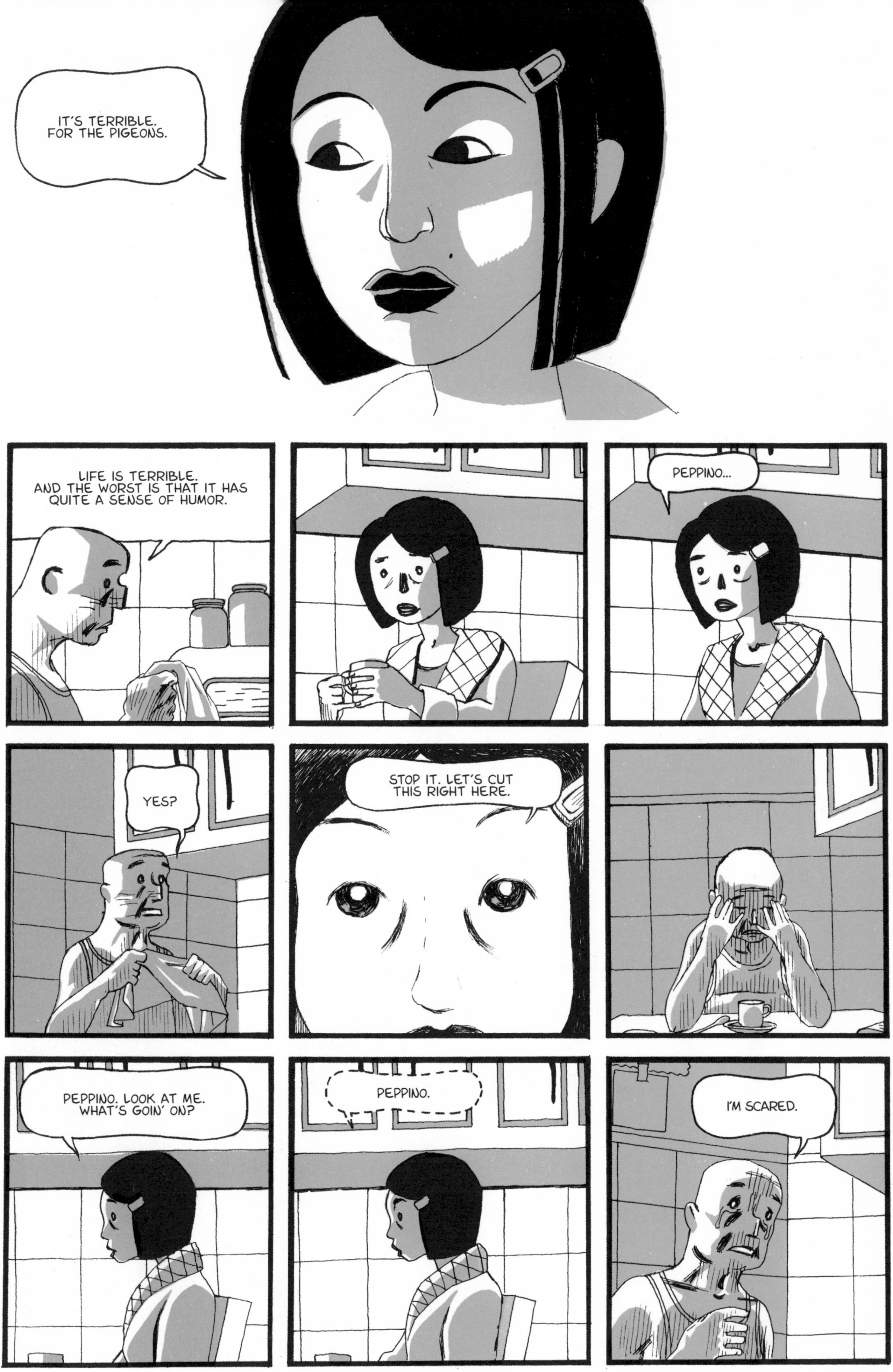
IT'S TERRIBLE. FOR THE PIGEONS.
LIFE IS TERRIBLE. AND THE WORST IS THAT IT HAS QUITE A SENSE OF HUMOR.
PEPPINO...
YES?
STOP IT. LET'S CUT THIS RIGHT HERE.
PEPPINO. LOOK AT ME. WHAT'S GOIN' ON?
PEPPINO.
I'M SCARED.

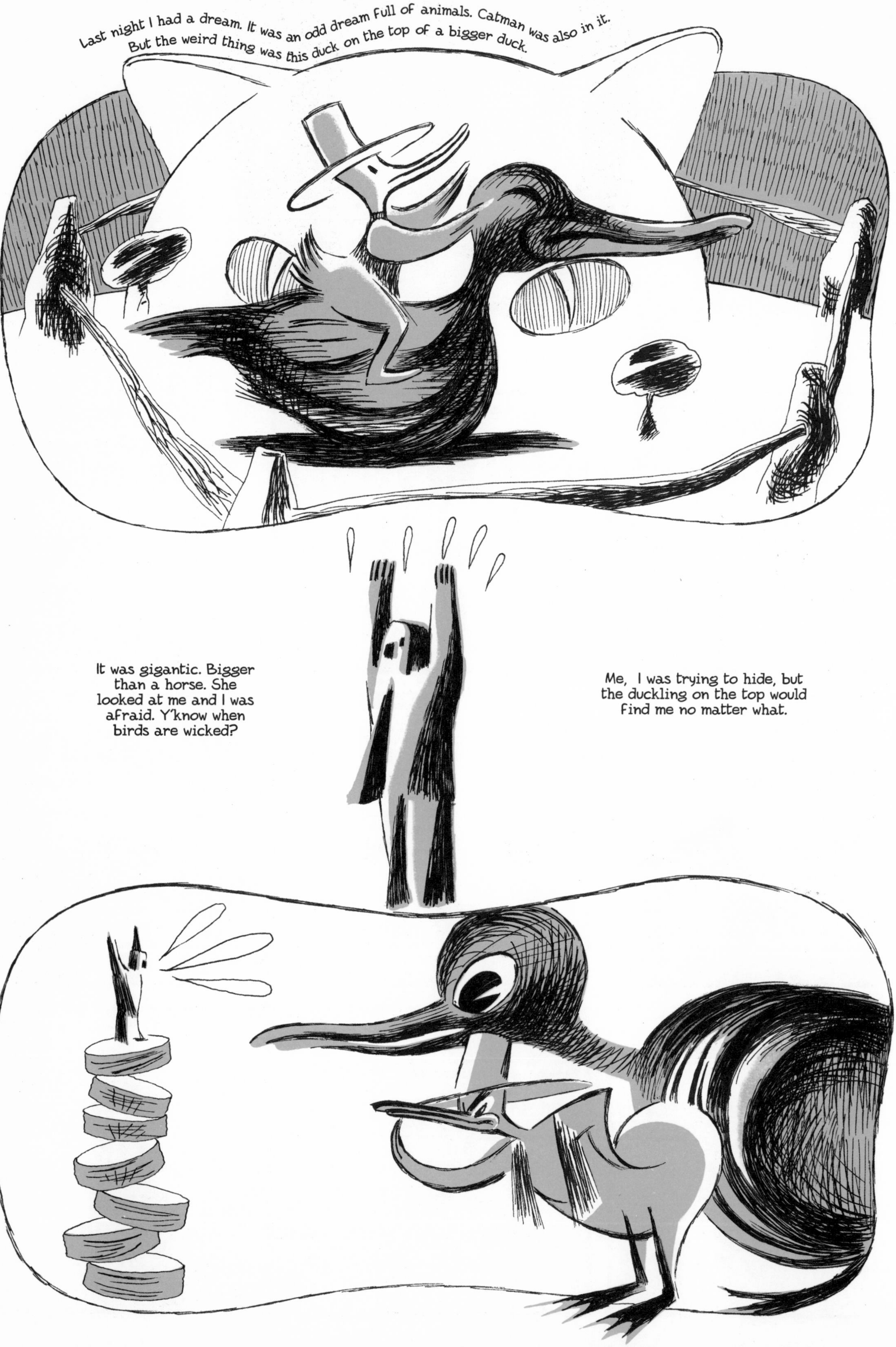
Last night I had a dream. It was an odd dream full of animals. Catman was also in it.
But the weird thing was this duck on the top of a bigger duck.
It was gigantic. Bigger than a horse. She looked at me and I was afraid. Y'know when birds are wicked?
Me, I was trying to hide, but the duckling on the top would find me no matter what.

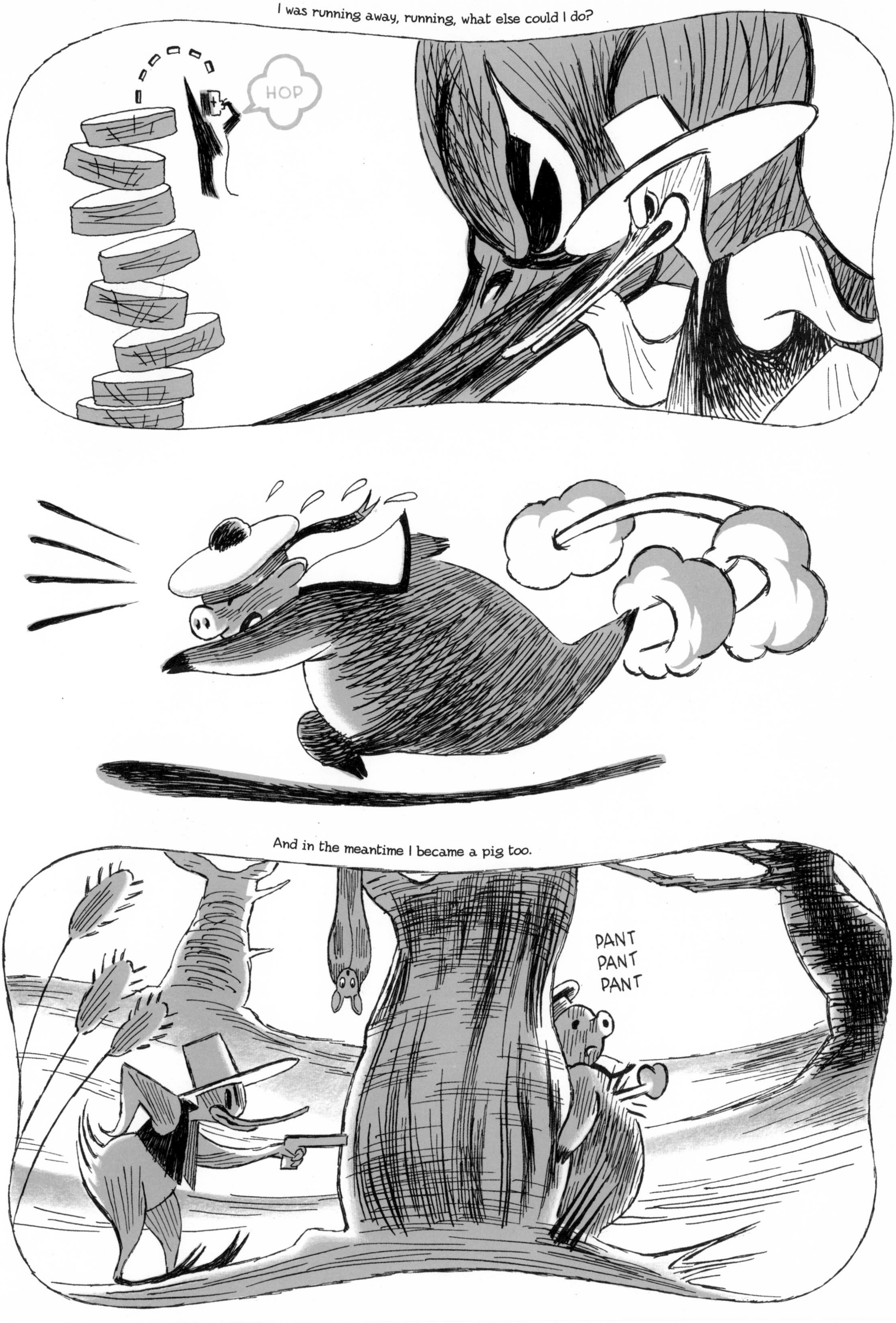
I was running away, running, what else could I do?
HOP
And in the meantime I became a pig too.
PANT
PANT
PANT

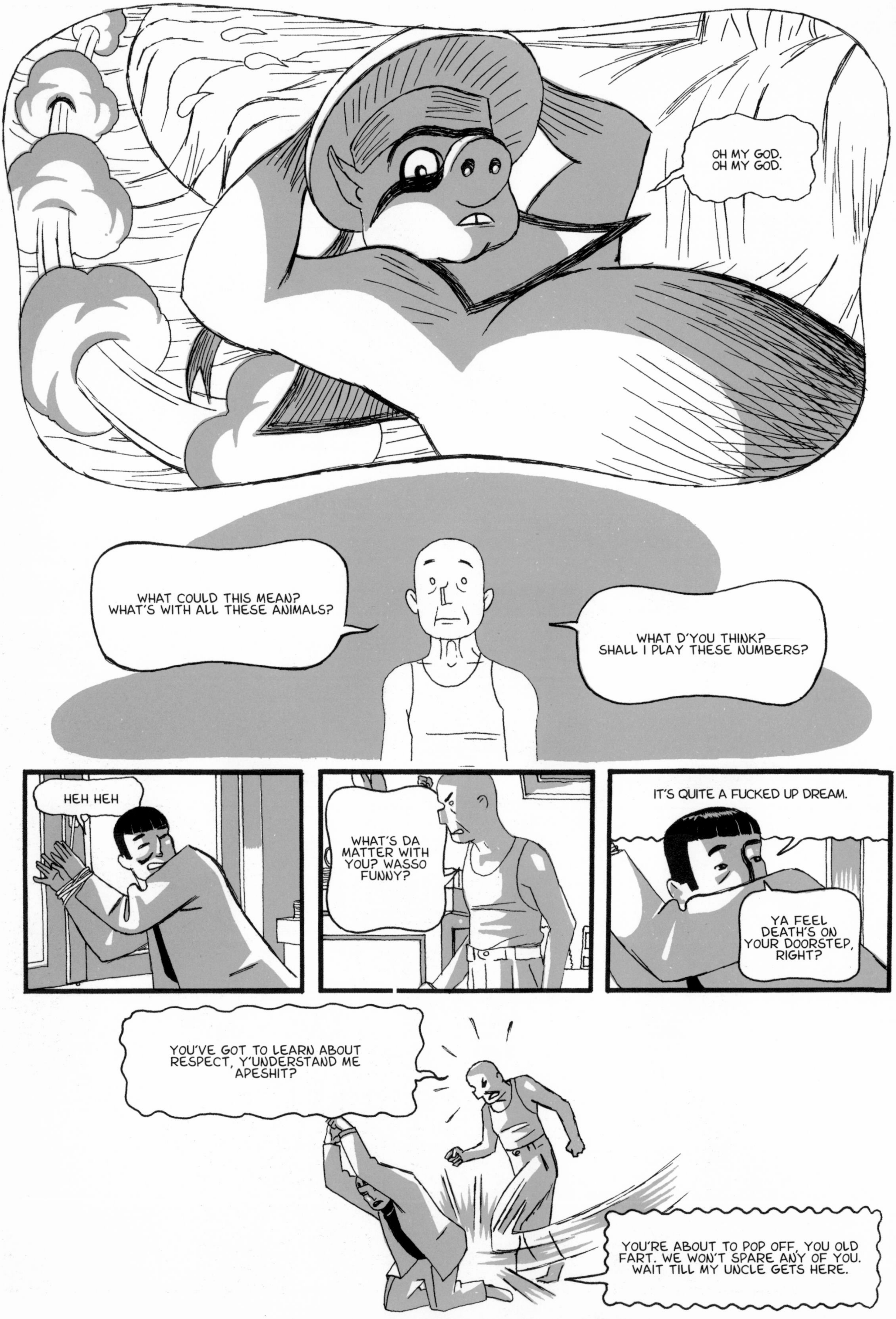
OH MY GOD.
OH MY GOD.
WHAT COULD THIS MEAN? WHAT'S WITH ALL THESE ANIMALS?
WHAT D'YOU THINK? SHALL I PLAY THESE NUMBERS?
HEH HEH
WHAT'S DA MATTER WITH YOU? WASSO FUNNY?
IT'S QUITE A FUCKED UP DREAM.
YA FEEL DEATH'S ON YOUR DOORSTEP, RIGHT?
YOU'VE GOT TO LEARN ABOUT RESPECT, Y'UNDERSTAND ME APESHIT?
YOU'RE ABOUT TO POP OFF, YOU OLD FART. WE WON'T SPARE ANY OF YOU. WAIT TILL MY UNCLE GETS HERE.

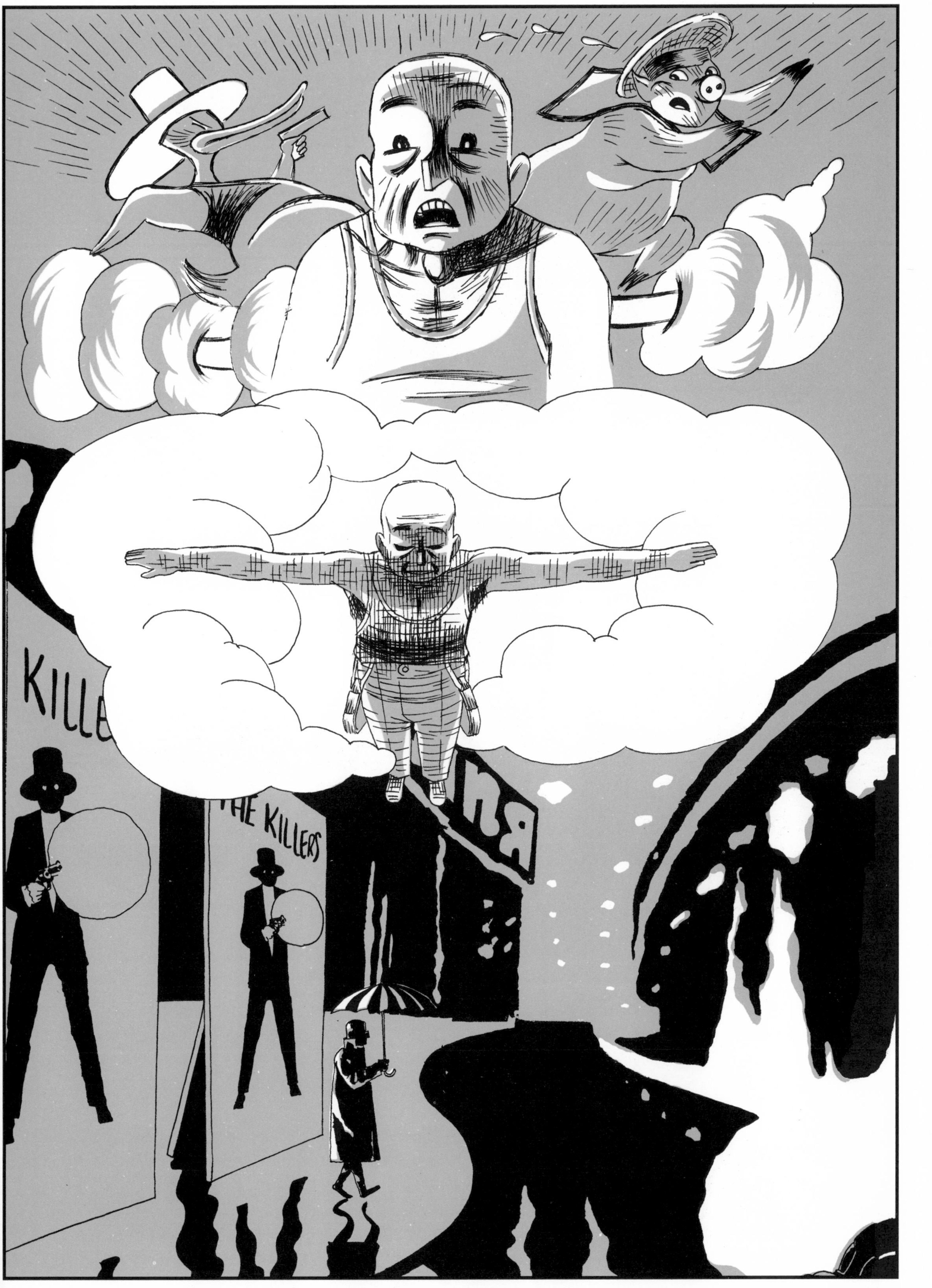
KILLE
THE KILLERS

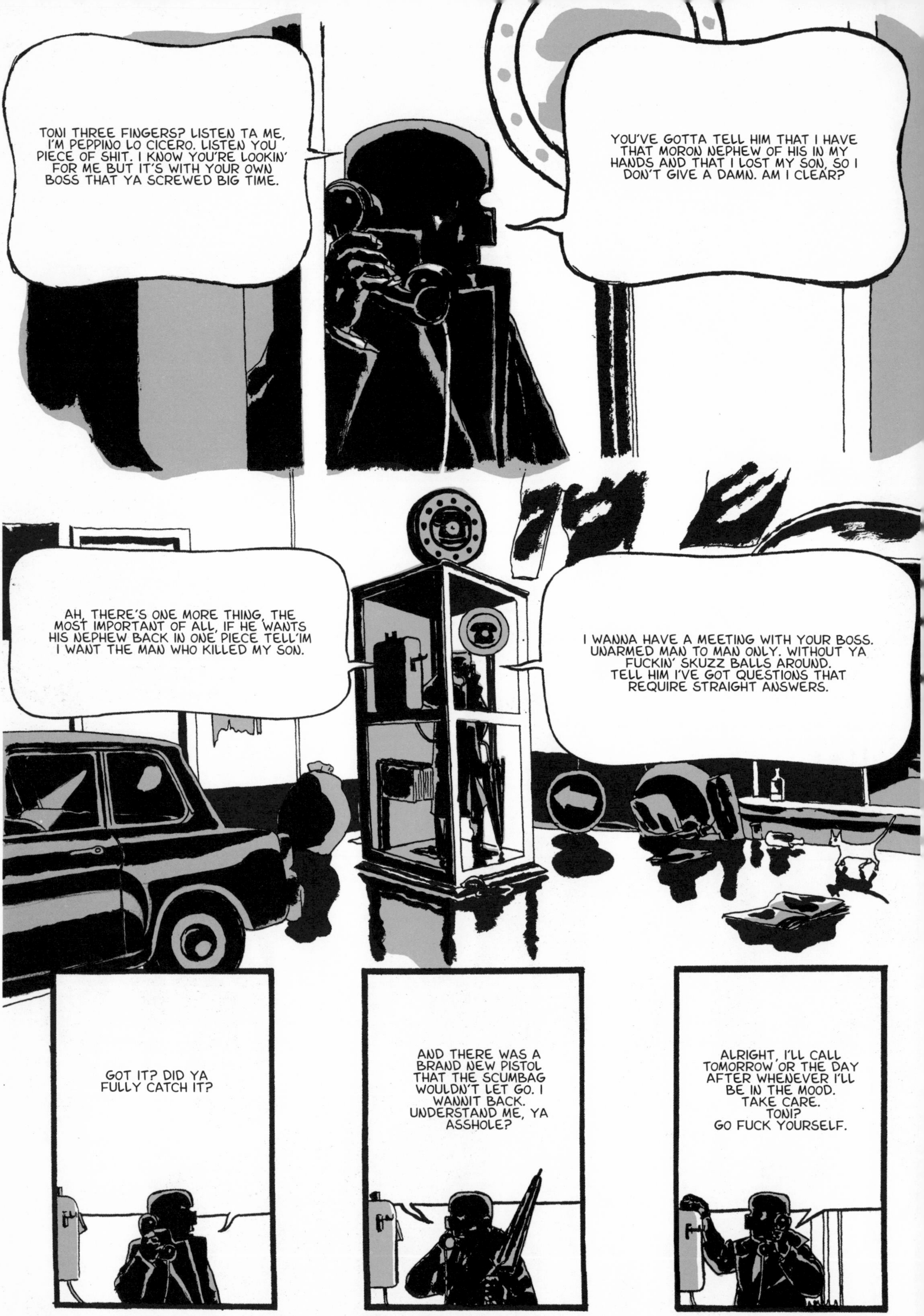
TONI THREE FINGERS? LISTEN TA ME, I'M PEPPINO LO CICERO. LISTEN YOU PIECE OF SHIT. I KNOW YOU'RE LOOKIN' FOR ME BUT IT'S WITH YOUR OWN BOSS THAT YA SCREWED BIG TIME.
YOU'VE GOTTA TELL HIM THAT I HAVE THAT MORON NEPHEW OF HIS IN MY HANDS AND THAT I LOST MY SON, SO I DON'T GIVE A DAMN. AM I CLEAR?
AH, THERE'S ONE MORE THING, THE MOST IMPORTANT OF ALL, IF HE WANTS HIS NEPHEW BACK IN ONE PIECE TELL'IM I WANT THE MAN WHO KILLED MY SON.
I WANNA HAVE A MEETING WITH YOUR BOSS. UNARMED MAN TO MAN ONLY. WITHOUT YA FUCKIN' SKUZZ BALLS AROUND. TELL HIM I'VE GOT QUESTIONS THAT REQUIRE STRAIGHT ANSWERS.
GOT IT? DID YA FULLY CATCH IT?
AND THERE WAS A BRAND NEW PISTOL THAT THE SCUMBAG WOULDN'T LET GO. I WANNIT BACK. UNDERSTAND ME, YA ASSHOLE?
ALRIGHT, I'LL CALL TOMORROW OR THE DAY AFTER WHENEVER I'LL BE IN THE MOOD. TAKE CARE. TONI? GO FUCK YOURSELF.
CLIK

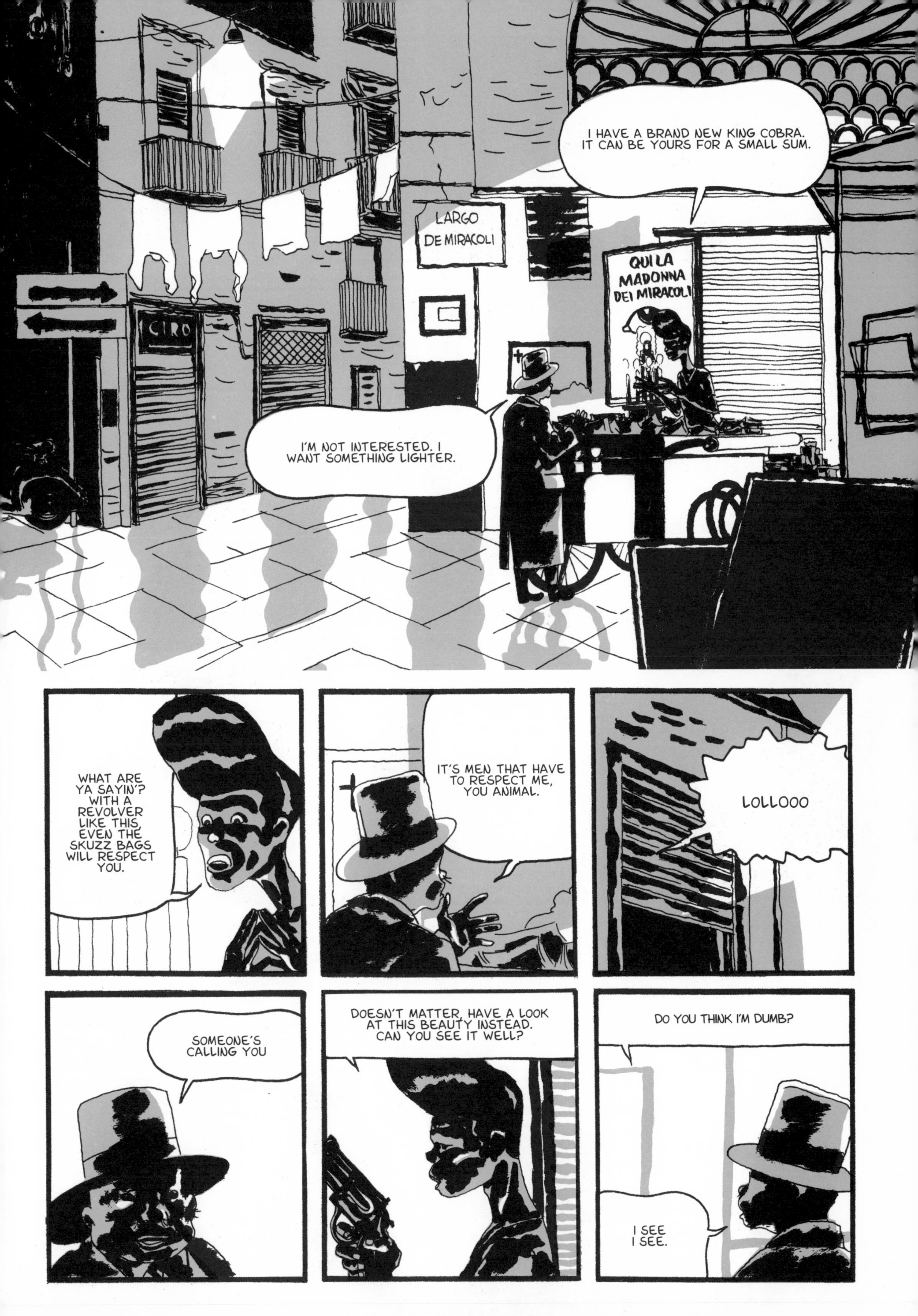
LARGO DE MIRACOLI
CIRO
QUI LA MADONNA DEI MIRACOLI
I HAVE A BRAND NEW KING COBRA. IT CAN BE YOURS FOR A SMALL SUM.
I'M NOT INTERESTED. I WANT SOMETHING LIGHTER.
WHAT ARE YA SAYIN'? WITH A REVOLVER LIKE THIS, EVEN THE SKUZZ BAGS WILL RESPECT YOU.
IT'S MEN THAT HAVE TO RESPECT ME, YOU ANIMAL.
LOLLOOO
SOMEONE'S CALLING YOU
DOESN'T MATTER, HAVE A LOOK AT THIS BEAUTY INSTEAD. CAN YOU SEE IT WELL?
DO YOU THINK I'M DUMB?
I SEE I SEE.

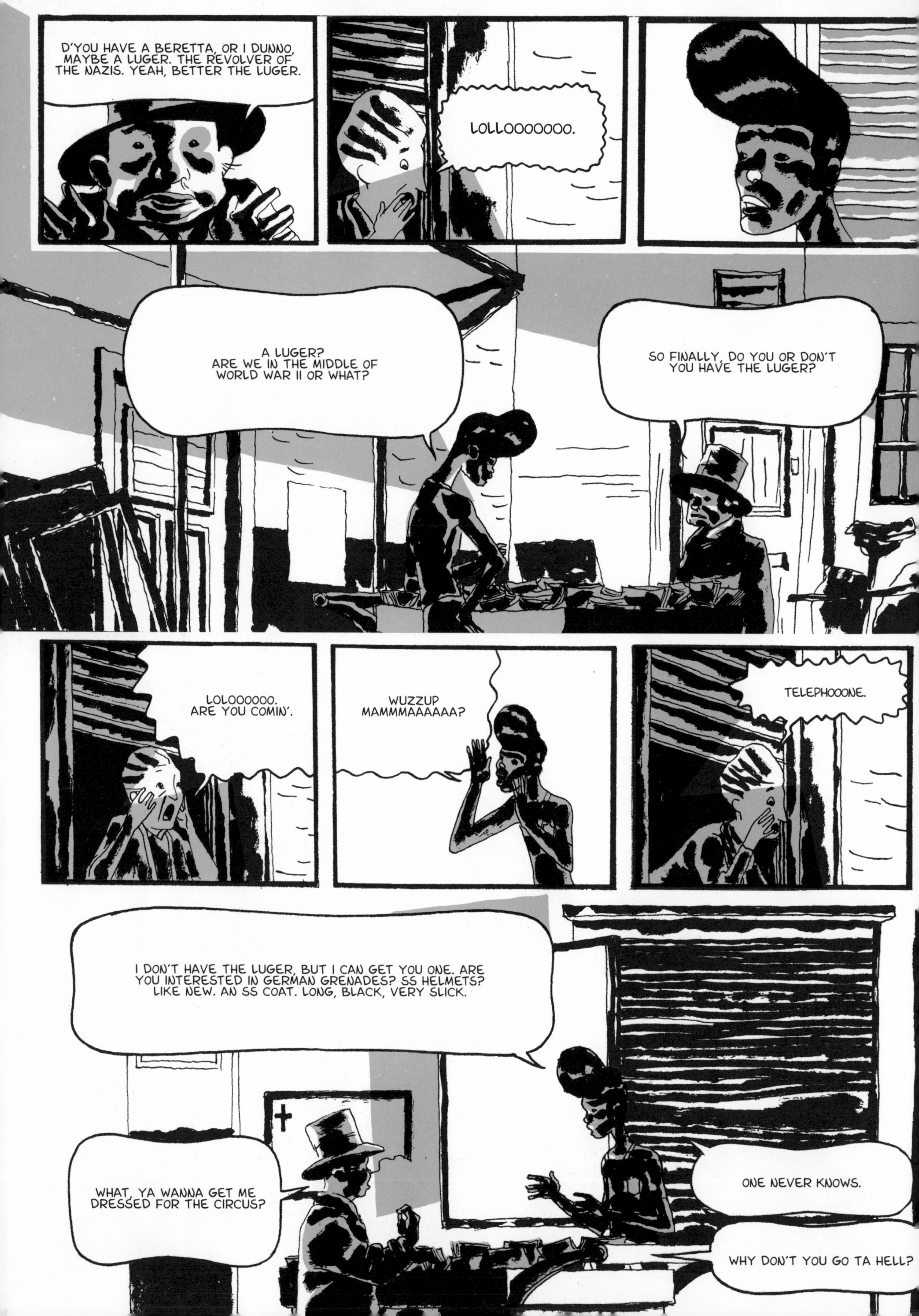
D'YOU HAVE A BERETTA, OR I DUNNO, MAYBE A LUGER. THE REVOLVER OF THE NAZIS. YEAH, BETTER THE LUGER.
LOLLOOOOOOO.
A LUGER? ARE WE IN THE MIDDLE OF WORLD WAR II OR WHAT?
SO FINALLY, DO YOU OR DON'T YOU HAVE THE LUGER?
LOLOOOOOO. ARE YOU COMIN'.
WUZZUP MAMMMAAAAAA?
TELEPHOOONE.
I DON'T HAVE THE LUGER, BUT I CAN GET YOU ONE. ARE YOU INTERESTED IN GERMAN GRENADES? SS HELMETS? LIKE NEW. AN SS COAT. LONG, BLACK, VERY SLICK.
WHAT, YA WANNA GET ME DRESSED FOR THE CIRCUS?
ONE NEVER KNOWS.
WHY DON'T YOU GO TA HELL?

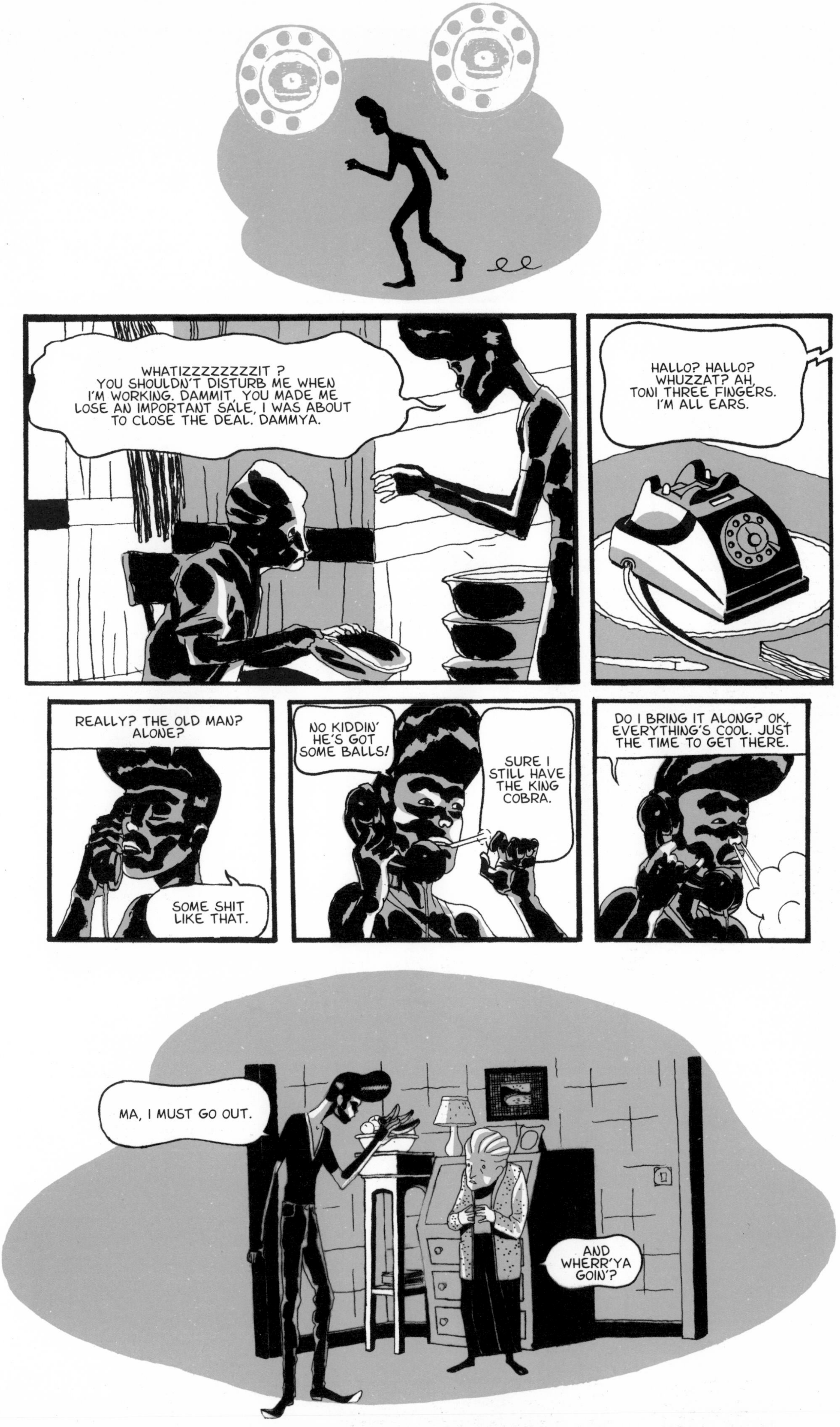
WHATIZZZZZZZZIT ? YOU SHOULDN'T DISTURB ME WHEN I'M WORKING. DAMMIT, YOU MADE ME LOSE AN IMPORTANT SALE, I WAS ABOUT TO CLOSE THE DEAL. DAMMYA.
HALLO? HALLO? WHUZZAT? AH, TONI THREE FINGERS. I'M ALL EARS.
REALLY? THE OLD MAN? ALONE?
SOME SHIT LIKE THAT.
NO KIDDIN' HE'S GOT SOME BALLS!
SURE I STILL HAVE THE KING COBRA.
DO I BRING IT ALONG? OK, EVERYTHING'S COOL. JUST THE TIME TO GET THERE.
MA, I MUST GO OUT.
AND WHERR'YA GOIN'?

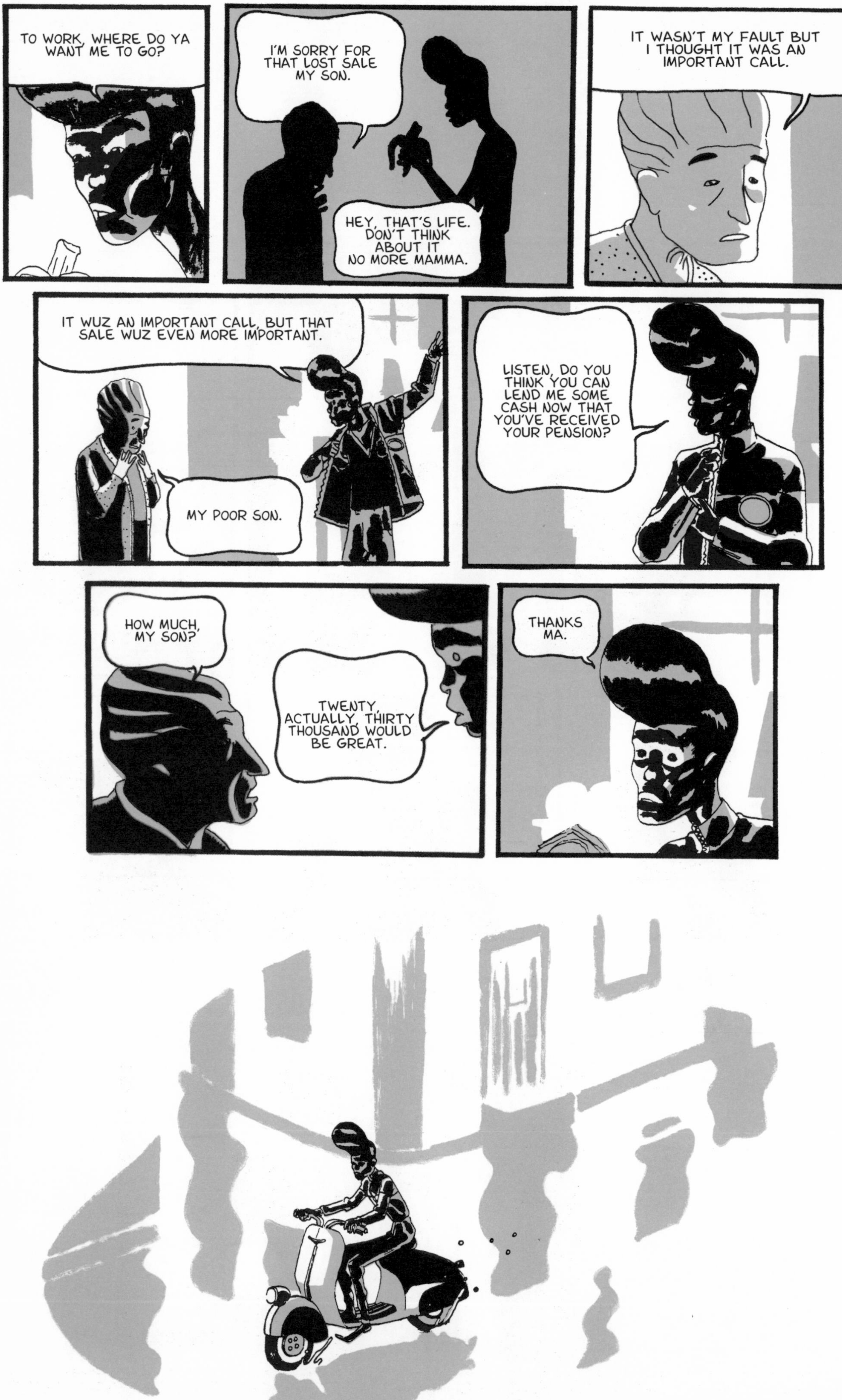
TO WORK, WHERE DO YA WANT ME TO GO?
I'M SORRY FOR THAT LOST SALE MY SON.
HEY, THAT'S LIFE. DON'T THINK ABOUT IT NO MORE MAMMA.
IT WASN'T MY FAULT BUT I THOUGHT IT WAS AN IMPORTANT CALL.
IT WUZ AN IMPORTANT CALL, BUT THAT SALE WUZ EVEN MORE IMPORTANT.
MY POOR SON.
LISTEN, DO YOU THINK YOU CAN LEND ME SOME CASH NOW THAT YOU'VE RECEIVED YOUR PENSION?
HOW MUCH, MY SON?
TWENTY, ACTUALLY, THIRTY THOUSAND WOULD BE GREAT.
THANKS MA.

chapter four
the smile of death

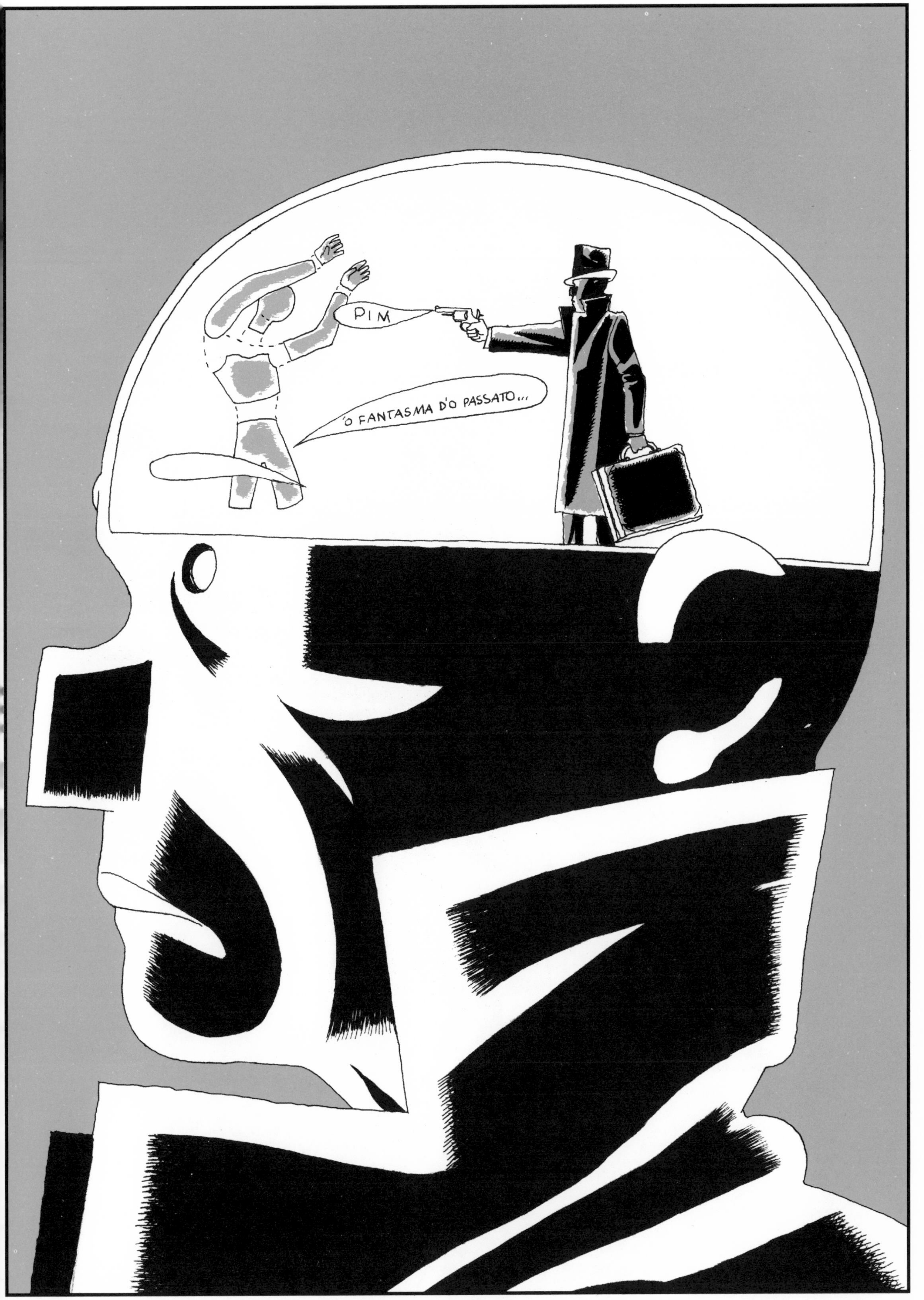
PIM
'O FANTASMA D'O PASSATO...

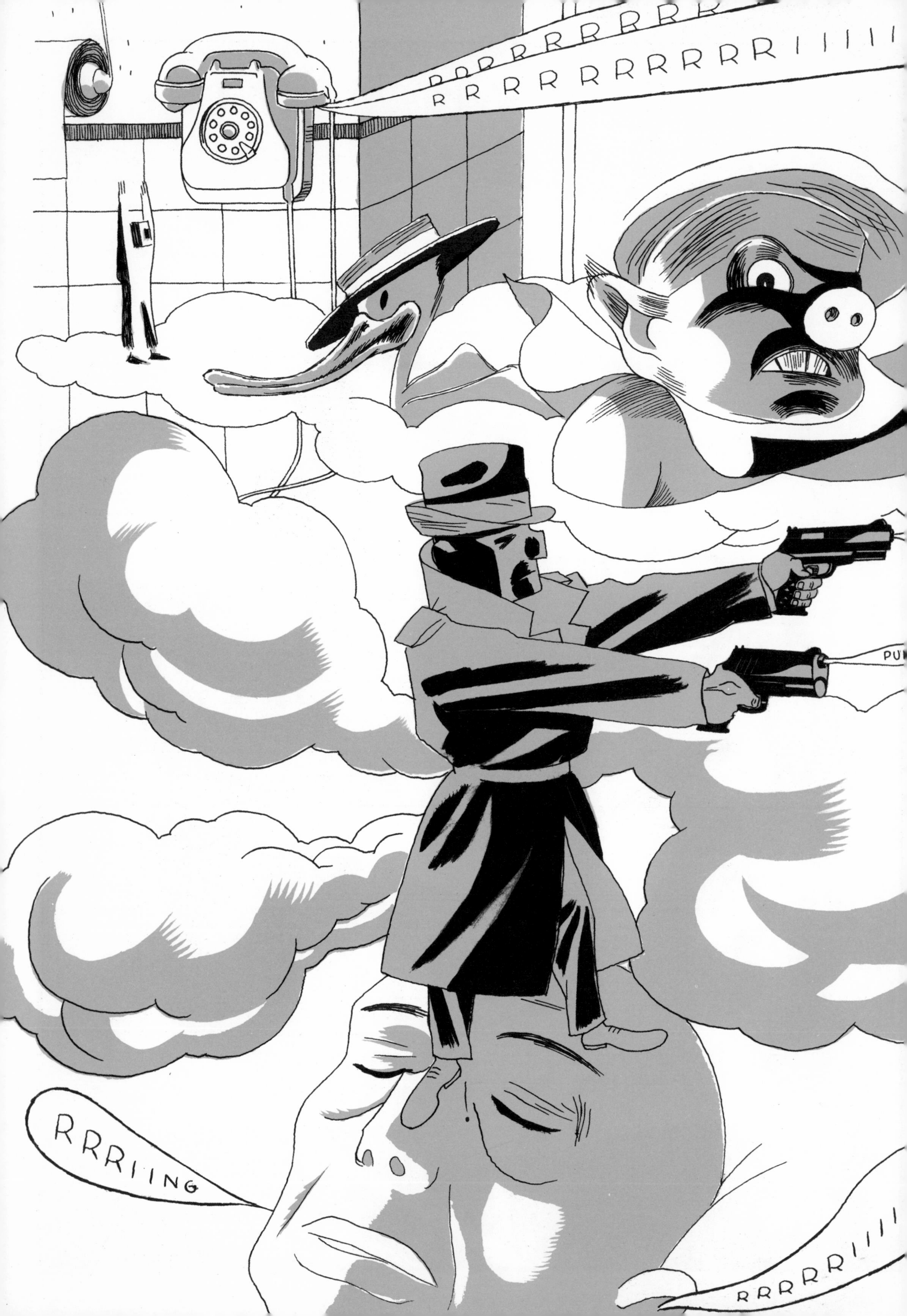
RRRRRRRRRRIIIII
RRRIIING
RRRRRIIIII

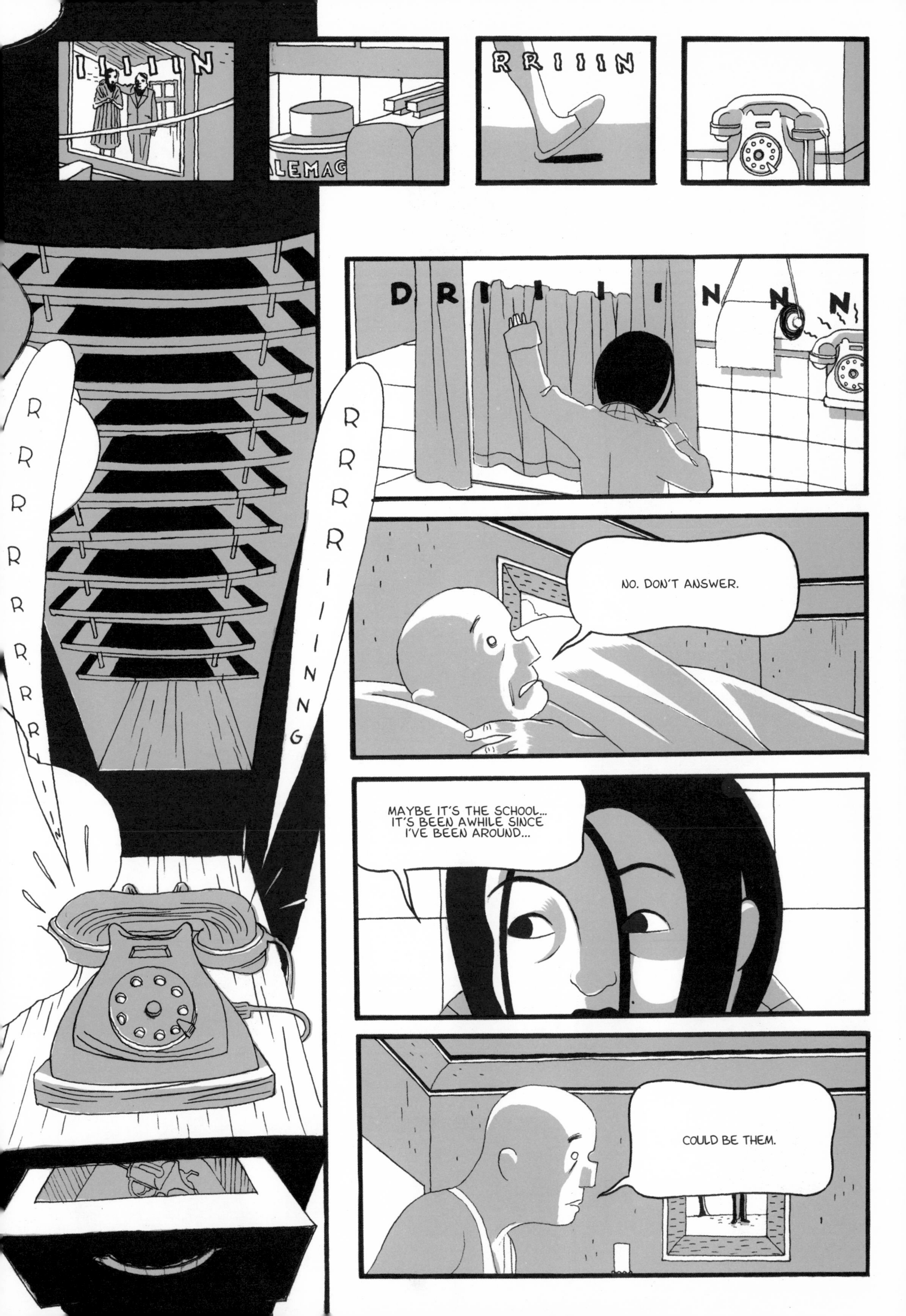
IIIIIN
LEMAG
RRIIIN
DRIIIINNN
RRRRRRRR
RRRRRIIIINNG
NO. DON'T ANSWER.
MAYBE IT'S THE SCHOOL... IT'S BEEN AWHILE SINCE I'VE BEEN AROUND...
COULD BE THEM.

THEY'LL FIND US, PEPPINO. WHAT D'YA THINK? YOU REALLY BELIEVE IT MAKES A DIFFERENCE IF YOU DON'T ANSWER THE PHONE?

HOW YA' FEELIN' TODAY SALVATO'?

LIKE A WALKING CORPSE.

C'MON, WE'VE BEEN THROUGH MUCH WORSE.

REMEMBER THAT TOTO MOVIE WHERE EVERYBODY THINKS HE'S DEAD? REMEMBER IT?

HE HAD GONE TO RUSSIA TO FIGHT AND HIS WIFE GOT REMARRIED. EVERYBODY THOUGHT HE WAS DEAD BUT HE CAME BACK HOME AND CAUSED A GREAT DEAL OF SHIT.

YA THINK THIS IS A JOKE, EH PEPPINO?

NO, I ONLY THINK THAT WE CAN'T STOP NOW. SEEMS LIKE YESTERDAY. REMEMBER? WE SPENT A LIFETIME TAKING CARE OF BUSINESS FOR DON GUARINO AND ALL THAT.

WE WUZ HAVING FUN, EH?

ADMIT IT.

YEAH, WE WUZ HAVING FUN.

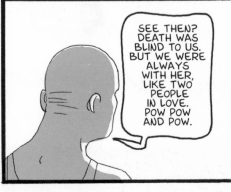

SEE THEN? DEATH WAS BLIND TO US. BUT WE WERE ALWAYS WITH HER, LIKE TWO PEOPLE IN LOVE. POW POW AND POW.

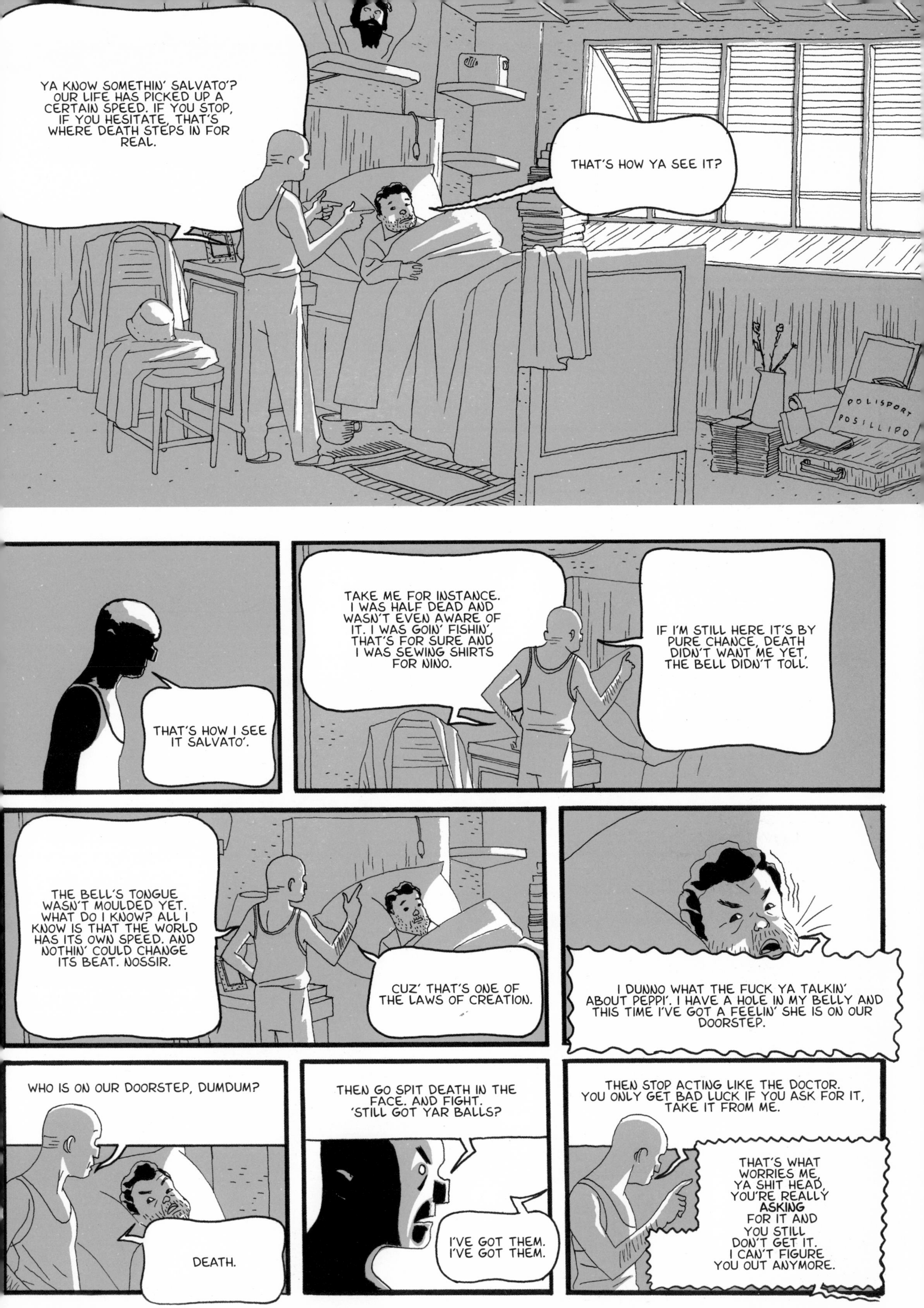
YA KNOW SOMETHIN' SALVATO'? OUR LIFE HAS PICKED UP A CERTAIN SPEED. IF YOU STOP, IF YOU HESITATE, THAT'S WHERE DEATH STEPS IN FOR REAL.
THAT'S HOW YA SEE IT?
POLISPORT
POSILLIPO
THAT'S HOW I SEE IT SALVATO'.
TAKE ME FOR INSTANCE. I WAS HALF DEAD AND WASN'T EVEN AWARE OF IT. I WAS GOIN' FISHIN', THAT'S FOR SURE AND I WAS SEWING SHIRTS FOR NINO.
IF I'M STILL HERE IT'S BY PURE CHANCE, DEATH DIDN'T WANT ME YET, THE BELL DIDN'T TOLL.
THE BELL'S TONGUE WASN'T MOULDED YET. WHAT DO I KNOW? ALL I KNOW IS THAT THE WORLD HAS ITS OWN SPEED. AND NOTHIN' COULD CHANGE ITS BEAT. NOSSIR.
CUZ' THAT'S ONE OF THE LAWS OF CREATION.
I DUNNO WHAT THE FUCK YA TALKIN' ABOUT PEPPI'. I HAVE A HOLE IN MY BELLY AND THIS TIME I'VE GOT A FEELIN' SHE IS ON OUR DOORSTEP.
WHO IS ON OUR DOORSTEP, DUMDUM?
DEATH.
THEN GO SPIT DEATH IN THE FACE. AND FIGHT. 'STILL GOT YAR BALLS?
I'VE GOT THEM. I'VE GOT THEM.
THEN STOP ACTING LIKE THE DOCTOR. YOU ONLY GET BAD LUCK IF YOU ASK FOR IT, TAKE IT FROM ME.
THAT'S WHAT WORRIES ME, YA SHIT HEAD, YOU'RE REALLY ASKING FOR IT AND YOU STILL DON'T GET IT. I CAN'T FIGURE YOU OUT ANYMORE.

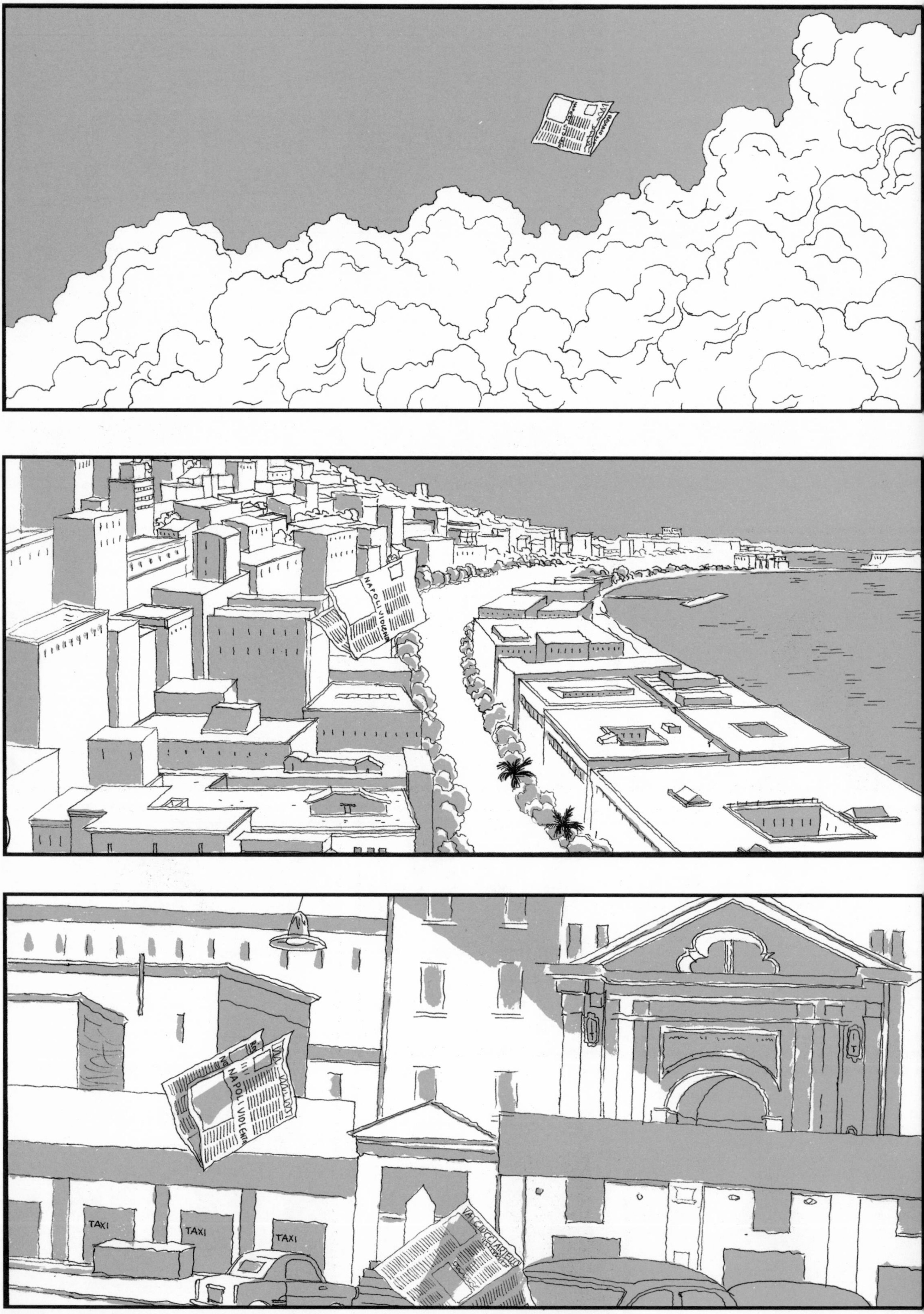
NAPOLI VIOLENTA
NAPOLI VIOLENTA
TAXI
TAXI
TAXI

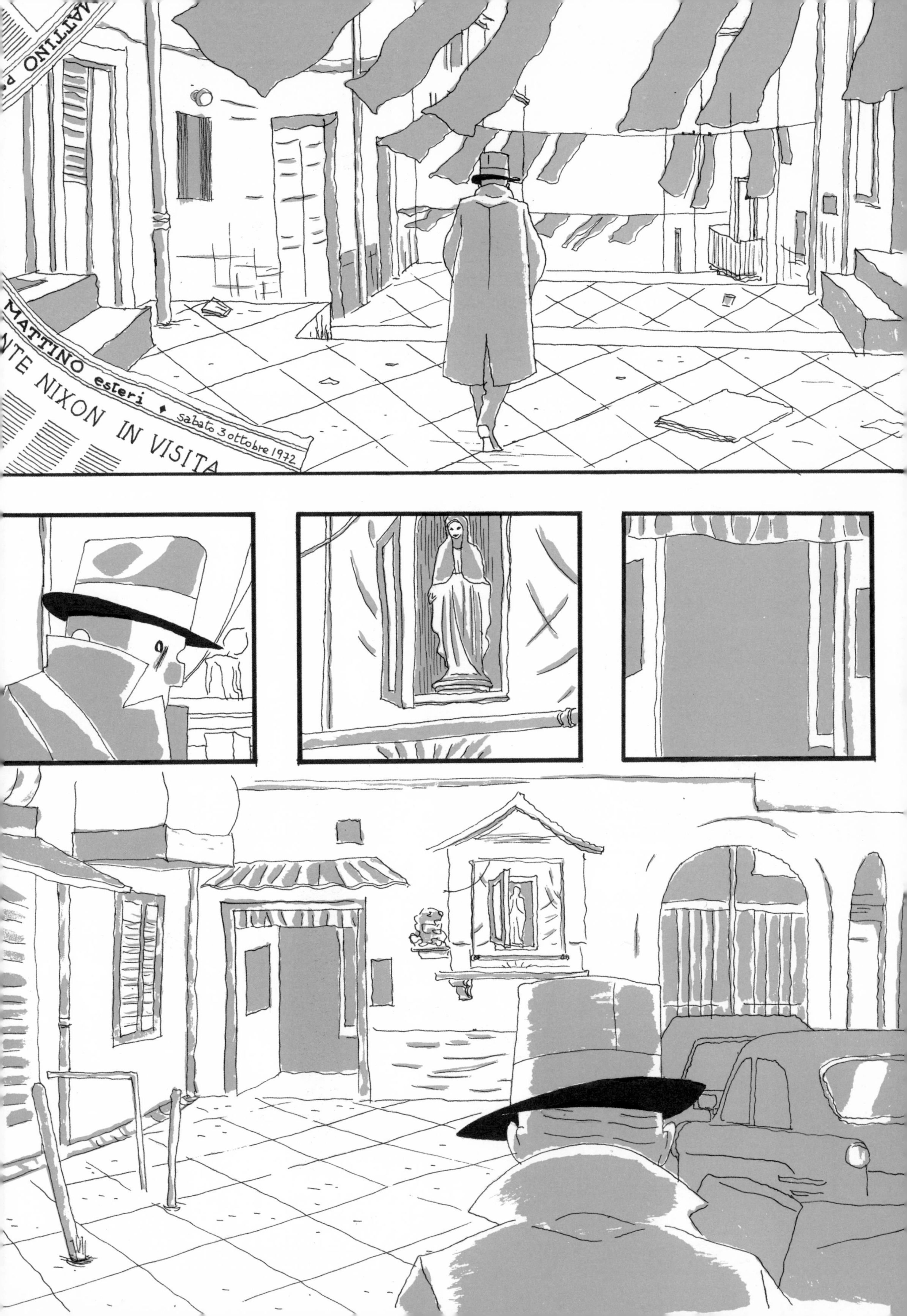
MATTINO
MATTINO esteri ♦ sabato 3 ottobre 1972
NTE NIXON IN VISITA

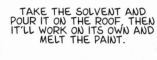
'O SOLE MIOO ♪

CARUSO.

TAKE THE SOLVENT AND POUR IT ON THE ROOF, THEN IT'LL WORK ON ITS OWN AND MELT THE PAINT.

WHEN THE SCUMBAG GETS TO THE CAR AND SEES THAT, HE'S GONNA EAT HIS HEART OUT.

EASY, NO? WHO SAID ANYTHING? IT'S A PIECE 'A CAKE.

OF COURSE. THE ONLY PROBLEM IS THAT YOU THREW THE SHIT ON THE WRONG CAR, YOU PRICK.

NOW THAT'S A PROBLEM, YA HEAR WHAT I'M SAYIN', THAT'S A REAL PROBLEM. NOW, WE'VE GOT TO FIND MORE SOLVENT.

IS IT YOU THAT'S GONNA TELL SALVO? HUH? HUH? LET'S SEE HOW YOU GONNA EXPLAIN THAT TO HIM?

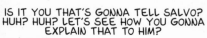
YOU'RE SUCH AN ASSHOLE. GET YAR ASS THERE AND FIND ANOTHER FIVE KILO TIN, YA MORON. YOU MAKE ONE MORE MISTAKE AND I'M GONNA KICK YAR FUCKING ASS REALLY HARD. WHAT DID I TELL YA?

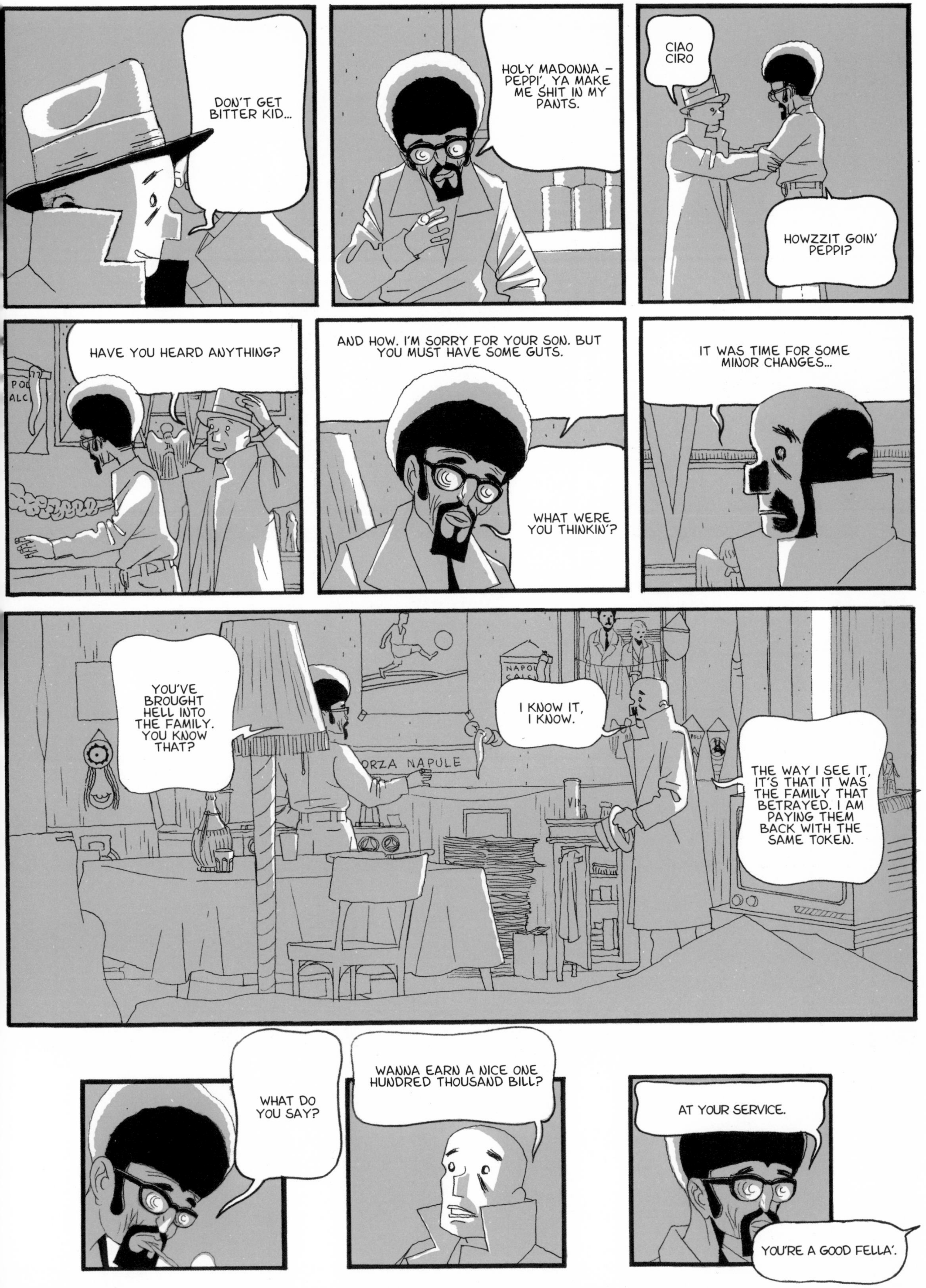
DON'T GET BITTER KID...
HOLY MADONNA – PEPPI', YA MAKE ME SHIT IN MY PANTS.
CIAO CIRO
HOWZZIT GOIN' PEPPI?
HAVE YOU HEARD ANYTHING?
AND HOW. I'M SORRY FOR YOUR SON. BUT YOU MUST HAVE SOME GUTS.
WHAT WERE YOU THINKIN'?
IT WAS TIME FOR SOME MINOR CHANGES...
YOU'VE BROUGHT HELL INTO THE FAMILY. YOU KNOW THAT?
FORZA NAPULE
I KNOW IT, I KNOW.
THE WAY I SEE IT, IT'S THAT IT WAS THE FAMILY THAT BETRAYED. I AM PAYING THEM BACK WITH THE SAME TOKEN.
WHAT DO YOU SAY?
WANNA EARN A NICE ONE HUNDRED THOUSAND BILL?
AT YOUR SERVICE.
YOU'RE A GOOD FELLA'.

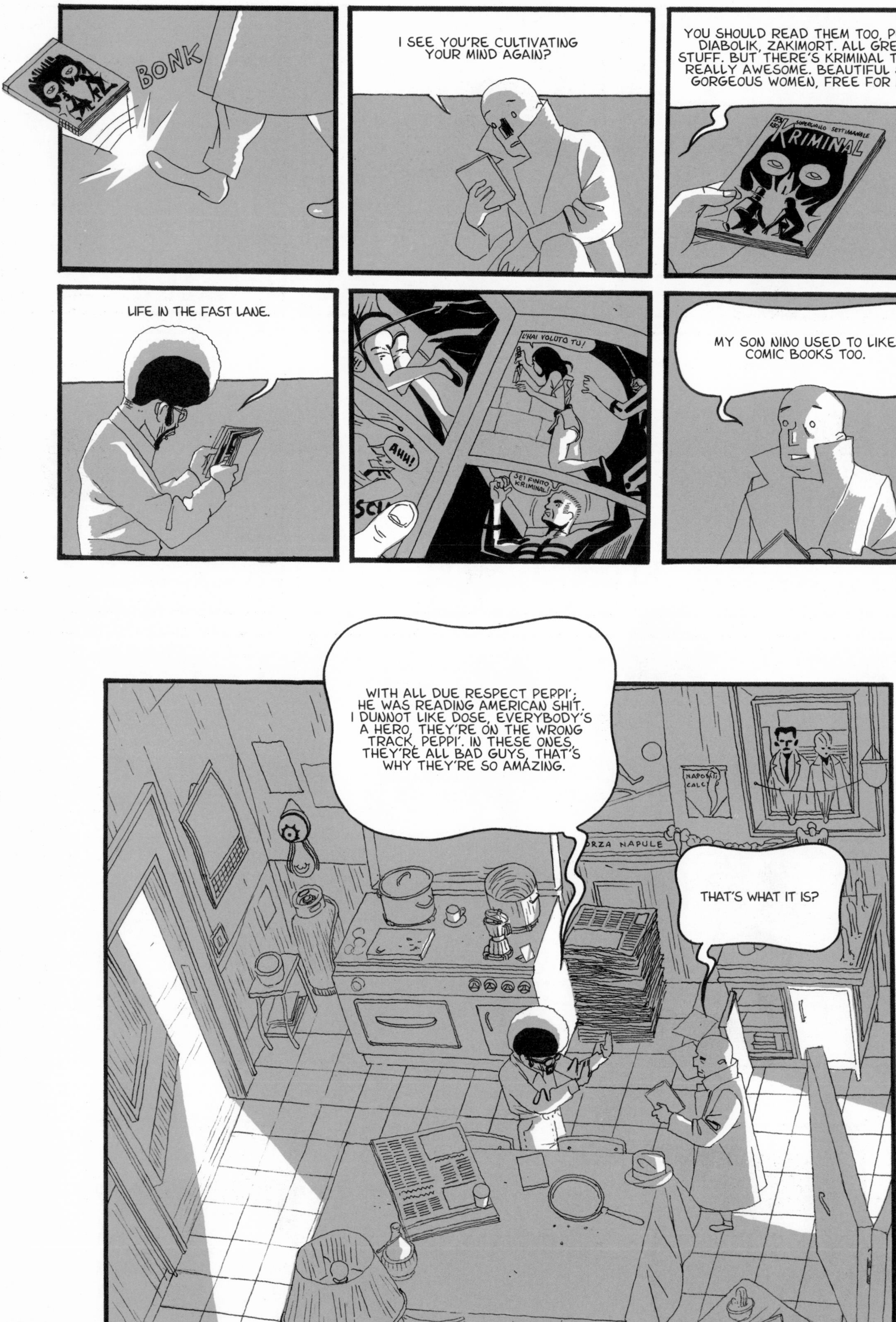
BONK
I SEE YOU'RE CULTIVATING YOUR MIND AGAIN?
YOU SHOULD READ THEM TOO, PEPPI'. DIABOLIK, ZAKIMORT. ALL GREAT STUFF. BUT THERE'S KRIMINAL THAT'S REALLY AWESOME. BEAUTIFUL SUIT, GORGEOUS WOMEN, FREE FOR ALL.
KRIMINAL
LIFE IN THE FAST LANE.
L'HAI VOLUTO TU!
AHH!
SEI FINITO KRIMINAL!
MY SON NINO USED TO LIKE COMIC BOOKS TOO.
WITH ALL DUE RESPECT PEPPI': HE WAS READING AMERICAN SHIT. I DUNNOT LIKE DOSE, EVERYBODY'S A HERO, THEY'RE ON THE WRONG TRACK, PEPPI'. IN THESE ONES, THEY'RE ALL BAD GUYS, THAT'S WHY THEY'RE SO AMAZING.
THAT'S WHAT IT IS?

THE AMERICANS HAVE NEVER HAD A CLUE.

LISTEN TA ME. THERE MIGHT BE SOMETHING THAT YOU COULD DO FOR ME. D'YOU REMEMBER THE DALLARA BUILDING IN THE SANITA' AREA?

WELL...WE SHOULD ORGANIZE A LITTLE EXCHANGE OF PRISONERS.

NO SHIT! GREAT. LET ME HAVE A LOOK.

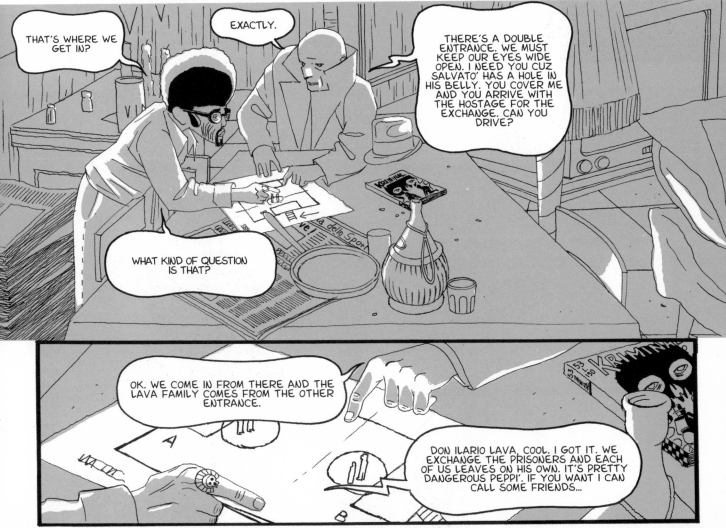
THAT'S WHERE WE GET IN?

EXACTLY.

THERE'S A DOUBLE ENTRANCE. WE MUST KEEP OUR EYES WIDE OPEN. I NEED YOU CUZ SALVATO' HAS A HOLE IN HIS BELLY. YOU COVER ME AND YOU ARRIVE WITH THE HOSTAGE FOR THE EXCHANGE. CAN YOU DRIVE?

WHAT KIND OF QUESTION IS THAT?

OK. WE COME IN FROM THERE AND THE LAVA FAMILY COMES FROM THE OTHER ENTRANCE.

DON ILARIO LAVA, COOL. I GOT IT. WE EXCHANGE THE PRISONERS AND EACH OF US LEAVES ON HIS OWN. IT'S PRETTY DANGEROUS PEPPI'. IF YOU WANT I CAN CALL SOME FRIENDS...

BETTER NOT. PLEASE, FIX YOUR HAIR, THEY CAN RECOGNIZE YOU.

YOU'RE THE BOSS.

I'LL GIVE YA A CALL.

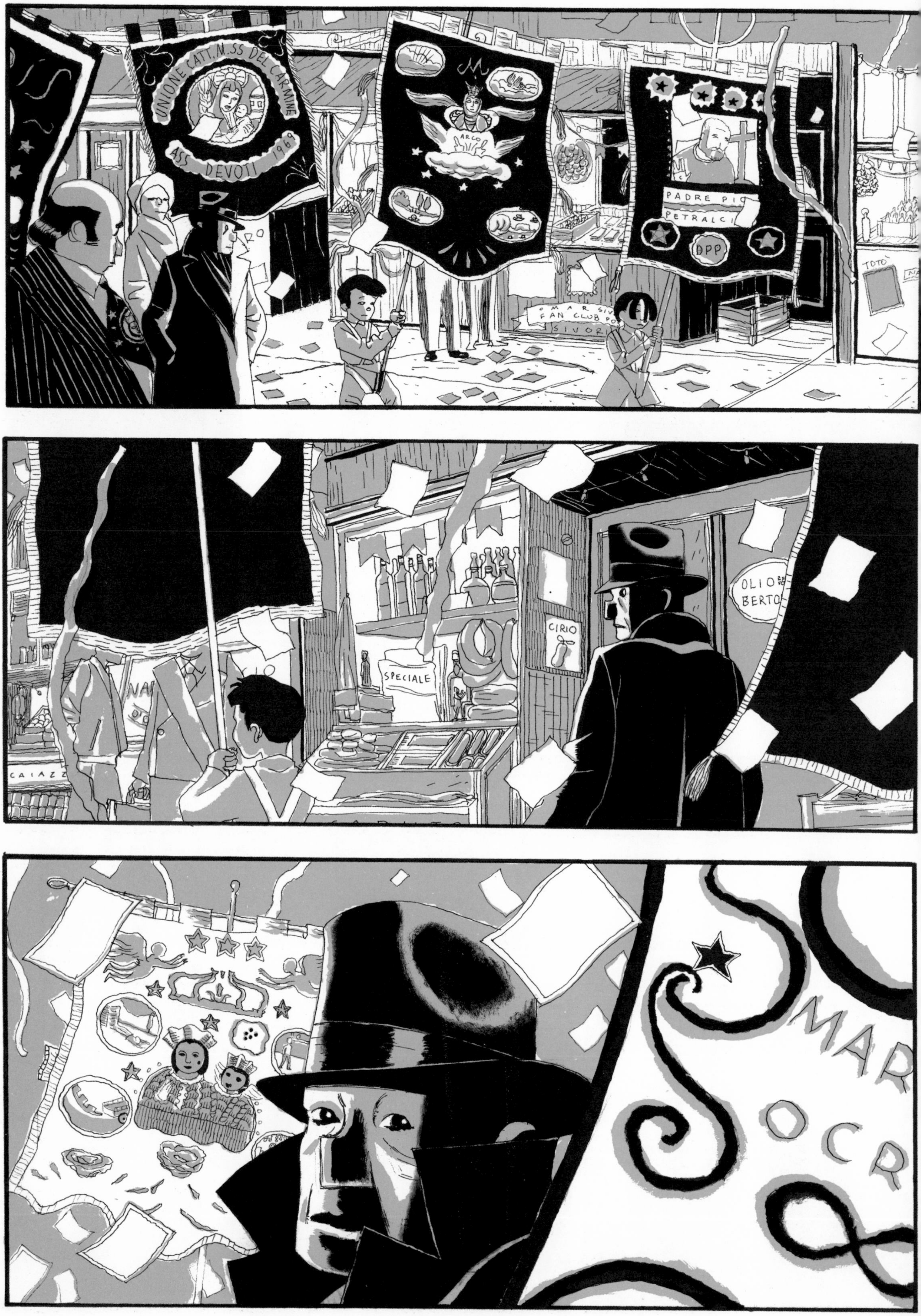

UNIONE CATT. M.SS DEL CARMINE
ASS DEVOTI 1969
ARCO
PADRE PIO
PETRALCI
DPP
FAN CLUB
SIVORI
TOTÒ
SPECIALE
CIRIO
OLIO
BERTO
CAIAZZ
MAR
OCR

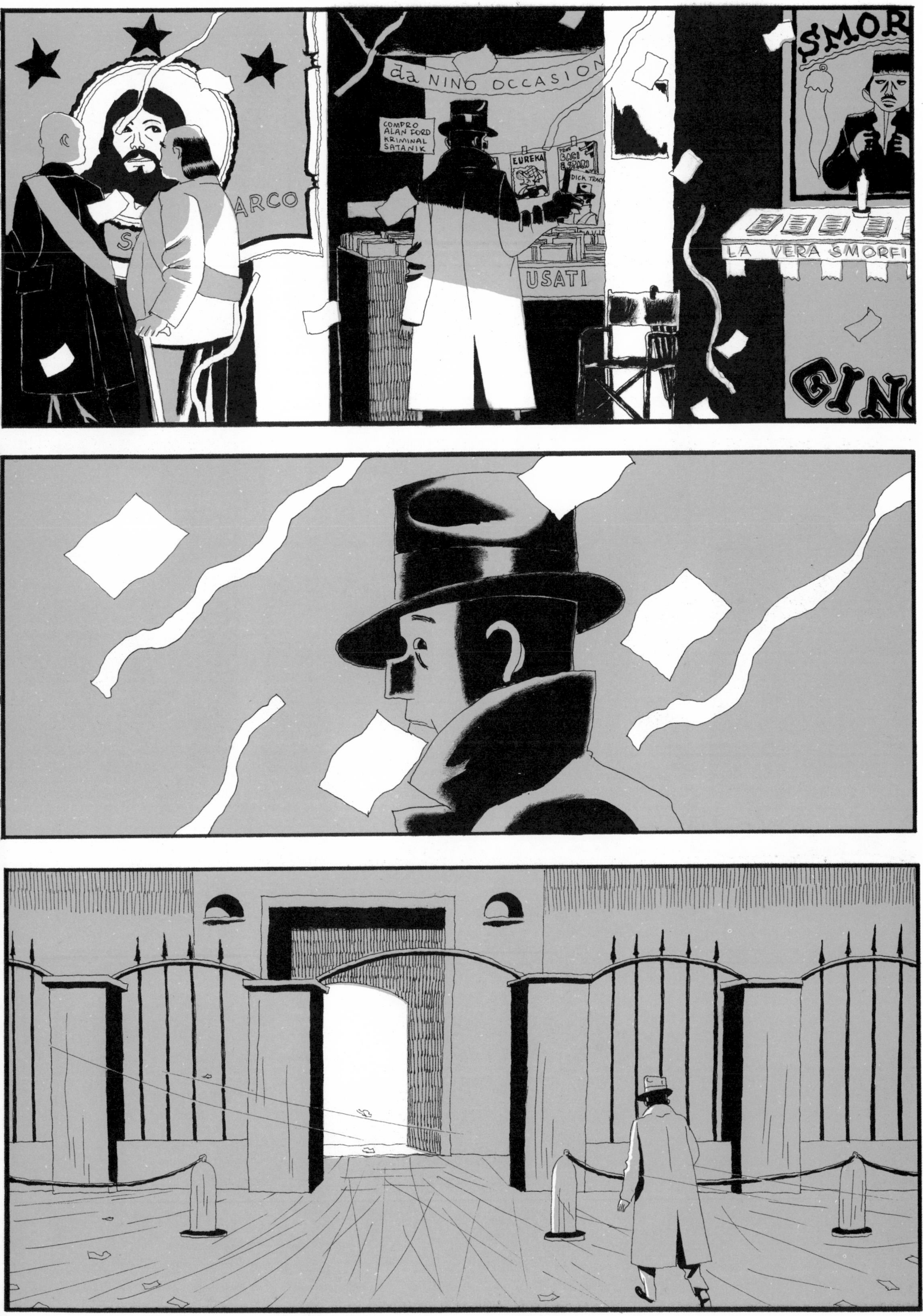

ARCO
da NINO OCCASION
COMPRO ALAN FORD KRIMINAL SATANIK
EUREKA
BACI E SPARI
DICK TRACY
USATI
SMOR
LA VERA SMORFI
GINO

HELP ME BECOME THE MAN I USED TO BE. AND FORGIVE ME FOR WHAT I'M NOT.

AMEN.

YOU TOOK AWAY THE MOST PRECIOUS THING THAT I'VE GOT IN THE WHOLE WORLD, MADONNA MIA. IS MY NINO UP THERE ALREADY? DO YOUR BEST TREAT HIM WELL, WOUDDYA?

I'M COUNTING ON IT.

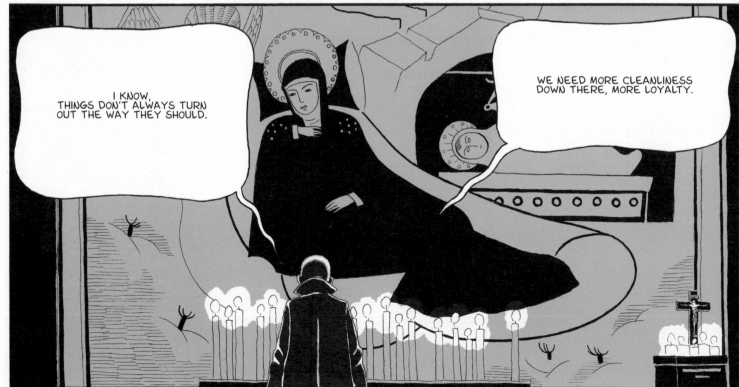

I KNOW, THINGS DON'T ALWAYS TURN OUT THE WAY THEY SHOULD.

WE NEED MORE CLEANLINESS DOWN THERE, MORE LOYALTY.

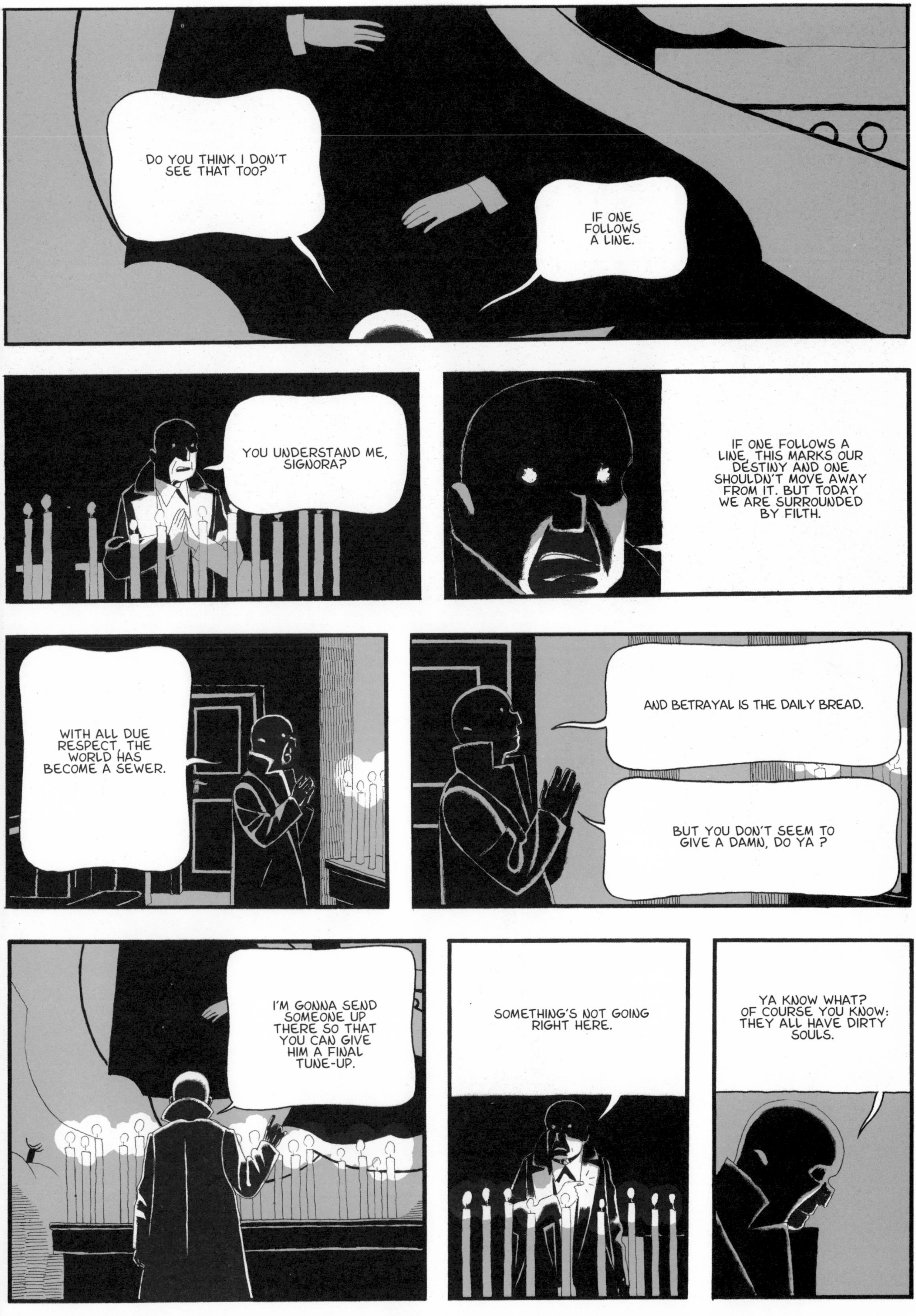
DO YOU THINK I DON'T SEE THAT TOO?
IF ONE FOLLOWS A LINE.
YOU UNDERSTAND ME, SIGNORA?
IF ONE FOLLOWS A LINE, THIS MARKS OUR DESTINY AND ONE SHOULDN'T MOVE AWAY FROM IT. BUT TODAY WE ARE SURROUNDED BY FILTH.
WITH ALL DUE RESPECT, THE WORLD HAS BECOME A SEWER.
AND BETRAYAL IS THE DAILY BREAD.
BUT YOU DON'T SEEM TO GIVE A DAMN, DO YA ?
I'M GONNA SEND SOMEONE UP THERE SO THAT YOU CAN GIVE HIM A FINAL TUNE-UP.
SOMETHING'S NOT GOING RIGHT HERE.
YA KNOW WHAT? OF COURSE YOU KNOW: THEY ALL HAVE DIRTY SOULS.

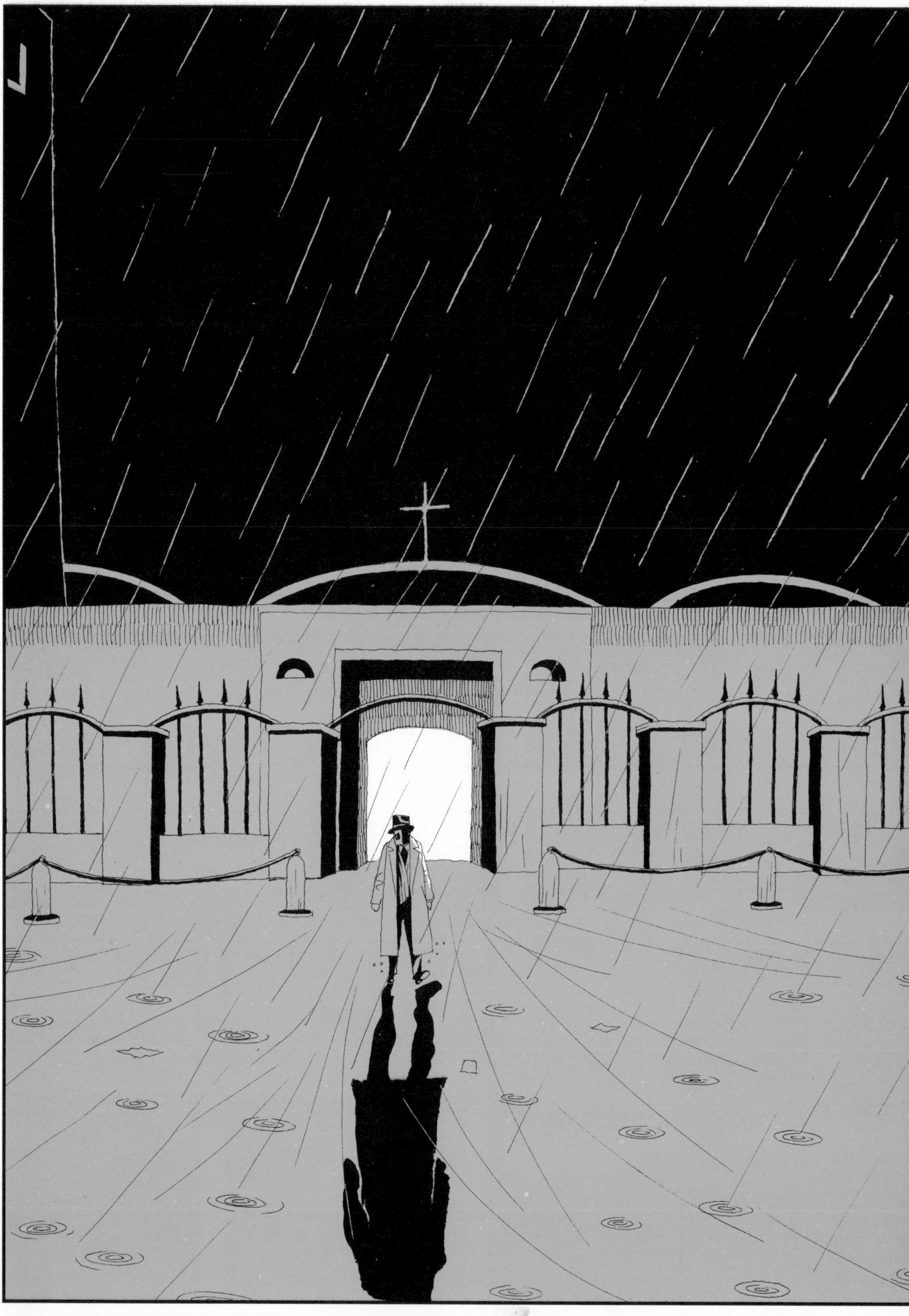

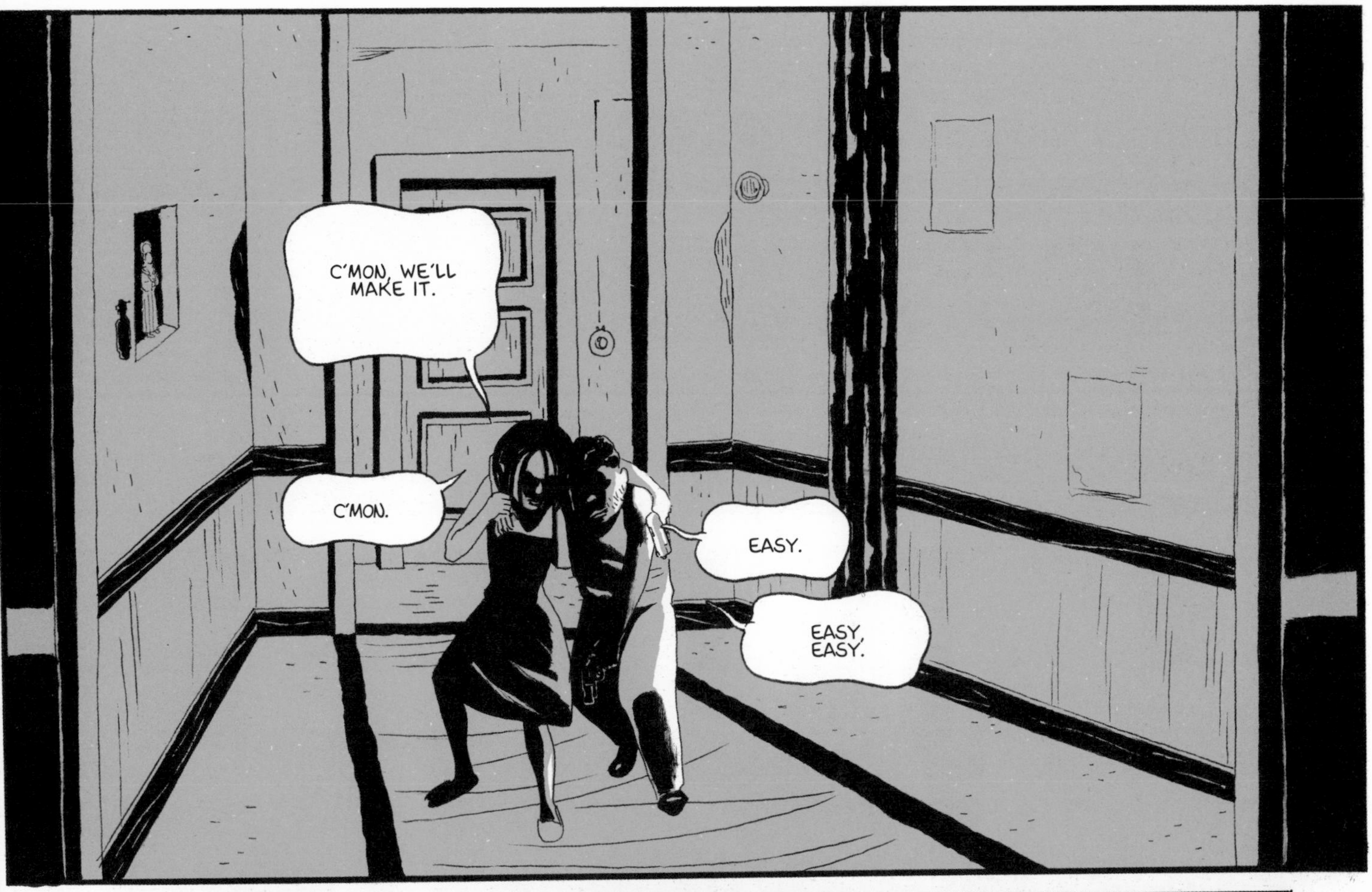
C'MON, WE'LL MAKE IT.
C'MON.
EASY.
EASY, EASY.

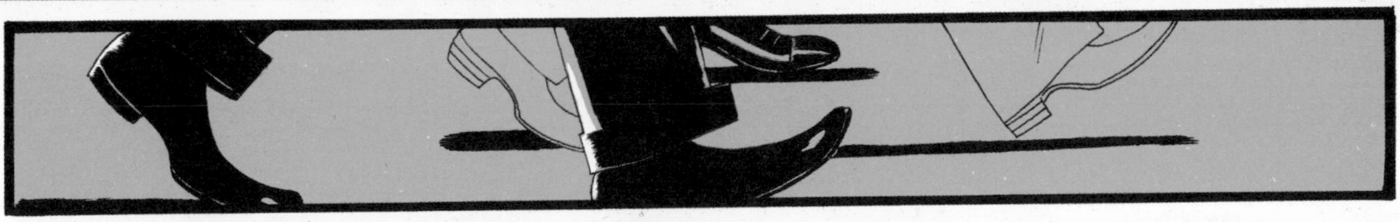

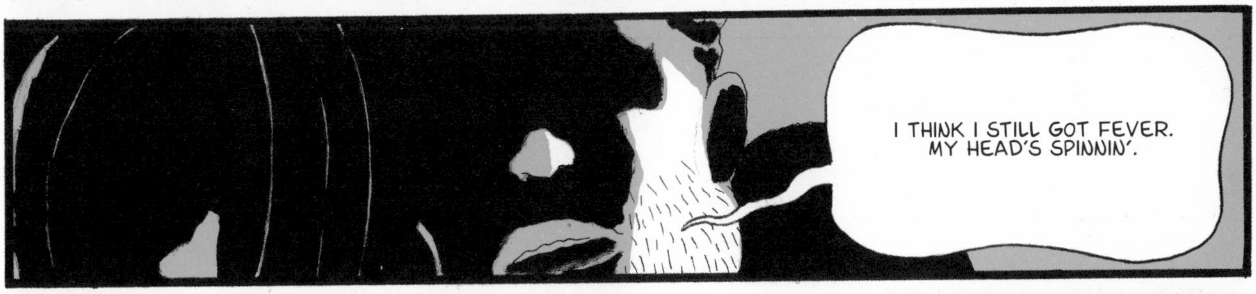
I THINK I STILL GOT FEVER. MY HEAD'S SPINNIN'.

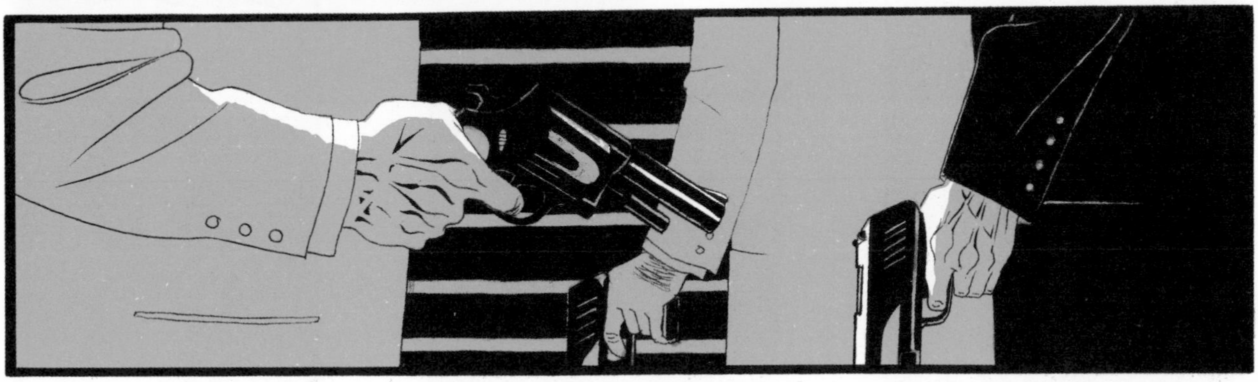

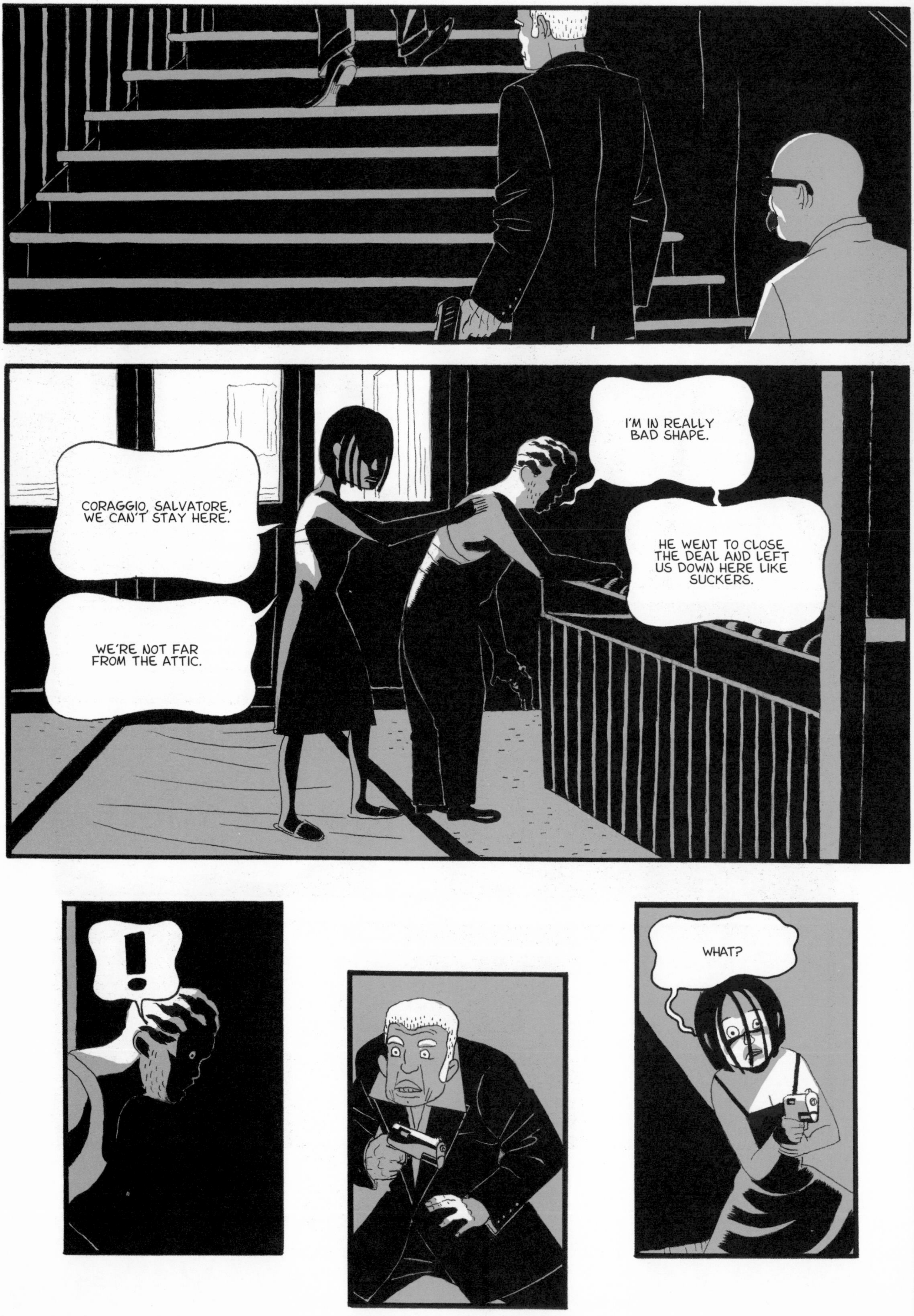
CORAGGIO, SALVATORE, WE CAN'T STAY HERE.
I'M IN REALLY BAD SHAPE.
HE WENT TO CLOSE THE DEAL AND LEFT US DOWN HERE LIKE SUCKERS.
WE'RE NOT FAR FROM THE ATTIC.
!
WHAT?

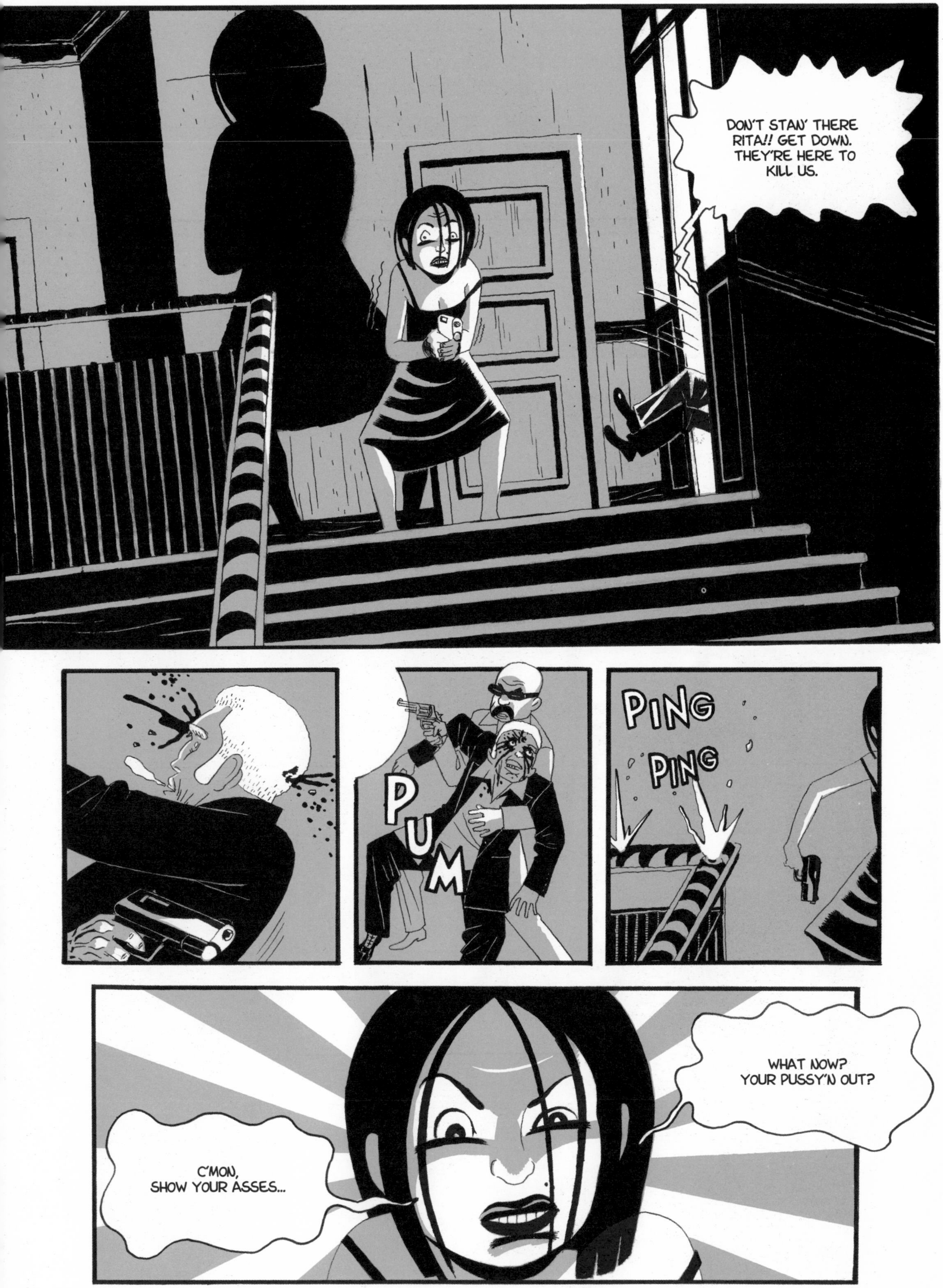
DON'T STAN' THERE RITA!! GET DOWN. THEY'RE HERE TO KILL US.
PUM
PING
PING
WHAT NOW? YOUR PUSSY'N OUT?
C'MON, SHOW YOUR ASSES...

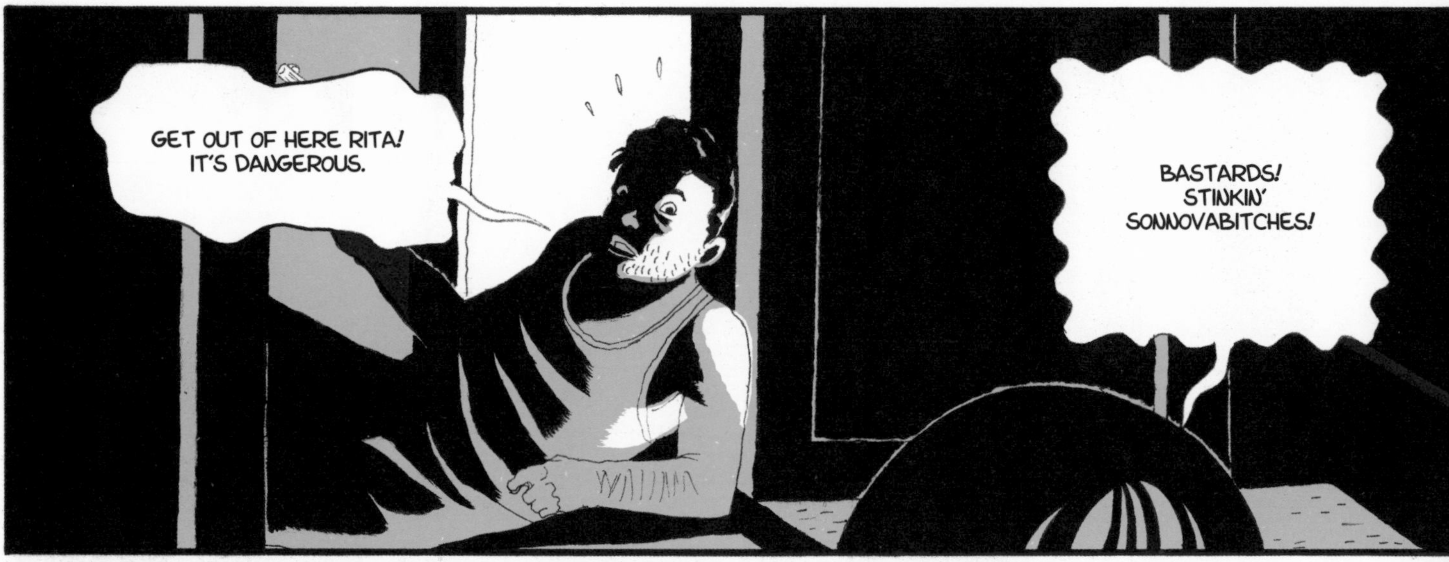
GET OUT OF HERE RITA! IT'S DANGEROUS.
BASTARDS! STINKIN' SONNOVABITCHES!

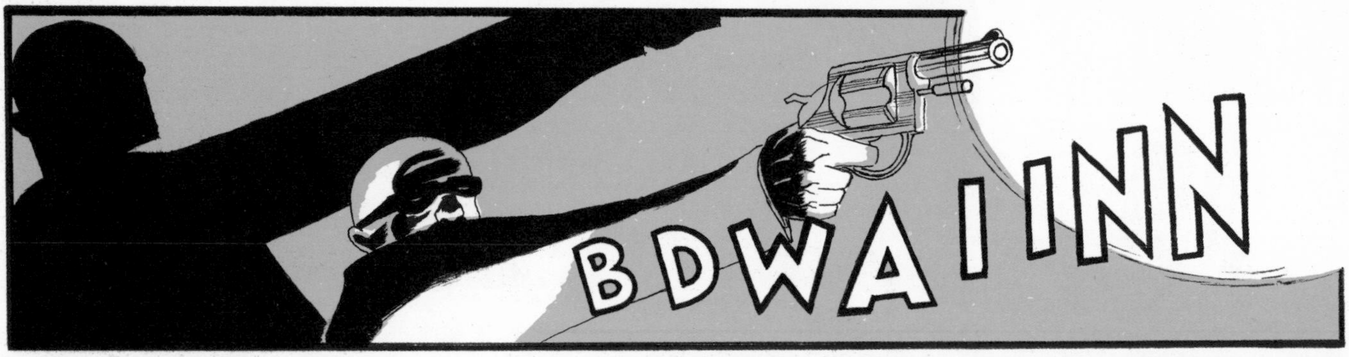
BDWAIINN

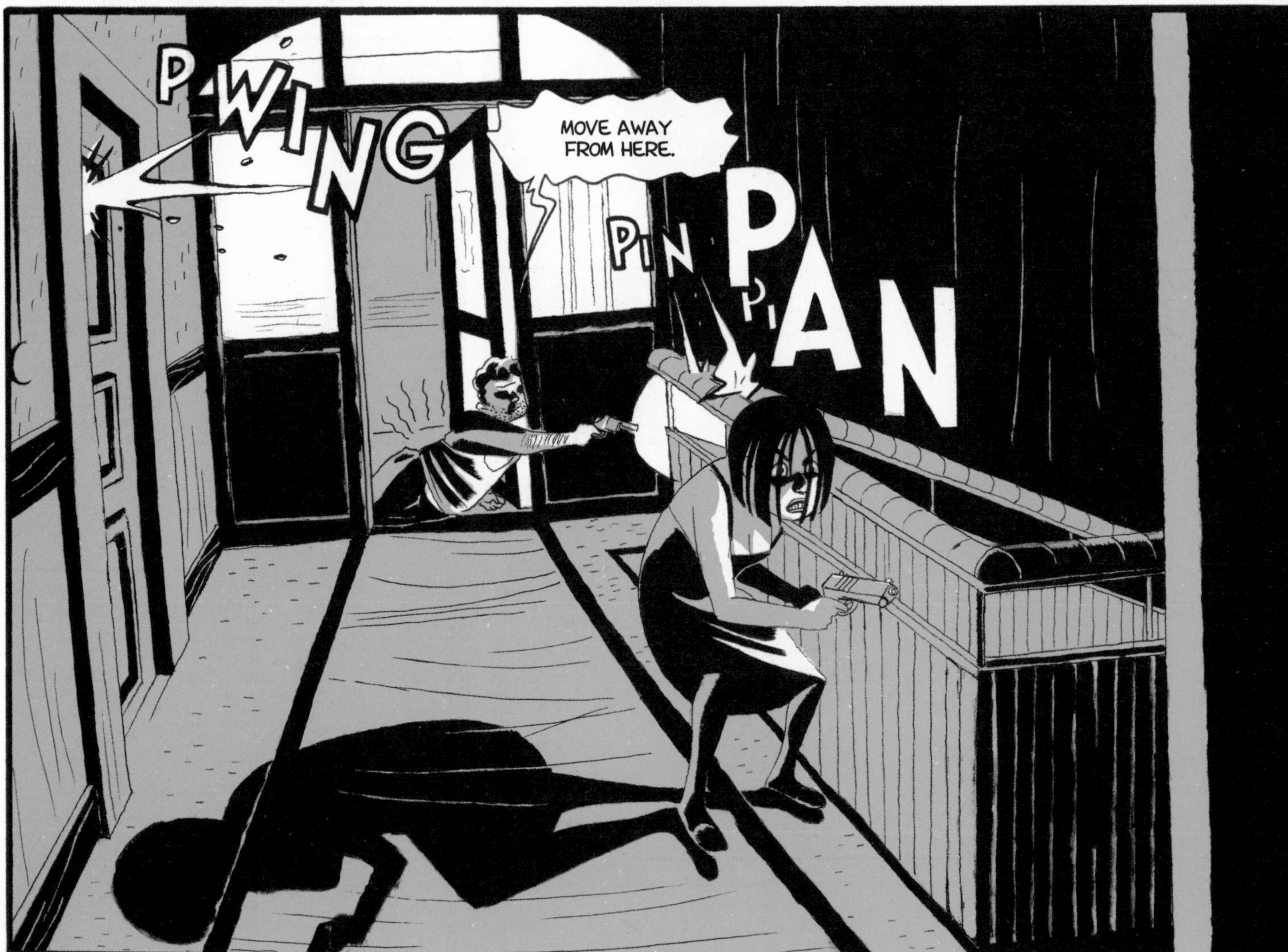
PWING
MOVE AWAY FROM HERE.
PIN
PI
PAN

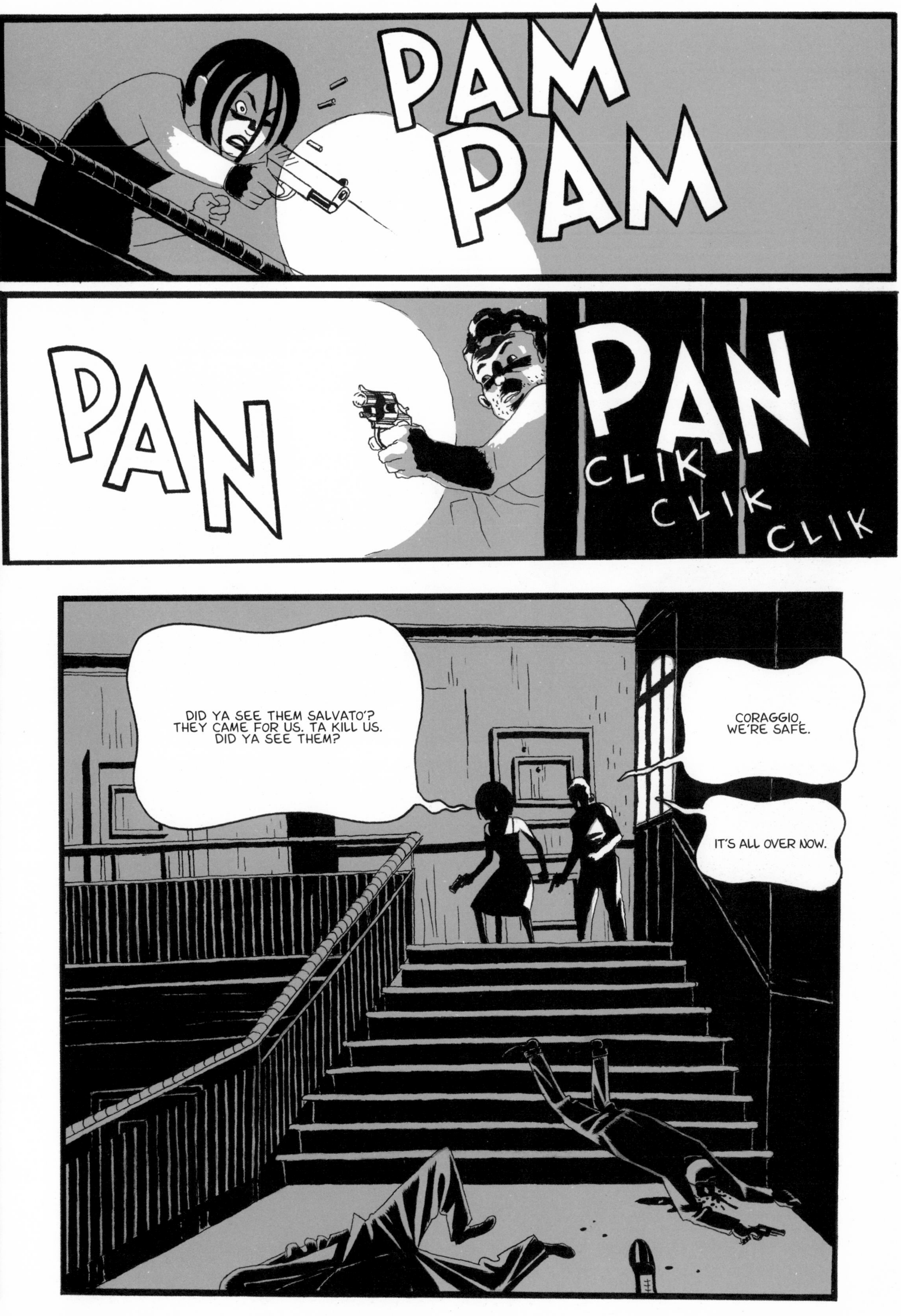
PAM
PAM
PAN
PAN
CLIK
CLIK
CLIK
DID YA SEE THEM SALVATO'? THEY CAME FOR US. TA KILL US. DID YA SEE THEM?
CORAGGIO. WE'RE SAFE.
IT'S ALL OVER NOW.

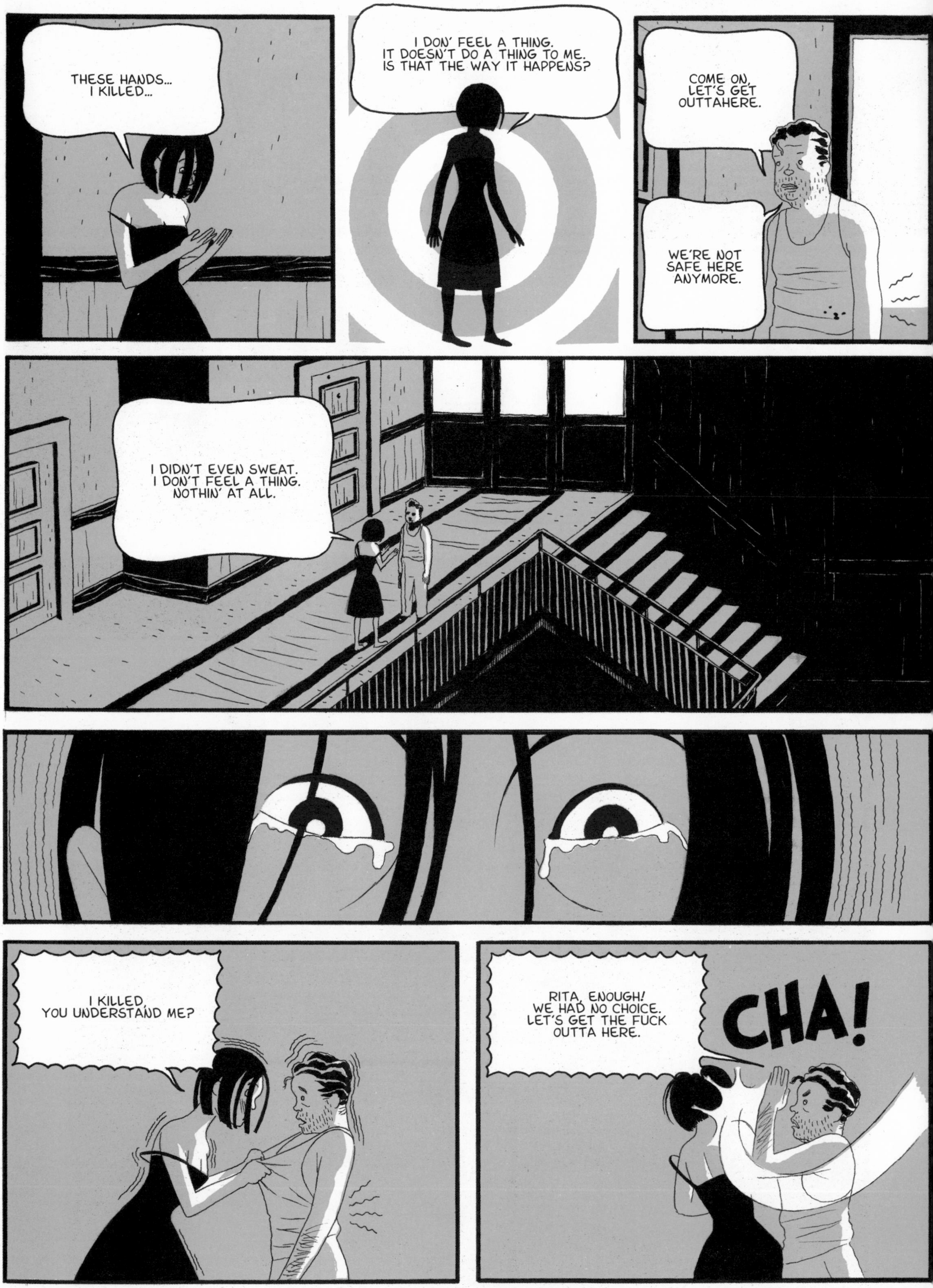

THESE HANDS... I KILLED...
I DON' FEEL A THING. IT DOESN'T DO A THING TO ME. IS THAT THE WAY IT HAPPENS?
COME ON, LET'S GET OUTTAHERE.
WE'RE NOT SAFE HERE ANYMORE.
I DIDN'T EVEN SWEAT. I DON'T FEEL A THING. NOTHIN' AT ALL.
I KILLED, YOU UNDERSTAND ME?
RITA, ENOUGH! WE HAD NO CHOICE. LET'S GET THE FUCK OUTTA HERE.
CHA!

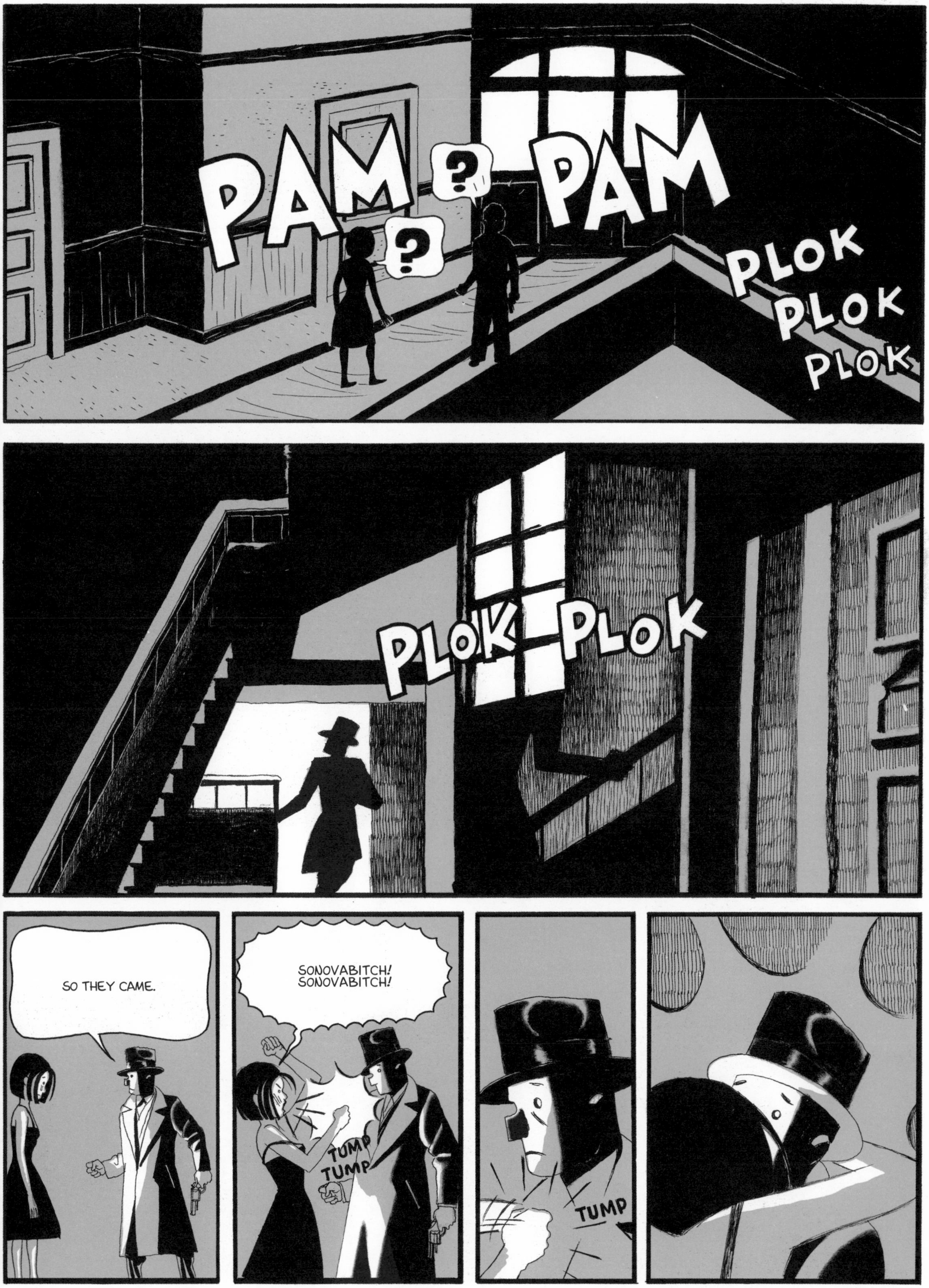
PAM
?
?
PAM
PLOK
PLOK
PLOK
PLOK PLOK
SO THEY CAME.
SONOVABITCH!
SONOVABITCH!
TUMP
TUMP
TUMP

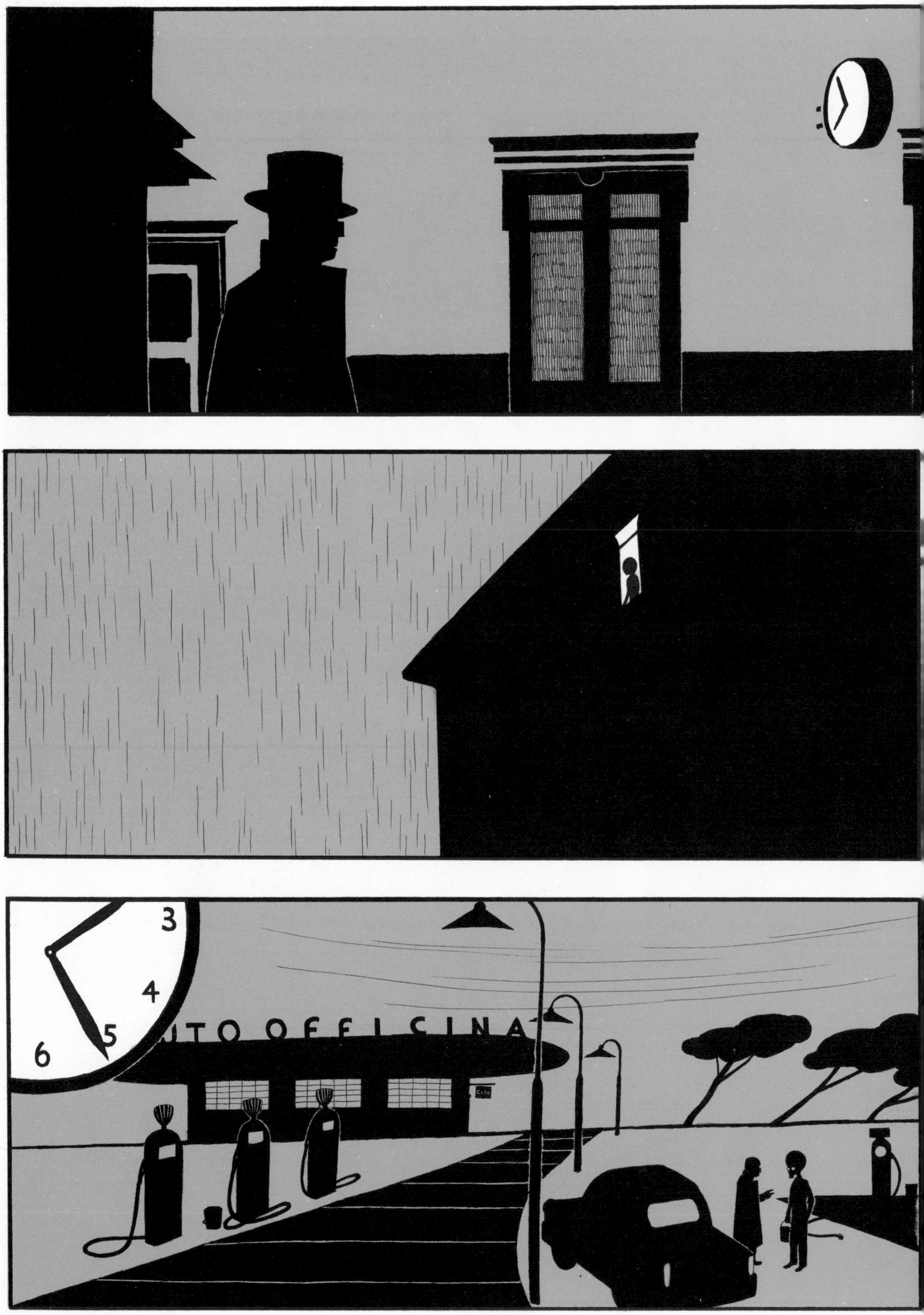
UTO OFFICINA

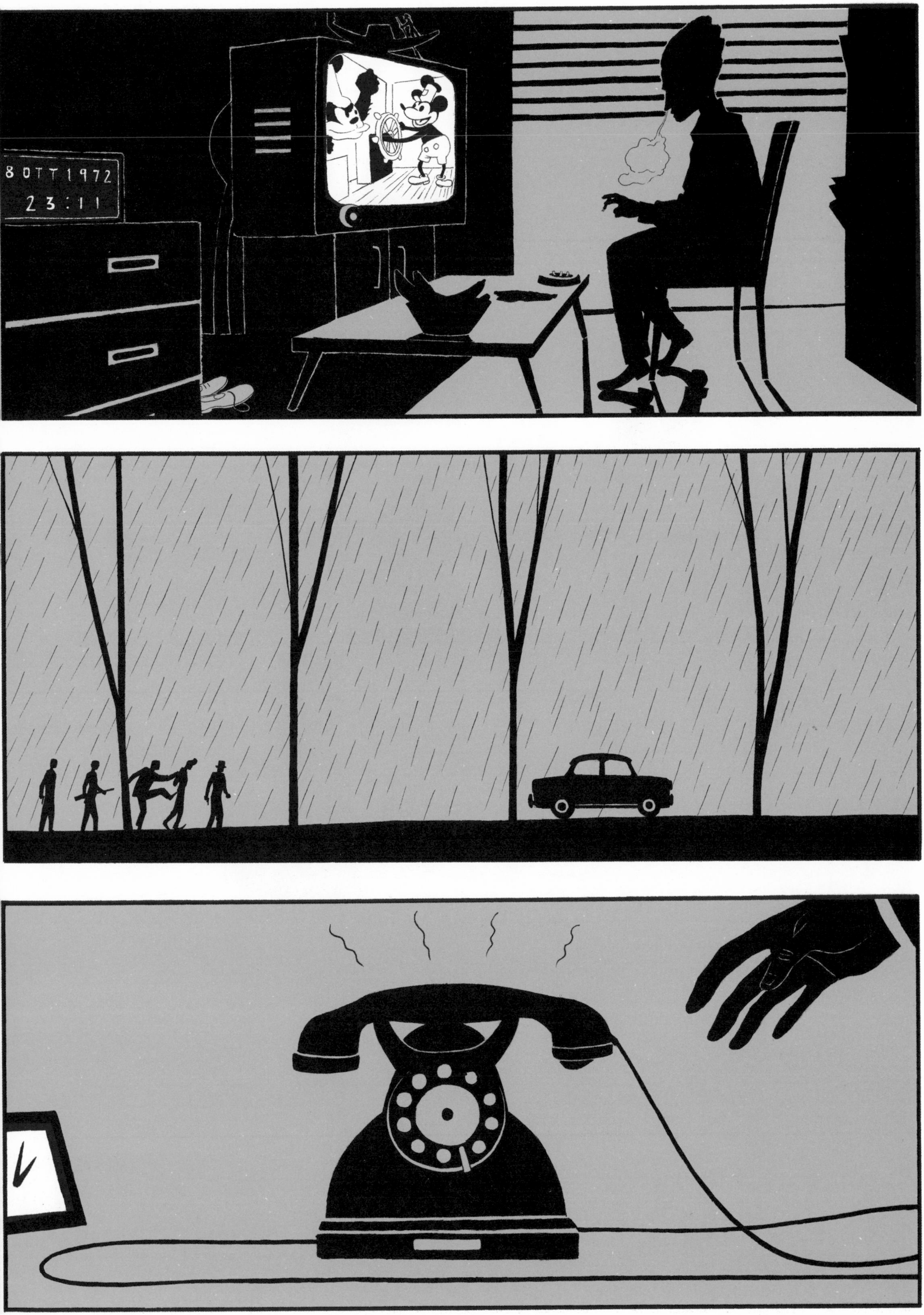
8 OTT 1972
23:11

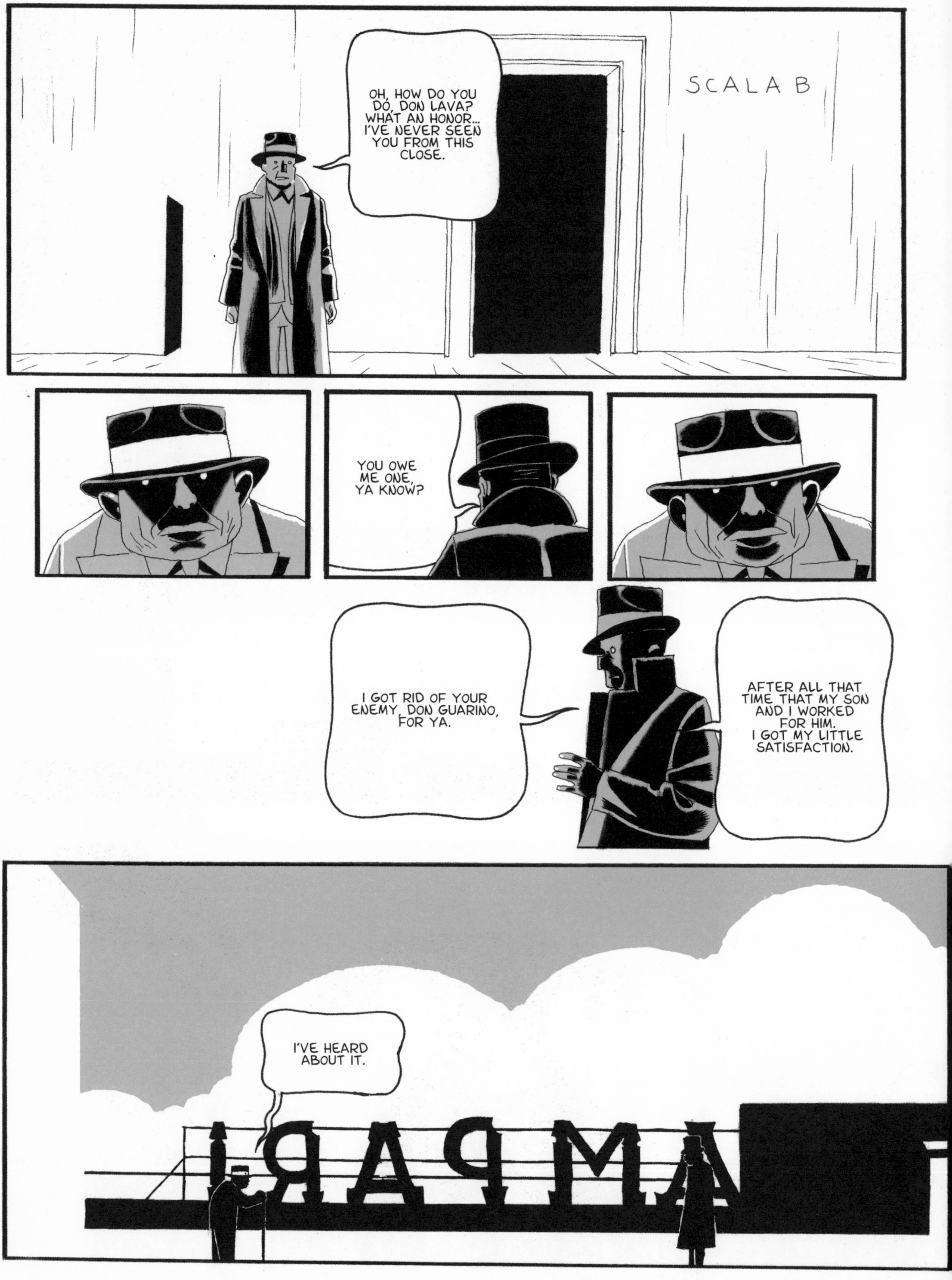
OH, HOW DO YOU DO, DON LAVA? WHAT AN HONOR... I'VE NEVER SEEN YOU FROM THIS CLOSE.
SCALA B
YOU OWE ME ONE, YA KNOW?
I GOT RID OF YOUR ENEMY, DON GUARINO, FOR YA.
AFTER ALL THAT TIME THAT MY SON AND I WORKED FOR HIM. I GOT MY LITTLE SATISFACTION.
I'VE HEARD ABOUT IT.

Y'KNOW? I NEVER DARED TO THINK BIG.

A YESMAN'S LIFE. BAM BAM, ALWAYS SHOOT UNDER SOMEONE ELSE'S ORDERS. WHO COULD HAVE GUESSED THAT I WOULD START ON MY OWN IN MY OLD AGE?

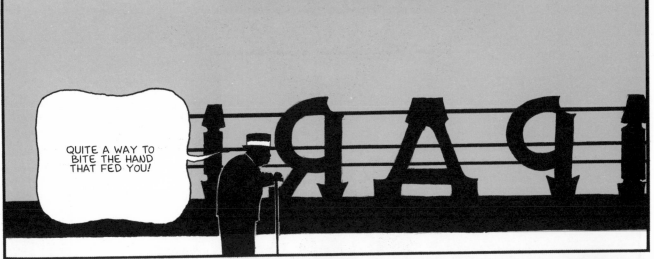

QUITE A WAY TO BITE THE HAND THAT FED YOU!

WELL, BRAVO PÉPPI.

I USED TO GO UP THERE WHEN I WAS A KID. Y'KNOW THAT DON LAVA?

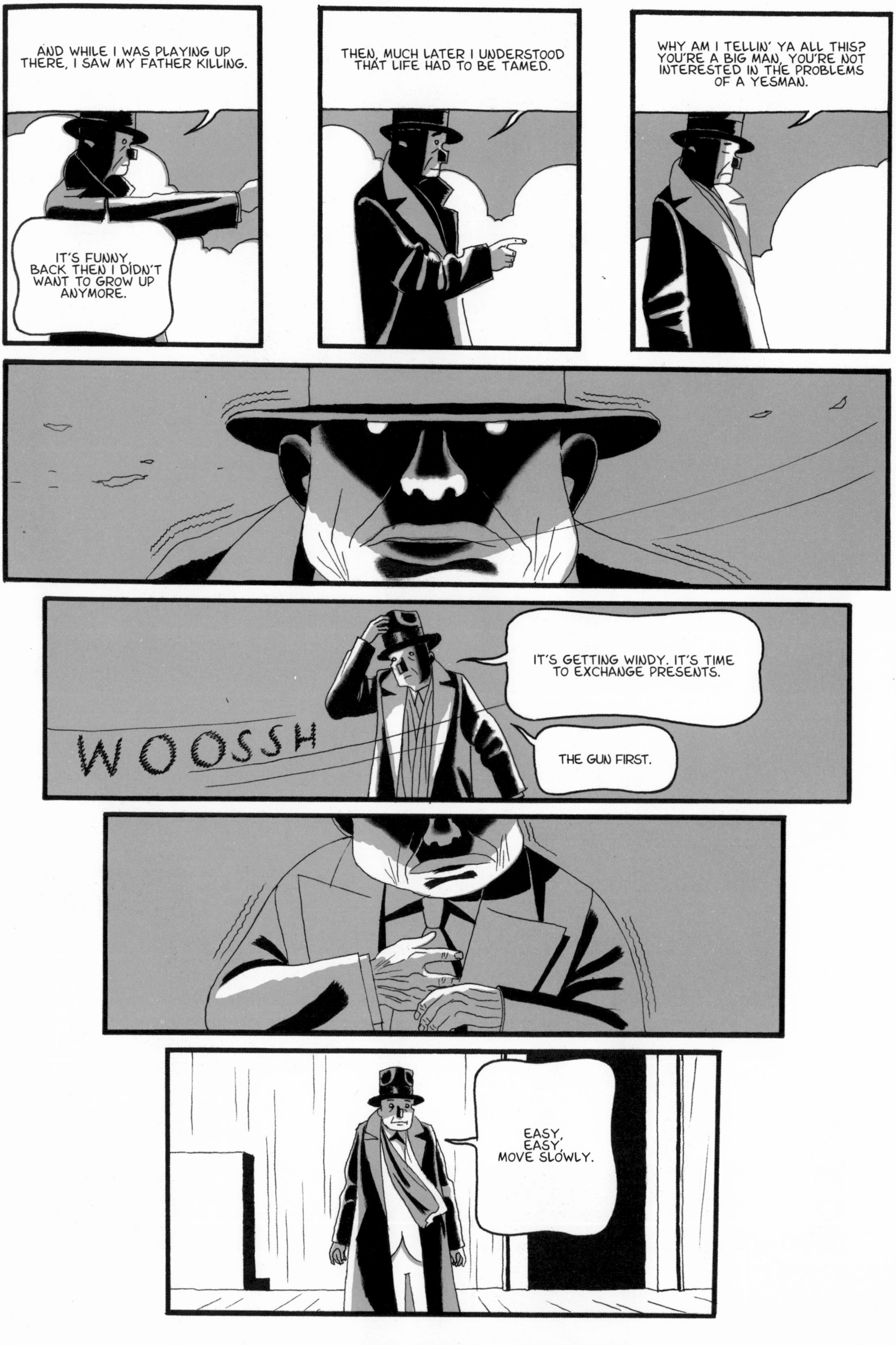
AND WHILE I WAS PLAYING UP THERE, I SAW MY FATHER KILLING.
IT'S FUNNY, BACK THEN I DIDN'T WANT TO GROW UP ANYMORE.
THEN, MUCH LATER I UNDERSTOOD THAT LIFE HAD TO BE TAMED.
WHY AM I TELLIN' YA ALL THIS? YOU'RE A BIG MAN, YOU'RE NOT INTERESTED IN THE PROBLEMS OF A YESMAN.
WOOSSH
IT'S GETTING WINDY. IT'S TIME TO EXCHANGE PRESENTS.
THE GUN FIRST.
EASY, EASY, MOVE SLOWLY.

YOU'LL HAVE TO FORGIVE ME BUT I MUST ASK YOU TO PUT THE GUN DOWN SLOWLY ON THE GROUND. JUST LIKE THAT. PUT IT DOWN AND MOVE AWAY, DON LAVA.

I WANT TO SEE MY NEPHEW.

SCALA **A**

YOU'LL SEE HIM, DON LAVA, YOU'RE GONNA SEE THAT SPOILED BRAT NEPHEW OF YOURS.

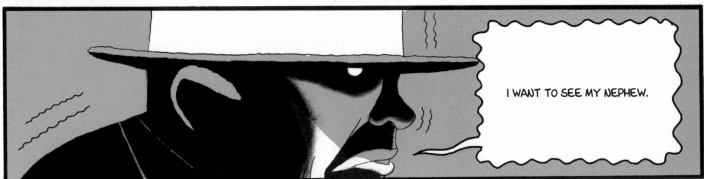

IF ANYTHING HAPPENED TO HIM I'M GONNA TEAR OUT YOUR EYES WITH MY BARE HANDS.

LET IN THAT BASTARD WHO KILLED MY SON.

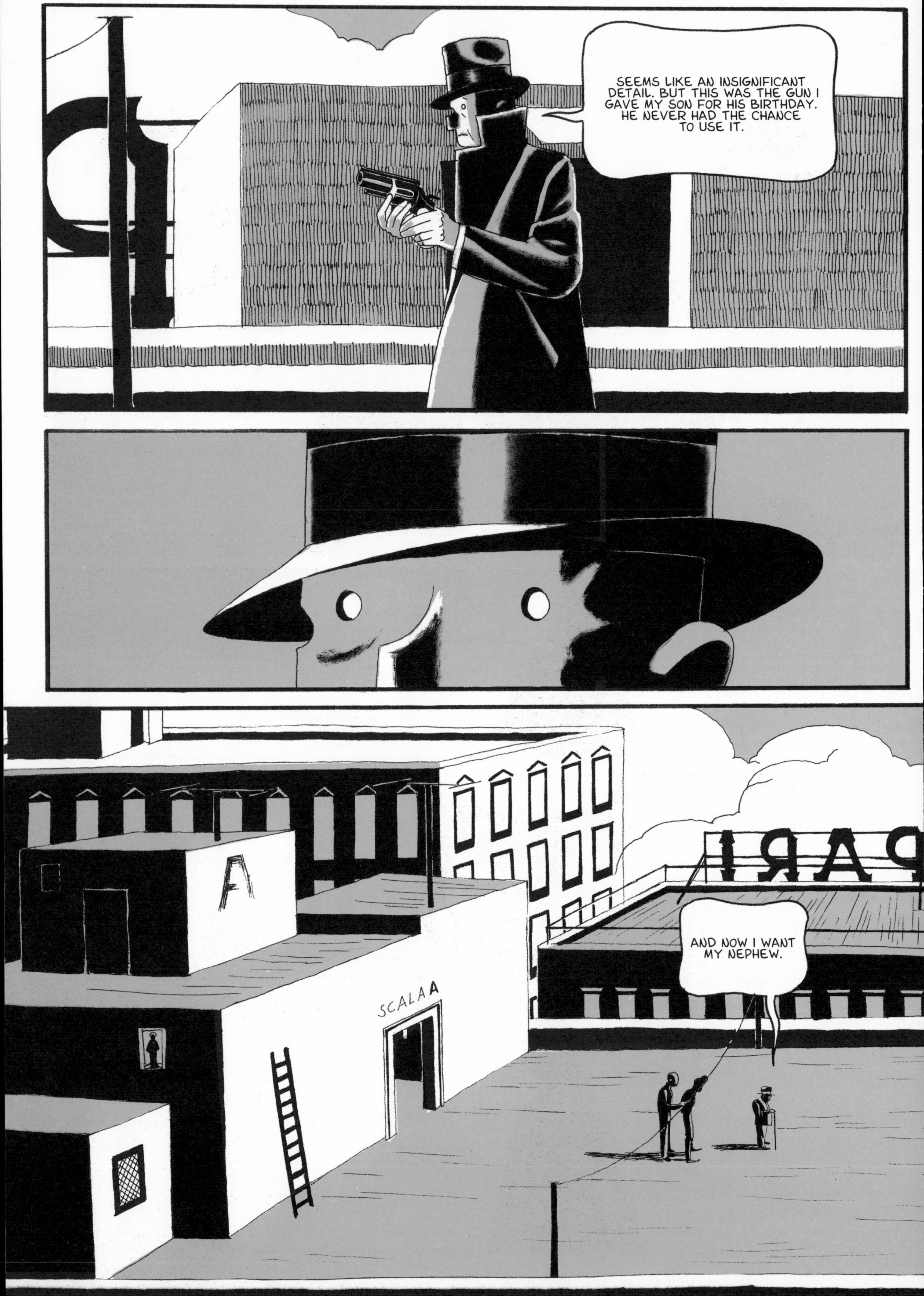
SEEMS LIKE AN INSIGNIFICANT DETAIL. BUT THIS WAS THE GUN I GAVE MY SON FOR HIS BIRTHDAY. HE NEVER HAD THE CHANCE TO USE IT.
A
SCALA A
AND NOW I WANT MY NEPHEW.

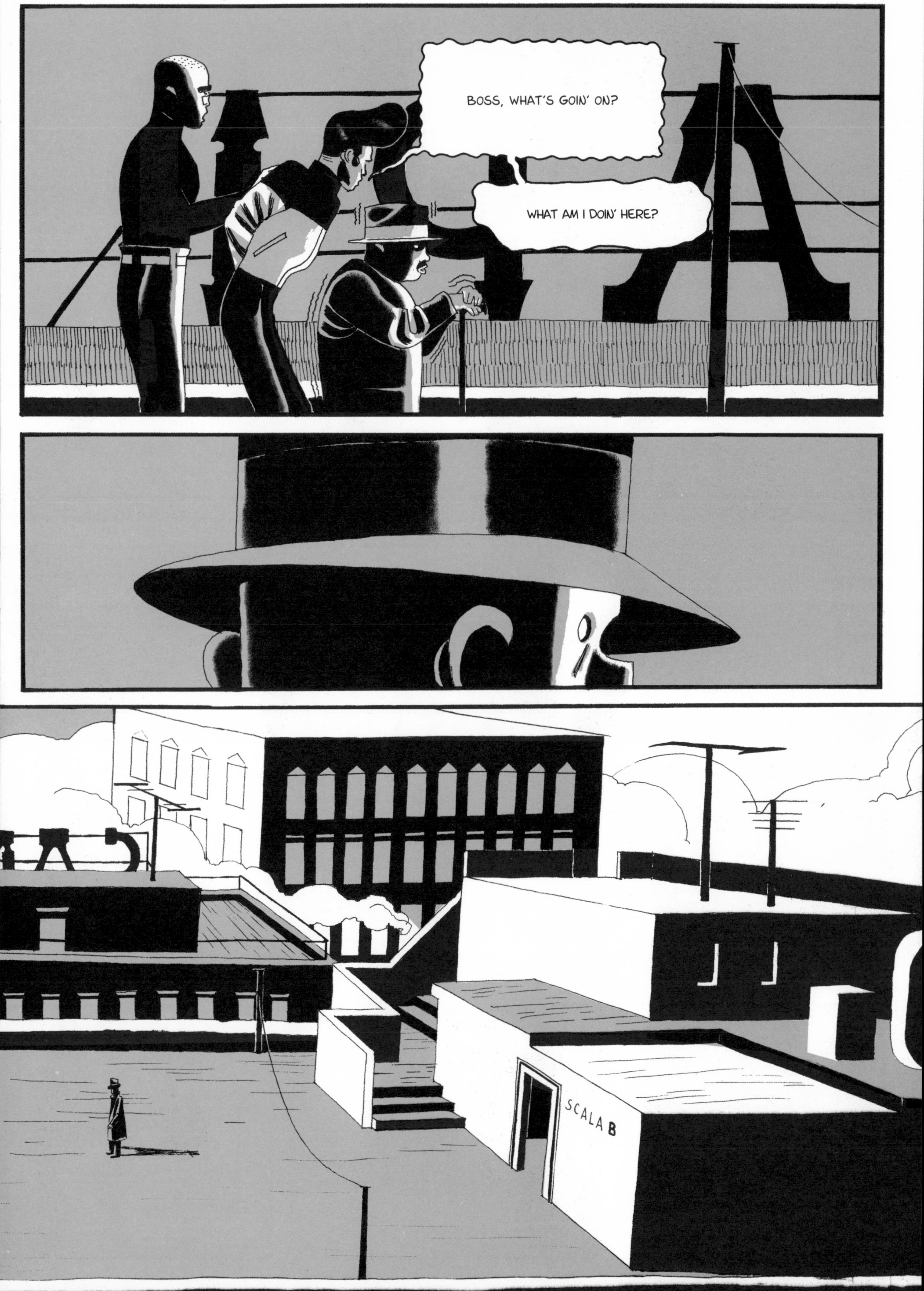
BOSS, WHAT'S GOIN' ON?
WHAT AM I DOIN' HERE?
SCALA B

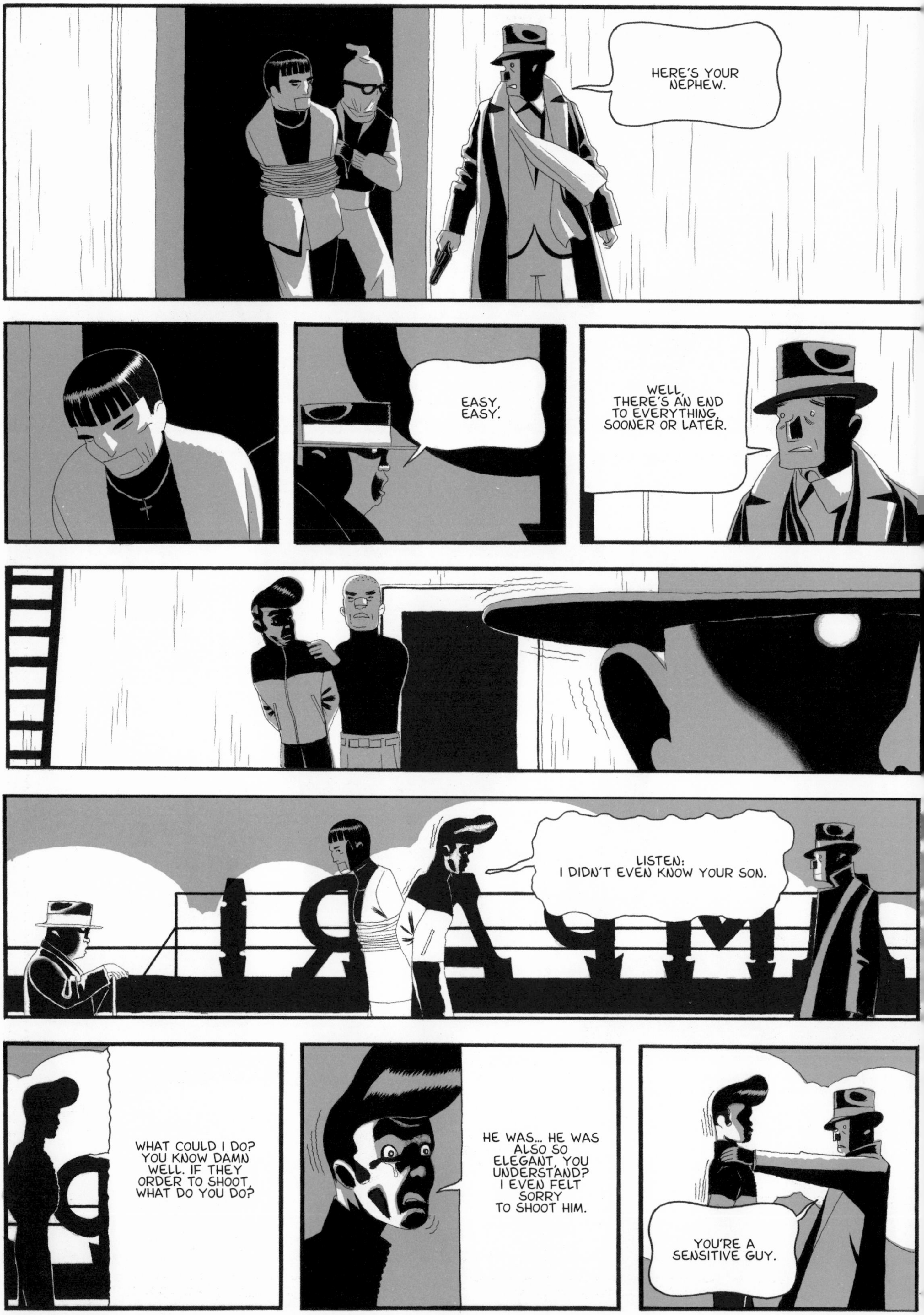
HERE'S YOUR NEPHEW.
EASY, EASY.
WELL, THERE'S AN END TO EVERYTHING SOONER OR LATER.
LISTEN: I DIDN'T EVEN KNOW YOUR SON.
WHAT COULD I DO? YOU KNOW DAMN WELL. IF THEY ORDER TO SHOOT, WHAT DO YOU DO?
HE WAS... HE WAS ALSO SO ELEGANT, YOU UNDERSTAND? I EVEN FELT SORRY TO SHOOT HIM.
YOU'RE A SENSITIVE GUY.

chapter five
5 is the perfect number

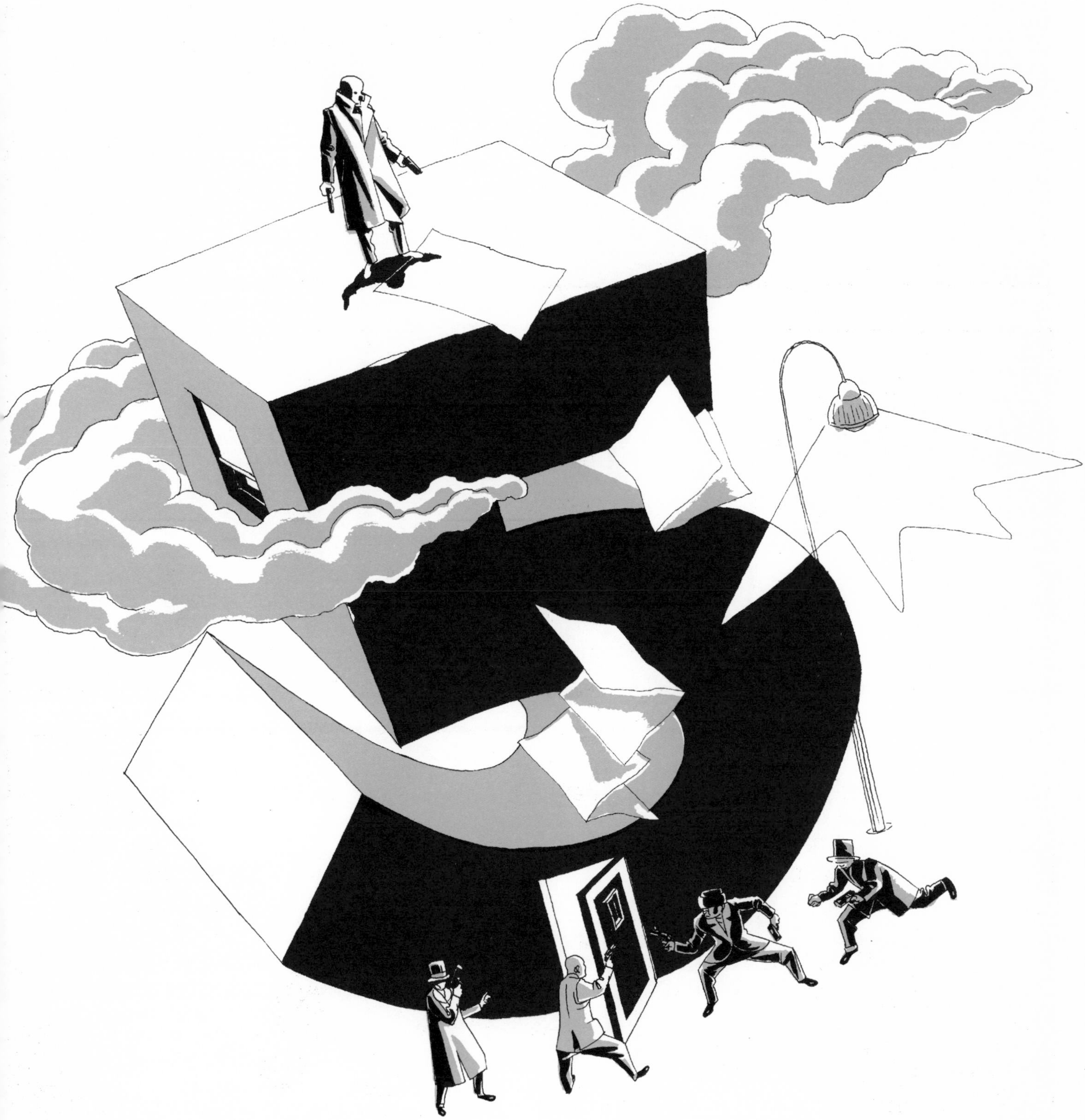

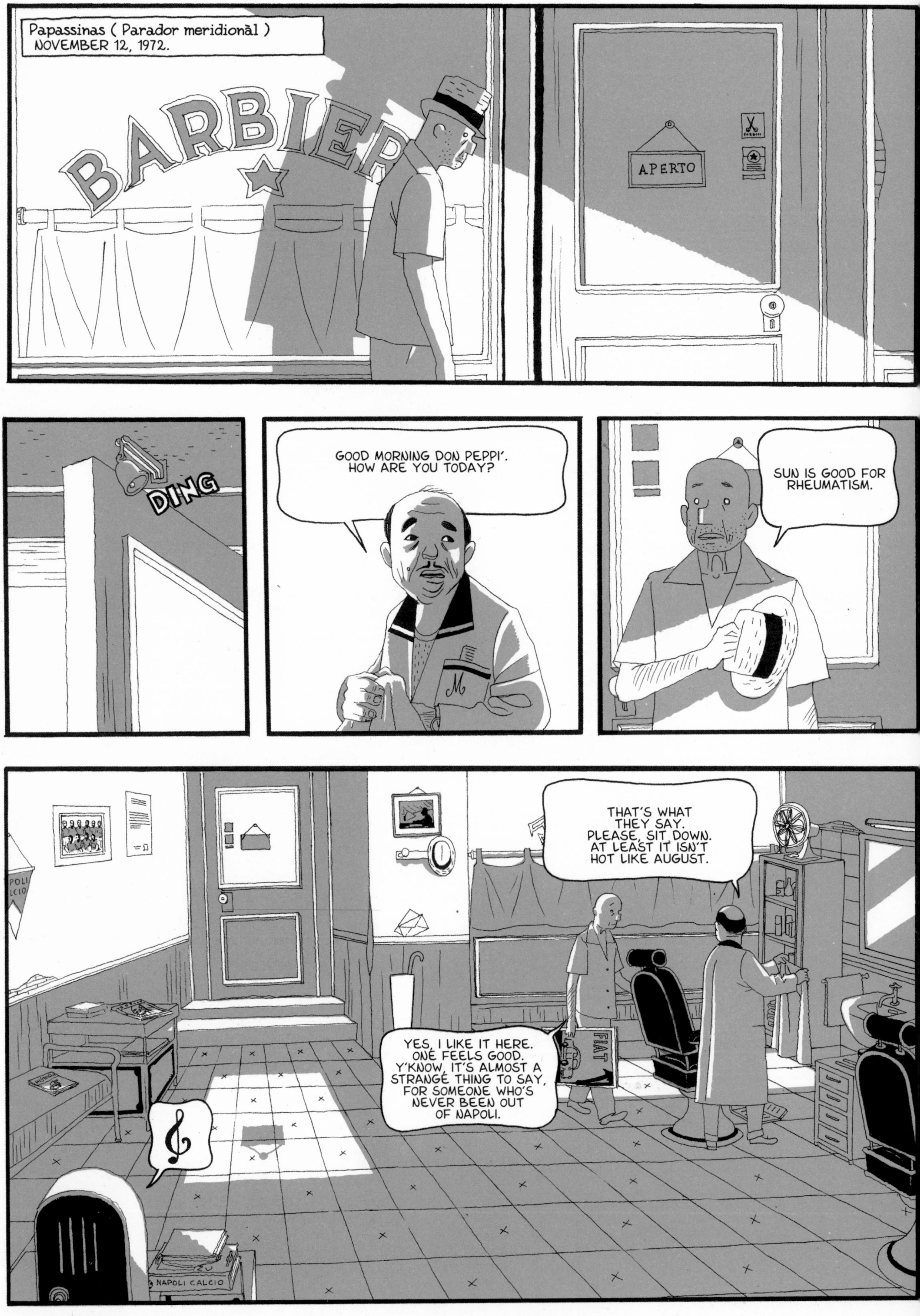
Papassinas (Parador meridionàl)
NOVEMBER 12, 1972.
BARBIER
APERTO
DING
GOOD MORNING DON PEPPI'. HOW ARE YOU TODAY?
SUN IS GOOD FOR RHEUMATISM.
THAT'S WHAT THEY SAY. PLEASE, SIT DOWN. AT LEAST IT ISN'T HOT LIKE AUGUST.
YES, I LIKE IT HERE. ONE FEELS GOOD. Y'KNOW, IT'S ALMOST A STRANGE THING TO SAY, FOR SOMEONE WHO'S NEVER BEEN OUT OF NAPOLI.
FIAT
NAPOLI CALCIO

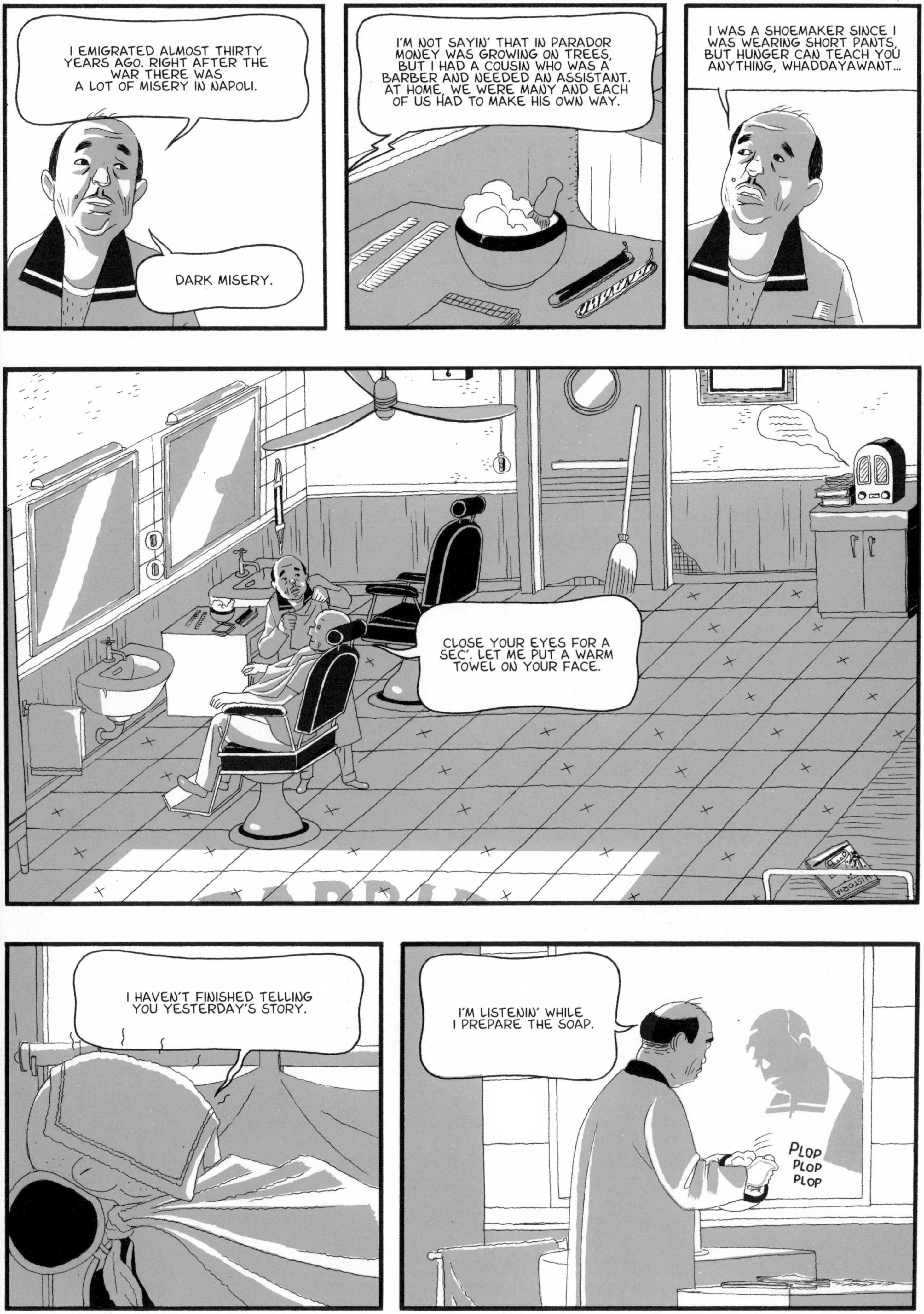
I EMIGRATED ALMOST THIRTY YEARS AGO. RIGHT AFTER THE WAR THERE WAS A LOT OF MISERY IN NAPOLI.
DARK MISERY.
I'M NOT SAYIN' THAT IN PARADOR MONEY WAS GROWING ON TREES, BUT I HAD A COUSIN WHO WAS A BARBER AND NEEDED AN ASSISTANT. AT HOME, WE WERE MANY AND EACH OF US HAD TO MAKE HIS OWN WAY.
I WAS A SHOEMAKER SINCE I WAS WEARING SHORT PANTS, BUT HUNGER CAN TEACH YOU ANYTHING, WHADDAYAWANT...
CLOSE YOUR EYES FOR A SEC'. LET ME PUT A WARM TOWEL ON YOUR FACE.
HISTORIA
I HAVEN'T FINISHED TELLING YOU YESTERDAY'S STORY.
I'M LISTENIN' WHILE I PREPARE THE SOAP.
PLOP
PLOP
PLOP

As I wuz sayin' to you, I did my best to get the man who killed my son delivered to me. That was a pretty delicate moment. One prisoner exchange outta three usually ends up in bloodshed.

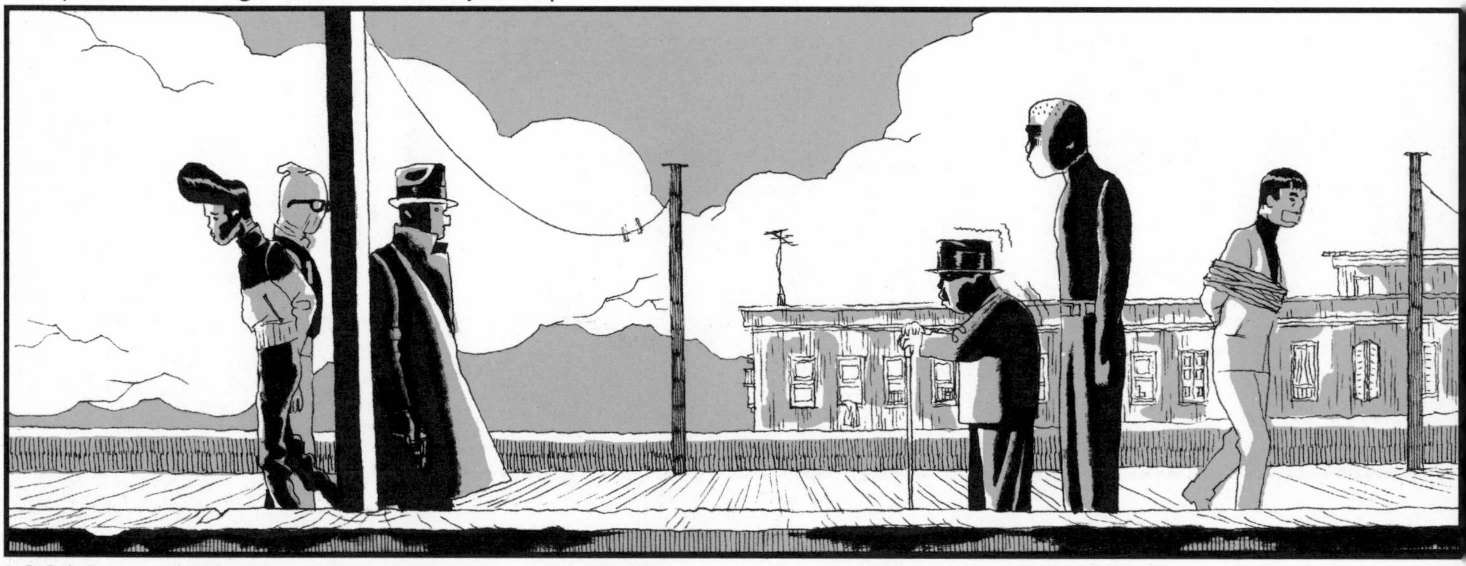

I didn't know it at the time, but it was a set-up; in the building across the street they were getting ready for an ambush. Did I tell ya who gave me back my man? Was Don Lava in person, the boss of the Spanish quarters.

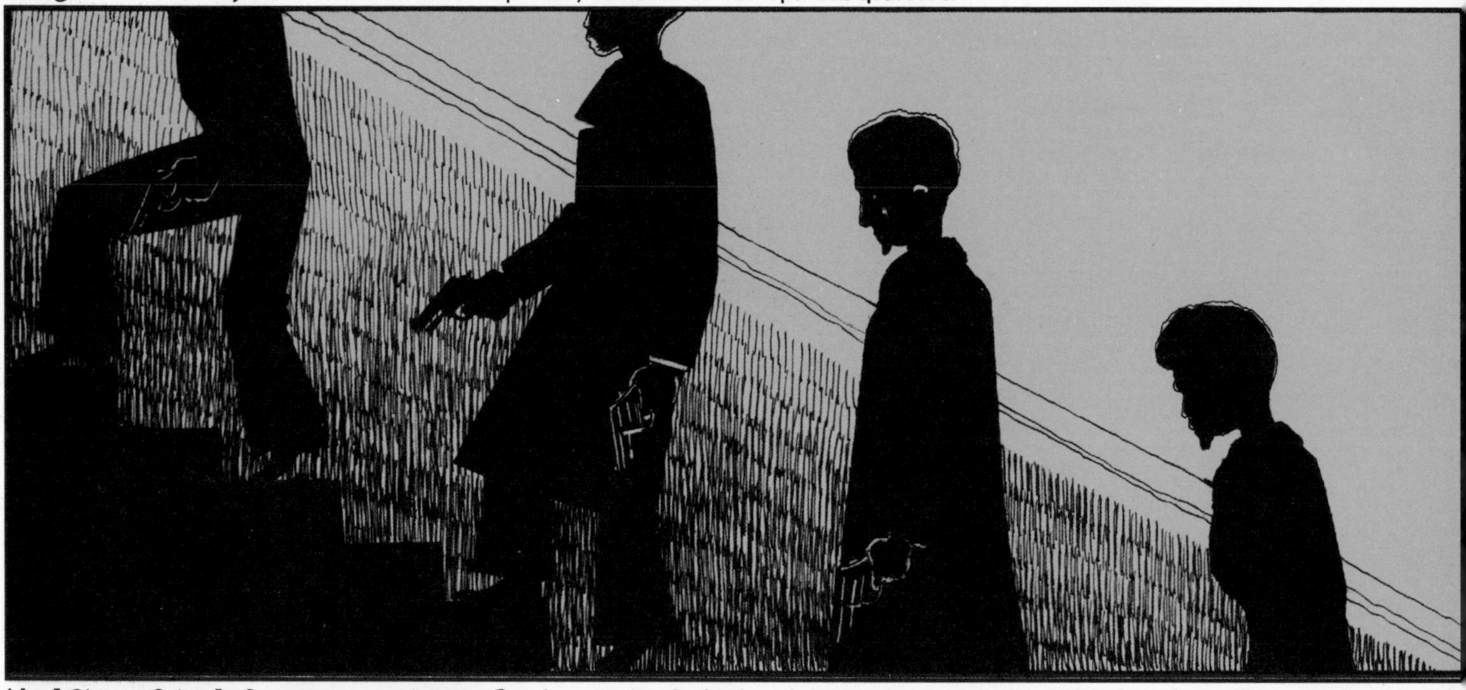

I had Ciro, a friend of my son, covering me. Don Lava got a fuckin' zealot. We were watching each other doggedly, we were really exposed, an easy target.

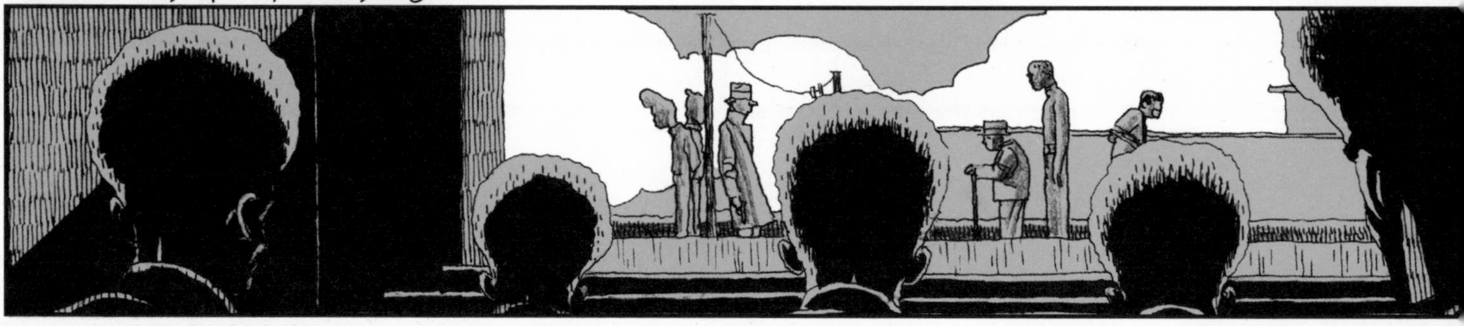

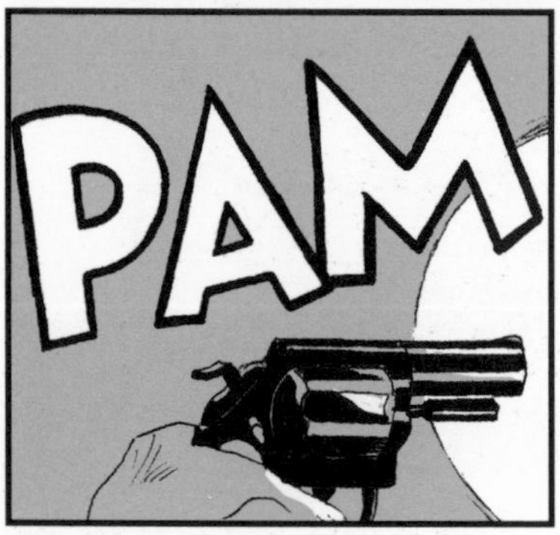
PAM

They started to shoot from the opposite building. We were so close that they were using revolvers. It was Don Lava they wanted to ice, I was just an insignificant detail.

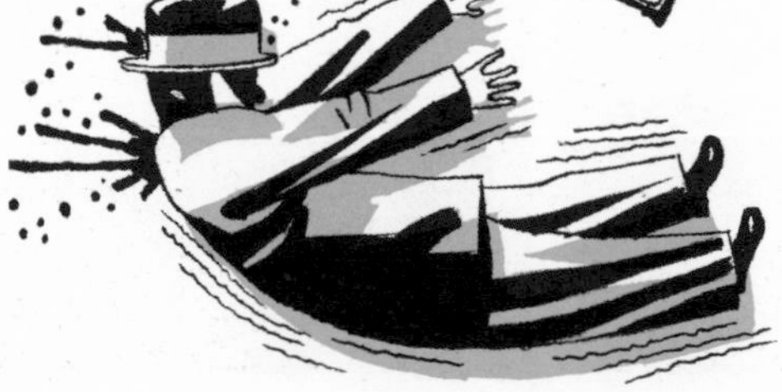

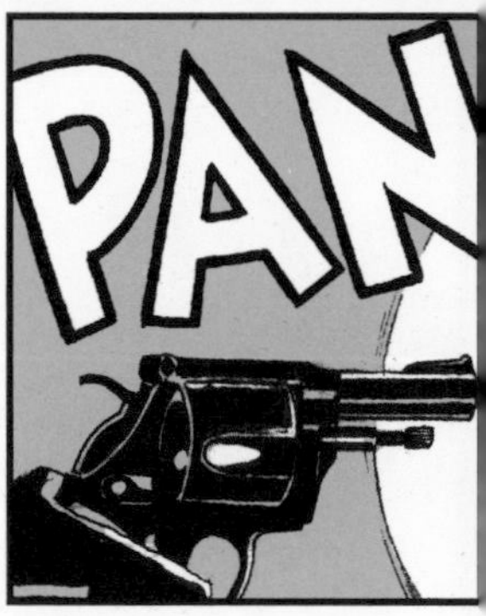
PAM

To make a long story short; I went down, besides tearing my trench coat, I got nothing. Nothin' at all. We escaped by the stairs. We wuz runnin' like mad.

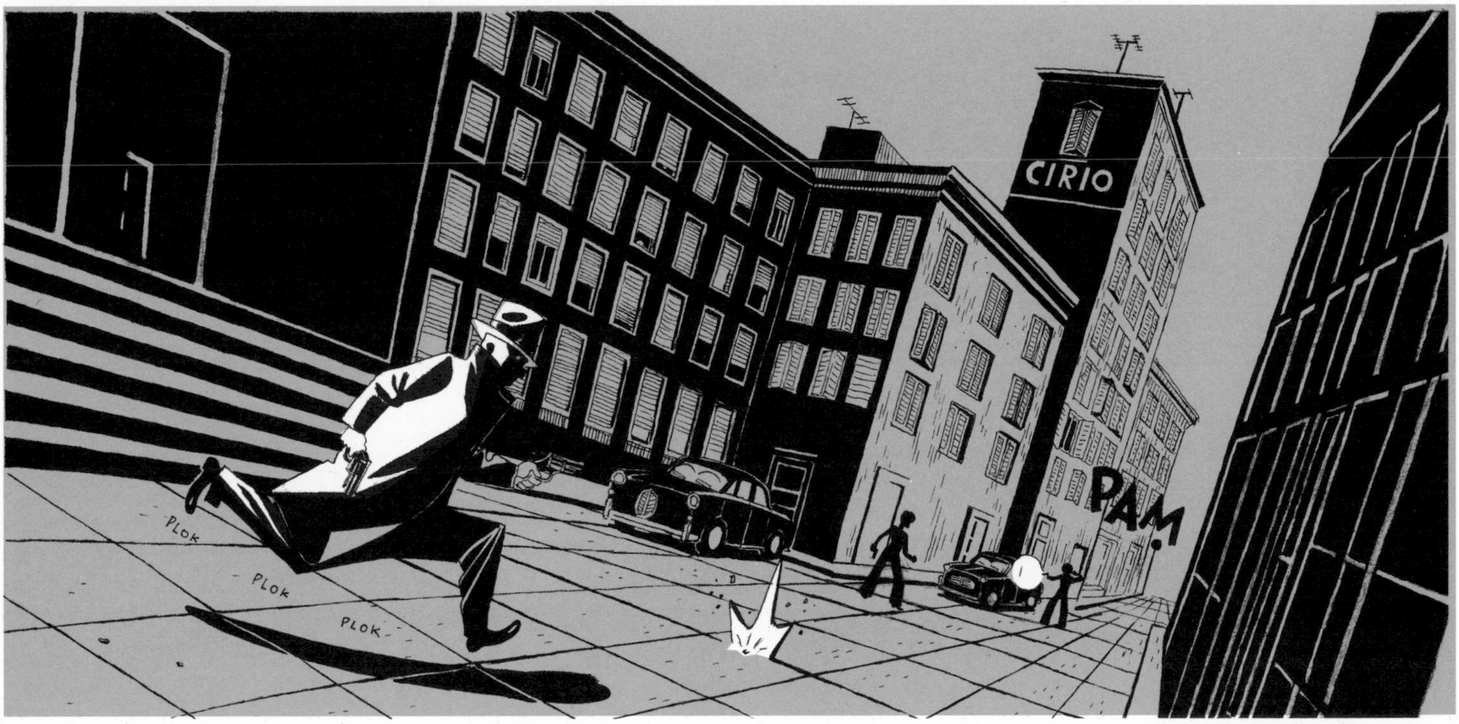
CIRIO
PLOK
PLOK
PLOK
PAM

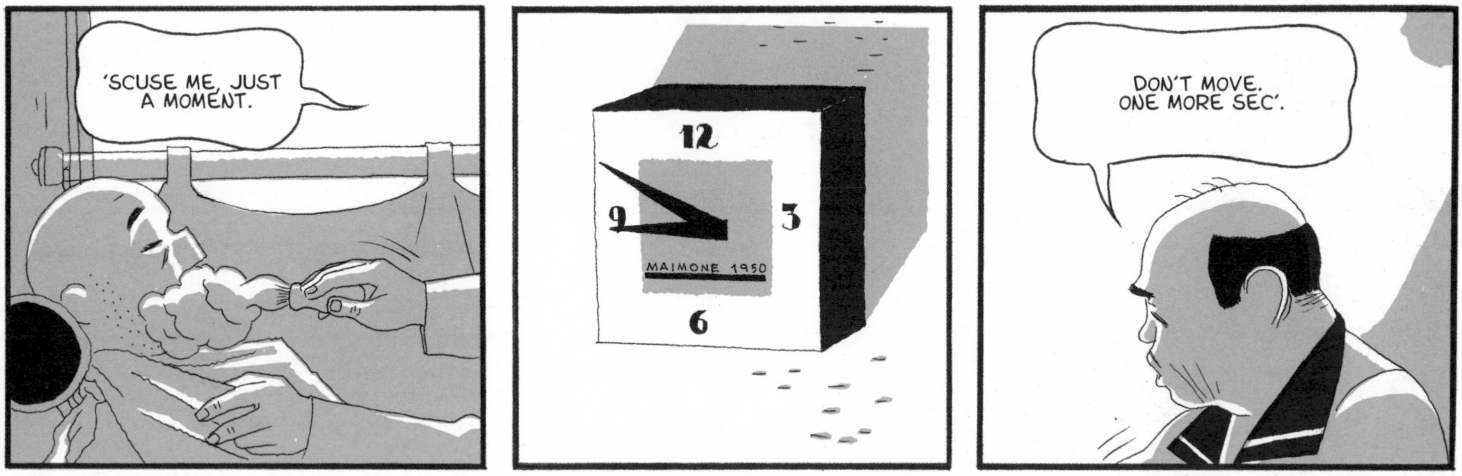
'SCUSE ME, JUST A MOMENT.
12
9
3
6
MAIMONE 1950
DON'T MOVE. ONE MORE SEC'.

Once outtathere, we decided to go in different directions. For me, things turned out bad. I was stuck, I couldn't run, there were armed men all over the place. I thought...

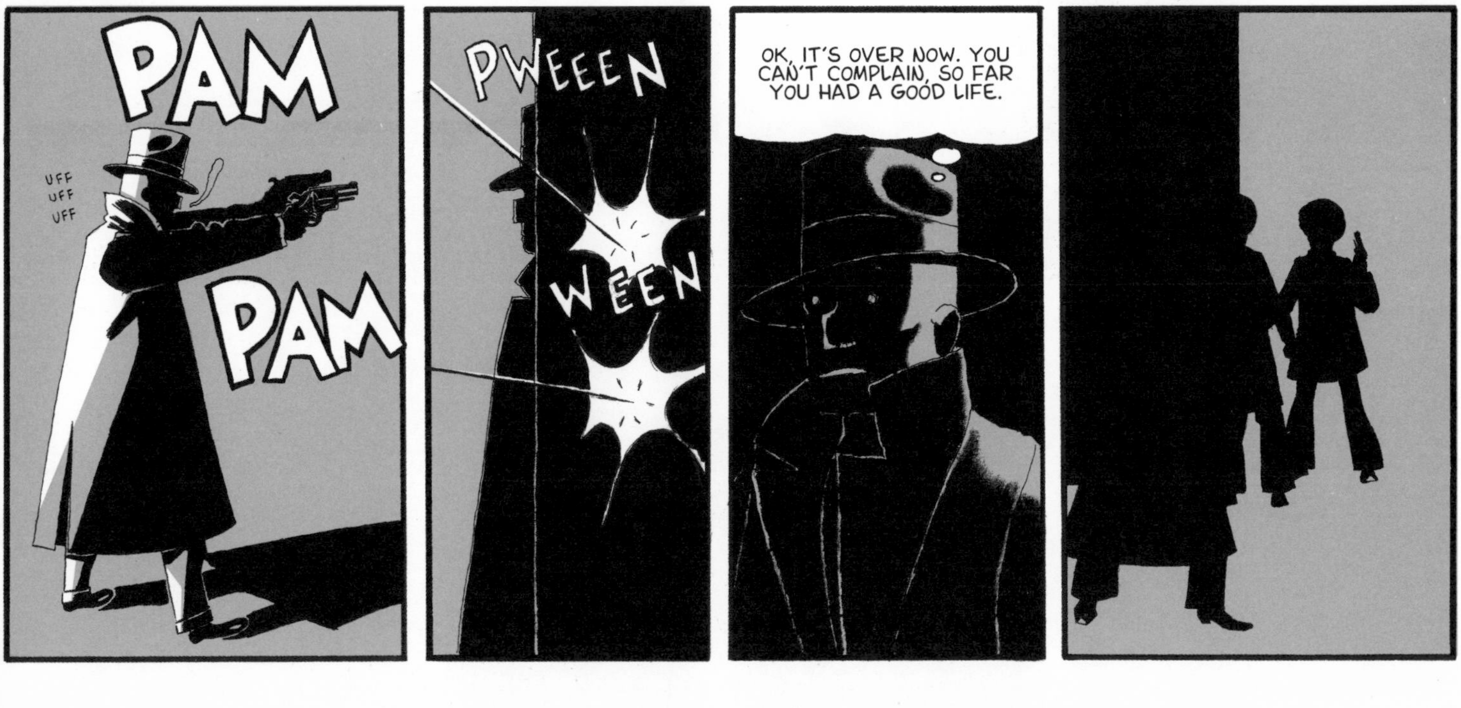
PAM
UFF
UFF
UFF
PAM
PWEEEN
WEEN
OK, IT'S OVER NOW. YOU CAN'T COMPLAIN, SO FAR YOU HAD A GOOD LIFE.

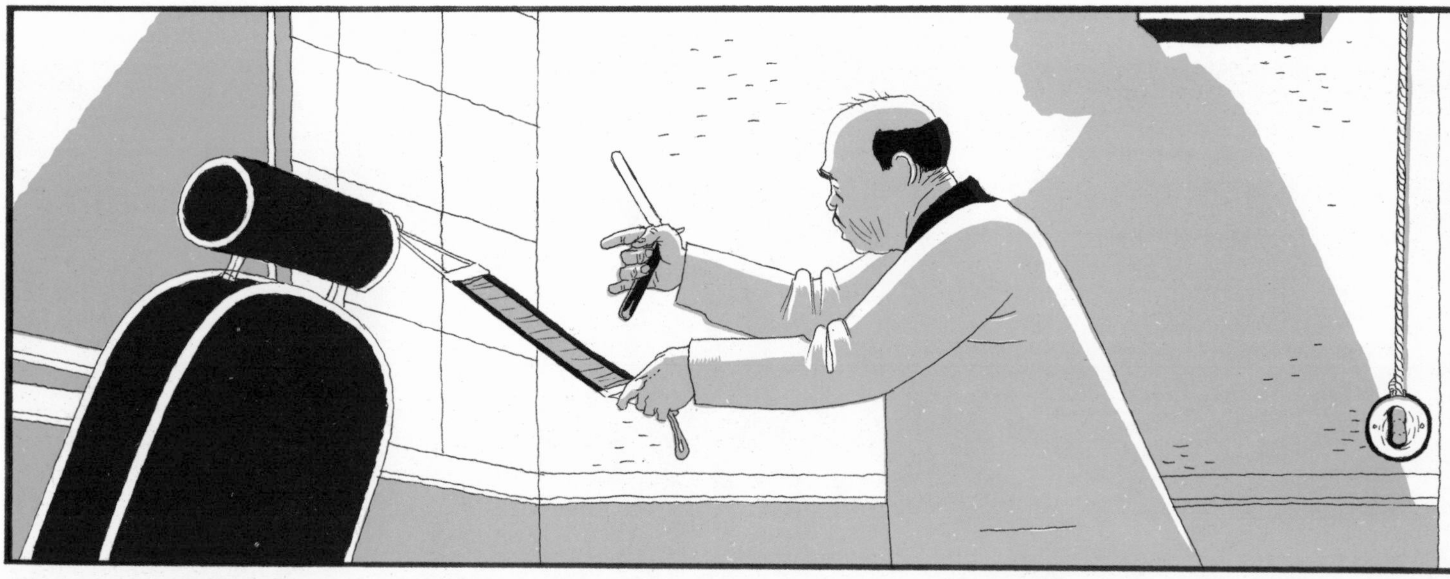

I was lost. Then, a car arrived at full speed and created some confusion. The killers jumped to the side, so they wouldn't get run over. The car was my son Nino's bianchina. But it couldn't have been him, that's for sure. It's clear as day, dead people don't drive cars.

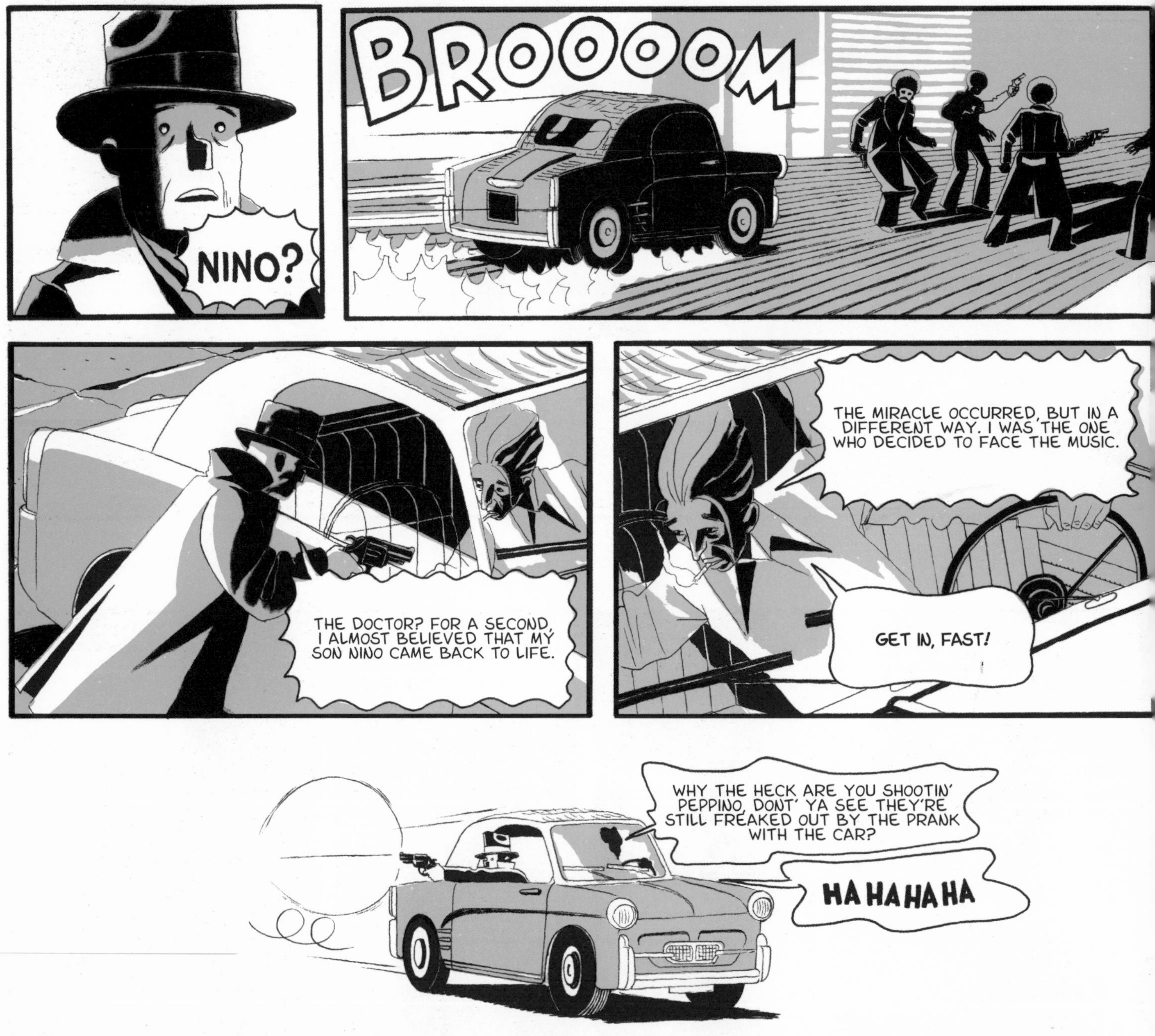
NINO?
BROOOOM
THE DOCTOR? FOR A SECOND, I ALMOST BELIEVED THAT MY SON NINO CAME BACK TO LIFE.
THE MIRACLE OCCURRED, BUT IN A DIFFERENT WAY. I WAS THE ONE WHO DECIDED TO FACE THE MUSIC.
GET IN, FAST!
WHY THE HECK ARE YOU SHOOTIN' PEPPINO, DONT' YA SEE THEY'RE STILL FREAKED OUT BY THE PRANK WITH THE CAR?
HA HA HA HA

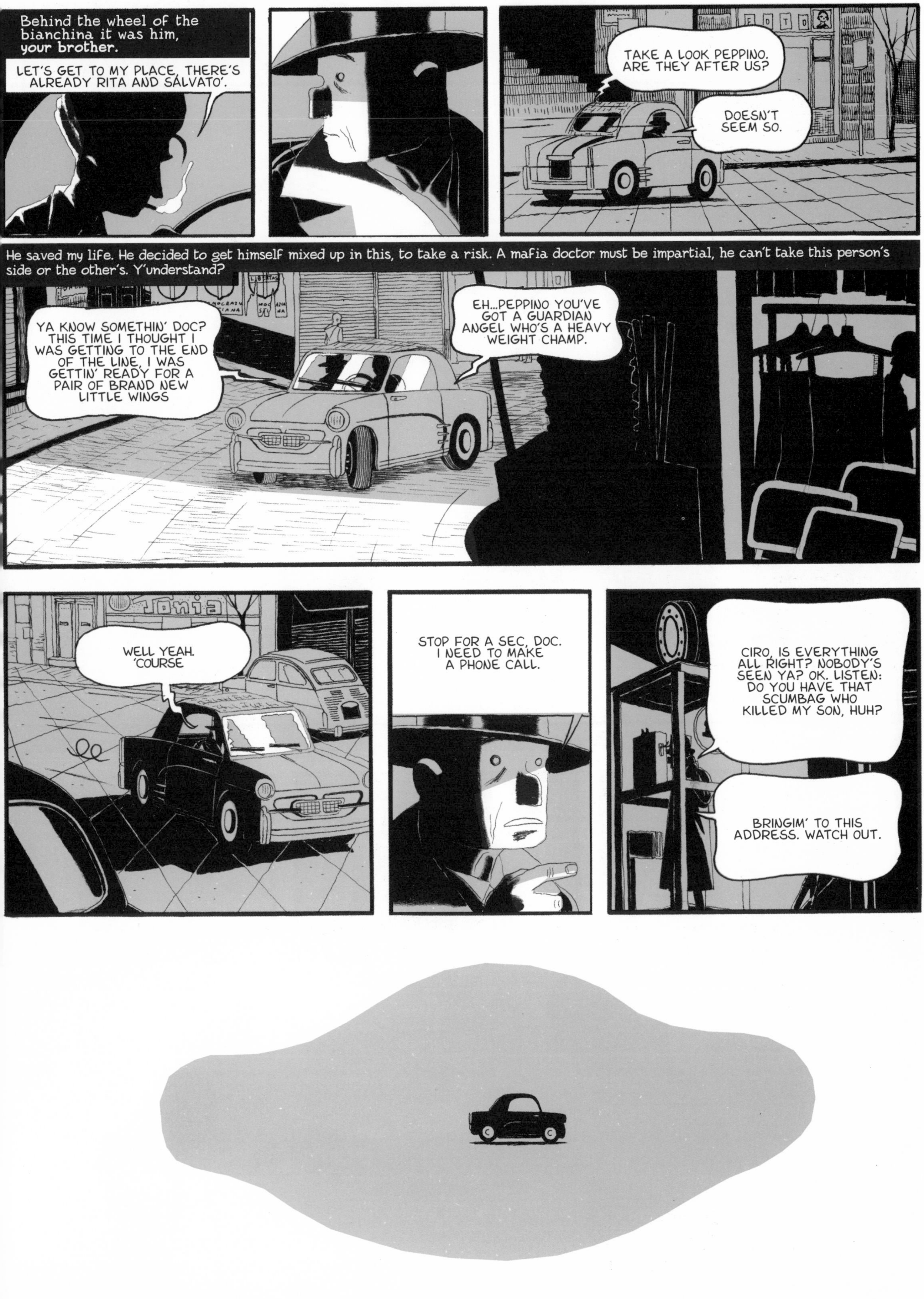
Behind the wheel of the bianchina it was him, your brother.
LET'S GET TO MY PLACE, THERE'S ALREADY RITA AND SALVATO'.
TAKE A LOOK PEPPINO. ARE THEY AFTER US?
DOESN'T SEEM SO.
He saved my life. He decided to get himself mixed up in this, to take a risk. A mafia doctor must be impartial, he can't take this person's side or the other's. Y'understand?
YA KNOW SOMETHIN' DOC? THIS TIME I THOUGHT I WAS GETTING TO THE END OF THE LINE, I WAS GETTIN' READY FOR A PAIR OF BRAND NEW LITTLE WINGS
EH...PEPPINO YOU'VE GOT A GUARDIAN ANGEL WHO'S A HEAVY WEIGHT CHAMP.
WELL YEAH. 'COURSE
STOP FOR A SEC, DOC. I NEED TO MAKE A PHONE CALL.
CIRO, IS EVERYTHING ALL RIGHT? NOBODY'S SEEN YA? OK. LISTEN: DO YOU HAVE THAT SCUMBAG WHO KILLED MY SON, HUH?
BRINGIM' TO THIS ADDRESS. WATCH OUT.

Got there, found also Rita and Salvatore. Then finally Ciro arrived with the man who killed my son. Just by looking at him, I could tell he wasn't even a man, he looked like he was still in diapers. Shit. If it wasn't for that fucking rock' n' roll hairdo I would have thought he was sixteen years old, more or less. I was trying to force myself into thinkin' that thanks to this little cocksucker my son Nino was riddled with lead.
IT'S TIME FOR THE LAST CIGARETTE.
RITA, CALM DOWN.
PHILCO
linus
L'EUROPEO
ATLAS
I was there, I had him at gunpoint, I could just go bam and I was done, feeling lighter. I had to get my revenge, what else?
ZKFF
FFF
FREEZE!

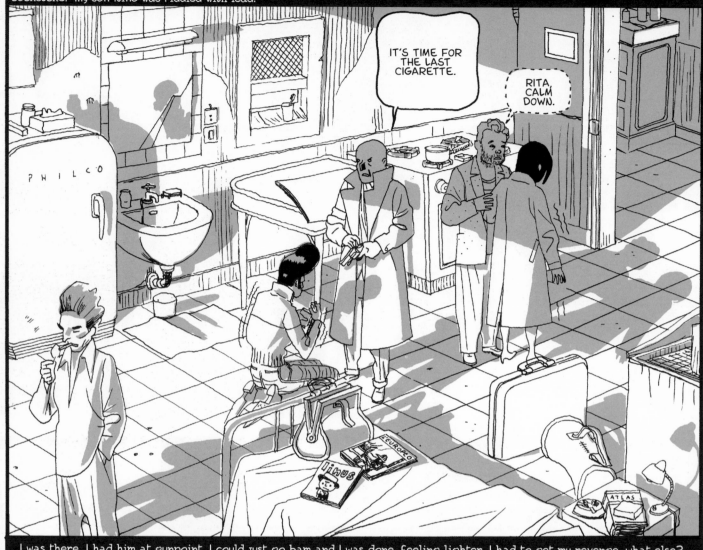

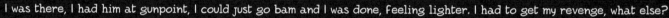

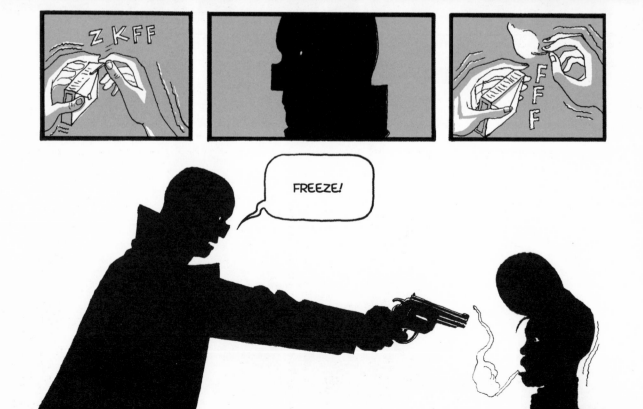

At your brother's place, the atmosphere was pretty heavy. He was there, smoking nervously. I don't think he liked the situation. Nobody did. Life can sometimes get you in the gut.

RRCLICK

NOPE

NOPE

I just couldn't. I looked the scumbag who killed my son straight in the eyes and told him:

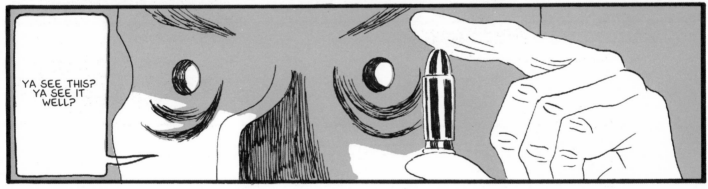

YA SEE THIS? YA SEE IT WELL?

THIS IS THE HAND YOU KILLED MY SON NINO WITH.

THIS IS THE BULLET THAT SHOULD HAVE KILLED YOU. TAKE IT. NOW SCRAM. I DON'T WANT TO SMELL YOUR STENCH ANY LONGER. GETOUTTA HERE.

SCRAM! I DON'T WANT TO SMELL YOUR STENCH ANY LONGER. GET OUTTA HERE!!!

I can still hear the words as if it wasn't me who uttered them.

IL GRANDE TOTO'

HE STOOD THERE STILL, AND KEPT REPEATING: WHAT? WHAT?

I HAD TO THROW HIM OUTTA THERE BY THE PANTS.

WAIT A SEC', DON'T MOVE, THERE'S A SMALL CUT. LET ME PUT SOME "STYPTIC" ON IT TO STOP THE BLEEDING.

MAYBE THIS WAS A TRAGIC MISTAKE. I DUNNO, BUT THE MAGIC WAS GONE. Y'KNOW MICHELE, AT THAT TIME, IT WAS A RELIEF FOR ALL OF US, I GUESS.

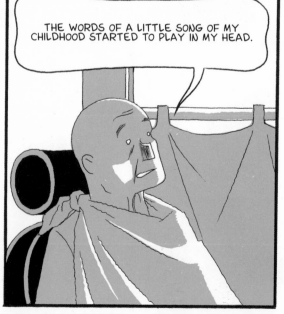

THE WORDS OF A LITTLE SONG OF MY CHILDHOOD STARTED TO PLAY IN MY HEAD.

I BELIEVE I HAD A STUPID SMILE ON MY FACE.

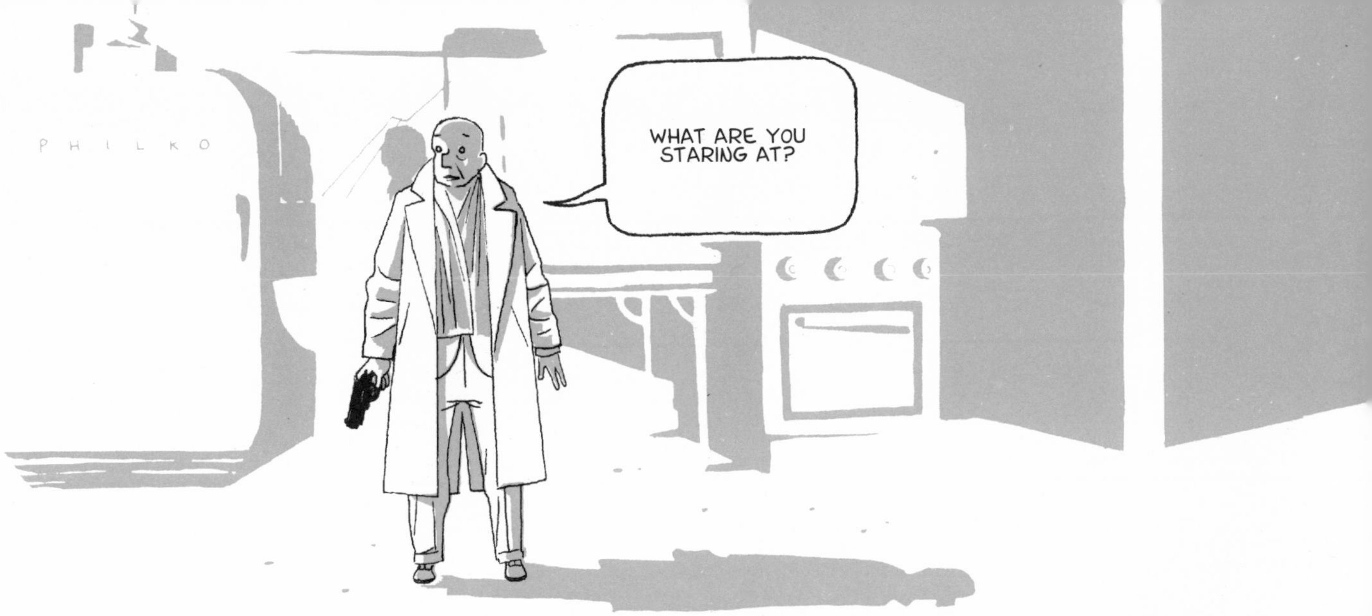
P H I L K O
WHAT ARE YOU STARING AT?

They were staring at me, not a single word was spoken. Heh Heh. I can understand them. Everybody was looking at the closed door; that's where my son's assassin had just made his exit. I had to go through hell to find him and then paff. There was a great silence. Rita was basically still in a panic.

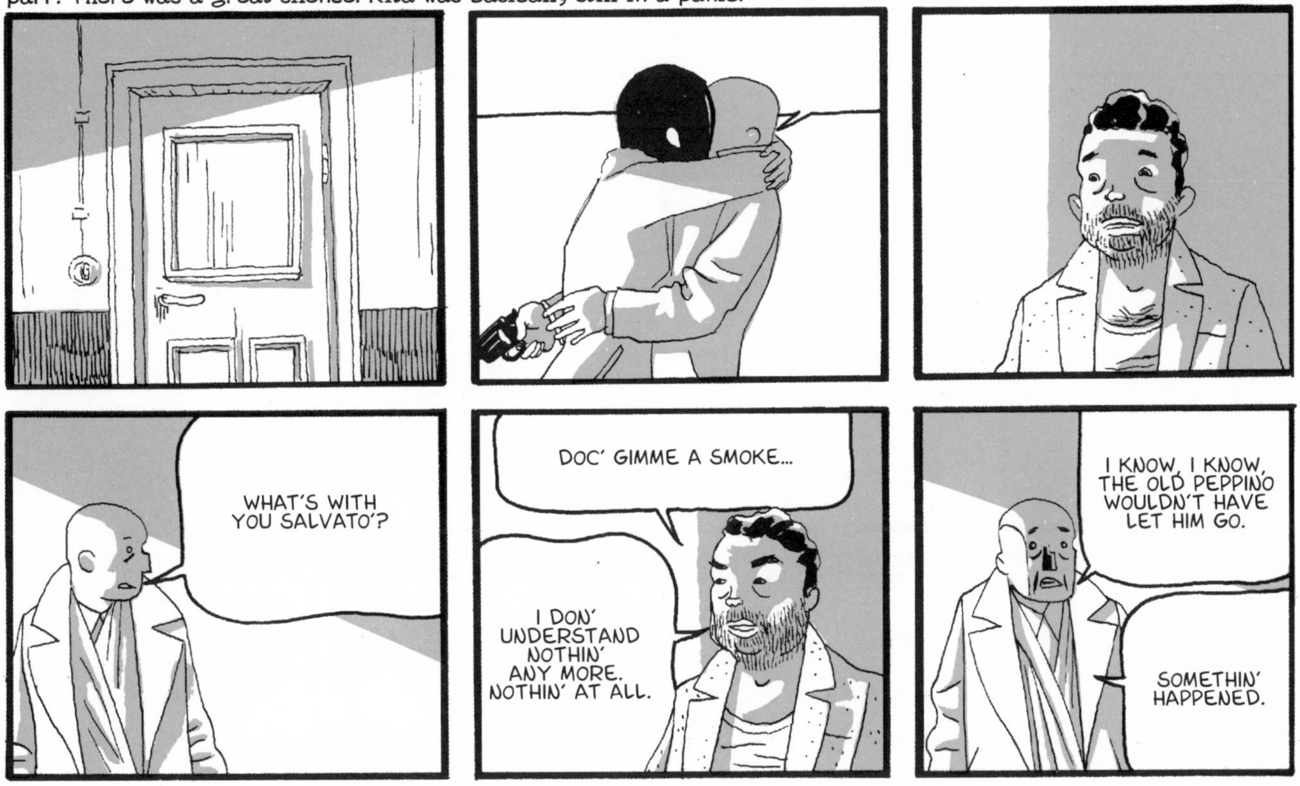
WHAT'S WITH YOU SALVATO'?
DOC' GIMME A SMOKE...
I DON' UNDERSTAND NOTHIN' ANY MORE. NOTHIN' AT ALL.
I KNOW, I KNOW, THE OLD PEPPINO WOULDN'T HAVE LET HIM GO.
SOMETHIN' HAPPENED.

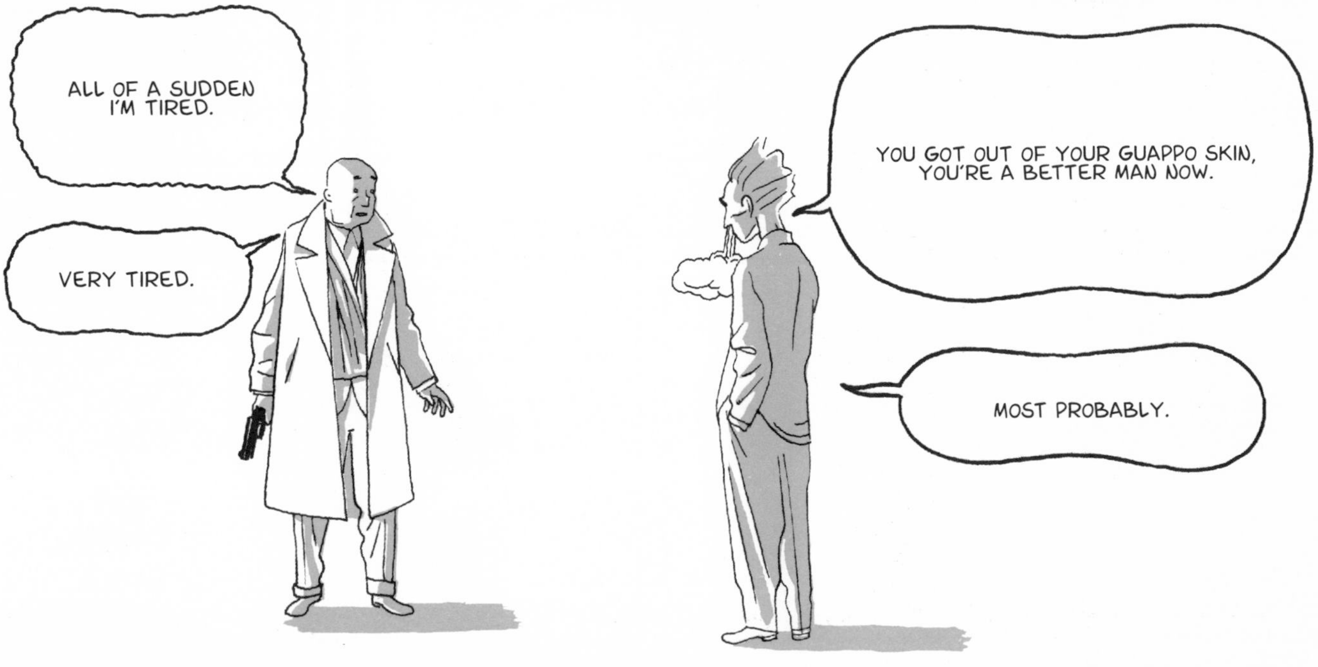
ALL OF A SUDDEN I'M TIRED.
VERY TIRED.
YOU GOT OUT OF YOUR GUAPPO SKIN, YOU'RE A BETTER MAN NOW.
MOST PROBABLY.

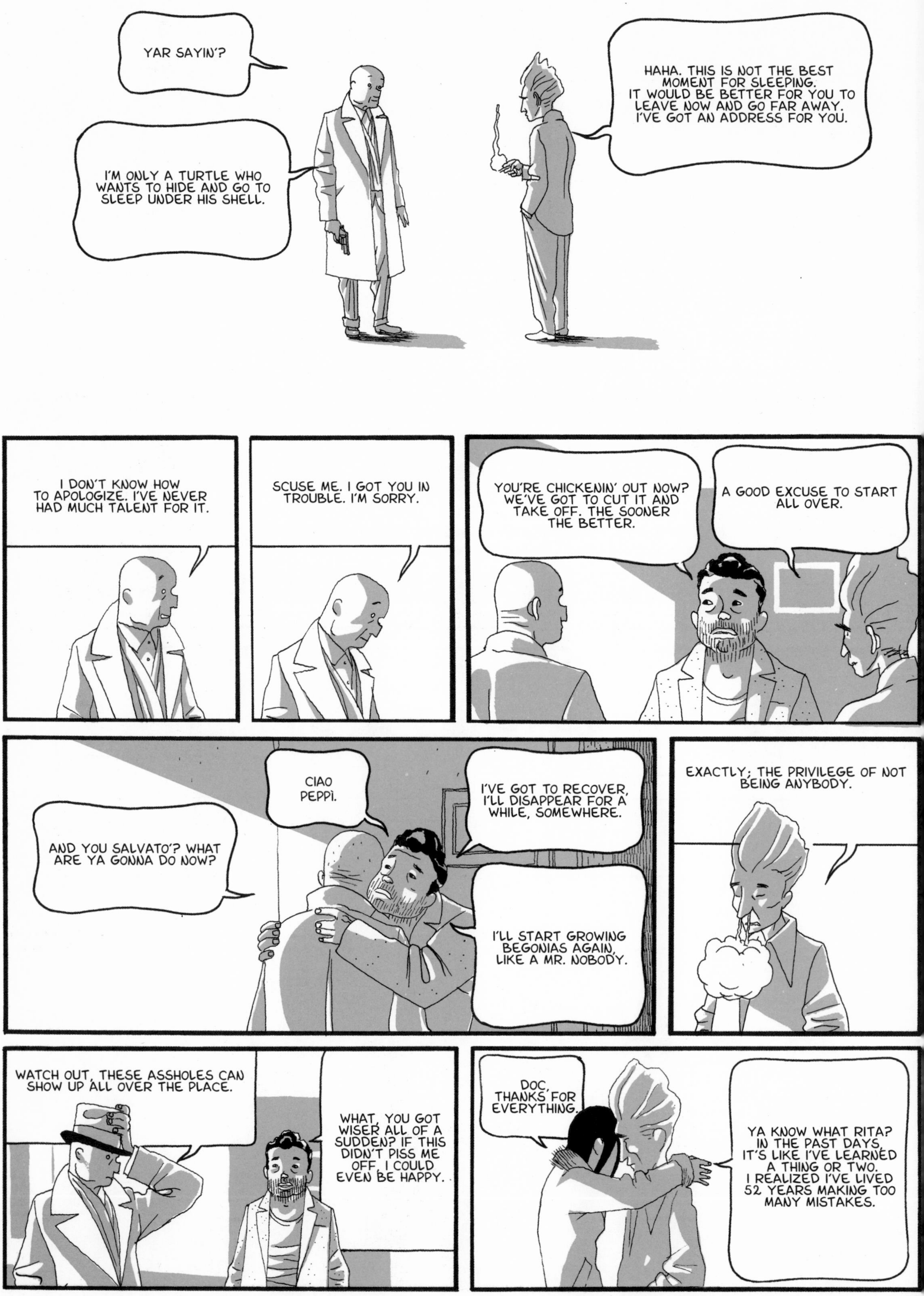
YAR SAYIN'?
I'M ONLY A TURTLE WHO WANTS TO HIDE AND GO TO SLEEP UNDER HIS SHELL.
HAHA. THIS IS NOT THE BEST MOMENT FOR SLEEPING. IT WOULD BE BETTER FOR YOU TO LEAVE NOW AND GO FAR AWAY. I'VE GOT AN ADDRESS FOR YOU.
I DON'T KNOW HOW TO APOLOGIZE. I'VE NEVER HAD MUCH TALENT FOR IT.
SCUSE ME. I GOT YOU IN TROUBLE. I'M SORRY.
YOU'RE CHICKENIN' OUT NOW? WE'VE GOT TO CUT IT AND TAKE OFF. THE SOONER THE BETTER.
A GOOD EXCUSE TO START ALL OVER.
AND YOU SALVATO'? WHAT ARE YA GONNA DO NOW?
CIAO PEPPÌ.
I'VE GOT TO RECOVER, I'LL DISAPPEAR FOR A WHILE, SOMEWHERE.
I'LL START GROWING BEGONIAS AGAIN, LIKE A MR. NOBODY.
EXACTLY; THE PRIVILEGE OF NOT BEING ANYBODY.
WATCH OUT, THESE ASSHOLES CAN SHOW UP ALL OVER THE PLACE.
WHAT, YOU GOT WISER ALL OF A SUDDEN? IF THIS DIDN'T PISS ME OFF, I COULD EVEN BE HAPPY.
DOC, THANKS FOR EVERYTHING.
YA KNOW WHAT RITA? IN THE PAST DAYS, IT'S LIKE I'VE LEARNED A THING OR TWO. I REALIZED I'VE LIVED 52 YEARS MAKING TOO MANY MISTAKES.

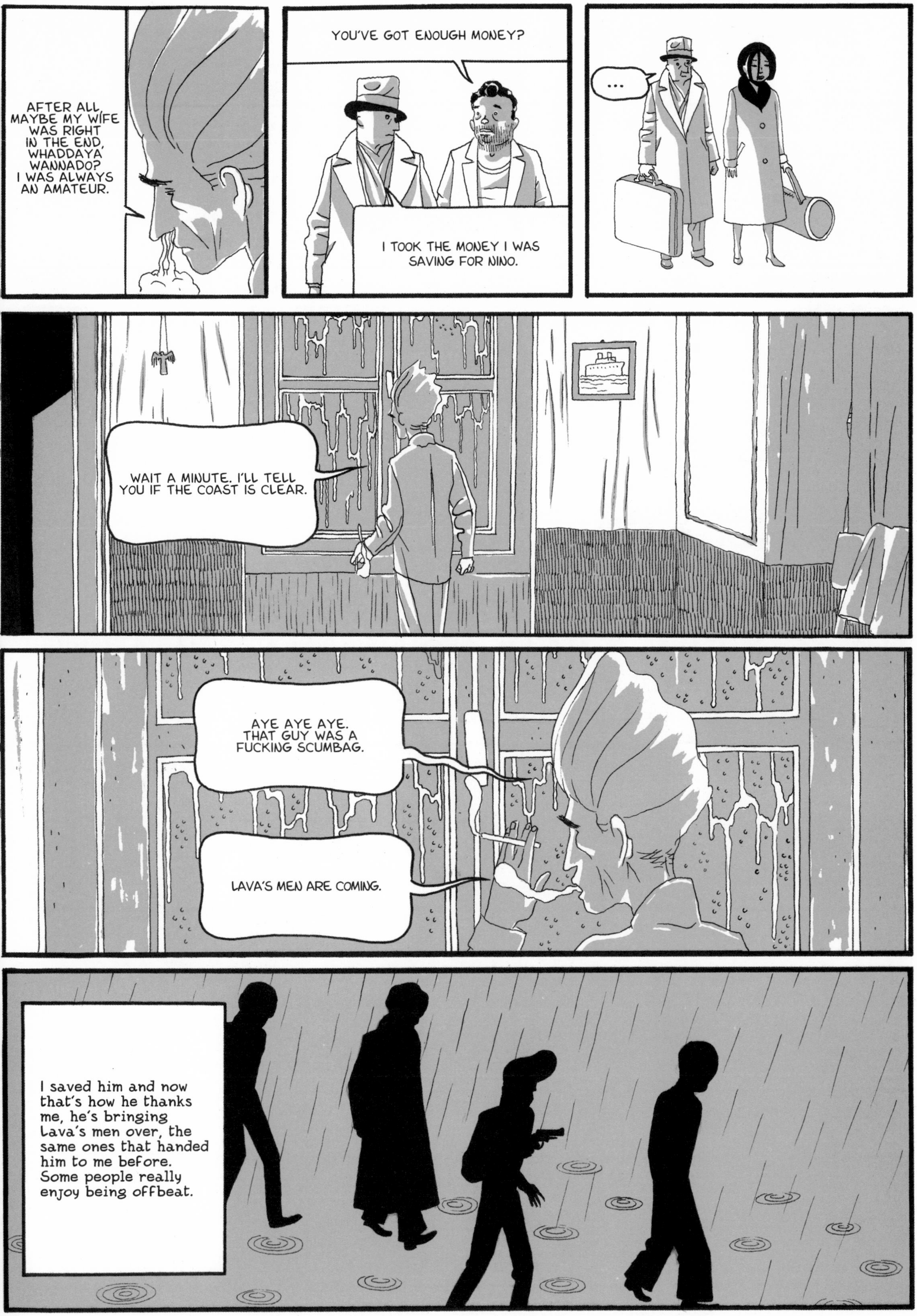
AFTER ALL, MAYBE MY WIFE WAS RIGHT IN THE END, WHADDAYA WANNADO? I WAS ALWAYS AN AMATEUR.
YOU'VE GOT ENOUGH MONEY?
I TOOK THE MONEY I WAS SAVING FOR NINO.
...
WAIT A MINUTE. I'LL TELL YOU IF THE COAST IS CLEAR.
AYE AYE AYE. THAT GUY WAS A FUCKING SCUMBAG.
LAVA'S MEN ARE COMING.
I saved him and now that's how he thanks me, he's bringing Lava's men over, the same ones that handed him to me before. Some people really enjoy being offbeat.

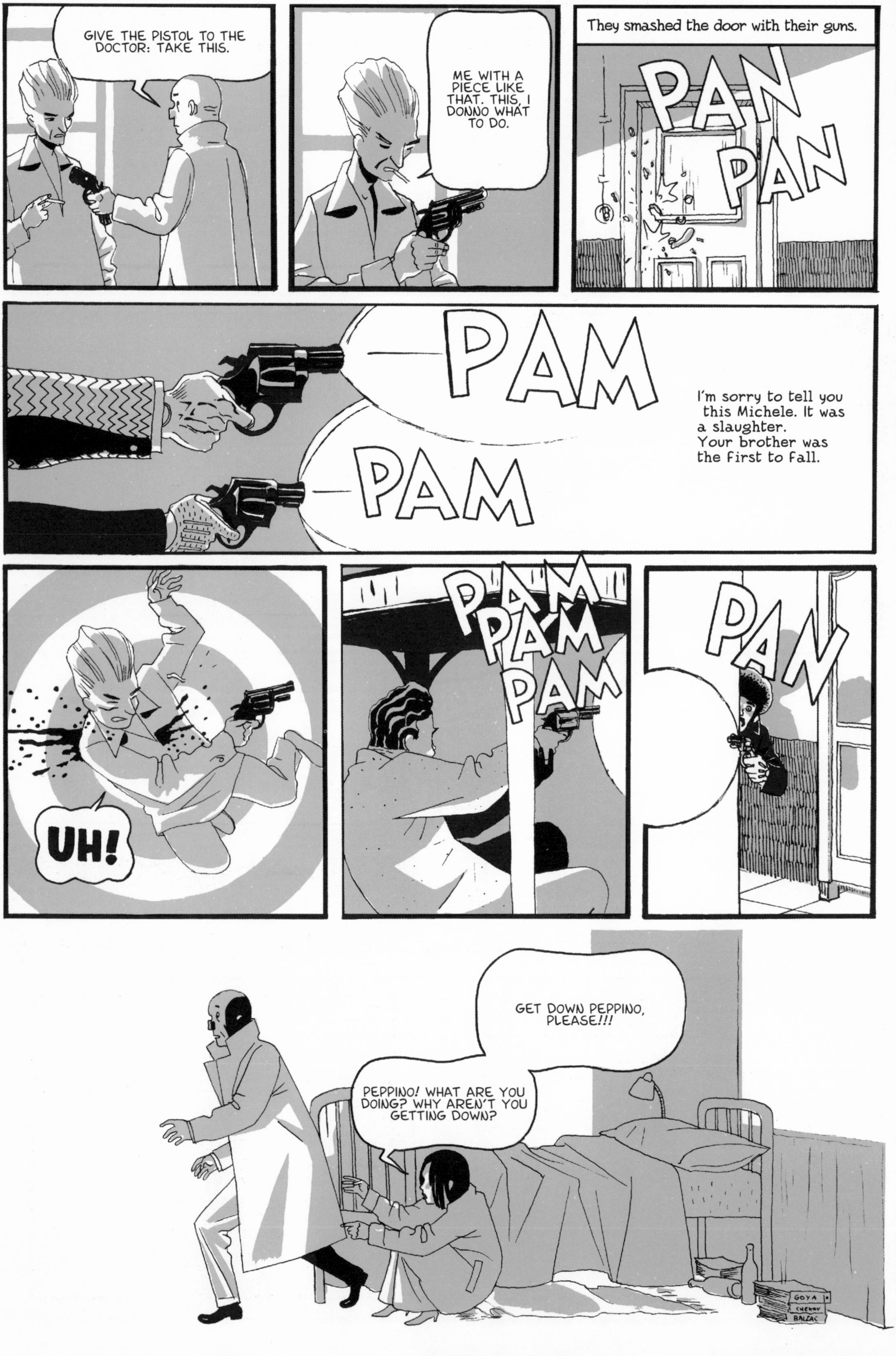
GIVE THE PISTOL TO THE DOCTOR: TAKE THIS.
ME WITH A PIECE LIKE THAT. THIS, I DONNO WHAT TO DO.
They smashed the door with their guns.
PAN PAN
PAM
PAM
I'm sorry to tell you this Michele. It was a slaughter. Your brother was the first to fall.
UH!
PAM PAM PAM
PAN
GET DOWN PEPPINO, PLEASE!!!
PEPPINO! WHAT ARE YOU DOING? WHY AREN'T YOU GETTING DOWN?
GOYA
BALZAC

I was moving like an idiot in the middle of flying bullets. Like a sleepwalker. I was out of place, y'understand Michele? Sometimes I think that if I were dead at least, I wouldn't feel the weight of what I've done. All of a sudden, everything seemed to be such nonsense. All I knew is that there was a wounded man lying down on the floor. I had to find out if he was still alive. Don't get me wrong; there's nothing heroic about all this, just the selfishness of an old man who knew that he caused trouble.

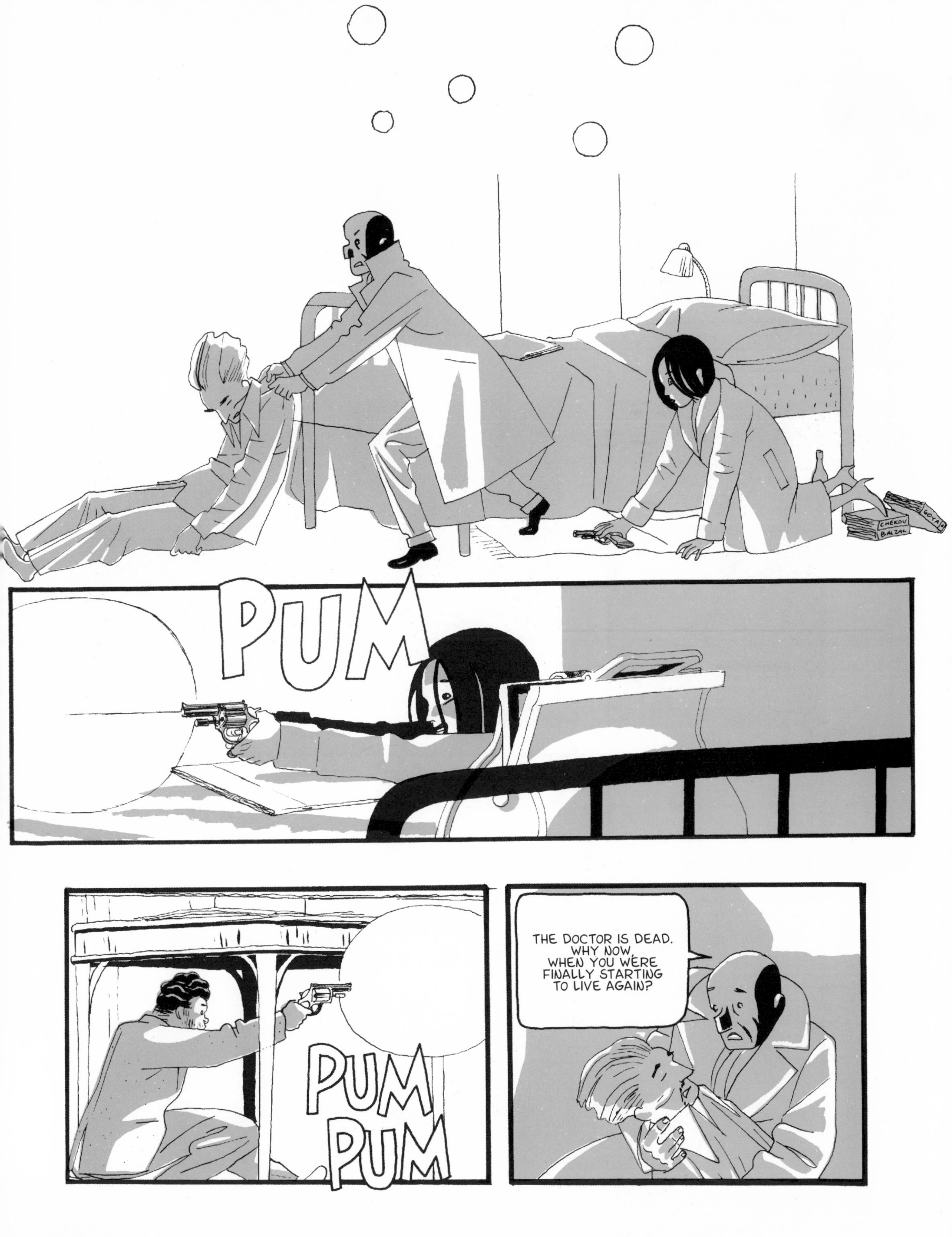
PUM
PUM PUM
THE DOCTOR IS DEAD. WHY NOW, WHEN YOU WERE FINALLY STARTING TO LIVE AGAIN?

Salvatore was shooting and screaming like a fury. He killed almost everybody. He took us to the car. Me? I was feeling weak, like a baby. I felt out of place. It made me sick to my stomach if I thought about how I dealt with things in the past few days. What a waste of energy, what an awful thing to realize that I blew everything.

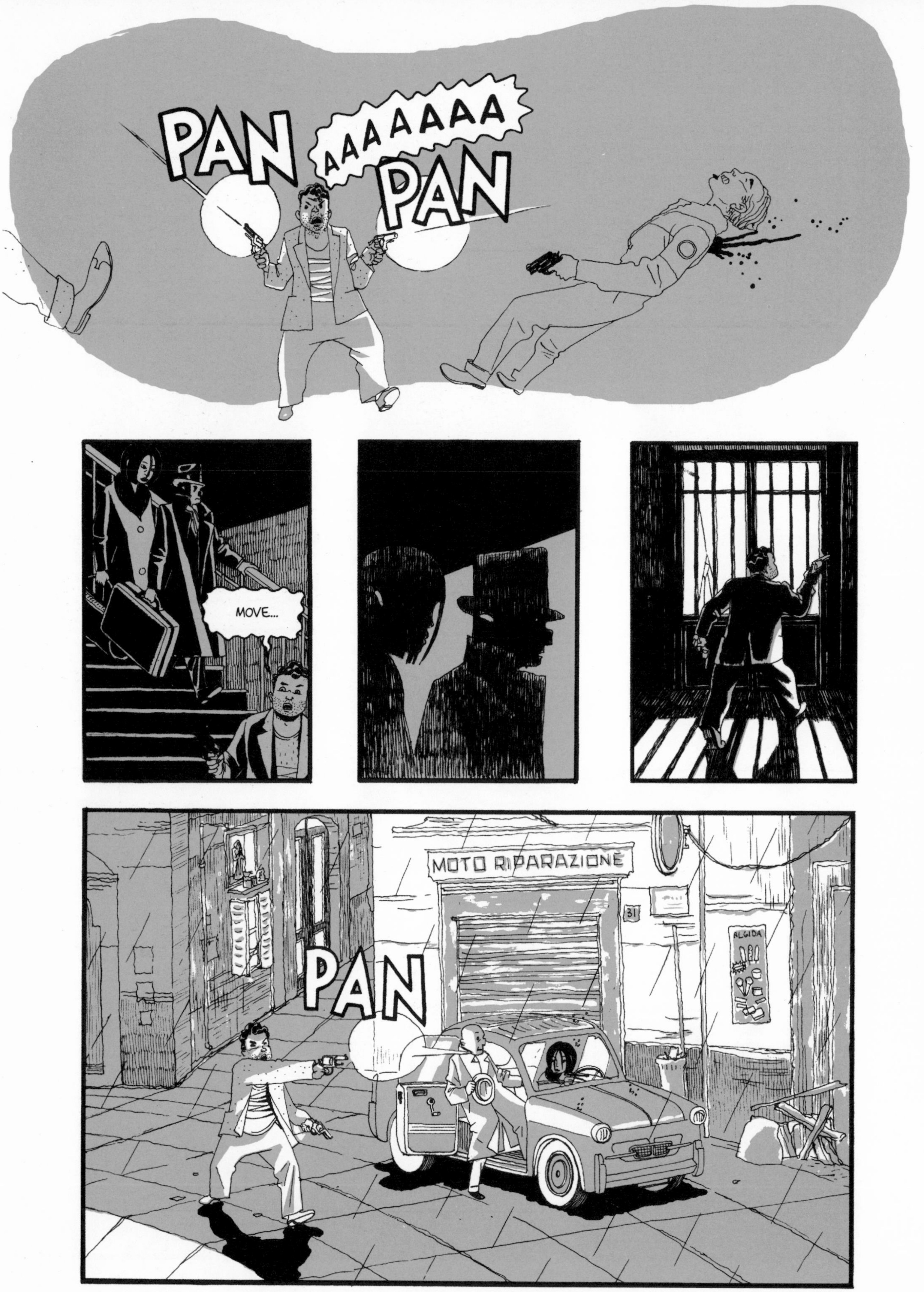

PAN
AAAAAAA
PAN
MOVE...
MOTO RIPARAZIONE
31
ALGIDA
PAN

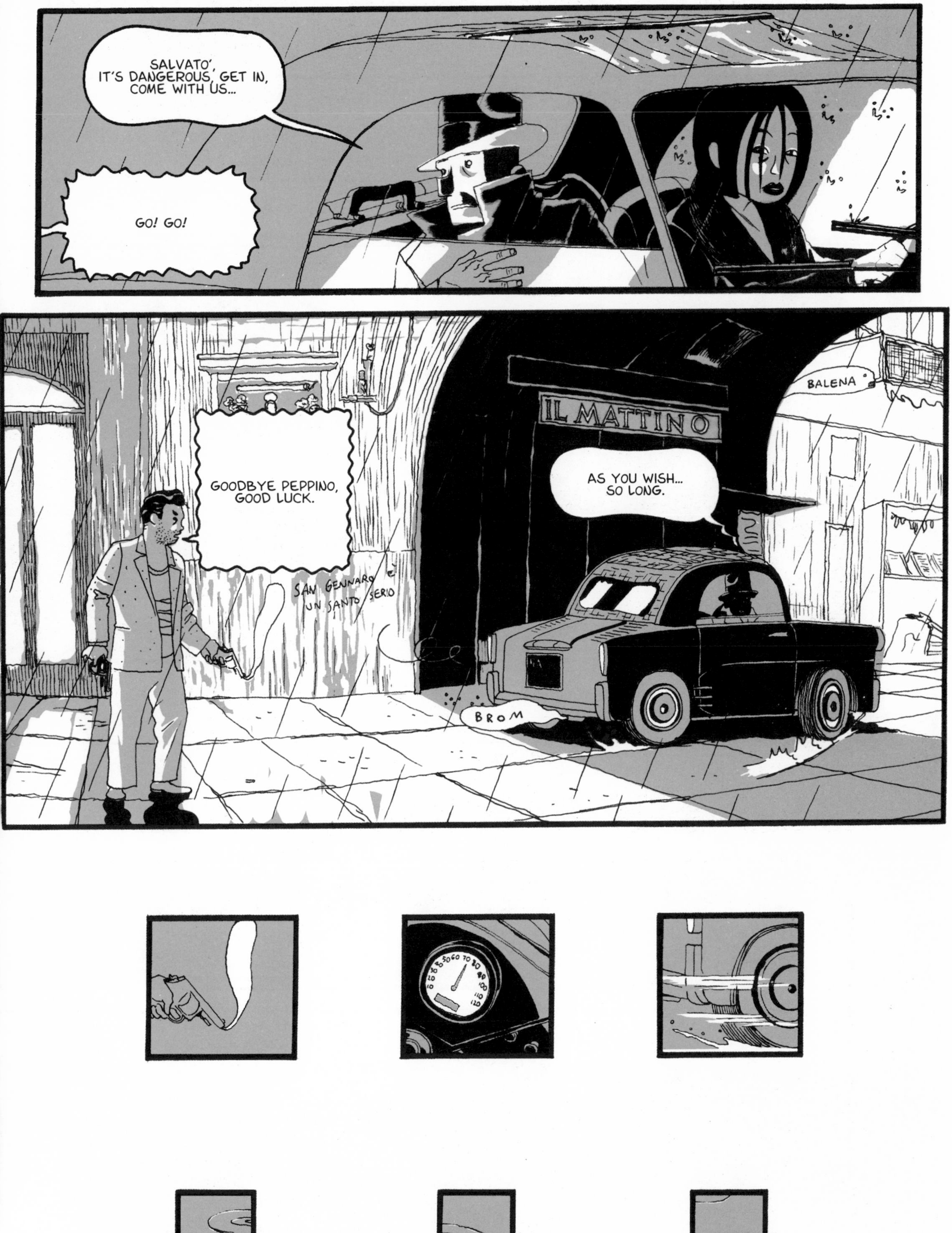
SALVATO', IT'S DANGEROUS, GET IN, COME WITH US...
GO! GO!
IL MATTINO
BALENA
GOODBYE PEPPINO, GOOD LUCK.
AS YOU WISH... SO LONG.
SAN GENNARO È UN SANTO SERIO
BROM

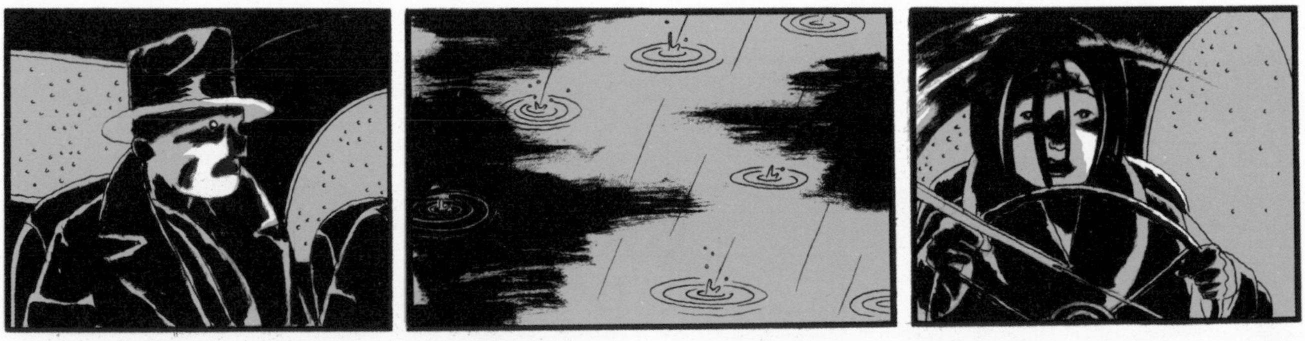

Salvato' stayed to cover us, risking his life one more time. I was... I was like in shock. I remember that it was raining. Lots of water
I never realized that I liked rain .

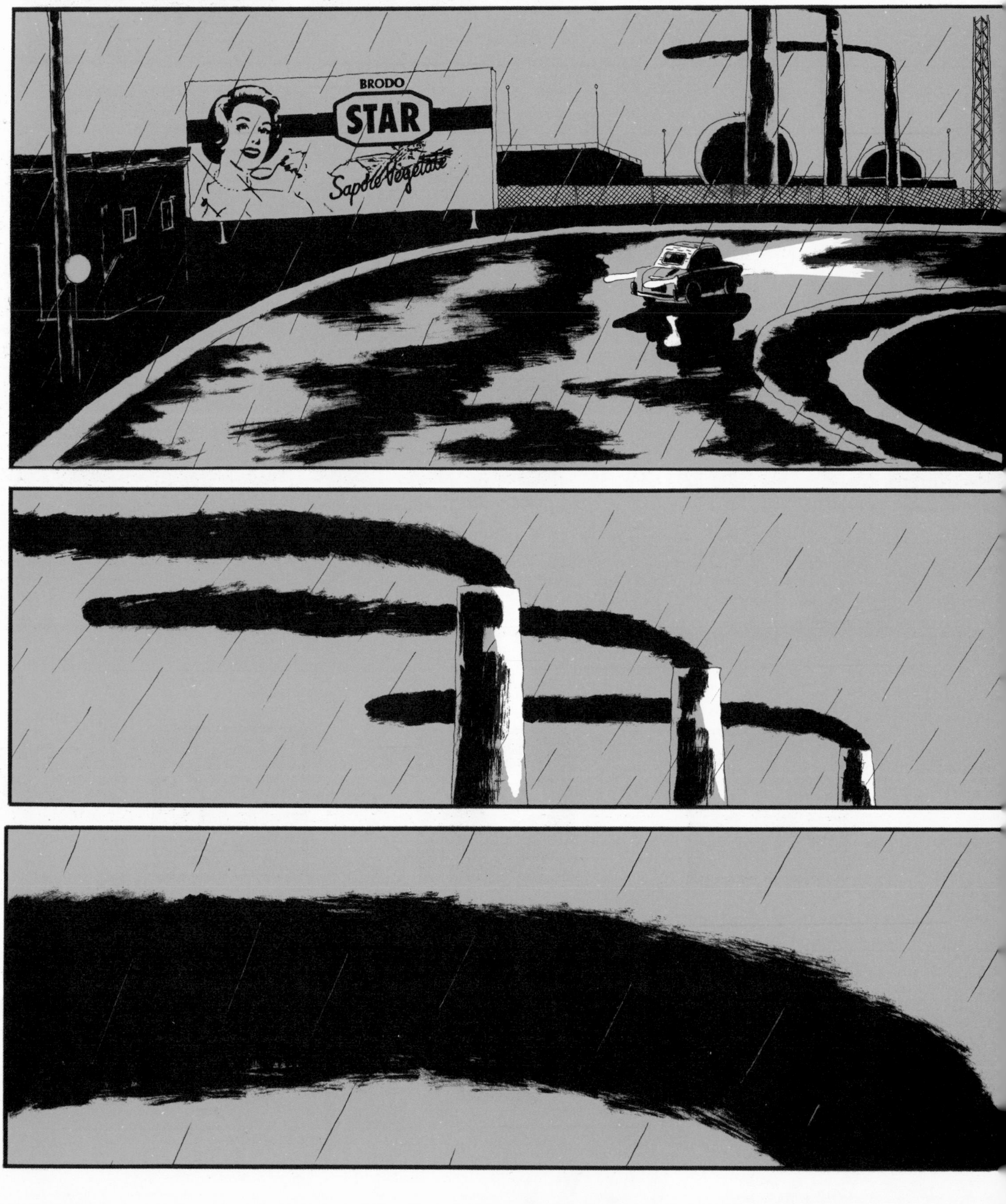
BRODO
STAR

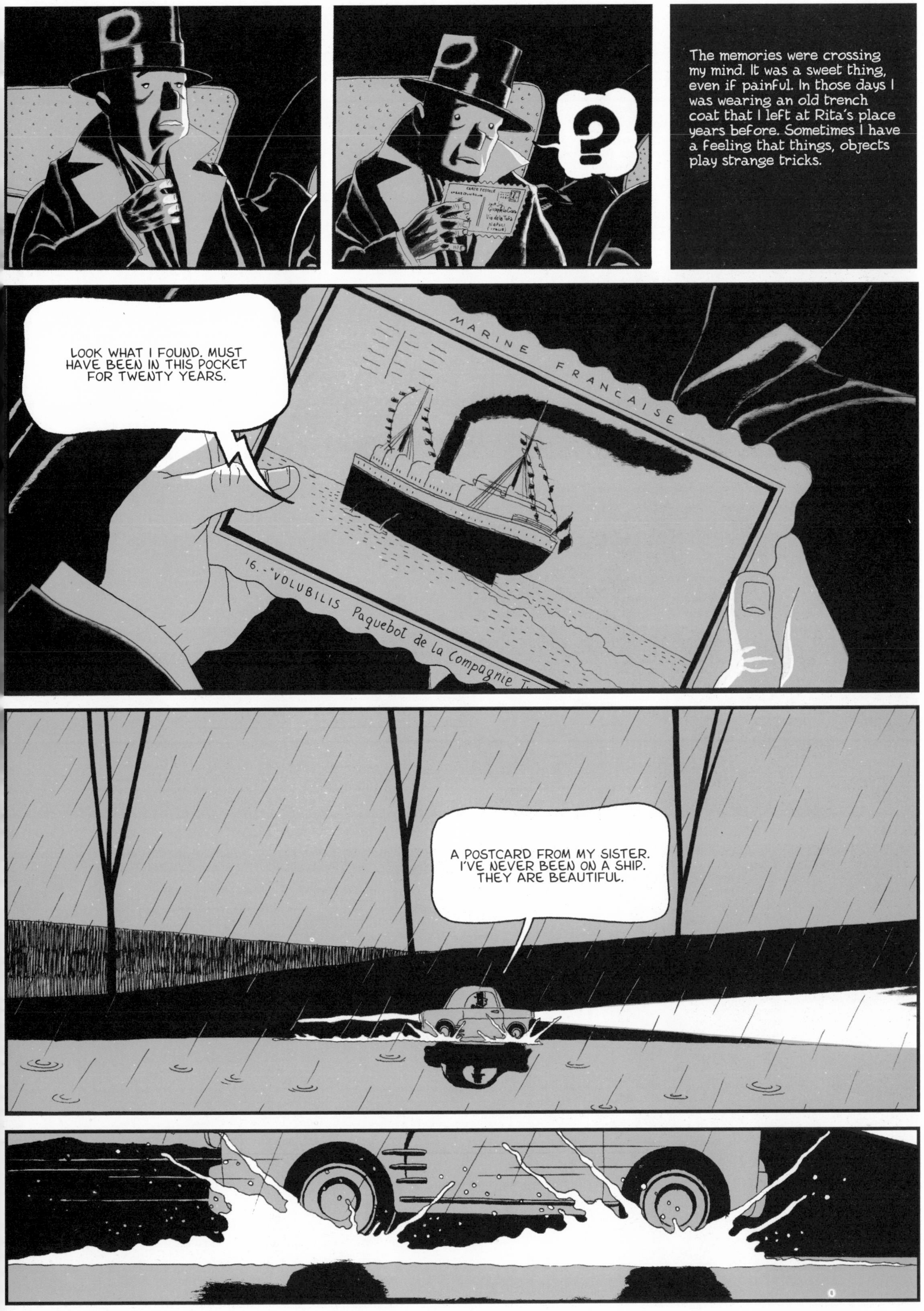
?
The memories were crossing my mind. It was a sweet thing, even if painful. In those days I was wearing an old trench coat that I left at Rita's place years before. Sometimes I have a feeling that things, objects play strange tricks.
LOOK WHAT I FOUND. MUST HAVE BEEN IN THIS POCKET FOR TWENTY YEARS.
MARINE FRANCAISE
16.-"VOLUBILIS Paquebot de la Compagnie
A POSTCARD FROM MY SISTER. I'VE NEVER BEEN ON A SHIP. THEY ARE BEAUTIFUL.

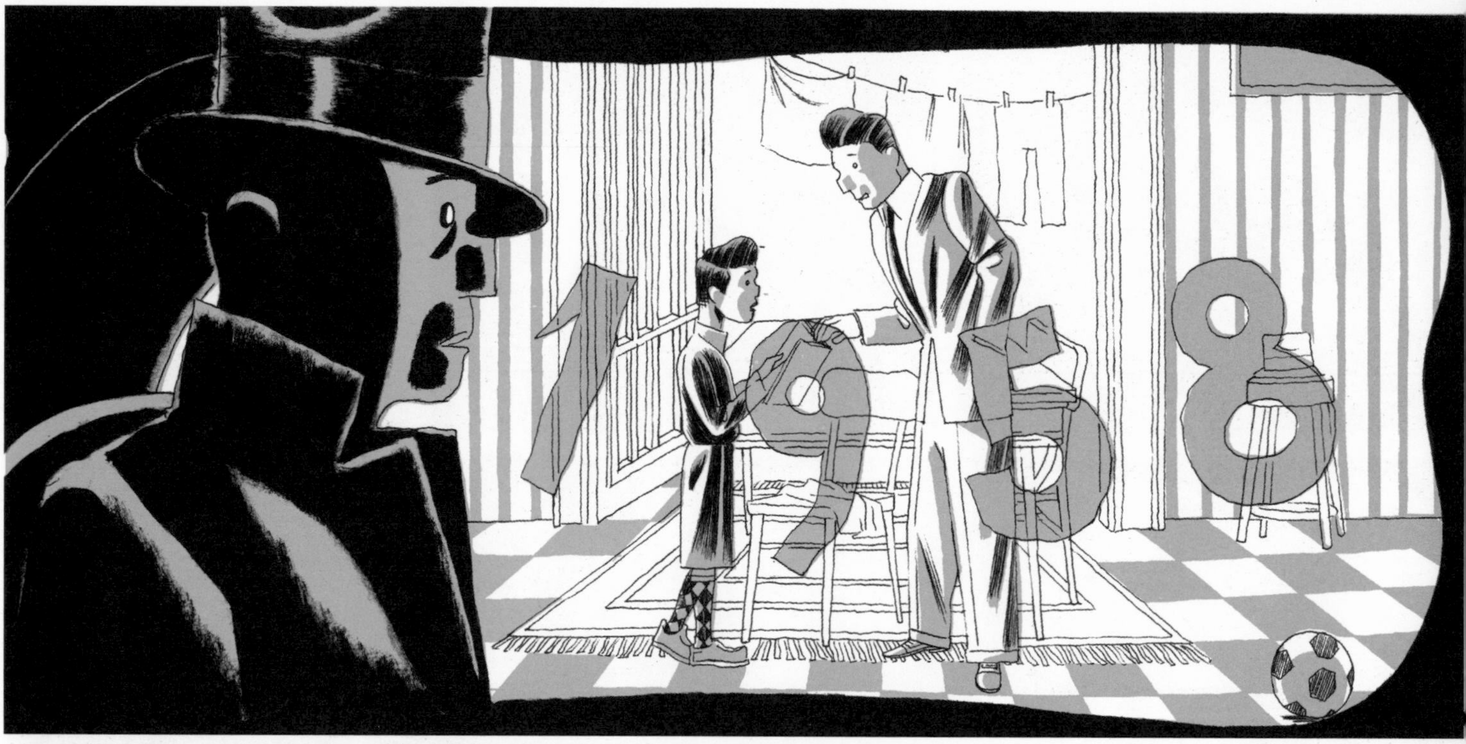

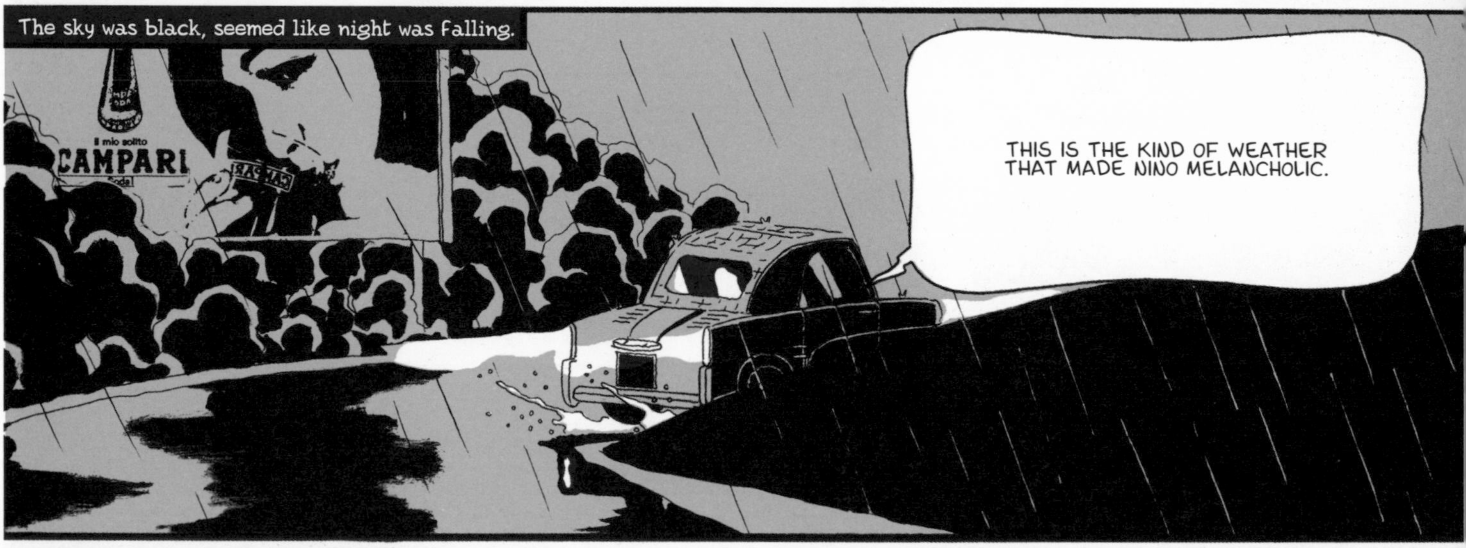
The sky was black, seemed like night was falling.
CAMPARI
THIS IS THE KIND OF WEATHER THAT MADE NINO MELANCHOLIC.

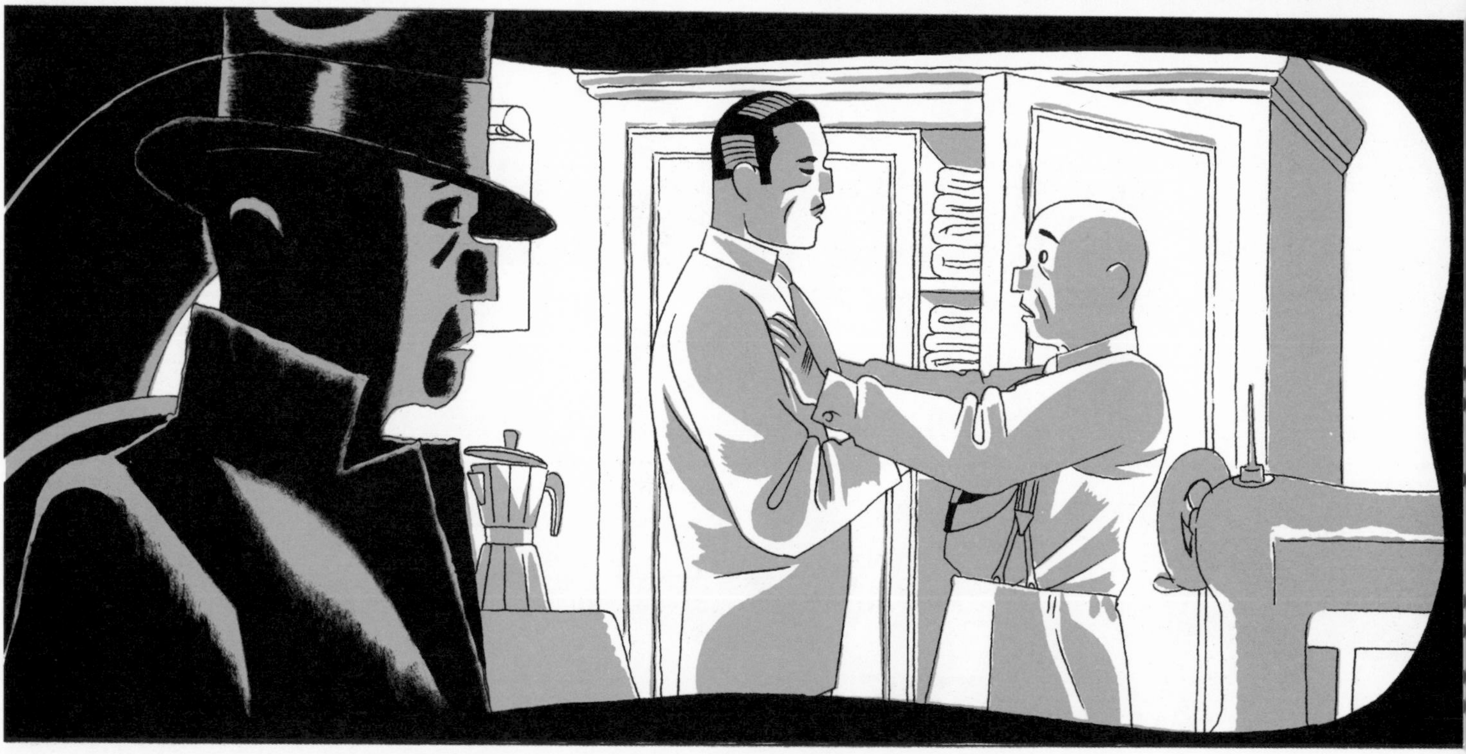

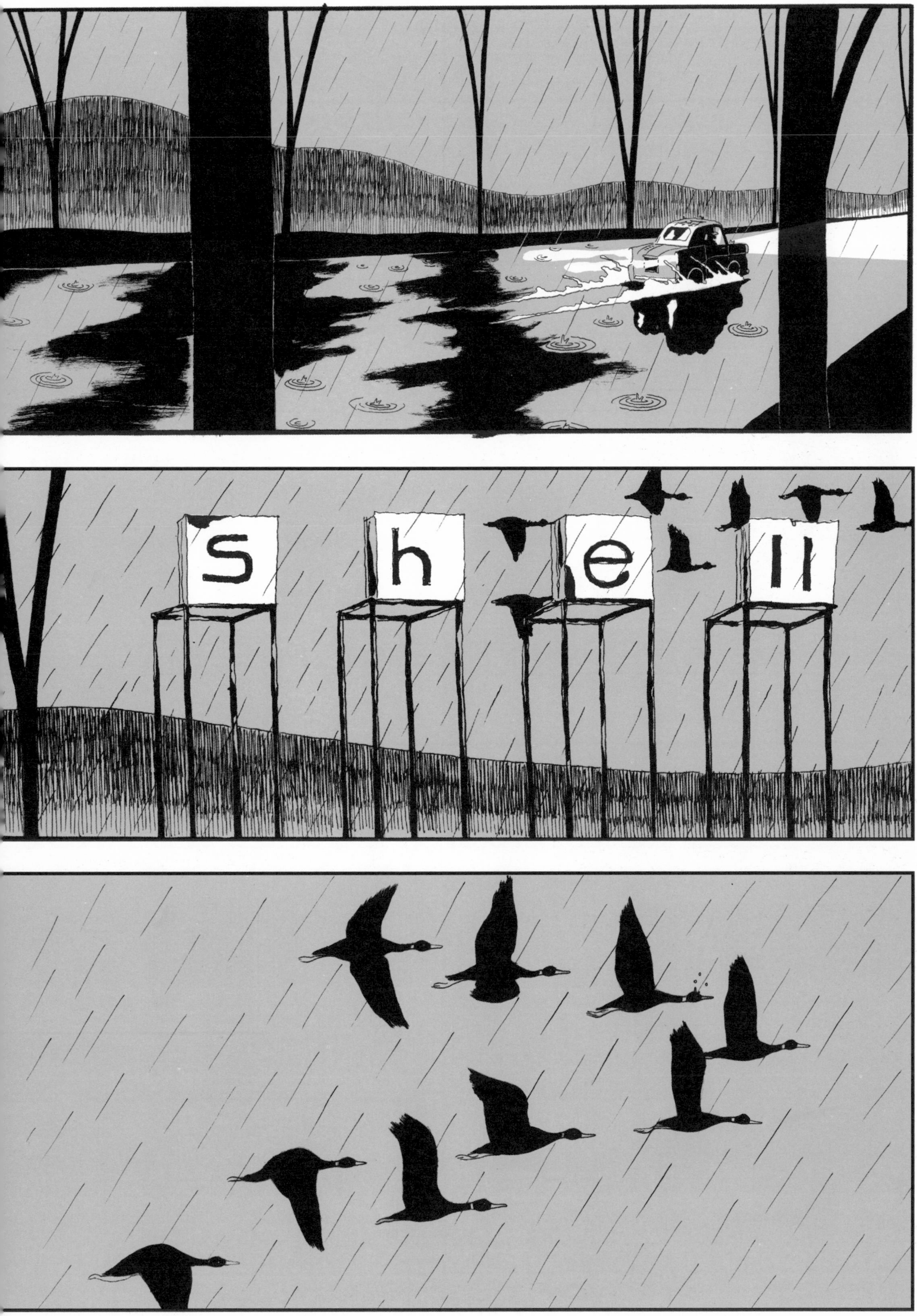
s h e ll

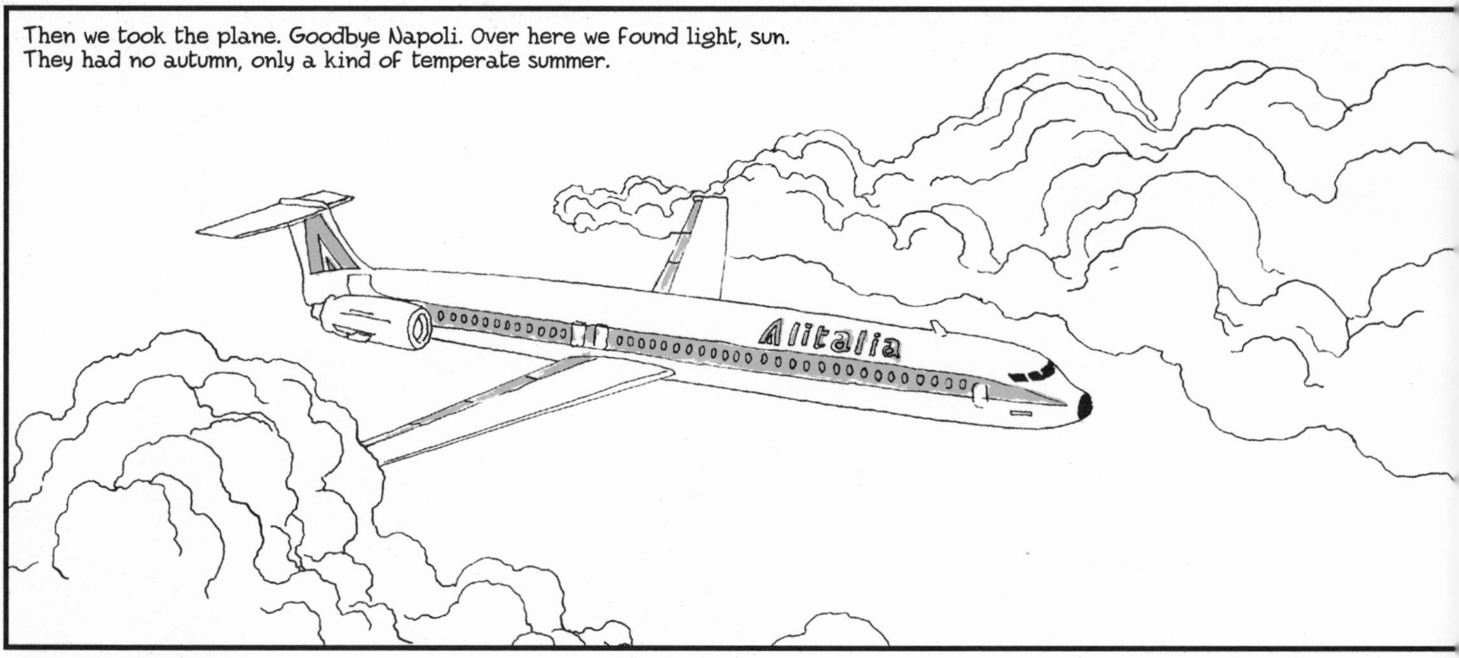
Then we took the plane. Goodbye Napoli. Over here we found light, sun.
They had no autumn, only a kind of temperate summer.
Alitalia

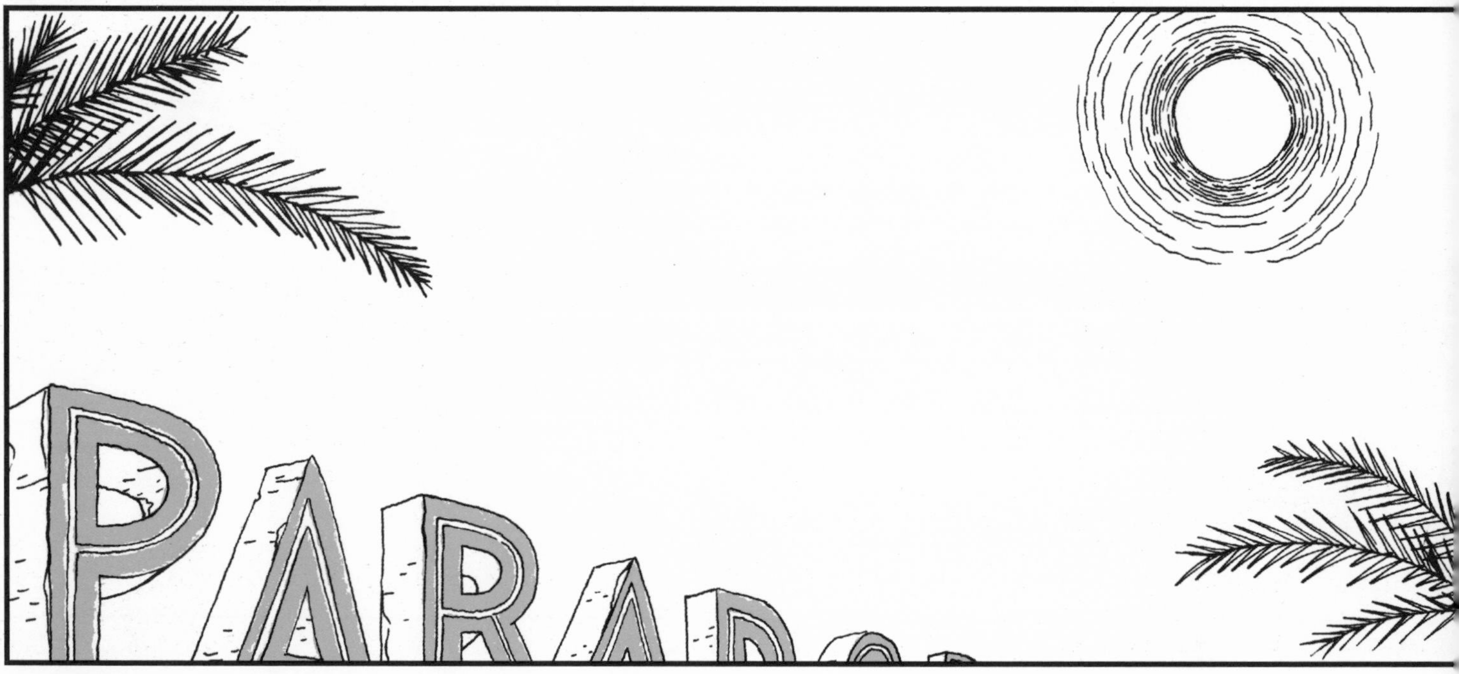

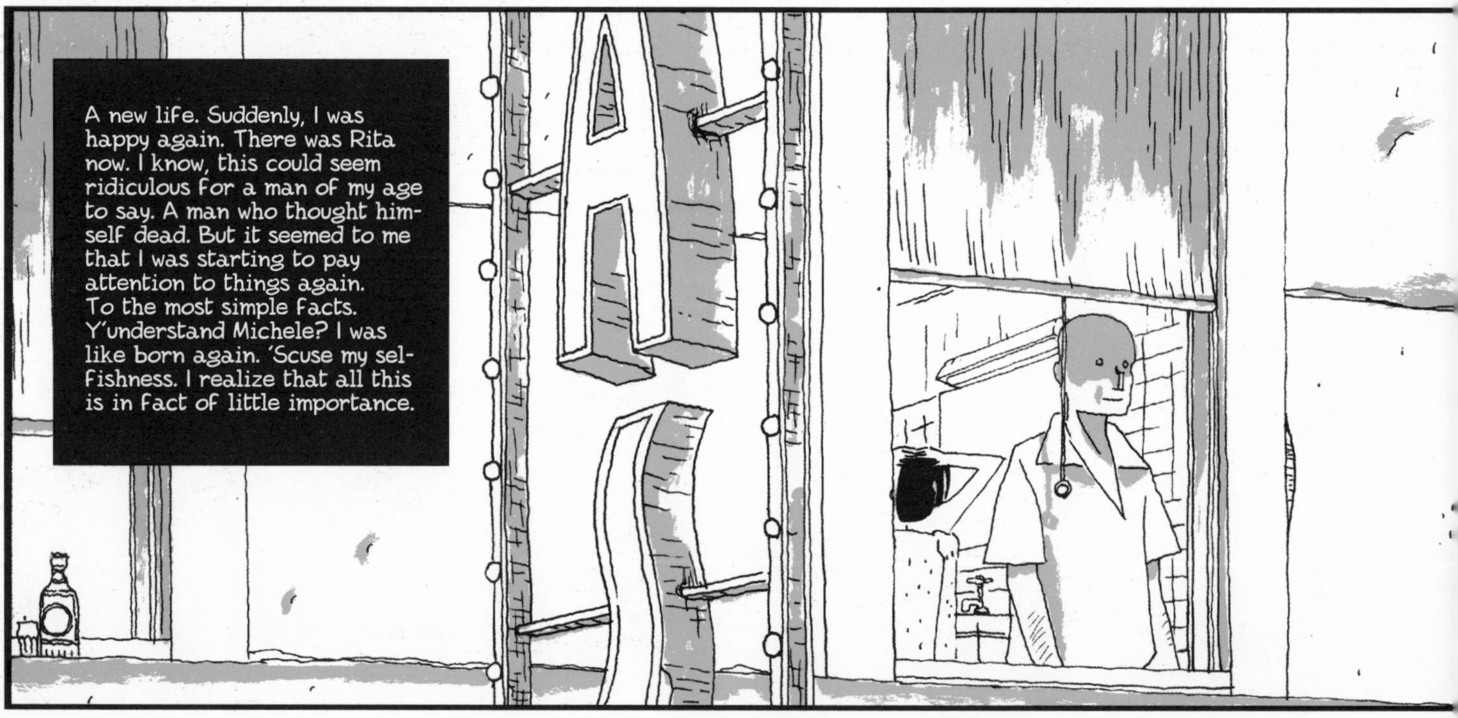
A new life. Suddenly, I was happy again. There was Rita now. I know, this could seem ridiculous for a man of my age to say. A man who thought himself dead. But it seemed to me that I was starting to pay attention to things again. To the most simple facts. Y'understand Michele? I was like born again. 'Scuse my selfishness. I realize that all this is in fact of little importance.

Time was going by and I was trying to forget. I didn't have the guts to come and see you. To tell you what, in the end? Hello, I'm Peppino Lo Cicero. Your brother died because of me.

That's why I hesitated for almost a month.

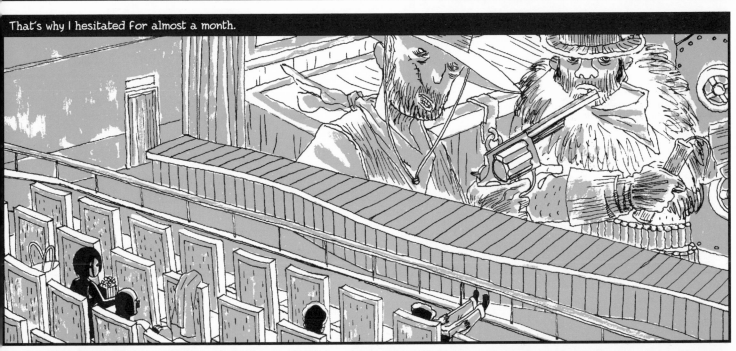

Then I thought that the doctor would have liked us to meet. I didn't know you were not in touch for such a long time...

MORE THAN TWENTY FIVE YEARS, FOR SUCH A STUPID REASON, A WOMAN... WE WERE SUCH IDIOTS...

I HAVE TO TELL YOU THIS. YOUR BROTHER WAS A GOOD MAN, MICHELE, A RARE BIRD.

'SCUSE ME. I DIDN'T MEAN TO RUIN YOUR DAY.

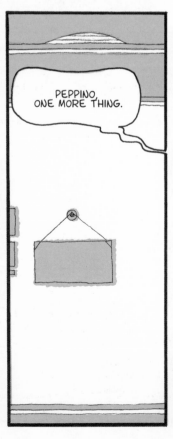

PEPPINO, ONE MORE THING.

TELL ME.

HOW WAS HE? FAT? SLIM? DID HE LOOK LIKE ME?

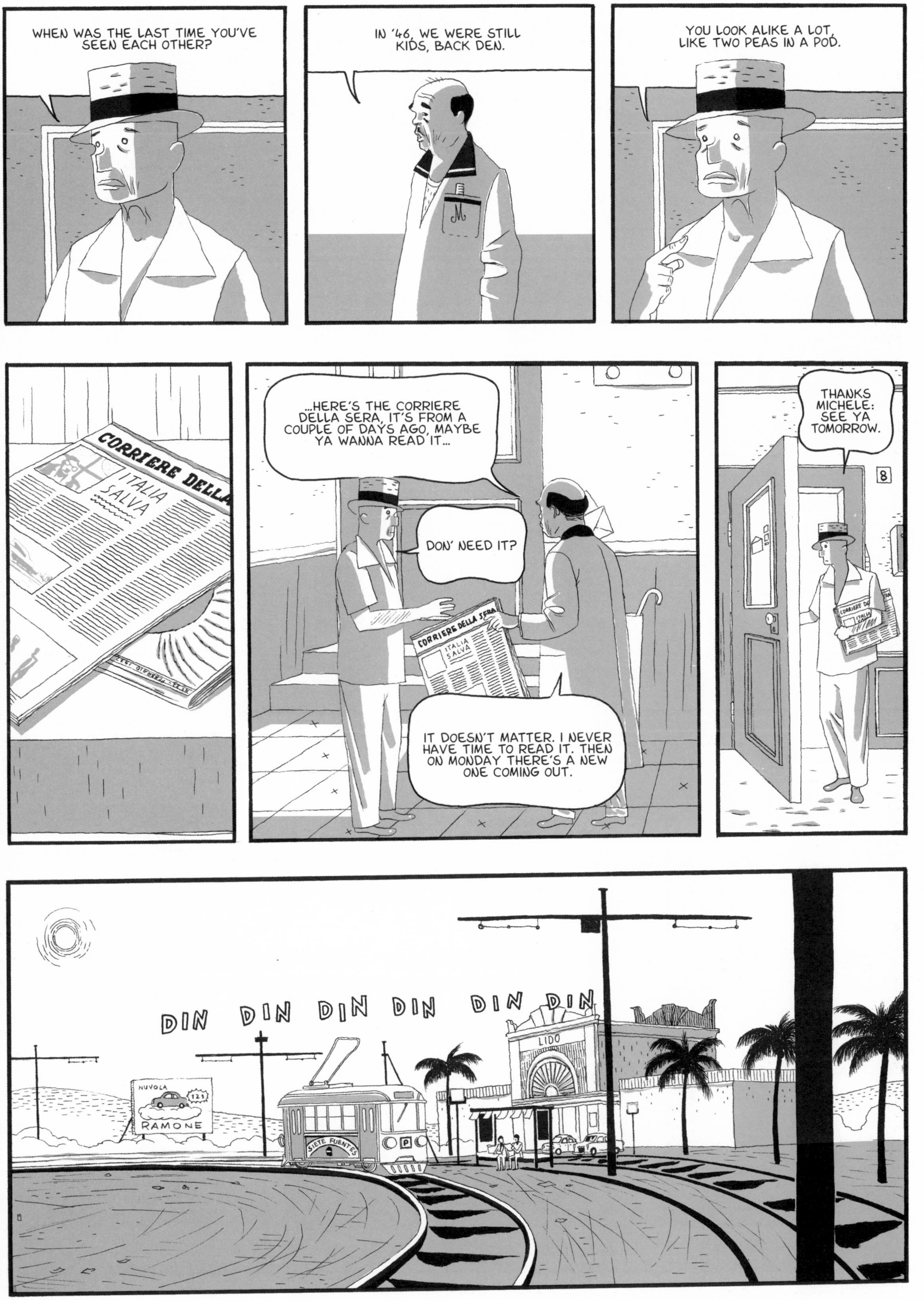
WHEN WAS THE LAST TIME YOU'VE SEEN EACH OTHER?
IN '46, WE WERE STILL KIDS, BACK DEN.
YOU LOOK ALIKE A LOT, LIKE TWO PEAS IN A POD.
CORRIERE DELLA
ITALIA SALVA
...HERE'S THE CORRIERE DELLA SERA, IT'S FROM A COUPLE OF DAYS AGO, MAYBE YA WANNA READ IT...
DON' NEED IT?
CORRIERE DELLA SERA
ITALIA SALVA
IT DOESN'T MATTER. I NEVER HAVE TIME TO READ IT. THEN ON MONDAY THERE'S A NEW ONE COMING OUT.
THANKS MICHELE: SEE YA TOMORROW.
8
DIN DIN DIN DIN DIN DIN
LIDO
NUVOLA
121
RAMONE
SIETE FUENTES
P

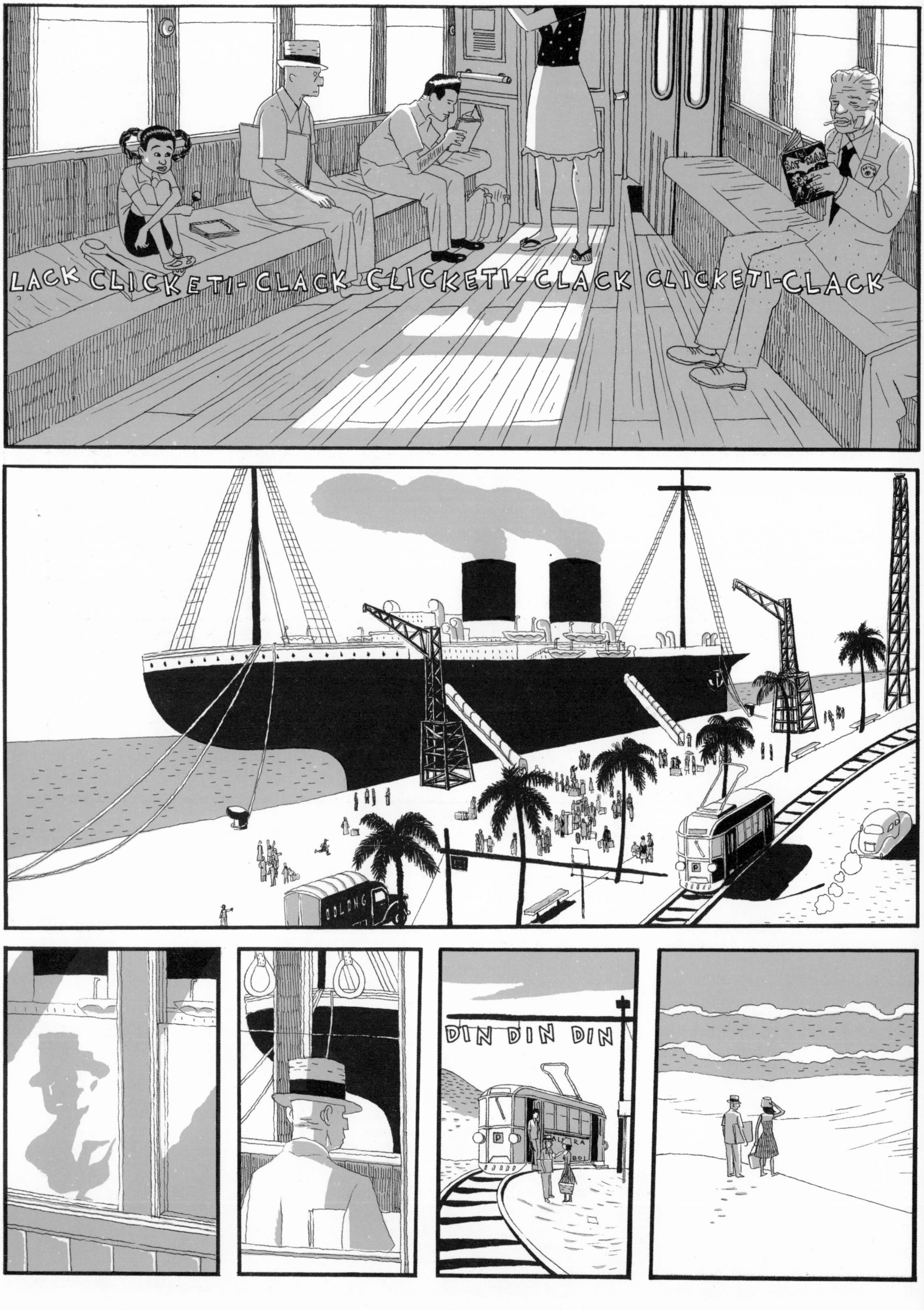
LACK CLICKETI-CLACK CLICKETI-CLACK CLICKETI-CLACK
BAT MAN
OOLONG
DIN DIN DIN

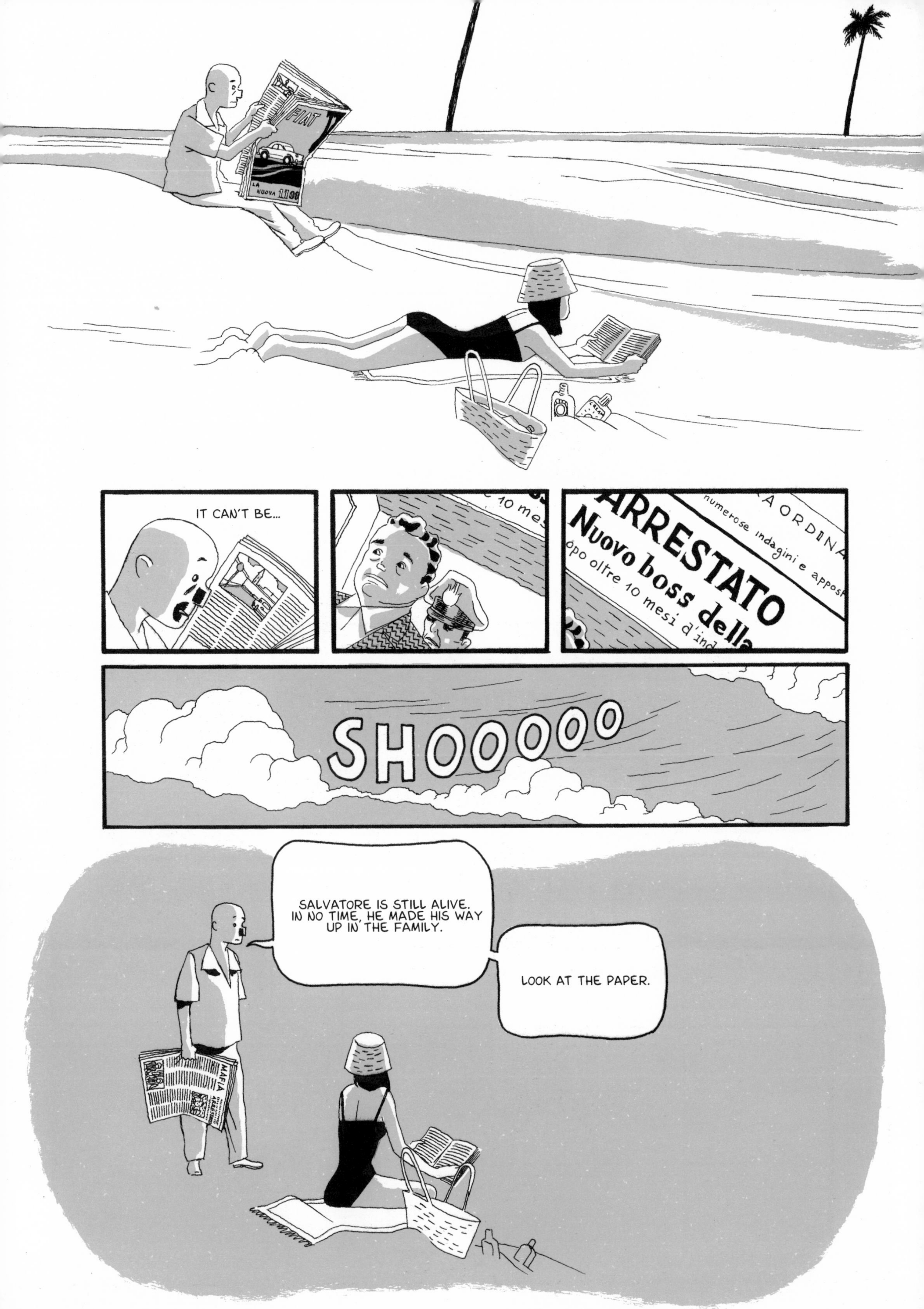
FIAT
LA NUOVA 1100
CREAM
IT CAN'T BE...
10 mes
ARRESTATO
Nuovo boss della
numerose indagini e apposi
opo oltre 10 mesi d'ind
SHOOOOO
SALVATORE IS STILL ALIVE. IN NO TIME, HE MADE HIS WAY UP IN THE FAMILY.
LOOK AT THE PAPER.
MAFIA

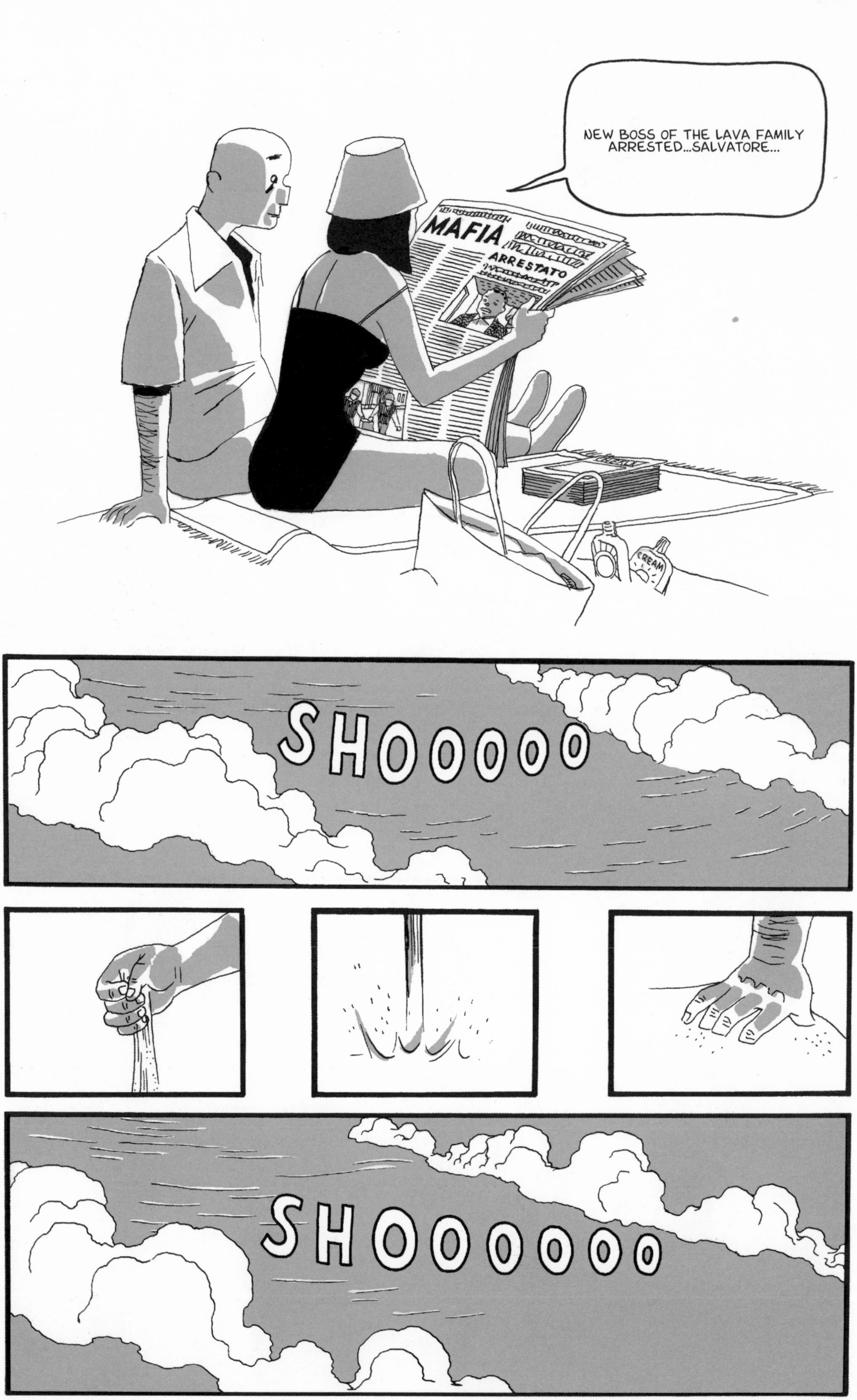
NEW BOSS OF THE LAVA FAMILY ARRESTED...SALVATORE...
MAFIA
ARRESTATO
CREAM
SHOOOOO
SHOOOOOOO

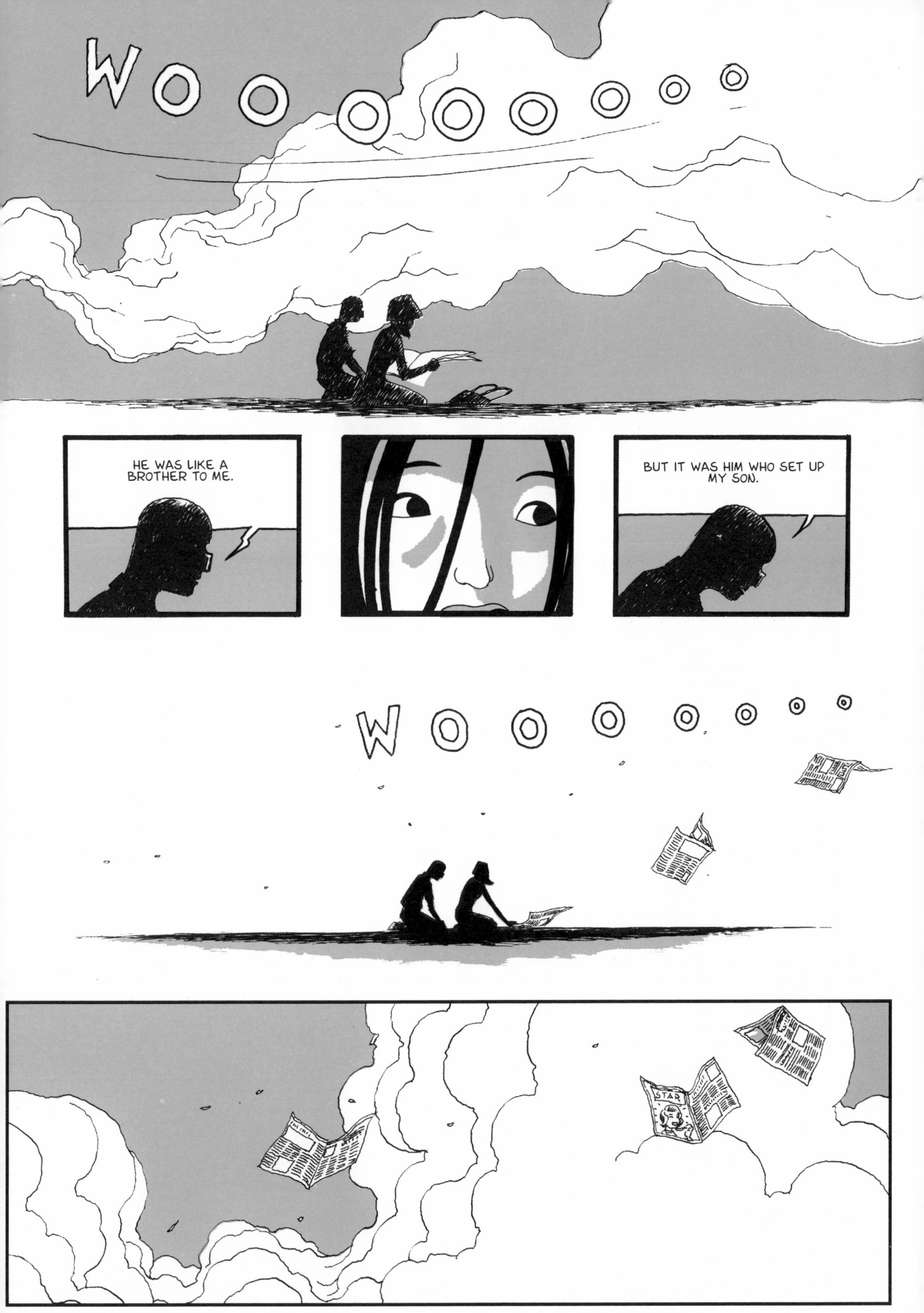
WOOOOOOOO
HE WAS LIKE A BROTHER TO ME.
BUT IT WAS HIM WHO SET UP MY SON.
WOOOOOOO
STAR

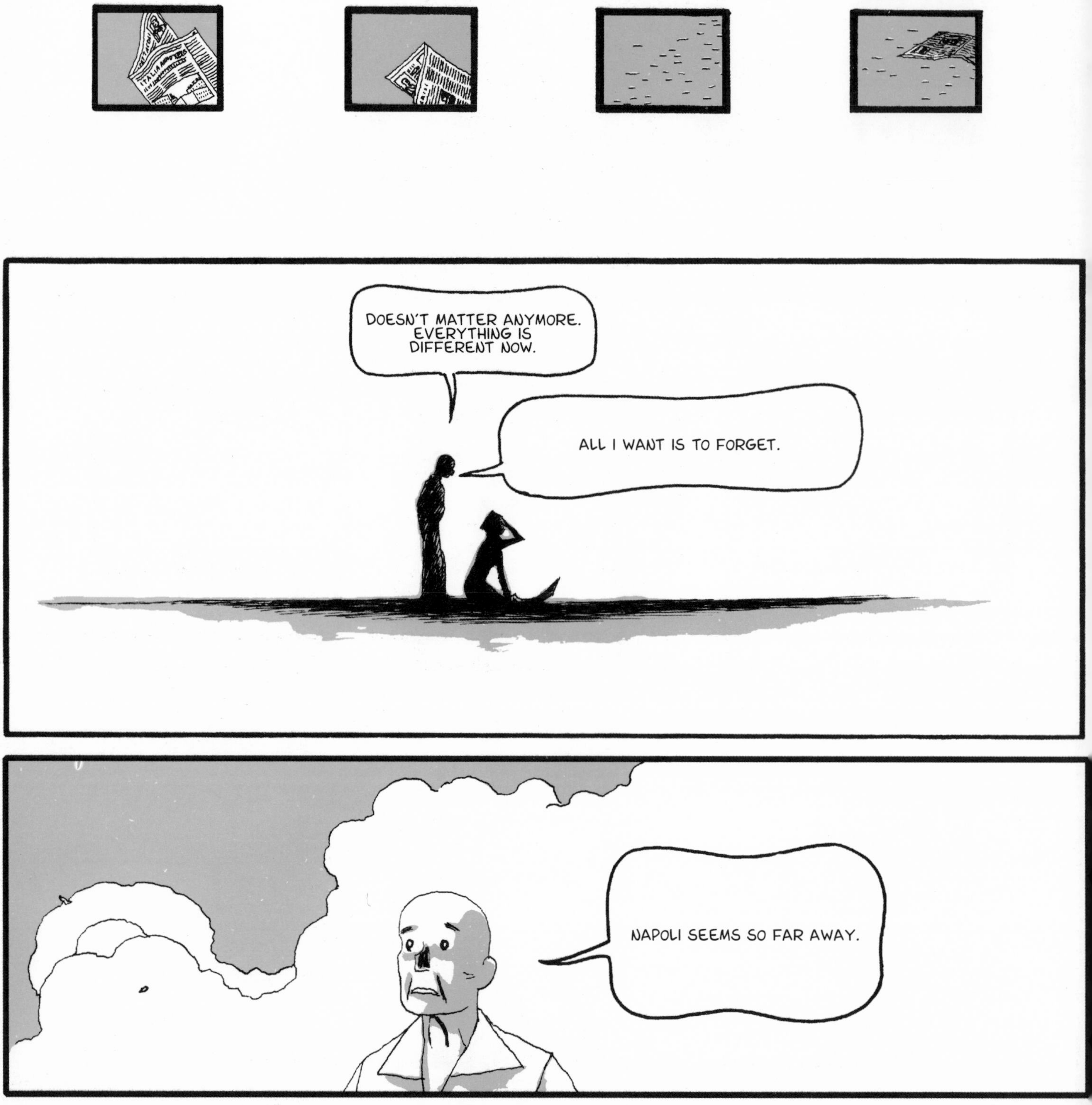
DOESN'T MATTER ANYMORE. EVERYTHING IS DIFFERENT NOW.
ALL I WANT IS TO FORGET.
NAPOLI SEEMS SO FAR AWAY.

SHOOOOO

SHOOOO

SHOOOO

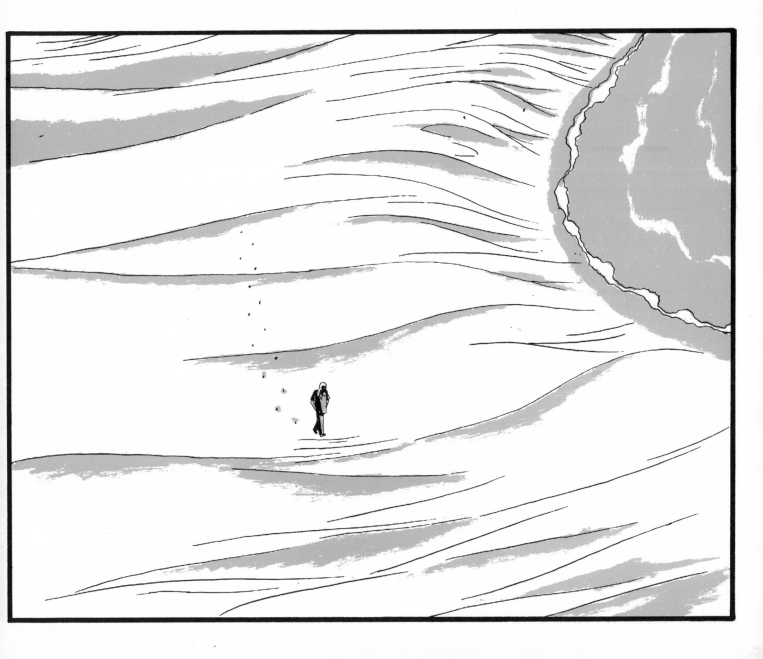

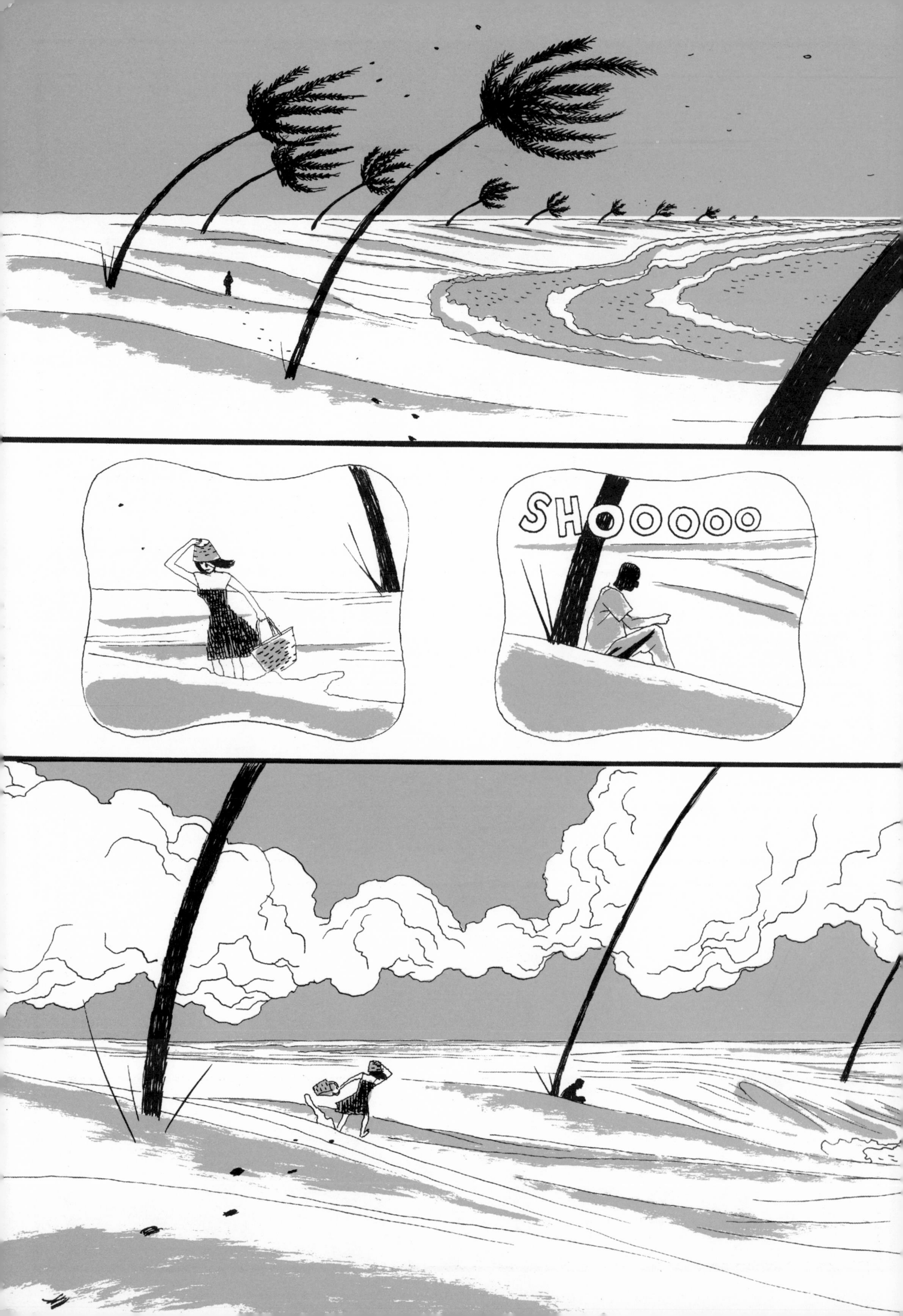
SHOOOOO

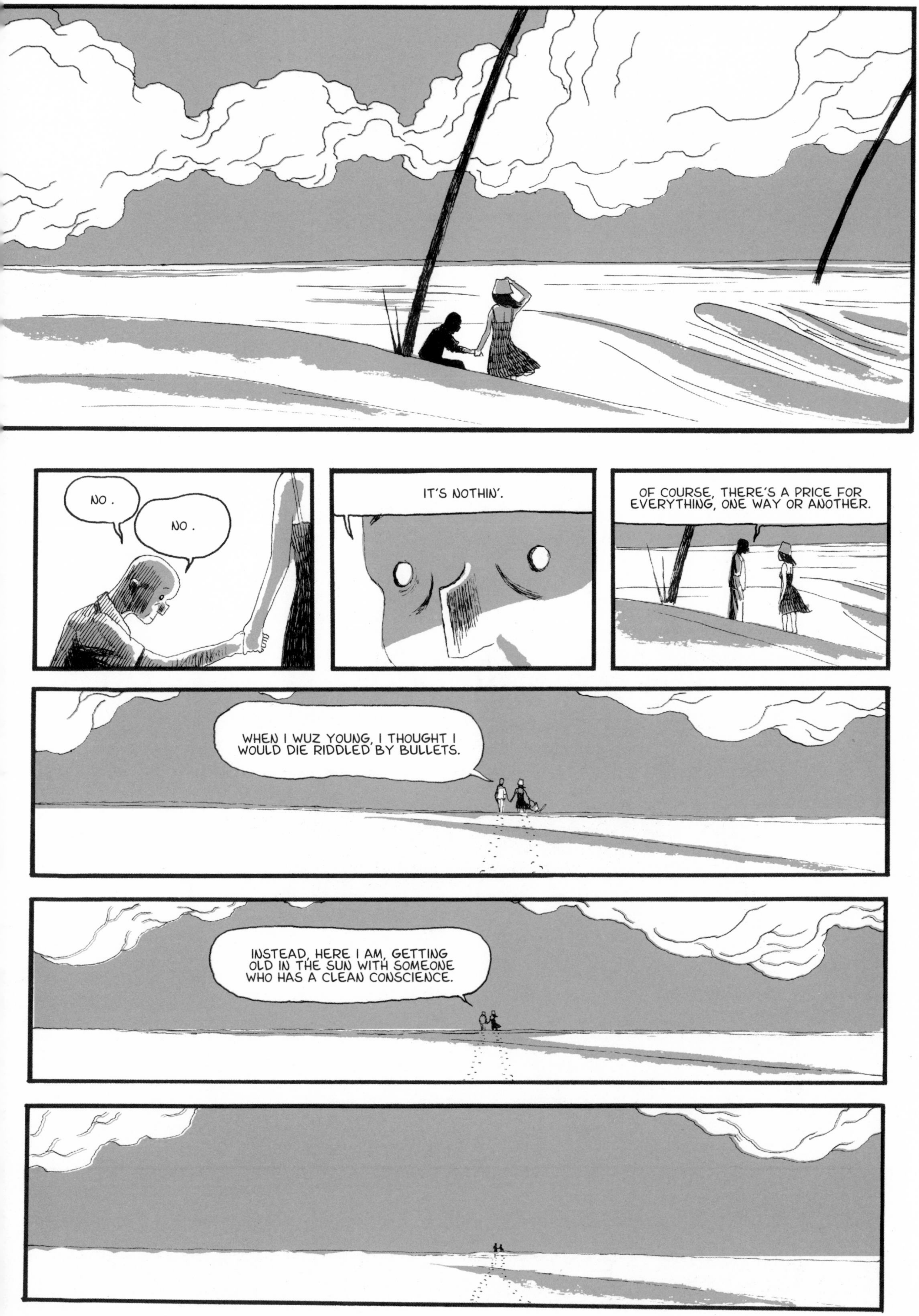
NO.
NO.
IT'S NOTHIN'.
OF COURSE, THERE'S A PRICE FOR EVERYTHING, ONE WAY OR ANOTHER.
WHEN I WUZ YOUNG, I THOUGHT I WOULD DIE RIDDLED BY BULLETS.
INSTEAD, HERE I AM, GETTING OLD IN THE SUN WITH SOMEONE WHO HAS A CLEAN CONSCIENCE.

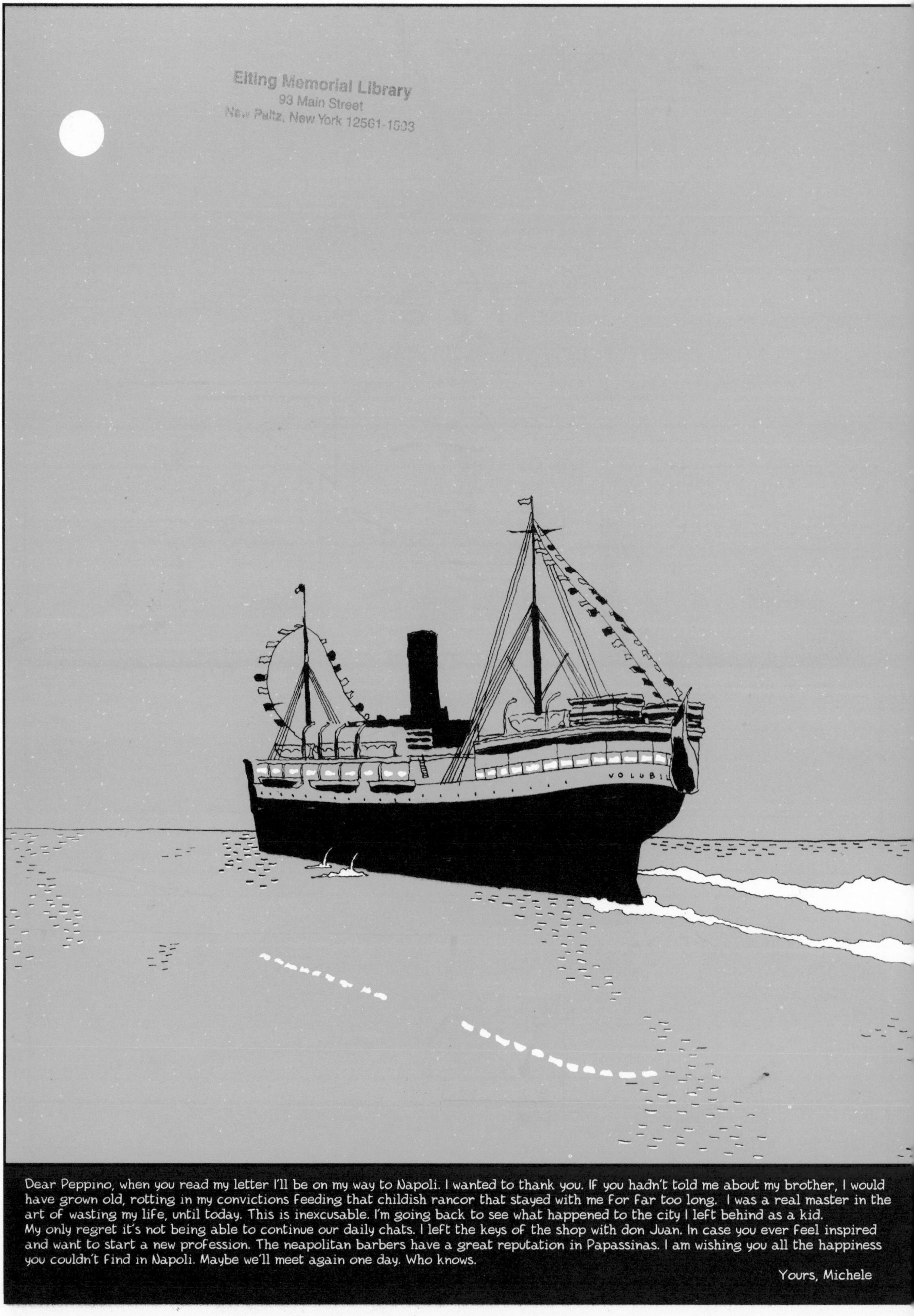
Dear Peppino, when you read my letter I'll be on my way to Napoli. I wanted to thank you. If you hadn't told me about my brother, I would have grown old, rotting in my convictions feeding that childish rancor that stayed with me for far too long. I was a real master in the art of wasting my life, until today. This is inexcusable. I'm going back to see what happened to the city I left behind as a kid.
My only regret it's not being able to continue our daily chats. I left the keys of the shop with don Juan. In case you ever feel inspired and want to start a new profession. The neapolitan barbers have a great reputation in Papassinas. I am wishing you all the happiness you couldn't find in Napoli. Maybe we'll meet again one day. Who knows.
Yours, Michele